Daily Life in Revolutionary China

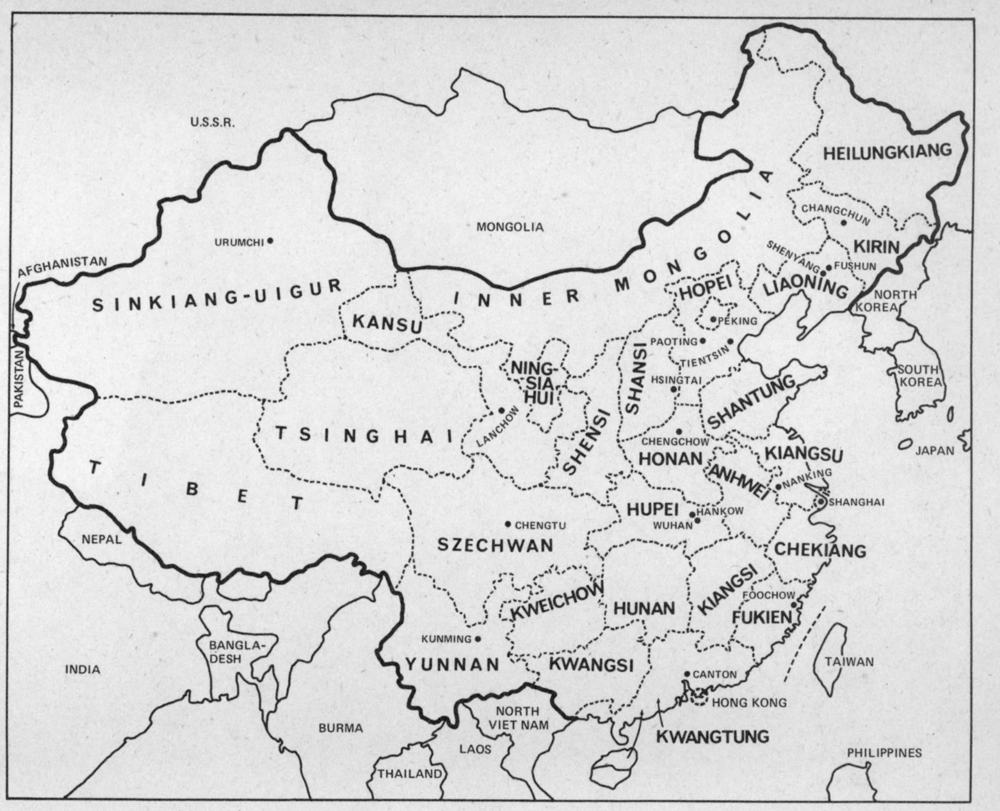
U.S.S.R.
MONGOLIA
HEILUNGKIANG
CHANGCHUN
KIRIN
SHENYANG
FUSHUN
LIAONING
NORTH KOREA
SOUTH KOREA
JAPAN
AFGHANISTAN
URUMCHI
SINKIANG-UIGUR
INNER MONGOLIA
HOPEI
PEKING
PAOTING
TIENTSIN
HSINGTAI
KANSU
NING-SIA-HUI
SHANSI
SHANTUNG
PAKISTAN
TSINGHAI
LANCHOW
SHENSI
CHENGCHOW
HONAN
KIANGSU
ANHWEI
NANKING
SHANGHAI
TIBET
HUPEI
HANKOW
WUHAN
CHENGTU
SZECHWAN
CHEKIANG
NEPAL
KWEICHOW
HUNAN
KIANGSI
FOOCHOW
FUKIEN
KUNMING
BANGLA-DESH
INDIA
YUNNAN
KWANGSI
TAIWAN
CANTON
HONG KONG
NORTH VIET NAM
BURMA
KWANGTUNG
LAOS
PHILIPPINES
THAILAND

Daily Life in Revolutionary China

Maria Antonietta Macciocchi

Monthly Review Press
New York and London

PUBLISHER'S NOTE

In order to prepare this volume for publication as rapidly as possible, the work of translating was divided among the following six people: Kathy Brown, Alfred Ehrenfeld, Lynn Garafola, Bobbye Ortiz, Malcolm Reid, and Jane Werner. The translation as a whole was then reviewed by Alfred Ehrenfeld and Frank Kehl, and Professor Kehl also checked the translation of Chinese names, terms, slogans, etc. The publisher wishes to thank all of the above for their dispatch and cooperation, without which the speedy realization of this project would have been impossible.

Library of Congress Catalog Card No.: 72–81757

First Modern Reader Paperback Edition 1973
Fourth Printing

Monthly Review Press
62 West 14th Street, New York, N.Y. 10011
21 Theobalds Road, London WC1X 8SL

Manufactured in the United States of America

Contents

Introduction to China

I took the Paris-Shanghai plane on October 26, 1970, at 1:30 P.M. Destination Peking. Until I actually boarded the Air France DC-8, I felt as though I was leaving for Mars. But everything went smoothly. The plane took off for Shanghai via Athens, Cairo, and Karachi. Four hours after leaving Karachi the jet plunged into the dawn we had been pursuing, and I experienced a first, rather violent, emotion as I watched the chestnut- and ochre-colored desert regions of southwest China. The giant stretched out below us looked available, inviting, accessible at last. Feeling the need to unburden myself, I approached the Chinese diplomat who had been travelling with us from Paris. I sat down beside him, nodded toward the window, and said: "Do you know, my husband and I are the first Communists to return to China after a ten-year freeze in relations, or should I call it a ten-year split . . ." "You are certainly good friends of China," he answered briefly, following a typically Chinese dialectical procedure which consists less in giving an answer than in summing up, in jumping two or three intermediate conversational steps so as to reach an immediate conclusion.

I recall other moments of equally powerful emotion. I had a similar experience as a young woman in Brest Litovsk when I first met a Soviet army soldier who had entered the train at the border to collect our passports. We had hardly emerged from the underground resistance struggle and the soldier represented victorious Communism, "hard as steel," "pure as a diamond." There are many today who say that Communism with a "C" can be found here, in the heart of Asia, an all-powerful safeguard against the disillusionments, temporizations, and stagnation of the struggle in the West.

But aren't we still haunted by Prague, by the vise-like grip of the two world powers, by the split in the workers' movement, by the great theoretical and political dispute which concerns not only Moscow and Peking but the struggle for socialism everywhere?

I don't think that we should cling to the Chinese experience as blindly as we did to that of the USSR in the fifties, or transfer to China the hopes placed earlier in the Soviet Union. One historical error cannot be redeemed with another. One and one is still two. We must do our utmost to make a serious study of the vast subject which is Mao Tse-tung's China. Will I succeed?

In the plane the sixteen Chinese with whom we had been travelling from Paris wake, converse rapidly with one another, are visibly happy: they are *home*. During the flight they maintained a kind of astonished silence toward the French stewardesses. They refused the offers of liquor, rarely left their seats, and spoke only when absolutely necessary. Now, however, they tell us that they have come from Africa, Algeria, Congo-Brazzaville, that they are technical workers assisting the underdeveloped nations. They live like the workers in those countries. They get the same pay, and no distinction is made between engineers and unskilled laborers, for the division of labor into higher and lower grades has been abolished in China and they act abroad as they would in their own country. It would be difficult, in fact, to distinguish in this group between the Arabic-speaking chauffeur working in Algeria and the diplomat who heads a delegation in Paris. Their relations show no trace of the hierarchical attitude which, in the West, is considered the hallmark of success and brandished like a sign. During the ten-hour flight I could observe them closely. It was my first direct experience of an unknown world.

But now I have forgotten these travel companions and concentrate on discovering what I can about China from an altitude of 33,000 feet. I am experiencing a mixed and contradictory sensation of profound agitation and overwhelming joy. My return to China after sixteen years—from September-October 1954 until today, October 26, 1970—is due less to personal merit than to a fortuitous set of circumstances.

First (personal) prologue to China

The first question a Chinese asks you when you meet him abroad is: "Have you visited China?" If the answer is affirmative the conversation becomes less constrained simply because he knows that your attitude toward a world as complex as China is not merely bookish or theoretical but the result of a practical experience, however modest. "If you want to know the taste of a pear, you must bite into it," says Mao. I had had a taste of China in 1954, but it was only later that I fully understood how important that experience had been for me. My trip to China (forty-five days, from Mukden to Shanghai) had set off a powerful ferment within me. For many months after my return I was unable to adjust to my accustomed life. I was suffering from "China sickness." I don't think this ever happened to me in any other country, except for much more marginal or personal reasons. If I had been asked to work in China at that time, when I was twenty-five, I would have accepted. But political life took me elsewhere. A party activist cannot devote herself to Sinology but must remain faithful to certain political options. The turmoil within me resulted from what was in fact a political choice. During my 1954 trip I had felt in a confused way that China would eventually give a powerful impulse to the world revolution, and that its strategy would have an impact on the entire movement. Historically, the implantation of Marxism-Leninism in this country did not merely represent one more socialist revolution in a vast country, which then numbered 600 million inhabitants, but also the revolution of an autonomous, highly developed, five-thousand-year-old civilization. It marked the birth of a global force with an impact similar to that attributed to Greek or Roman civilization in centuries past. But with a difference—this was the civilization of socialism.

On this trip I have brought with me the articles I wrote in 1954. They are extremely enthusiastic. Today there is nothing I would change in what was then a basic intuition on my part. I will quote them very briefly:

> China, for the colonizers, adventurers, and wives of Western capitalists, exemplified the vast gap between their own high degree of hu-

> manity and the *low degree of humanity of the coolie, the cheapest human flesh in the world along with that of the blacks. . . .* But it is precisely this land, where people were treated as dirt, that produced the movement of revolt against English, French, German, and American colonialism and gave the "white man" his first taste of defeat. The "white man" resorted in vain to his tanks, aircraft carriers, and bombers. The Chinese drove him out, along with his gambling houses, brothels, opium dens, spies, and courtesans. He is now raving in America and Britain, asserting that China has fallen into the hands of bloodthirsty, lawless revolutionaries. He advocates a war for the liberation of China so that it may again have the "freedom" to enjoy brothels, opium dens, gambling houses, and epidemics. So that the world may be delivered from the "Yellow Peril." The Chinese Revolution represents the historical defeat of imperialism.

I understand now that for the generation which had come out of the underground resistance, the Chinese Revolution was also the personal experience of an earlier October. As Mao advanced toward Shanghai, Chiang Kai-shek, disguised as a sailor and protected by the Americans, abandoned his yellow villa and fled by junk on the Hwang-Po toward Formosa. The guerrillas fought with weapons captured from the enemy. We in the Western European countries who were forced to surrender our weapons were psychologically redeemed by the Chinese. China was not affected by the division of the world into spheres of influence at the Yalta Conference; more precisely, China had already disrupted the logic of blocs. If one wishes to find a constant in Chinese policy since this period, it will be found in the stubborn, uncompromising refusal to become subordinated to either bloc. Mao against Stalin, that advocate of the united front with Chiang Kai-shek until the eve of defeat. Stalin against Mao, whom he regarded as a mere "rebellious peasant chief."

When I visited China in 1954 there was no indication of future developments. I recall the platform on Tien An Men square in Peking on October 1, on the occasion of the seventh anniversary of Liberation. Surrounded by a thousand other guests, I saw Mao Tse-tung come forward with Khrushchev, then secretary of the Russian Communist Party. The Soviet Union and China were on excellent terms.

Mao and Khrushchev stood side by side as they saluted the red masses of Peking. They waved their caps at the schoolchildren who were launching hundreds of kites, miniature airplanes which rose like swallows, covering the sky with red dots. I saw Mao again in the reception room of the Great Hall of the People. Khrushchev was still at his side, following him wherever he went. None of us at the time paid any particular attention to Khrushchev, and yet within hardly more than two years he would make his secret report to the Twentieth Congress. Who would have thought that Khrushchev, the head of the great friendly socialist nation, would be speaking of a "Yellow Peril"?

Mao made an unexpected appearance at the Peking hotel reception. The day before yesterday I reread the following memo in my appointment book: "This is a wonderful moment . . . Chairman Mao arrived unannounced through a side door, dressed modestly in his everyday gray . . . He was greeted affectionately in every imaginable language. He responded by raising his glass and toasting his guests . . . Seen at close range, his face seemed luminous: smooth skin, no wrinkles, a pervasive light irony."

Chou En-lai, then Minister of Foreign Affairs, had approached our delegation (we were seven delegates from the union of Italian women—Communists, Socialists, Catholics) and asked me whether we were enjoying our trip. After a short speech to the delegations attending the reception, he had again gently approached us, raised his glass, and said: "To the health of Italy." (Who would have thought that it would take Italy sixteen more years to establish diplomatic relations with Peking?) I had already met Chou En-lai and his wonderful co-worker Kung Peng (my only Chinese woman friend, who died in Peking just a month ago) in Geneva in the spring of 1954, during the conference on Indochina at which China made its official comeback on the stage of history.

Other links have been established between China and myself. After October 1956, I asked Curzio Malaparte to take a trip to China for *Vie Nuove*, the Italian Communist Party weekly which I then edited. I remember visiting Malaparte in his Capri villa, which reminds one of a red heron wading into the sea. During his trip, already stricken with cancer, he had become hopelessly ill. He had been hospitalized and attended for three months by Peking doctors. Returning to Italy shortly before his death, he had willed his villa to China: he wanted it to become a study center for Chinese intellectuals. His last words on leaving China were: "I love the Chinese." He said this in the Chinese he had learned in Peking: *Wo ai chungkuo jen.* But to the government authorities China was not a "legal entity" and could not receive a bequest. The villa is still there, solitary, as if waiting.

Change of scenery. Paris 1964. General de Gaulle's press conference in the Elysée Palace. When the general announced the diplomatic recognition of China, I was in the Salle des Fêtes, seated in the midst of a thousand journalists who were awaiting the historic event. I was correspondent for *Unità.* Whereas for the others this announcement was no more than a simple news item to be recorded and transmitted, I felt carried away listening to de Gaulle's words in the historic context of vast China's triumphant socialism. I fixed my eyes on my notebook. From now on there would be either silence or polemics between us. And here this bourgeois general was throwing *our China* in our faces!

Second (less personal) prologue to China

> . . . in dealing with questions of party history we should lay the stress not on the responsibility of certain individual comrades but on the analysis of the circumstances in which the errors were committed, on the content of the errors and on their social, historical and ideological roots . . .
>
> —Mao Tse-tung, *Our Study and the Current Situation*

I am flying to China. This sixteen-year absence is minute in terms of the Chinese way of measuring time, yet it represents an immense span of years and experiences. One of its most traumatic events was the calculated split with China, which began in 1960 with the recall of Soviet technicians, and continued with the campaign to "excommunicate" China and the unleashing of anti-Chinese propaganda. The last *Unità* correspondent had left China in 1961.

Many of us (as the storm grew more violent) continued to believe in China's immense revolutionary vitality. Not intellectually or through a privileged intuition, or because we took no stock in Reuters, the Associated Press, and Tass. But simply because in our lives as political activists there were two fixed elements: the October Revolution and the Chinese Revolution. This conviction was shared by many party members. It was certainly not the Soviet Union's unilateral cancellation of its contracts with China, which caused very serious difficulties for the Chinese economy, that made us differ. Nor was it the dramatic Tenth Congress of the Italian Communist Party (CPI) in December 1962, where we participated officially in the consummation of what one Communist leader likened to "the schism between the Church of Rome and the Church of Byzantium, one which may last just as long"—for there the 1,020 delegates rose and vigorously applauded the speech by the Chinese delegate, Chao Yi-ming. I think that in this manner we, like thousands of others, demonstrated our rejection of the condemnation.

Little more than a year later Palmiro Togliatti, then head of the Italian Communist Party, while not sharing the views of the Chinese, became concerned over the widening split and its repercussions within the workers' movement. He advocated a more flexible attitude toward China, which he set forth in his famous article, "The Chinese Challenge." Certain French Communists like Jeannette Vermeersch (wife of Maurice Thorez, head of the French Communist Party), however, regarded this as a clearly pro-Chinese gesture by the Italian Communists. She denounced it at the Seventeenth Congress of the French Communist Party (CPF), and called the Communist student periodical, *Clarté,* to account for wishing to reprint the article: "This publication should not be called 'Clarity' but confusion," she said ominously.

I had direct evidence of the fact that Togliatti, although profoundly hostile to the Chinese strategy, experienced moments of profound uncertainty at the end of his life. I had gone to see him at his home in Rome after the Seventeenth Congress of the CPF. He talked about his article on China, and then, as though addressing a much more important audience, he said: "The discussion within the international workers' movement has been seriously undermined by the split with the Chinese leaders. It has become impoverished and onesided, almost lifeless." He was very animated, and he voiced a political esteem for the Chinese which contrasted sharply with Khrushchev's vulgarity at that time.

Togliatti wanted to gain time and initiate a discussion of the Chinese theses so as to refute them theoretically and, above all, delay the convocation of a world congress of Communist parties, which Khrushchev wanted to turn into a tribunal that would excommunicate China. As one commentator explained: "A new world congress following those of 1957 and 1960 would find us with positions opposed to those of the Soviet comrades." *

Togliatti's last act was to take a trip "under the sign of uncertainty." Although ill and tired, he went to Moscow in August 1964 to urge Khrushchev to abandon his plan to "excommunicate" China, a plan which the CPI regarded as a mistake. Togliatti died in Yalta without having completed his mission and without even having met Khrushchev. ("The fact that he was not able to meet with Khrushchev made him worry even more; it seemed as if he viewed this as the symptom of an ambiguous situation," to quote the same commentator.) Expressing his profound misgivings about the validity of the policy of split, he refused to restore the lines that he had deleted in the document known as the *Yalta Testament.* Through one of those contradictions which keep recurring in the history of the workers' movement, this policy had found proponents at the Tenth Congress, people who were caught up in the atmosphere of subordination to Khrushchev's strategy. For the first time Togliatti clearly expressed his disapproval of Khrushchev's attack on China, declaring that "The workers' movement never understood why the Soviet technicians were recalled from China." It is well known that when Luigi Longo, who was to head the CPI after Togliatti's death, went to Moscow, he decided to publish the *Yalta Testament*: "This is the moment to publish it, we must make it public at once." This act, which disregarded Soviet opposition (Khrushchev and Brezhnev), was an important step in the development of autonomous policies within the international movement, a development which did not always proceed in linear fashion, but which eventually resulted in the condemnation of the Prague inva-

* A. Natta, *Ore di Yalta* (Rome: Editore Riuniti, 1970).

sion, and in the successive positions adopted by Enrico Berlinguer at the preparatory meetings for the congress of Communist parties and during the congress itself. The CPI leadership, moreover, wrote to Longo on August 18, 1964, while he was still in Yalta: "The document left by Togliatti clearly confirms the positions of our party concerning the current situation in the international Communist movement."

Given this background, it is perhaps easier to understand why in March 1966 the chief of *Unità*, Mario Alicata, asked me to take an official letter to the Chinese embassy in Paris, requesting permission for one of our correspondents to go to China to gather "first-hand information concerning Chinese life and the activities of the party." In those days I could not even gain admission to the embassy, which was located on the Boulevard Bineau. When I telephoned I was asked to spell my complicated name and that of my newspaper, and was finally asked: "What is *Unità?* Is it a Soviet publication?" "No, Italian Communist." "Did you say American?" And the like. The comrades stationed at the embassy gate would not let me enter. The diplomats refused to receive me, declaring that relations between the Chinese Communist Party and the Italian Communist Party had been broken off at the Tenth Congress. The Chinese rejected all my initiatives with the keen yet subtle irony they reserved for us.

I persevered, however, with "Chinese patience" until the day when I was told that since I was a journalist and since a newspaper was involved, I could present my letter to the Hsinhua News Agency—New China News Agency—which was also located on the Boulevard Bineau. This letter was never answered, although I personally called for an answer every two weeks. I was compensated, however, by the friendship I struck up with the comrades at the Hsinhua Agency—Communists always manage to find a common language. These "inscrutable Chinese," as they were called by the Parisian press, soon became my cordial and highly intelligent comrades who eventually enlightened me a little on the events of the Cultural Revolution. This was the period when *France-Soir* ran such huge headlines as "China in Chaos" or "Mao Doomed?", and *Le Figaro*—I remember this well—proclaimed: "Maoism Is Disintegrating." The comrade journalists of the Chinese agency sent me their newsletter regularly and even visited me at my home early in 1968. I was then about to leave Paris for Italy. There was no doubt in my mind that my "mission" for *Unità* had failed, but my agency comrades told me not to lose hope. We parted good friends. I was starting out on another life but would not forget them. They understood and wished me well. My free subscription to Hsinhua was transferred to my Rome address. We did not meet again until January 1970 when, at my request, my friend Charles Bettelheim introduced me to the same ambassador who had refused to receive me in 1967. The Chinese embassy was no longer in Neuilly. It was again housed in the handsome buildings on Avenue George V from which the Taiwan "representatives" had been expelled.

I never directly broached the subject of the China trip to the ambassador during this meeting, although he was quite aware of it. I adapted myself to his circuitous conversational ways and to his oblique questions, which led me into speaking of India, which I had visited the previous year, and of Europe, with which I had been concerned for years. Eventually I realized that he wanted to "understand" me. He was evaluating neither India, Europe, nor Japan (which he knew quite well), but me, my perspicacity, my political position. Everything was nuance and allusion. It is through this diplomat that I began to realize the difficulty of adapting our way of reasoning and understanding things (which is related to Cartesian rationalism) to the more complex and subtle way of the Chinese (which values the understanding of every nuance and allusion rather than our "logic of reasoning" which is frequently mere syllogistics).

The world was now contained within that drawing room, furnished with yellow sofas. An excellent interpreter translated from the French. The hours passed without the ambassador ever looking at his watch, and soon I was no longer aware of being surrounded by Paris and the harsh Western world. I was immersed in a beloved and distant China which beckoned dimly through the political finesse of this Communist diplomat. One of the outrageous things now being said about the Chinese is that they would like to split the Communist parties. Nothing is further from the truth. The Chinese, concrete in outlook, have been interested essentially in establishing a dialogue with those in the Western Communist parties who can be regarded as "friends of China." They want to break through the walls of distrust that have been raised between us, but without ever embarrassing anyone.

I met the ambassador only three times. He was then negotiating Italy's diplomatic recognition of China with Gardini, the Italian ambassador in Paris. (These negotiations, by the way, were successful.) On second thought it seems as if I met him innumerable times—a long series of meetings, reflections, and thoughts which, without my being aware of it, enabled me to come to grips with China as I began to see things in their true light. I informed the party of these meetings.

Then the Chinese launched their satellite on April 24, 1970. The management of *Unità* (headed now by Pajetta) published an article, written by Alberto Jacoviello, praising China's feat. *Le Monde* and the world press quoted it at length, offering various interpretations of our new attitude toward China. For the first time it seemed to me that the ambassador was really interested in us. "Who wrote the article?" he asked me. "My husband," I answered, blushing, and added: "Would you like to meet him?" "With pleasure," came the answer, "as soon as possible."

He was clearly familiar with a polemical article Alberto had written for the "free forum" of *Le Monde* in answer to the Soviet journalist Dadianze, who had called for a kind of Holy Alliance against the "Yellow Peril." I then realized that the Chinese diplomats and party leaders concerned with international affairs read everything dealing with other Communist parties. They were minutely informed about our public documents, our published accounts of Central Committee discussions, and knew of every line in *Unità* dealing with China.

After the regional electoral campaign, my husband and I went to Paris. The ambassador and the press attaché had invited us to lunch at the ambassador's residence on the Boulevard Bineau. This was in June. The heat was stifling, and the humid and close air of Paris was charged with dust. The ambassador had a very long conversation with my husband, an extraordinary political conversation ranging over Europe, Germany, the socialist camp, the Mediterranean, and the Near East. Alberto then officially requested a visa for *Unità*. The ambassador appeared in agreement but replied that this was a delicate matter that must be viewed in the context of the relations between the two parties.

In August, while I was unexpectedly detained in parliament as the honorable Colombo presented the cabinet that had emerged from successive crises, I received a note from the ambassador ("Dear Madam, dear Sir . . .") informing us that he wished to see us as soon as possible about an urgent message. I called the embassy in Paris to find out whether it was really urgent, especially since my husband was away on vacation. The interpreter made some inquiries and said yes, it was *urgent*. I consulted with the party leaders and took a plane on the morning of August 12, promising to be back that very evening. It never occurred to me that the visa might be granted. As always, the ambassador questioned me on my latest trips to Hong Kong, Japan, Ceylon. He let me talk at length, paying close attention, as though this were the principal object of our meeting. Finally he told me: "Peking informs me that the visas for you and your husband have been granted. These visas are granted to two friends of China. We realize, of course, that you are political activists. But you are not a party delegation, you have no party messages to communicate, and you are not official correspondents. On your return—and only on your return—you will be free to publish whatever and wherever you wish. You will be able to see anything you desire in China. You will be able to establish your own itinerary and stay wherever you wish for as long as you deem necessary. You are expected as soon as possible. In Peking you will be received by the tourist agency, for you will be the guests of neither the party nor the government. You are two friends of China, although your political allegiance is well known. The tourist agency will organize your trip, as it does for all foreigners."

"This is wonderful," I said. "This is a happy day." But I added immediately: "And what are we to do if there are difficulties?" The ambassador looked at me as though he were suddenly very far away. Then he said, weighing every word: "Well, in that case we will postpone the trip until more auspicious times."

My husband and I wanted to leave at once, but things were not that simple. After so many years of polemics, a trip to China by a Communist deputy and by the chief of the foreign desk of *Unità* was an important political event that raised many problems. The party leaders wanted to consider the matter. Finally, consistent with the necessity they themselves had proclaimed to study all the experiences of the proletariat in power, it was decided (probably not unanimously) that we could proceed. The ambassador had been transferred to East Berlin at the end of August and was no longer in Paris; I think that one of his last diplomatic acts in Paris was to arrange this trip. Our visas were valid for two months, starting from October 20.

I fly to China

During the eighteen hours I have spent in this plane I have repeatedly gone over the events of the past—introduction and preamble to this trip—retrospectively thinking over many things, some more important than others. I should add that just before leaving I reread what our Italian newspapers have written since 1963 about the realities of the country I am about to observe with my own eyes. What struck me most was the deliberately casual manner in which our "house" expert on China dealt with a subject of such vast theoretical and political import. (Its "principal contradiction" opposes it to the Chinese, its "secondary contradiction" to the Soviet Union!) This casualness, to be sure, is common among the leaders of a great number of Communist parties and should, more precisely, be called improvisation. It ranges from the proclamation of "the errors of the Chinese Communists" to an abusive language without parallel in discussions of other societies. It can even be asserted that our party has never before displayed such lack of restraint, not even with respect to the United States. This is why it occurred to me on rereading these articles that they were based on a single assumption: that the Chinese "way" would collapse and Soviet tutelage over China be restored.

Others will undoubtedly deal with this matter more polemically than is appropriate for someone like myself, who is interested only in understanding the realities of the Chinese way. This must be done in the interest of all, for unity will not be restored without a serious examination of why the split occurred and then widened. As for myself, at a moment like this I cannot but believe that our attitude toward China reflected a particular historical relationship between our party and the Communist Party of the Soviet Union.

What, for instance, was the real reason why we first broke off and then resumed relations with Yugoslavia? There may have been any number of secondary reasons, but the main reason was our "faith" in the judgment of the Soviet leaders. We broke with Yugoslavia *after* the Cominform decision. We resumed relations *after* Khrushchev's visit to Belgrade. To be sure, we were less acrimonious toward Yugoslavia than were the Soviet Union and other Communist parties. Politically, however, we acted in the same manner. And this was true in the case of China as well. Others were absolutely shameless in talking of "Mao's line." The CPI press never went that far, but politically we had the same attitude. We ignored Khrushchev's remark that there was only one pair of trousers for every four Chinese, but we spoke of a "colossal Chinese crisis," and following the Ninth Congress of the Chinese Communist Party we insolently put forth the notion of "Lin Piao's Sino-centrism." Recently we went even further when certain leaders who had prided themselves on their "balanced" analysis of Chinese affairs hastily parroted the charge that the CCP leaders were guilty of "factionalism." They quite conveniently forgot that this "factionalism" in fact originated in the ruthless decision by Khrushchev's Communist Party, at a time when the Chinese were facing very severe difficulties, to recall its technicians and unilaterally cancel economic, scientific, and technical cooperation agreements. And yet, Togliatti's *Yalta Testament* had advised the CPI that this was an incomprehensible act. How then explain this return to the old theses and calumnies except in terms of the tendency to accept "uncritically" every Soviet pronouncement on China? The Chinese, for their part, did not mince words when they included our own party in their charge of revisionism.

I am thinking about all this as we fly over Peking. In my opinion, this attitude must be changed before an eventual critical position can be achieved. It seems grotesque at this moment to claim that we have an independent critical position without first clearing the ground of the *acritical method* we adopted when we accepted the Soviet views of China. I would like to further this end by making a modest contribution to our understanding of China—a first step toward a serious independent position. I think that the party shares this wish, for otherwise it would be incomprehensible that we are now, both of us, flying over China. We are both, as "friends of China," on our way to China with the consent and assistance of the party. This means essentially that there is a desire to respond with a gesture of good will to the willingness of the Chinese to grant us visas. There was this time, therefore, no waiting, as in the case of Belgrade, until a Soviet leader had disavowed the policies of his predecessors. Alberto made a point of this. *Unità* had sent him to Yugoslavia in 1955 to cover Khrushchev's visit of "reconciliation" and "self-criticism." This time we are not following a Soviet leader on the "road to Peking." We are in fact the first members of a Western Communist party to visit China since the split occurred.*

To appreciate this fact properly we remember that the CPI did once give solid evidence of its independence of Moscow—when it condemned the military intervention in Czechoslovakia. Time will tell how the party will react to the impressions and information we will bring back with us. They will be the result not of a few hours or days spent in China (which were sufficient for certain transient Communist journalists and leaders to make catastrophic judgments on China), but of an extended visit during which, in keeping with our agreement, we will be shown the *reality of China.*

My purpose is not to write an erudite treatise on China, in the manner of Byzantine Sinologists, but to "tell the story" of China after the Cultural Revolution. My dear friend Charles Bettelheim, to whom I owe a great deal in connection with this trip, said to me in Paris: "You know, it's terrible that current writings on China are so frequently dull, pedantic, and entirely devoid of interest to ordinary people. Our writings are of interest only to specialists, they are lifeless and esoteric. In my opinion, what is needed at present is the *story of China,* told simply and movingly, just as the country would be seen by millions of European activists."

And on the eve of my departure Simone de Beauvoir said to me: "You know, we no longer know anything about China. Whatever

* And we are the first anywhere—together with Edgar Snow who has been in Peking for the past month—to be invited to China for the express purpose of *observing and reporting.*

you write about your personal experiences, whatever direct dialogue with the Chinese you report, whatever you tell us about their views, will be a contribution. We are totally ignorant about China." "But will eight weeks be long enough?" I asked. "Why not? One must write regularly, tenaciously, daily. As though one were writing letters, as in your book on Naples." *

A well-known television reporter who lives in Hong Kong told me: "When I describe a man shaving on the moon, people go wild. China is our moon. People want to know the most ordinary things about the Chinese. There is a vague feeling, especially among the youth, that China represents the future, but there is a great deal of uncertainty as to what that future is."

"Letters from China," suggested some young comrades in Naples. "Why don't you write letters from China?"

"But to whom?"

"Not to anyone in particular," said another, "just letters addressed to all comrades, friends as well as opponents."

No, not letters, but I will write plainly and candidly—from China after the Cultural Revolution.

---

* *Lettere dall' interno del PCI* (Milan: Feltrinelli, 1971).

1
In Peking

China is not yet a great power.
—Mao Tse-tung

October 27, 1970: arrival in Shanghai and Peking.

Still dazed by the twenty-hour jet flight, I try to order my first impressions of China conscientiously, objectively. It is not easy. This is the country of the Cultural Revolution. This is the China of Mao Tse-tung—anti-imperialist, anticapitalist, antirevisionist, the revolution enshrined in its red heart.

At the Shanghai airport a huge Mao cast in polished plaster extends his right arm in greeting; in his left hand he holds a sheet of paper the way the ancient Romans held the *volumen*. Behind him, lettered in gold against a red background, is the following message of welcome in Chinese and English addressed to the traveller and designed to politicize him from the start, be it ever so mildly: "The hour of the collapse of imperialism and of the march of socialism toward victory has arrived." Airports usually project a characteristic image: the frivolity of perfumes and silk goods, famous liquors, *foies gras*, Japanese cameras and watches, Oriental pearls, German photographic equipment, even tulip bulbs. This airport is stubbornly filled with sweaters, wool caps, politics. Little books of Mao's thoughts, the works of Mao, illustrated magazines, all are stacked high on a red table. There are all the Chinese publications translated into English, Spanish, Italian, Vietnamese, Korean, Russian, Japanese, French, etc. There is something for everybody. We eagerly stuff our pockets. "Help yourself freely," reads a sign, and we are not slow to respond.

First image: *the forward march of socialism in the world*. Second image: *politicization*. Lined up in two orderly rows, young girls wave Mao's little book at us right under the wings of the Air

France DC-8. Are they expecting someone? Our travel companions perhaps, the technicians returning from Africa? In any case, it is normal for Red Guards to welcome the plane from the West. I could hardly expect not to see these girls with their red armbands, so familiar from millions of photographs. The only thing that still surprises me is that I am here.

Very young girls are polishing the arrival lounge, which already gleams like a jeweler's display case. Others serve tea. They are dressed in blue: felt footwear, white socks, Mao badge, small cap pulled down over the eyes. Still others busy themselves about the airport. They announce hours of departure, check passports, vaccination certificates, currency—it seems as if schoolgirls have playfully occupied the largest airport in China.

Another image: *an antitechnocratic world,* an antimodel of industrial hyperdevelopment (not its slavish imitation, as in other countries). This is evident from a single glance at the airport shopping area filled with sweaters, wool berets, fur-lined jackets, embroidered tablecloths, small handkerchiefs, thermos bottles, watches, fountain pens, cameras.

On July 13 Mao had made the following declaration to French Minister Bettencourt when he congratulated Mao on China's immense achievements (last Wednesday, by the way, China exploded a three-megaton atomic bomb in the region of Lob-Nor, in northwest China): "China is not yet a great power; the newspapers say that it is, but I don't believe them . . . As yet China does not carry much weight." The successful launching of a space satellite? This, said Mao, is not "a great achievement." And he added: "The two great powers alone have orbited more than two thousand satellites. France has launched some, and so have other countries." *

China? At first sight, to offer a composite image, it is a country which never attempts to disguise itself in any way whatever. An

* As quoted in *Le Monde* on October 16, 1970. On January 1, 1971, *People's Daily* stated editorially that "the world is facing a great revolutionary change . . . the revolutionary situation is developing more quickly than anticipated. . . . According to the teachings of Chairman Mao, China stands firmly on the side of the proletariat and the people, as well as of the oppressed nations throughout the world. . . . *Never, and under no circumstances, will China behave like a superpower, neither today nor in the future.*" (Italics mine.)

overwhelmingly agricultural country with 500 million peasants in a population which will soon number 750 million (some, like Snow, estimate this figure at 800 million); a country which is described perfectly in Mao's little red book, which I have just picked up at the Shanghai airport:

> Things develop ceaselessly. It is only forty-five years since the revolution of 1911, but the face of China has completely changed. In another forty-five years, that is, in the year 2001, or the beginning of the twenty-first century, China will have undergone an even greater change. It will have become a powerful socialist industrial country. And that is as it should be. China is a land with an area of 9,600,000 square kilometers and a population of 600 million people, and it ought to have made a greater contribution to humanity. Its contribution over a long period has been far too small. For this we are regretful.
>
> But we must be modest—not only now, but forty-five years hence as well. We should always be modest. In our international relations, we Chinese people should get rid of great-power chauvinism resolutely, thoroughly, wholly, and completely.

We go to the airport foreign exchange office to buy yuan. "What kind of currency do you have?" asks the comrade who met us. "You may change any currency except dollars. In China we do not accept or change dollars." Why not? "We are struggling against American imperialism. Why should we accept American currency?" The dollar is a "paper tiger."

Stewardesses and stewards: Red Guards

In the Chinese Shanghai-Peking plane, which leaves two hours after the weekly arrival of the Air France Paris-Shanghai flight (the fastest way of getting to China from Western Europe), the young stewardesses sit down on the armrests and chat with the passengers. They question the chauffeur who spent three years in Algeria and made the flight with us from Paris. How many miles does he drive daily? What do Algerians look like? What about the climate and the food? The questions reflect their seriousness and eagerness to learn.

It is frequently said in the West that the Chinese are self-absorbed or that, as the Americans claim, they "withdraw into a shell." We soon discover, however, that they are extremely interested in everything about other countries, not in order to imitate them—never to imitate—but in order to understand, take apart, put together again, and perfect, as they do with machinery.

One stewardess is also a Red Guard: she is under eighteen and refuses to give her age. She took part in the Cultural Revolution, of course, but is working now. The steward is eighteen, lived in Sian and participated in the Cultural Revolution in his middle school. He went twice to Peking to attend the Red Guard rallies. For the past two years he has been working as a steward.

Young men and women are dressed like the soldiers of the People's Liberation Army, the ultimate model for the youth. This is not a question of fashion but of politics. The crews of China's passenger planes chose, at a meeting called to discuss the matter, the air force uniform—green jacket and blue trousers—and rejected the existing outfits of the stewardesses and stewards as being "too different from those of the people."

The plane begins its descent. It flies over Peking—tiny lights patterned in rows and rectangles. Pointing to an illuminated square, perhaps the Forbidden City, the Red Guard from Sian says with a knowing smile: "There . . . Mao Tse-tung is there."

Everything now happens with unexpected speed. Three men come toward us in the small airport lounge. To my surprise the youngest addresses us in perfect Italian: "On behalf of the tourist agency I bid you welcome to China. My name is Lu. This is the representative of the China International Travel Service, and this is Comrade Chao, also from the agency." I am astonished. Everybody has said that there are no Italian interpreters in China. Sixteen years ago I had a French interpreter with a rather shaky command of the language. He would say things like: "You will find the soup in the bathroom." (He meant "soap," of course.)

"When did you learn Italian?"

"During the Cultural Revolution. Before that we had a few courses taught by a Radio Peking teacher. After that we studied by ourselves, we corrected and practiced on one another. . . . We must rely on ourselves."

"Why did you choose Italian?"

"It is, in my opinion, useful to the cause of world revolution."

"Do you like it?"

"It's a beautiful language, but so are Spanish, French, and English."

We are seated at a table in the now-deserted airport, alone with our hosts. They address us: "We represent the China International Travel Service; you are tourists and friends of China. Our agency hopes that you will enjoy your stay here. Are you well? Do you like Chinese food? We will try to please you. In any case, it is important that we know your desires." And turning toward me: "You have been in China before, haven't you?"

They don't call us comrades and, except for Lu, the interpreter, whose gentle voice radiates friendliness, they seem at a loss, distant. We are soon embarrassed by the constant stress on tourism, on our tourist status, on the program prepared by the tourist agency which will be submitted for our approval tomorrow.

"Your embassy in Paris has already transmitted our letter containing our political requests . . ."

"We have heard of it . . . but we represent the tourist agency. Anything that does not fall within the scope of the tourist agency becomes the concern of the appropriate department . . . The tourist agency can do no more than forward your political requests."

I feel like saying: "We are not tourists. We all know that this is a fiction. You know very well that we are Communists, comrades." But Alberto kicks me under the table; he wants me to drop the subject. The comrades help us carry our suitcases. This is a token of great friendship: nobody in China carries the luggage of a foreigner. There are no porters.

Sixteen years later

A car with drawn white curtains—a big Soviet Zim—receives us into its capacious interior. Pushing the curtains aside, I can see row upon row of buildings. We are travelling along an endless avenue which, it seems, is twenty-two miles long; it is bordered on both sides by innumerable façades visible behind green trees arranged like bowling pins. I now realize, much better than if I had devoured tons of statistics, that the Peking I knew sixteen years ago is today part of a vast and unknown city in which the old style, with its rows of green ceramic animals running along ceramic-tiled roofs, has given way to a simple and functional architectural style. So much so that I have the impression of passing through the outskirts of some North or Central European city where modern architects have initiated a new kind of urban planning.

"Do you think that Peking has changed? You were here in 1954 and you can compare. The city now has 4 million inhabitants."

"Yes, things have changed, but not only in Peking. The changes that have occurred in China during these sixteen years will help me understand not only the topography of the city, but everything else."

The new city extends all around the Peking which Schickel, the German scholar, described to us as follows: "Peking is a rectangle crisscrossed by streets. Closed off and surrounded by walls that meet at right angles, the city is spread out beyond the walls of the Forbidden City like a geometrically shaped fruit around a stone seed. . . . Behind walls covered with green tiles, tall, pensive-looking trees rustle gently above the sculptured stone slabs and tombs." Peking is certainly one of the most beautiful cities in the world.

At the Hsin Chiao Hotel the lights have been dimmed. A white statue of Mao, similar to the one at the airport, greets us with the familiar raised-arm gesture and seems to give off light. The place reminds me of a party school when the students are asleep. A comrade who speaks French and appears to be the hotel manager—we later find he is actually a political worker for the tourist agency—approaches and asks politely: "Did you have a good trip, Madam?"

Our room on the fourth floor is as spacious as an apartment. It is divided by a faded green curtain: beds on one side, living room on the other. It looks austere, it contains nothing superfluous, as though it were meant to house studious political activists. On the wall, carefully copied and framed, a saying of Mao's: "Political power grows out of the barrel of a gun."

We are left alone. Alberto and I are left alone, very much alone. We look at each other and the happy excitement of the trip now gives way to a sense of political responsibility. We feel that a trip to China today by two Communists from *revisionist Western Europe* is a challenge, a kind of political test of our ability to understand the Chinese outlook.

Writing from China

This is by no means an easy task. We are handicapped by a *historical void.* When one "rediscovers" China after a sixteen-year interval, the initial reaction is one of humbleness when faced with the "curtain of ignorance" (the title of Felix Greene's book on China) that divides us. The sense of responsibility I feel is not ambiguous but real. How can I write *from China?* How am I to interpret China and convey its meaning to our people? Is it simply a question of "describing" it as it is? A mere glimpse of Shanghai, a quick ride across Peking, were enough for me to witness a rare phenomenon for a traveller from the West: politics as a mass passion, as an absorbing interest of millions of people. If I write in this vein, however, I will surely be criticized for being superficial or for fabricating myths about China. I am overcome with a desire to be coldly objective—to write like a moon-based observer describing Earth: to provide raw data for a historical and geographical atlas. For instance, it is untrue that the Chinese have only one leg or square heads. But someone behind the "curtain of ignorance" is sure to object: "Even if they have two legs, it is possible that one is shorter than the other. Watch out! Your vision of China is not critical, you are too impressionable." Yes, but how am I to measure the legs of 750 million Chinese? Those six thousand miles away advise me to use a "critical method," and the most cultivated minds tell me that I should follow our customary method of making a critical analysis of a socialist society. It remains to be seen whether it is, in fact, either *customary* or *critical.*

There is still another question to be considered. None of us, arriving in China, are able to write *for the Chinese*—this is a common flaw which underlies "leftist gibberish"; we can write only for *us,* for ill-informed people living in the distant Western world. Should I adopt the vantage point of an observer, of a chronicler?

Yes, but this is not enough; people want me to take a position, to choose, they don't like reservations. And where is it written that one may no longer express enthusiasm for anything touching on socialism? If it is true that there are forms of socialism which are flawed—"not presentable," as they say in France—this is no reason for sanctioning detached pedantry as the only way of making a sound evaluation of a socialist society. Emotion does not mean hagiography. All these difficulties in dealing adequately with China reflect an objective inability to achieve real understanding, and the difficulty derives not so much from "forms of racism" as from mental habits and unconscious reflexes rooted in the conviction that our world represents, in the words of Candide, "the best of all possible worlds."

While I lie on my bed under Mao's phrase—"Political power grows out of the barrel of a gun"—trying to sort out these thoughts on how to write *from China* in keeping with our responsibility as the first Communist political "explorers" from the West, there is a polite but insistent knocking on the door.

The comrades have returned to discuss the program that has been planned for us. It is a rigorous itinerary covering a period of almost two months. In addition to the two long stays in Peking and Shanghai that we requested, it includes a 3,500-mile trip with stopovers in Tientsin, Nanking, Hangchow, Shaoshan, and Canton (Kwangchow), from where we will return to Hong Kong before Christmas. Unlike on my 1954 trip, Manchuria (where it is now several degrees below zero) is missing; on the other hand, we will visit Canton for the first time and make a tour of Honan. In each city, they explain, the tourist agency will consult us before planning further activities with the assistance of the appropriate local representatives.

The Peking program turns out to be an eventful political plunge into China at the end of the Cultural Revolution: there will be a daylong visit to Tsinghua University, followed by a discussion with the university revolutionary committee. We will visit the May 7 School, where party and state administration cadres have been being re-educated since the Cultural Revolution. No Western Communist has ever visited these two institutions. We will visit the school for deaf-mutes, who are being treated with an experimental acupuncture method pioneered by the People's Liberation Army. Contemporary revolutionary plays, discussion of which sparked the Cultural Revolution, and a visit to the heavy machinery factory mentioned in the Central Committee communique following the Ninth Party Congress will round out the program. It is obvious that these activities have nothing to do with tourism. They are strictly political and quite in keeping with the desires we voiced in Paris. (We also requested a discussion with a factory party committee, which will take place later on in Shanghai.)

Scrupulously honest, the comrades ask us whether the agency rates are acceptable: forty yuan* per day per person—about $32 for both of us, including hotels, meals, and the use of a car in every city. The additional charge for trips not included in the itinerary will be 214 yuan each. The tourist agency is graciously placing two interpreter-guides at our disposal: young Lu, who speaks Italian, and the forty-year-old Chao, who speaks French and appears to be in a position to provide the political explanations we are constantly seeking. They will accompany us throughout our trip, but in every city other guides—always acting as representatives of the tourist agency—will join us.

"Generally," says the representative of the International Travel Service meaningfully, "we include neither guides nor interpreters, which are charged to the traveller. In our country, the tourist agency is directed by the party. This is a socialist country."

It is left entirely to us to realize that we are definitely not being treated as tourists, and that our program is not the customary one for tourists but rather for Communist guests. The Chinese approach becomes gradually clearer as we shed our Western habits—it is a way of sounding us out. They are, in fact, asking us to make a constant effort at understanding, to go beyond the surface of things. The extraordinary intuition which is required in China is not easily achieved, not only because we are unaccustomed to making this effort, but also because we must do several things at once: pay close attention to the interpreter, take notes, reflect on our observations, and come to grips with layer upon unknown layer of

---

* At the official rate of exchange, the yuan is worth about $.40; it is divided into 10 mao and 100 fen.—*Trans.*

Chinese behavior. Since the Chinese reality is primarily political, however, the Marxist-Leninist method enables one to grasp the *essence* of this reality. This essence can be summed up in a simple axiomatic truth: China is living through a great revolution which has been achieved yet continues to pervade everything—the Proletarian Cultural Revolution. The climate, the very atmosphere we breathe, are revolutionary.

Our impressions blend with those which, through reading and theoretical study, we have formed of other revolutionary situations—the Paris Commune, the October Revolution, etc. They make us able to understand the feverish tension, the sudden leap by millions of ordinary people toward the future of a world they are helping to change.

Compared with what I saw sixteen years ago, Peking seems now quite different: it is as undisguised and natural-looking as the faces of the women. Gone are the old, inlaid Chinese shop signs; gone the gold and silver glitter of precious fabrics; gone the flashy colors of ceramic figures on the house façades; gone the deeply slit satin skirts; gone coquetry, luxury, superfluity. The difference appears mainly in the toning down of colors, which from frenzied have turned into a uniform gray. This is what I wrote in 1954:

> The houses have yellow glazed ceramic-tile roofs, red architraves and columns, doors covered with yellow latticework and decorated with storied ceramic panes. The decor reminds me of a vividly colorful country drenched by a blazing sun which intensifies all colors a hundredfold. Small ceramic animal figures run along the roofs, heading toward the façades framing the shops, thousands of shops stretched along endless streets. There are no dreary-looking shops in Peking; even the coffin merchants display colorful lettered signs and silk-shaded lanterns above their doors. Most unforgettable are the dentists' shop-offices whose windows are decorated with enormous paper dentures exhibiting pearly white teeth against a background of prominent red palates; and since all these dentures are aligned in one long continuous row, the whole creates the image of one huge smile of happiness. Memorable also are the publicity signs on the bakeries, clothing stores, photographers, and funeral parlors. What a joy to be able to have teeth again—this was impossible a few years ago—or to be able to buy a handsome coffin! And everywhere there are pictures

and posters showing fat Chinese men and women urging people to buy.

The display windows these days belong to a different world. They are plastered with portraits of Mao, with quotations from Mao, with posters devoted to revolutionary works, with pictures of People's Liberation Army soldiers. They exhibit Mao badges of every size and kind, carefully aligned like watches and almost completely hiding the few pieces of merchandise. It is impossible, if one cannot read the Chinese characters, to distinguish between the shops of a watchmaker and a pharmacist, a shoemaker and a baker, a newsstand and a fabric store. The crowds in the streets do not look regimented, but rather seem to be a commune of seven million inhabitants. The people all dress alike in blue cotton (it should be remembered that this is an old Chinese custom), felt slippers like those worn by dolls, and carry small plastic bags displaying a printed thought of Mao Tse-tung: "The people, and the people alone, are the motive force in the making of world history."

Peking looks like a capital of austere revolutionary purity, the capital of a society of equals. There is an endless succession of political parades. Groups of children, preceded by Mao's portrait, walk to school to the sound of drums; after school they are often seen carrying chairs on their way to a lecture or speech, or to dance and sing revolutionary works. On entering Peking one immediately notices the posters of People's Liberation Army soldiers carrying bags of rice to a commune, working in the fields, or fighting on the banks of the Ussuri, the boundary between China and the Soviet Union. They parade endlessly through the streets in close ranks, frequently loaded down with knapsacks and blankets; they are mostly young, seventeen or twenty at the most.

In brief, Peking strikes me as a city dominated by the tension of politicization and of an unresolved, continuing struggle. Politics dominates everything. I recall the Hoping (Peace) Hotel in Peking, where I stayed sixteen years ago, with its parties, receptions, foreign guests, and constant din of singing, speechmaking, and clinking glasses. I went to see it again. It is now exactly like the Hsin Chiao: dim lights, gold tarnished with age, faded colors, the usual colossal statue of Mao. A certain conception of a hotel—as an urban symbol of comfort—has been abandoned. A hotel is now a place which lodges people who have no other place to stay; it is no longer the haunt of a high-living and offensive elite. Everything is comfortable, the service is excellent, but there is no luxury. Even where foreigners are concerned, there is no sign whatever of conformity to Western practices, no hint of our way of life. Everything is sober, as befits the attempt to diminish class contrasts. The hotel boasts two restaurants—Chinese on the ground floor, Western on the top floor. They look like cafeterias but have excellent food. The menu is headed with a thought of Mao attacking revisionism and imperialism. The meal hours, which are reminiscent of the Salvation Army, are those of a society which has simplified its ways in keeping with rigid hygienic requirements and the demands of a diligent and laborious life that begins very early in the morning. People dine between 6 and 8 P.M. at the latest, and go to bed between 7 and 10 P.M. No entertainment starts later than 7:15 P.M. or ends later than 10 P.M.

They wake you at 7 A.M., graciously but insistently, so that you can wash and dress comfortably and still have a long, profitable day.

From time to time the restaurant lounge is suddenly invaded by a crowd of young people—the hotel workers. Carrying their little Mao books, they disappear into a neighboring room where they hold a political meeting at which they analyze events and engage in criticism and self-criticism. We can hear them at the end of the meeting, intoning Mao's most famous sayings or singing a gay popular marching song, such as "The helmsman guides the ship, Mao Tse-tung guides the revolution."

A newcomer at the hotel immediately arouses the curiosity of the guests—customers, businessmen, diplomats, journalists—who are bored to death and whose entertainment consists largely in discussing the arrival of new personalities. A swarm of indiscreet remarks and whispered bits of information buzzes about your head, and juicy items arc passed on promptly, like news bulletins. Someone cautions us that the rooms have concealed microphones that record the slightest whisper. These people are already trying to make us suspicious of everything.

Our eager informants show us, not very far from our room—

which, they say, is one of those reserved for "important guests"—the room in which a Reuters correspondent, charged with dispatching what was regarded as false information about the Cultural Revolution, was confined for a year. His room was guarded around the clock by two soldiers (male and female) but, of course, good care was taken of his health—he was allowed a morning constitutional so that his appetite and morale would not be adversely affected.

With the advent of the Cultural Revolution, the manager of the Hsin Chiao became a floor waiter; he now works on the fifth floor where we are staying. He is plump, friendly, and modest. Previously, it seems, he had been conceited, but now, re-educated as a worker, he does his job to the satisfaction of his fellow workers. He is the waiter we see most frequently. He brings us large thermos bottles of hot water, advises me not to put too much tea in my glass, takes care of the linen, and exchanges a few words with us in English. Occasionally we hear him singing at the desk where the room keys are kept. He looks so relaxed that I wonder whether it really is more pleasant to be a boss. One of the first things we were told is that managerial posts in China are considered justified only in terms of wholehearted devotion to the collectivity, and that even the slightest tendency toward careerism is incompatible with full commitment to revolutionary tasks. "I do not aspire to a party membership card in order to become a bureaucrat or build a career, but in order to become an exemplary revolutionary fighter"—we heard this frequently, even from very old peasant women.

In an absolutely egalitarian society such as China appears to be, there are no grade levels of any kind. Distinctions of rank have been abolished in the army as well as in the universities, hospitals, factories, and offices. The young woman who waits on us in the restaurant on the eighth floor of the hotel speaks perfect Spanish and has completed her middle school studies. She is now spending two years working as a waitress. Her fellow workers will decide whether she is to attend the university, and this will depend on whether she achieves a creative understanding of revolutionary politics and of Mao's thought. A few Western diplomats in the hotel bemoan her "horrible fate."

At this point some general remarks are in order. The traveller who judges China by Western standards will understand nothing and be at a complete loss. Like a cultural mandarin he or she will lament the closing down of museums, and will desperately and vainly search for Western expressions of his or her own status as an intellectual. A Texan will exclaim in horror that since they don't have Cadillacs, the bicycle-riding Chinese are starving. Khrushchev, to cite a specific example, spread slogans that gained wide currency in the West concerning the poverty of the Chinese, such as, "Two Chinese share one bowl of rice, and four Chinese one pair of trousers." Even today there are no Chinese who do not remember these words as so many slaps in the face. But their very anger has enabled them to absorb, in their very souls, Chairman Mao's famous precept: "We should rely on our own strength."

And they appear to have been quite successful. The revolution has triumphed. Thus in China the simplest Chinese is visibly proud of having overcome economic and political pressures from a hostile world. But I repeat, any attempt to judge the Chinese in terms of our customary notions of *living standard* and *technological development*—which, as we know, are frequently misleading—will lead to very serious blunders. I do not mean to suggest that our traditional value judgments are easily abandoned. We are the children of another society and culture, and many of our conceptions are like epithelial cells. *Relearning to see* (making the revolution on the level of *superstructure*) is a hard and sometimes even traumatic undertaking for us as well. Even the most dedicated "revolutionary" among us soon feels paralyzed in the presence of this total self-devotion, this individual and collective heroism, this self-effacing effort inspired by the beautiful motto: "Be resolute, fear no sacrifice."

In short, when they say in China that all points of reference change, this may appear obvious from afar, but it is never obvious to those of us who are there.

"We must make our own revolution, every day, every moment," says Lu.

"That's a saying that does not exist in our language," I respond.

"There are words which do not exist at first, but which emerge from historical experience."

Understanding Asia

Anyone who knows India and Asia as I know them—I recommend this southern itinerary to anyone wishing to go to China liberated from narrow Western modes of thought—has the appropriate framework for understanding the immense effort undertaken by the largest country in the world to solve the problems of underdevelopment, food, clothing, health, education, and national unity.

In 1953 a trade-union delegation stated that China would "never" produce enough to feed its people or to be able to run the port of Shanghai in the absence of Anglo-Franco-American management. Both assumptions proved false; and China has even launched a satellite. A similar fate awaits our Euro-centric chauvinism and all the banalities poured out by American computers.

We leave our Soviet Zim for a walk in the Summer Palace.

The streets of Peking are incredibly crowded with bicycles. There are many more of them now than when I was here last: the means of transportation were then poorer, more modest—wagons, carts, rickshas. The buses and cars can hardly move, these days, for the millions of bicycles—there are always four or five bicycles in front of every vehicle. I watched two of them collide and their riders fall violently to the ground where they lay almost unconscious. The traffic policeman on his little tower blew his whistle and traffic came to a halt; the two men were given first aid and the policeman took their names and addresses. Our Zim slowly made its way through the mass of bicycles. The driver sounded his horn as though he were on a fire engine. The bicyclers, the most reckless in the world, made us gasp as we watched them zigzagging just in front of the hood or jumping like grasshoppers in order to get ahead of the car. I heard a story about an unfortunate British diplomat in Peking who had applied for a driver's license and taken the required test. "You know how to drive," he was told, "but we can't give you a license yet because you don't sound the horn enough."

"In my country, you see, sounding the horn is not allowed."

"That's probably because there isn't much traffic."

At the Summer Palace, where I had taken copious notes in 1954, all the works of art have been carefully removed—the museum no longer exists. The five pavilions, aligned in tiers along the grassy slopes that descend toward the artificial lake, used to rival each other in splendor. There were gilded alcoves belonging to I no longer remember which imperial dynasty, knickknacks, jewels, high-backed chairs encrusted with precious stones, tapestries. I remember the portrait of Empress Tsu Hsi, adorned from head to toe with pearls set into the paint and wearing on the ring and little fingers of her right hand the two gold, claw-shaped thimbles with which she used to slash her eunuchs.

All this has vanished. There only remains, on the lake covered with white water lilies, the stone ship which Tsu Hsi had built with funds earmarked for the fleet. I cannot see it from where I am standing, and I tell myself that it must have weighed anchor all by itself and sailed away heavy with all the ancient art works. The five pavilions now contain large statues of Mao and works depicting the life and heroism of the masses. In the central pavilion one sees two huge, life-sized papier-mâché groups glorifying two examples of collective sacrifice: soldiers of the People's Liberation Army rescuing Red Guards from a storm which has sunk their boat face miners saving their comrades by containing the walls of a collapsing tunnel with their backs.

Chao asks me: "What do you find changed here since your last visit to the Summer Palace in 1954?"

"I don't know," I answer prudently. I reflect, and add sincerely: "What I find changed, perhaps, is that these gardens are no longer filled, as they were in 1954, with women whose tiny bound feet struck the ground like those of birds."

Famous museums and restaurants

It should never be forgotten that an entire generation has already disappeared. What will happen in the next ten years? I have been told that the famous art works of the Summer Palace are all in the museums of the Forbidden City, carefully preserved and catalogued. I ask whether it is possible to see the museum which I visited in 1954 in the Forbidden City, where I had been struck by the divine pagoda and its twenty-foot-high gold Buddha with his enigmatic and cruel smile. I am told that it is still closed. * From the "Coal Hill" where we are walking with our friends we can see the outline of the wall enclosing the most famous Chinese monument, the Forbidden City, which Marco Polo described in the seventeenth century when Peking was still called Cambaluc. The silent pavilions inside look uninhabited. But we know that Mao, Lin Piao, and most party and government leaders live there, abiding by the rules of collective living.

On the subject of art and the museums closed for reorganization, Chao says this: "Liu Shao-chi wanted to preserve the entire past indiscriminately. He was a depoliticized technocrat who no longer believed in the genius of the masses. The difference between Mao and Liu, and it applies also to art, is the difference between two lines, two classes—between socialism and revisionism."

In front of the gates with their crouching lions, a foreign journalist informs us: "You surely know that there were nine such gates around Peking. Now there are only six. The other three were torn down during the Cultural Revolution. Sections of the Great Wall have suffered the same fate."

Every fact, every episode of this first day leads us to one and the same conclusion: a genuine, new, and difficult revolution has occurred here.

We are thoughtful as we return to the hotel and the noble Zim, the only car in Peking with a serious political past, gets parked among the other small and insignificant cars. It looks like a monument, its curtains casting mysterious glances. A well-informed socialist diplomat tells us that the car reveals our status as "honored guests," which is rendered in Chinese as "*kueiping.*" The telltale sign is not only the kind of trip we are taking, but this Soviet-made car which dates from the period of friendship between China and the USSR, and which now, of course, belongs to the party Central Committee. Our very itinerary is that of "honored guests," and the preferential rates granted us are those reserved for Communists,

* The Forbidden City and its museums were reopened to the public in the summer of 1971.—*Trans.*

however misguided. The others, the bourgeois, pay almost twice as much, not counting the additional charge for interpreters. The charges and rate of exchange, in spite of all divergences, reflect socialist political criteria. The dollar is a paper tiger and has no value. And in spite of China's violent ideological polemic with Moscow, the ruble is the favored currency in Peking and enjoys the highest rate of exchange. If one has rubles, say the diplomats, there are no problems. One must recognize these subtle differences in treatment—the first encountered by a foreign Communist—to understand much more than is stated.

"The Soviet radio," Lu tells me the next day, "has announced once again that famine is raging in China."

We take a walk through the narrow streets where, between 11:00 and 12:30, people take their noon meals. For twenty fen (about eight cents) one gets rice, fish, vegetables, and various kinds of soup. In the covered market of Hsitan, where everything imaginable is sold, open-air restaurants lined up like stands at a fair offer steaming broths, fritters, meats, fish, soups. The chopsticks move rapidly to and from the silently chewing mouths. Tens of thousands of Chinese spend not more than a few cents for a meal that does not have to be cooked by a member of a family: everybody works, it is cheaper, and it prevents additional fatigue. Contrary to the stories about the bowl of rice, the Chinese have abundant and varied food. At noon no one is satisfied with a mere snack, for the Chinese are hearty eaters. Between 11:00 and noon Peking becomes a huge fried-food shop which feeds several million hungry guests who are served quickly and then disappear. The whole meal takes between ten and thirty minutes. Jean Esmein, who has written a good book on the Cultural Revolution,* told me: "Remember, when you go to China, that there are three facts that you must cling to as to an ideological axiom: people there eat abundantly for almost nothing; they all have adequate clothing; and they passionately love politics, political philosophy."

The restaurants formerly reserved for the elite are crowded at this hour with the same kind of worker who eats in the open taverns along the streets or under the porticos of Hsitan. At the Pe-

* *La révolution culturelle* (Paris: Editions du Seuil, 1970).

king Duck, which serves the most famous glazed duck in Peking, or at the Little Mongol, it is difficult to get a table. Reservations must be made several days in advance. These places now cater to women with children, soldiers, young people, workers, peasants from nearby and very distant communes wearing white hats like those of the Tachai brigade, a few grandmothers, and couples—in brief, a crowd such as can be found in the New York subway during the evening rush hour. And here are all these people, perfectly at ease amid the ebony and mother-of-pearl embellishments, the sculptured ceilings and massive black furniture. Every revolution projects its particular imagery, and my first "images" of China are of these sumptuous restaurants crowded with ordinary people instead of wealthy customers.

2

The Cultural Revolution in the Universities

The Red Guards and revolutionary tradition

The Chinese schools and universities began to function again between the end of 1968 and the summer of 1970. The first institution to open its doors was the scientific institute in Peking where courses were resumed in June 1970. We are very excited at the prospect of visiting it, for it provides the first concrete example of revolution in the superstructure. The Red Guards are back at their studies or working in the fields, communes, factories, hotels, planes (where we first met them), everywhere. The Communist Youth League is being reconstituted, as in Shanghai. Meanwhile the party is calling an increasing number of provincial congresses.

I have been told that the youths now returning to work have changed profoundly, as happens to youths who have waged war or made a revolution. The Red Guards are not an organization (even though millions of young people wear the distinctive armband) but a generation of Chinese between the ages of fourteen and twenty-five. They are very much like the young people who made the Long March, the generation of Yenan and of the war against the Japanese. They can still be appealed to, as Mao did recently when he gave the initial impulse to the Cultural Revolution.

Every revolution has its Red Guards. I think that the phenomenon is as old as Communism. Westerners who were shocked by the appearance of these "hoodlums," "vandals," and "destroyers of hierarchy," have forgotten history. There were Red Guards during the revolutionary civil war in the thirties and forties. In 1946 the Chinese Red Army was renamed the People's Liberation Army. The Soviet army became the "Red Army." John Reed speaks of the

Red Guards in Russia in 1905 and 1917, men ill-prepared and undisciplined but full of revolutionary dynamism. The National Guard of the Paris Commune was *red* and *armed* (see Lissagaray's account), and the Commune can also be compared to this Cultural Revolution in another respect: "The Revolution spoke through placards, of the greatest variety of color and opinion, posted on all the walls," wrote Lissagaray.

The Red Guards will probably remain an inalienable revolutionary heritage of the Chinese, even though their role was a temporary one—it lasted for little more than two years. But this is only the first cultural revolution. Mao has predicted that there will be others, so that "China will not change its color, not only in the next five, ten, twenty years, but in the next hundred, thousand, ten thousand years." The most striking aspect of this upheaval consists in the attempt to steel the will of those whom Mao calls the "successors to our revolutionary cause" in a revolution in which they themselves are the actors. There is nothing clearer or more dramatic in this connection than what Mao told André Malraux in an interview in July 1965:

> If we make of the revolution a feeling of the past, everything will fall apart. Our revolution cannot be simply the stabilization of a victory. . . . The young are not born "red," they have not known the revolution. . . . Men do not like to bear the burden of the revolution throughout their lives. . . . Many youths are concrete-minded, resolute, prudent revolutionaries. On the other hand, there is a whole generation of dogmatic youths, and dogma is less useful than cow dung. One can make whatever one likes out of it, even revisionism . . .

In 1965 Mao had stressed the same point in an interview with Edgar Snow:

> I hope that the new generation will continue the revolution and carry it through on the basis of a proletarian line that will have to be revitalized through an uninterrupted revolution. Otherwise, we risk repression, the restoration of capitalism, and even the return to power of Chiang Kai-shek within ten years. But we cannot foresee how the youth will act in the future. They will have to decide themselves.

The revolutionary transformation of the youth is filtered through the schools—primary schools, middle schools, and the university. It is in this area of the superstructure that an attempt was made to effect thoroughgoing change. Mao's pronouncements in the field of education must be included in this account of our visit to the university in order to understand the cultural background against which the schools were reconstructed after having been destroyed. I transcribe them here. They date from 1966 and 1967. The headings are mine.

The superstructure and the proletariat

The proletariat must exercise total dictatorship over the bourgeoisie in the domain of the superstructure, including all the cultural sectors.

Current teaching methods are like those at the time of the imperial examinations

The programs today are excessive. They kill people. The junior and senior middle school as well as university students live in a constant state of tension. At least half of the program must be eliminated. The examinations are set up like defenses against an enemy. They are ambushes, full of esoteric and bizarre questions. This is nothing but the method used in the imperial examinations with their "eight-legged essays."

The workers and peasants must lead the schools

To accomplish the proletarian revolution in education, it is essential to have working-class leadership; the masses of workers must take part in this revolution and, in cooperation with People's Liberation Army fighters, form a revolutionary three-in-one combination with the activists among the students, teachers and workers in schools and colleges, who are determined to carry the proletarian revolution in education through to the end. The workers' propaganda teams should stay permanently in the schools, take part in all the tasks of struggle-criticism-transformation there and will always lead these institutions. In the countryside, it is the poor and lower-middle peasants, the staunchest allies of the working class, who must occupy themselves with the schools.

Give attention to the re-education of the teaching staff

We must give particular attention to re-educating the large numbers of university and middle school graduates who started work quite some time ago, as well as to those who have just begun to work, so that they will integrate themselves with the workers and peasants. . . . These people should be publicized in order to encourage them and others. Those who are really impossible, that is, the diehard capitalist roaders and bourgeois technical authorities who have incurred the intense wrath of the masses and therefore must be overthrown, are very few in number. Even they should be given a way out. It is not the policy of the proletariat to deny people a way out. The abovementioned policies should be applied to both new and old intellectuals, whether working in the arts or sciences.

Decentralization of young graduates

It is essential that young intellectuals be re-educated in the countryside by the poor and lower-middle peasants. The urban cadres must be persuaded to send their children who have completed junior and senior middle school, or the university, to the countryside where the comrades in the various rural regions must give them a warm welcome.

Roundtable discussion at Tsinghua

Tsinghua University is the most famous scientific institute in China. Visiting it is like making a pilgrimage to a battlefield, for this was the scene of one of the pathbreaking political struggles in the unfolding Cultural Revolution.

Our discussion takes place in a vast room flooded with light streaming through four arched windows—the president's reception room. We face each other across a massive, barricade-like, thirty-foot-long oak table: on one side, the foreign visitors with their interpreters and companions; on the other, the members of the university revolutionary committee and other participants.

It should be stressed that these "round"-table discussions, increasingly common in China since the Cultural Revolution, are by no means staged or ritualistic affairs. Our previous encounters with them in socialist countries, and even in China in that far-off year of 1954, strike me as of an altogether different kind. Someone would speak and the others would merely parrot what had been said, or remain tongue-tied, as if mummified. In those days tongues loosened only during the drinking bouts that followed the political discussions. Over gargantuan meals, people would give each other friendly pokes in the back and the "Russian soul," à la Gogol and Tolstoy, would then emerge in all its duality, compounded of both melancholy and magnanimity. Chinese discussions nowadays are of a very different order.

This new style, which reflects a profound seriousness of purpose—its dialectical character derives from four or five years of Cultural Revolution and stems naturally from the Chinese political tradition—makes it possible to combine maximum individual and group participation in the discussion, as advocated by Engels in his later years. On the other hand, the "charter" of the Cultural Revolution, the "Sixteen-Point Decision," states that "in the course of debate, every revolutionary should be good at thinking things out for himself and should develop the Communist spirit of daring to think, daring to speak and daring to act." *

As one listens to the Chinese speak, interrupt each other, and answer all questions without the slightest hesitation, it becomes obvious that they do not mince words, and that they are more interested in exposing our lack of information as Westerners than in *pleasing us,* as demanded by the old standards. On other occasions, as we shall see, we frequently became irritated. This never hap-

* This is Point 6 of the famous "Decision of the Central Committee of the Chinese Communist Party Concerning the Great Proletarian Cultural Revolution," adopted in August 1966.

pened to them. They never failed to use formal expressions (such as "Great Proletarian Cultural Revolution" instead of "Cultural Revolution," or "struggle between two classes, two lines, two roads" instead of a single expression which would save time), but this was done because these were clearly defined concepts—as required by the precise graphic aspects of the Chinese characters—and would mean the discussion would proceed from the *lowest common denominator*.

At the start of the meeting a comrade, dressed in blue, his hands crammed in his sleeves against the cold, bids us welcome, hails our presence in the name of renewed relations between China and Italy, and speaks glowingly of this visit as prefiguring the future friendship and mutual understanding between our two peoples. Diplomatic relations had been resumed the day before, and this rapid acceptance of the most immediate reality clearly reflects an antibureaucratic mind.

These are the members of the revolutionary committee and the other participants as they were introduced to us:

Lin Ping. Deputy first secretary of the party committee before the Cultural Revolution, and one of the official representatives of the university revolutionary committee. Re-elected party deputy first secretary after the Cultural Revolution, he is an outstanding political personality in the struggle in the Chinese universities. He has an angular, bespectacled face, and nervous hands. He looks between fifty and fifty-five.

Chien Pei-chang. Professor of dynamics, with a solid reputation both in China and abroad, author of works translated in various Western European countries and in the United States. He is one of the re-educated professors.

Shih Kuo-heng. Professor of sociology. Works at present in the university library, for sociology is no longer taught. His works used to enjoy a great reputation in China. Studied also in the United States, where his work is well known. He is also a re-educated professor.

Kuo Achin-fo. A Red Guard during the Cultural Revolution. He is a metallurgical engineer who graduated this year. His face is still pimpled and he is twenty-three at the most.

Lien Chi-ta. A Red Guard during the Cultural Revolution, she graduated in mechanics this year. She is twenty-two, a tiny woman who looks determined and intense.

(After completing their studies, these two Red Guards stayed on to work and study at the university. They are both members of the revolutionary committee.)

Ma Yun-hsiang. A young woman sailor chosen by her naval detachment to attend the university. Braids with ribbons, jovial round face, not over nineteen. Member of the revolutionary committee.

Juan Hsi-min. An official representative of the revolutionary committee.

Liu Min-yi. Worker, head of the Mao Tse-tung Thought Propaganda Team. May be forty but looks thirty. Very friendly, big hands unlike the usual slender hands of the Chinese. Wide face, high cheekbones. For all practical purposes, he is the head of the university.

The worker Liu Min-yi speaks first:

"We will make a report on the Great Proletarian Cultural Revolution in general, and more specifically on the manner in which it unfolded at the university. This is an industrial university. It is, in a sense, the product of cultural aggression by American imperialism. In 1911 the indemnities paid by China after the Boxer Rebellion were used by the United States to establish this university as a cultural weapon directed against the Chinese people.

"The university is fifty-nine years old. During the thirty-eight years preceding our liberation, its sole function and purpose was to produce comprador intellectuals, cultural puppets of the foreigners, and petty politicians of all sorts. After its liberation in 1948, the university became the scene of a sharp struggle between two classes, two lines, two roads. The university should have opened its doors to workers and peasants, but Liu Shao-chi, 'waving the red flag to oppose the red flag,' was agitating for the restoration of capitalism in the cultural domain. He found the agent he needed to push his revisionist line in the area of education in the person of president Chiang Nan-hsiang. For Mao's line on education these men substituted Western educational practices—European, American, and, subsequently, Soviet. They perverted the character of the party by packing it with bourgeois and reactionary professors who turned it into a 'professorial party' endowed with academic authority, with the result that the thirty-nine-member university party committee included fifteen bourgeois professors and not a single worker. At a time when the country was ruled by the dictatorship of the proletariat, Tsinghua University was under bourgeois domination.

"Chiang Nan-hsiang, who was both president and party secretary, became the ideological spokesman for the individualist theory of knowledge, for the notion of 'attending school to achieve a reputation,' and of 'becoming highly paid specialists and officials destined to occupy high posts in the social hierarchy.' His absurdities included the notorious slogan of 'the hunting rifle and food.' The schools, he said, provide the student with a 'hunting rifle' and not with 'food,' and while a food supply must sooner or later dwindle, a hunting rifle will always enable the hunter to procure food.* He justified these absurdities with the assertion that 'knowledge is an individual concern and serves to achieve reputation and success.' Furthermore, the notion that theory transcends everything led the workers and peasants to believe that simple things were in fact profound mysteries. The president stated that Tsinghua University was a 'cradle of engineers,' thereby belittling practical activity, and that 'the militants of the three great revolutionary movements can be adequately trained without leaving their laboratories.' ** In keeping with this view, the students began to hanker after bourgeois success and became separated both from the workers and peasants and from productive practical activity.

"This road is that of the 'three separations.' This poisonous line corrupted the youth. Grades were all-important. The prevailing grading system was such that anyone receiving the top grade of five in every course was considered a potential scholar and could thus aspire to become a university professor and study abroad. This obsession with grades as the foundation of success had tragic consequences. A girl-student of working-class origin had worked ex-

* A debate in Shanghai on June 12, 1970, included a roundtable discussion on the revolution in education (*Red Flag*, no. 8, 1970). To the arguments of the former president, one of the participants replied: "You would starve if you had nothing but a hunting rifle in Shanghai. What would you hunt in the midst of all that traffic? I mean that mere instruction cannot solve the problems of practical knowledge."

** The three revolutionary movements are the movements for production, for class struggle, and for scientific experiment.

tremely hard to receive top grades at the end of her course work; but on her examination she was given a three instead of a five, which was no more than the passing mark. She was convinced that she would never become a university teacher or be sent abroad, and was so ashamed of her inadequate performance that she sank into despair and refused to see anyone. She eventually hanged herself—a kind of holocaust of the revisionist line in education.

"Many students grew indignant over this degenerate reactionary orientation. Mao has always taught us that we must struggle against the old system of education which corrupts the youth, that courses must be shortened and their contents simplified, and that education must be profoundly revolutionized so that bourgeois domination in this area can be eliminated. We had reached a critical stage at Tsinghua. The struggle in the university between two lines, two classes, two roads, became inevitable. When Mao, in 1966, initiated and guided the Great Proletarian Cultural Revolution against a handful of revisionists so as to restore power to the people, we at Tsinghua started a revolt too."

Kuo Achin-fo, former Red Guard, currently a metallurgical engineer:

"On June 1, 1966, Mao decided to publish the first tatzupao at Peking University.* Its contents were broadcast by radio, published

---

* Tatzupao are big-character posters put up on walls, or laid on sidewalks, in factories, schools, and communes, which enabled Chinese public opinion to intervene in the Cultural Revolution. Mao has characterized them as the "cutting edge of the Revolution." On June 1, 1966, Mao approved the publication of the first Marxist-Leninist tatzupao. It was put up at Peking University and triggered the "liberation of the energies of the Great Proletarian Cultural Revolution and resulted in a mass movement whose principal target is a handful of men who hold powerful party positions and are opening up the road toward capitalism" (*People's Daily* editorial of January 1, 1967).

It is also possible to conclude from this editorial that after the Red Guards had taken the initiative in putting up their own tatzupao at the university on May 28, 1966, Mao *requested* its publication in *People's Daily* of June 1, 1966. The July 1, 1971, *People's Daily* editorial commemorating the fiftieth anniversary of the Chinese Communist Party, contained these details: "At the Eleventh Plenary Session of the Eighth Central Committee of the party in August 1966, Chairman Mao presided over the adoption of the *Decision Concerning the Great Proletarian Cultural*

by *People's Daily,* and widely diffused by the Hsinhua News Agency. The students and teachers at Tsinghua responded by initiating criticism of the president. They put up tatzupao denouncing the maneuvers and crimes of those taking the capitalist road. By means of tatzupao and meetings we openly attacked the president: 'Why do you oppose the study of Mao's thought and the Proletarian Cultural Revolution? Why did you undermine or disband the groups engaged in the study of Mao Tse-tung's philosophical thought? Why did you beat sons of working-class and peasant families, and proclaim the students an aristocracy and the university a place for the reproduction of class hierarchies?' "

The young Red Guard woman, a graduate in mechanics, speaks up:

"In short, everybody was confronted with this dilemma: is the president a revisionist or a Marxist? For us the answer was clear. He was one of the leaders taking the capitalist road. Within ten days we seriously undermined his autocratic power. He found it increasingly difficult to cover up his servile philosophy, his mealy mouthed parroting of foreign practices. Liu Shao-chi, the president's ally, was extremely irritated and worried over developments at Tsinghua, and personally dispatched a work team led by his wife, Wang Kuang-mei, who arrived at the university accompanied by party cadres belonging to various groupings with revisionist tendencies.*

"This work team had hardly arrived at the university when it began to propagate leftist positions—or rather, ultra-left positions, which are at bottom always rightist. The team wanted to strike at the many in order to protect the few. It branded more than 150 professors and students troublemakers and attacked them on the

---

Revolution and put up his tatzupao 'Bombard the Headquarters,' formally taking the lid off Liu Shao-chi's revisionist line. And so came the high tide of the Great Proletarian Cultural Revolution."

* These work teams, which had been formed in 1966 at the time of the Socialist Education Movement, either remained intact or were transformed by those who wanted to make use of them. Liu Shao-chi used them for his own ends between June and July 1966. They were openly disavowed after the Central Committee's August 1966 resolution. According to Joan Robinson, the work team at Tsinghua University included, among others, deputy prime minister Ho Lung and ex-Minister of Industry Po I-po, although according to Jean Daubier these two were merely "advisers."

basis of fabricated dossiers which charged them with harboring the sinister intention of destroying the party and which contained faked evidence of their counter-revolutionary character. More than 800 teachers and students who had composed tatzupao were accused of being rightists. Within Tsinghua, the work team tried to repress the revolutionary movement of criticism. For tactical reasons it removed the president, who had already been discredited in the eyes of the students, assumed his functions, and proclaimed itself the sole representative of the party. Liu Shao-chi's wife declared that anyone opposed to the team was opposed to the party itself. The work team took over the university. It assumed administrative control and eventually supplanted the party leadership and committee."

"But how were they able to do all this," I ask, addressing myself to the two Red Guards, "if the majority at the university were hostile to them? They must have had very effective slogans, they must have had real influence."

The young student-sailor breaks in:

"In those days Liu Shao-chi was head of the republic and deputy chairman of the party. Two factors obscured the real state of affairs: the presence of Liu's wife and the work team's claim to represent the party."

"But did the mere presence of this woman, even if she was the wife of Liu Shao-chi, suffice to convince the student and teacher activists that the team really represented the party, and that its activities reflected the will and line of the party?"

The Red Guard woman, Lien Chi-ta:

"That's right. But things were not that simple. Nobody had yet mentioned the name of Liu Shao-chi as that of the party person in authority heading the revisionist faction. Mao had written his tatzupao of August 5, 1966, 'Bombard the Headquarters';* but the

* *Bombard the Headquarters: My Tatzupao,* by Chairman Mao: "China's first Marxist-Leninist tatzupao and Commentator's article on it in *People's Daily* are indeed superbly written! Comrades, please read them again. But in the last fifty days or so some leading comrades from the central down to the local levels have acted in a diametrically opposite way. Adopting the reactionary stand of the bourgeoisie, they have enforced a bourgeois dictatorship and struck down the surging movement of the Great Cultural Revolution of the proletariat. They have stood facts on their

task of identifying and defeating the enemy lay with the masses and the movement of revolutionary criticism that was rapidly growing among the youth. We began to see things in their true light and to attack Liu Shao-chi by name in the wake of our struggle against the work team, and on August 18 our newspapers also attacked him directly.*

"The work team branded both of us Red Guards reactionaries. We were deprived of our right to express political disagreement or any other views. There was no discussion, only iron discipline. Anyone opposing the party was struck down. Many of us were forced to engage in self-criticism. But we were studying the works of Mao Tse-tung and had learned that one must not blindly assume the revolutionary character of a policy, that orders must not be carried out without prior discussion, and that it is our duty to resist and disobey misguided or deceitful directives. So we composed this slogan: 'They may threaten to cut off our heads, blood may flow, but we will not abandon the thought of Mao.' We wrote this slogan in blood, not only to achieve a dramatic effect, but also to make our determination absolutely clear."

Red Guard Kuo Achin-fo:

"We were beginning to grasp the idea that anyone opposing Mao's thought must be fought to the end without regard to his leading position in the party."

"But who was opposing Mao?"

The young Red Guard:

"Nobody opposed him openly; even the work team pretended to act in his name. We had to dig beneath the surface, make a close analysis of the situation, investigate events with great care. We were maturing in the course of our struggle. In our discussions we succeeded in uncovering the revisionist substance of their revolutionary rhetoric. The political struggle at Tsinghua was extremely

---

head and juggled black and white, encircled and suppressed revolutionaries, stifled opinions differing from their own, imposed a white terror, and felt very pleased with themselves. They have puffed up the arrogance of the bourgeoisie and defeated the morale of the proletariat. How poisonous! Viewed in connection with the Right deviation in 1962 and the wrong tendency of 1964 which was 'Left' in form but Right in essence, shouldn't this make one wide awake?"

* On August 18 the "Sixteen-Point Decision" disbanded the work teams.

important. Liu Shao-chi had come here with his wife on several occasions,* and not merely for reasons of gallantry. His purpose was to work out a repressive tactic that would be effective *in all the universities.* Tsinghua was to provide a model that could be reproduced and extended for the purpose of repressing the student revolt throughout the country."

"But Chou En-lai came to Tsinghua in July, only a few days, I believe, after Liu Shao-chi, and visited the student who had been jailed by the work team for being counter-revolutionary. Wasn't that a favorable turn of events?"

The Red Guard:

"Certainly. But it was Mao himself who, at our most difficult moment, on August 1, 1966, sent a letter to the Tsinghua Red Guards. After that . . ."

The young student-sailor breaks in eagerly; she wants to relate the events in which she played a principal role. (This is how we learned that she was one of the first Red Guards in China.)

"I was then attending the junior middle school attached to Tsinghua University—I graduated in 1968 before entering the navy. I was one of the first Red Guards in the entire country. Mao's letter was sent to my school. It arrived at an extremely difficult time, and when we received it we jumped for joy, for it was clear that the Chairman was supporting us. We began to shout 'Long live Mao!' in defiance of the work team, for we now had conclusive confirmation that our course was correct, that it was shared by Mao. In this letter [the girl opens a notebook] Mao wrote:

> The revolutionary actions of the Red Guards express indignation and denunciation of the landlord class, the bourgeoisie, imperialism, and revisionism as well as their jackals who exploit and oppose the workers, peasants, revolutionary intellectuals, and revolutionary groups and parties. You show that rebellion against reactionaries is justified. . . . I hereby give you my enthusiastic support. . . . While we support you, we also ask you to turn your attention to uniting with all those who can be united with. As for those who have made serious mistakes, after their mistakes have been pointed out to them, they too must be given a chance to work, to correct their mistakes, and to start life anew. Marx said that the proletariat must liberate not

* At any rate, on July 11 and 16.

only itself but all mankind. If it is unable to liberate all mankind, then the proletariat too will not achieve ultimate self-liberation. I would urge you comrades to heed this truth.

"But who told you to organize 'Red Guards'?" I ask.

The girl answers quietly and gently:

"Nobody. On May 29, 1966, a few of us in our school met in back of the gardens, where we used to go secretly for meetings and discussions, and constituted ourselves Red Guards. This was two days before the June 1 publication of Mao's tatzupao. During the interval we discussed a formal name for our group. There were several suggestions: *East Wind, Red Army, Forward Toward the East.* Finally we agreed on *Red Guards.* We chose this name unanimously. Why? *Hung wei ping* consists of three characters. The three characters making up *Red Guards* express the concept we had spent so much time discussing. *Hung* (red) means that 'Our red hearts are loyal to Mao'; *wei* (defense) means 'We are determined to defend Mao's line with our blood and lives'; *ping* (soldier) means 'We come from workers and peasants, we have always wanted to join the People's Liberation Army, and we know that we are called upon to bring about the liberation of humanity.' The bourgeois reactionaries in our school immediately attacked us Red Guards with their white terror. Even Red Guards of fourteen were branded reactionaries, but since they were studying the works of Mao they did not capitulate. Nor did those among us who were hardly ten years old. Mao teaches that there are many reasons for Marxist-Leninist struggle. At a given stage it is possible to say that rebellion is justified. It is necessary to rebel. This requires sacrifices, but the enemy must be destroyed regardless of the disguises he assumes. Such is the nature of revolutionary rebellion."

"How could they attack children of thirteen or fourteen?" I ask.

The young student-sailor:

"In the junior middle school the children had adopted various forms of rebellion against the reactionary line, such as belaboring the work team with loud shouts of 'you are reactionaries!' They also composed tatzupao attacking the work team.* The student

* Toward the end of July 1966 a very sharp struggle broke out within the leadership between Liu Shao-chi and Mao. According to Edgar Snow and Joan Robinson,

rebels were then the target of a full-scale rightist counterattack, but small groups of them continued to expose their opponents by means of tatzupao and meetings. As for the manner in which the young revolutionary rebels were repressed, this is what happened. They were prevented from putting up their tatzupao, other tatzupao were torn down, and they met with great obstacles in trying to form rebel organizations. They were sharply criticized at public meetings and forced to engage in self-criticism. They were refused the right to carry on political activities. The work team even expelled them from the party Youth League. But the children knew Lenin's precept: 'It is not sufficient to be a party member in name only, one must also have the courage of a communist.' Although we were young, we realized that unless we opposed the revisionist line it would win a total victory. On July 23 we composed three tatzupao entitled 'Long live the spirit of the proletarian revolution!' On July 28 we took them to the party Central Committee team in charge of the Cultural Revolution. These three tatzupao came to the attention of Mao, who replied with the letter I have already mentioned. It was addressed to us Red Guards."

The young Red Guard:

"Our most memorable experience occurred on August 18, 1966, when Mao met with the Red Guards on Tien An Men square. Mao's warm greeting filled us with tremendous pride and showed us the way to further struggle. On our return to school and university we adopted the slogan 'Down with Liu Shao-chi!' We had identified him, and we now attacked him by name. We were determined to sacrifice ourselves; it was absolutely necessary to defeat Liu. . . . There must have been over a million Red Guards from all over the country at the great rally."

"What did Mao say to you?" I ask.

The young woman Red Guard:

"He said 'Good day to you, comrades,' and waved to us."

The young man Red Guard:

"After Mao, deputy chairman Lin Piao spoke. Back at Tsinghua, we kicked the work team out of the university . . ."

Mao's supporters were at first in the minority. (On the question of the relationship of strength between Mao and his opponents, see Chapter 12.)

"Literally?" I ask.

"Yes," they answer laughing.

The Red Guard man continues:

"Studying Mao was our Long March. It enabled us to expose Liu and fan the revolutionary flame. Thirteen million Red Guards from all over the country rallied in Peking and met with Mao on eight different occasions during the Cultural Revolution. Young people throughout the country had the same motto: 'It is right to rebel against reactionaries.' "

"What did you regard as the main issue?" I ask.

"During the Cultural Revolution we came to understand that the central issue was the question of power. To wrest power from the clutches of the reactionaries. The Cultural Revolution was a struggle to win power for the dictatorship of the proletariat. On January 1, 1967, we won out at the university as a result of a great revolutionary alliance between 90 percent of the various newly formed organizations and the majority of the party cadres."

The worker Liu Min-yi:

"The Cultural Revolution turned Red Guards and even children into fighters. They were the vanguard and their great achievements are extremely praiseworthy. But the development of the struggle-criticism-transformation movement taught us a truth: intellectuals cannot by themselves carry through a revolution of the infrastructure. The working class has to intervene. Mao had launched his great appeal to the working class urging it to assume firm leadership of the revolution in education. 'To accomplish the proletarian revolution in education,' says Mao, 'it is essential to have working-class leadership; the masses of workers must take part in this revolution and, in cooperation with People's Liberation Army fighters, form a revolutionary three-in-one combination with the activists among the students, teachers, and workers. The workers' propaganda teams should stay permanently in the schools and colleges, take part in all the tasks of struggle-criticism-transformation there and will always lead these institutions.' Who will transform whom, and who will win out over whom? It is over these questions that a struggle broke out between two classes, two lines, two roads. Working-class leadership was strengthened in the course of the struggle. The workers at New China, the steel works where I work,* joined hands with the workers of more than sixty plants and with the People's Liberation Army, and together we organized a Mao Tse-tung Thought Propaganda Team. We arrived at the university on July 27, 1968. There were thirty thousand of us."

"Is it true that you had to fight with the students who were continuing to take matters into their own hands both inside and outside the university? To keep them from using force, to re-establish unity and make it possible for courses to resume?" (It seems that the Red Guards, who certainly played a revolutionary role, did at a certain point lapse into fanaticism, vandalism, and factionalism. When the workers arrived at the university, they found it occupied by two rival factions totaling some three hundred students.)

The Red Guard woman:

"There were rival groups among us. We accused each other of extremism and revisionism. We were so self-centered that we could no longer tell comrade from enemy. This enabled numerous class agents to infiltrate the organization. They said: 'The contradiction cannot be resolved. We must again resort to violence'; or 'Armed struggle is the highest stage of revolution.' We accused each other of being Kuomintang agents, ultra-left Trotskyists. On April 23, 1967, the university became a battlefield. This very building and the one opposite were the outposts of the factional war. Helmeted students fought each other with slings, spears, pikes, and sticks. We had made these weapons ourselves. The absurdity of it all was that although we attacked each other, we all wanted to get Liu Shao-chi. In short, we were all revolutionaries. Three hundred of us had stayed at the university to fight it out. Twenty thousand people had left. The university became a battleground and no longer played a vanguard role."

The worker, who has been looking absentminded, breaks in:

"We did not find it easy to deal with the situation. We had to put a stop to the fighting as well as to the factionalism, which was so much grist for the enemy's mill. We finally succeeded in halting this absurd battle between revolutionaries unable to distinguish be-

* The plant continues to pay this worker; he was assigned to the university by decision of his fellow workers.

tween friends and enemies. We undertook to administer the university in the name of the workers, but it is clear that we did this under the leadership of the Communist Party."

"But by the leadership of the party," I say, "you undoubtedly mean Mao's proletarian headquarters. After all, it seems that the party had abdicated its role at the university."

The worker:

"Yes, that's exactly what happened. We were not afraid to attack the problem at its root—the party. Faithful to Mao's directive, we thus advanced both the cause of the rectification and consolidation of the party and that of the revolution in education. On August 1, 1969, we formed the university revolutionary committee. On January 10, 1970, we reorganized the party committee. In the struggle-criticism-transformation movement we resolved the problem of the cadres. According to Liu's revisionist line, it was a party principle to humiliate or hit hard at the broad masses of cadres in order to protect a handful. In the situation confronting us at the university, we workers applied Mao's line on the question of cadres: the majority are good or comparatively good, whereas the bad ones constitute a tiny minority. We organized the revolutionary masses and rid the party of the bad cadres who had infiltrated it. The majority of the cadres today have been re-educated and are integrated with the masses. We succeeded in reconstituting the teaching staff almost in its entirety; its members have liberated themselves from revisionist attitudes and are now fully committed to the revolutionary line. The purpose of this re-education is to further the proletarian revolution."

(Two huge oil paintings on the wall depict the workers entering the university carrying red flags and posting the liberation program; these paintings are a vivid illustration of working-class loyalty to the Cultural Revolution.)

The worker continues:

"Over 95 percent of the 156 university cadres have returned to the revolutionary line. They have again begun, at different levels, to assume leadership tasks in the revolutionary committees which are based on the principle of the 'three-in-one combination,' which means they consist of leading revolutionary cadres, leaders of revolutionary mass organizations, and representatives of the People's

Liberation Army. Before the Cultural Revolution this university had 10,000 students. When it reopened its doors as a socialist university on June 15, 1970, it readmitted 800 students on the basis of new admission standards. Now, at the end of October 1970, there are 2,800 students. Students are selected by the factory collectives and communes in the light of criteria that are not individualist but mindful of the general interest, of the need to 'serve the people.' Forty-five percent of the students were selected by the factories, 40 percent by the communes, and 15 percent by the People's Liberation Army. Before the Cultural Revolution, 60 percent of the 10,000 students attending the university were of non-working-class origin."

"But between the end of 1966 and the end of 1968 this university did not function, and it is claimed in other countries that China suffered serious setbacks in the areas of education and research."

The worker:

"They can't understand. As a result of the Cultural Revolution and the mass democracy which made the minds of the youth receptive to dialectical materialism and Marxist research, the students have made a qualitative advance they could not have achieved in two or three years of university study. And their struggle against the class enemy has hardened a generation of youths who, unlike their predecessors, have no direct experience of the enemy. Now we must continue. We must deepen their consciousness of the need for an unending revolution that will assume new forms. As Mao has said, this is but the first of many cultural revolutions."

Lin Ping, deputy first secretary of the party at the university, deposed by the rebellious students and then re-elected, speaks up for the first time. This man has made quite a comeback.

"Before the Cultural Revolution I was deputy first secretary. I came to this university in 1965 with my comrade Wu Tien. Before that, I did high-level political work in the party. At the university we had to confront the key question of *who transforms whom.*

"We were in the forefront of the ideological struggle in the superstructure. How was this struggle to be carried on? Thinking back on the past, I now realize that I was ignorant. The question of *who transforms whom* hinged entirely on one point: what is the correct line regarding cultural education? Where the line is concerned, concessions or compromises are useless; it is absolutely true, as Mao teaches, that 'if the East wind abates, the West wind takes over.' The essence of a struggle of this kind is the question of leadership. Lin Piao teaches us that *leadership is power.* The university party committee had the choice of following either the proletarian line or the revisionist line.

"I had a long history behind me. I had participated in the revolutionary struggle since 1938, and had attended the Anti-Japanese Imperialism University. This university at Yenan was founded by Mao and headed by Lin Piao. Mao Tse-tung taught us philosophy at Yenan; together with the Chairman we studied his works "On Contradiction" and "On Practice." These widely known texts formed the subject matter of our studies. Lin Piao taught the military courses on the war of resistance, on the war of attack and counterattack against the Japanese. This was the most progressive university in the world and it was really my good fortune to have studied there . . ."

The worker nods vigorously. The young woman student-sailor reads a quotation from Mao to the other Red Guard, and their discussion of it is obviously related to the remarks of this eminent comrade who was taught by Mao in the most outstanding university in the world. They smile at each other.

Lin Ping continues:

"In 1946, the year of the Japanese capitulation, and nine years after its founding, the university at Yenan had educated over 100,000 revolutionary cadres. To have been steeped in the spirit of this university in Yenan was an exceptional experience: in addition to our studies we also learned agricultural production and military tactics, and were involved in practical activities. It was a way of life whose exemplary character is inspiring us again today. The soldiers participated in every task, struggled against selfishness, and developed morally, intellectually, physically. Many of them sacrificed themselves in armed struggle, and I recall many companions who died fighting the enemy.

"In his 'Talks at the Yenan Forum on Literature and Art,' Mao posed the central question: *for whom?* The basic question is to know whom to serve and how to serve. I remember this lesson perfectly. And then, after victory was won throughout the country, the question arose of whether it was still necessary to follow the tradition and revolutionary course of Yenan. This was a problem of line and therefore, as I said, of power.

"When they arrived at Tsinghua, Liu Shao-chi, who was then deputy first secretary of the party, and his ally, President Chiang Nan-hsiang, began to treat me contemptuously. Convinced that the working class is incapable of acting as a guide in the various areas of modern science, the professors told me with saccharine smiles: 'Think carefully, you did not attend a real university. What you learned in your courses is no longer valid, for that method is old fashioned, that method of research has been made obsolete by the problems of modern science.' The professors and rightist elements kept berating me: 'You are a simpleton, a hick in the most famous technological institute in China. What can you achieve here without scientific knowledge? You'd be better off somewhere else.' After innumerable humiliations, intimidated by famous professors, out of sheer weakness, beset by all these rightist pressures exerted from within the party, I finally gave in. I abandoned the Yenan road and began to parrot the bourgeois revisionist line. I am one of those 'communists incapable of resisting sugar-coated bullets,' as Mao put it at the Second Plenary Session of the Seventh Central Committee of the Chinese Communist Party. And at the Ninth Congress, Lin Piao urged us 'not to knuckle under to the sugar-coated bullets' of the bourgeoisie.

"I had studied all this but had not really understood what it was all about. I had arrived at Tsinghua from Honan Province to participate in the task of cultural leadership. Mao had taught me that the entire bourgeois system of education must be destroyed, but I had not understood him. I was unable to grasp the notion of a capitalist, revisionist line in education. I kowtowed to the president and imparted a bourgeois education to my students. I had really fallen for those sugar-coated bullets. I was not aware of my errors but, on the contrary, thought that the interests of the party required me to support such important university professors. The Cultural Revolution opened my eyes. Large numbers of students and teachers severely criticized my errors. Every day I saw the tatzupao put up by the Red Guards, or was subjected to fierce criticism at the meetings of the rebel students. At first I was furious and totally incapable of understanding the errors attributed to me.

"And then a subtle, almost involuntary, process of reflection set in: why were they after me? I learned to scrutinize and analyze every aspect of my life at Tsinghua. Why were the masses hurling such incredible charges at a Communist, a deputy secretary of the party? Why were they hounding me? And then I recalled Mao's teachings: we Communists are the force of the revolution, but we must not divorce ourselves from the masses and become party hacks without links to the people. The masses were against me. Why? These disturbing thoughts haunted me. They pursued me day and night, and gradually I began to understand where I had gone wrong.

"Marxists hold that the internal cause is decisive, and that conditions constitute the external cause. But under certain circumstances the external cause may also prove decisive. That is what happened in my case: the criticism from the revolutionary masses forced me to become conscious of my errors. Soon all traces of bitterness and discontent vanished. The connection between revolutionary criticism and error became a stimulating and even vital source of reflection—new horizons of thought were opening up.

"I began to go to the bottom of things. I raised my consciousness and gained a fresh understanding of the realities I had experienced. In a sense, I was making my way back to Yenan. I was, as it were, regaining my youth."

At this point the physics professor opens the little red book and becomes absorbed in it, as though he were alone. The university clocks strike noon and the chimes play "The East Is Red." The two girls observe our reactions to a party deputy secretary practicing self-criticism, talk to each other, grow thoughtful, and at times burst into laughter. I wonder what impression they have of us; they must surely think that we are riddled by those sugar-coated bullets. The sunlight is pouring through the four large windows of this vast icy room where we are all sitting bundled up in our coats, caps pulled down low over our eyes. Behind us, portraits of Marx, Lenin, and Engels—and, flanking them like a sentinel, the customary portrait of Stalin—are impeccably aligned. Mao's portrait, always apart from the others—he is generally depicted full face but sometimes in profile—hangs above the dais amid the crimson velvet curtains and six Chinese Communist flags, three on each side.

Lin Ping:

"At the propaganda meeting I studied the report of the Seventh Central Committee of the Chinese Communist Party and became more conscious and determined. The comrades of the People's Liberation Army and of the workers' propaganda team gave me a class education. We reflected on the past and recalled the miserable life of old China and the years during which I had followed Mao in the revolutionary war. I also reflected on the Yenan period, when I derived so much benefit from the teachings of Mao and Lin Piao, and on our struggles beside the heroes who fell in battle. Encouraged by all these discussions with workers and soldiers, I sifted every aspect of my life and completed my re-education. I awoke to the reality of the struggle between the two lines and two roads. I returned to the revolutionary road of Mao. The members of the party and the representatives of the revolutionary masses again elected me to the post of party deputy first secretary, and I now belong to the standing committee of the Tsinghua revolutionary committee."

Interruption of our roundtable discussion and visit to the factories of Tsinghua University

Tsinghua University was a pilot university designed to establish the new "three-in-one" combination—of education, scientific research, and production—in "open" universities which run their own factories.

It is clear that the Cultural Revolution is not intended simply to effect changes in distinct areas such as organizational structure, teacher re-education, or student selection, but to bring about an all-encompassing revolution based on the following principle: education must serve proletarian political ends and be furthered through productive work.

The members of the revolutionary committee with whom we have talked for over three hours now escort us to the workshops. What did the old counter-revolutionary president want? To turn

Tsinghua University into a "cradle of engineers," in the belief that they could become revolutionaries "without leaving their laboratories." The situation is quite different today. In the factories we see teachers, students, and workers side by side. They cannot be told apart, except sometimes by their age. But we also come across young workers instructing future engineers, and occasionally two handsome youths bending over the same machine. "Officers teach soldiers, soldiers teach officers, and the soldiers teach each other."

Mao's precept truncates the hierarchical pyramid in the field of education. As I had occasion to witness, it is applied even in the elementary schools, where it is consciously implemented by the children and their teachers. The university faculty, together with their students, has the task of combining practical and theoretical work. Education is rooted in practice and is losing its arid and abstract character. It has been noted, moreover, that the re-education of the teaching staff proves more successful when the teacher does not devote himself exclusively to manual labor, but alternates it with teaching tasks—if both go hand in hand. The aim is to have education, scientific research, and production develop at the same pace. In view of the requirements of specialization and the need to capitalize on available resources, a number of small- and medium-sized factories have been set up at Tsinghua. The three factories we are visiting specialize in the manufacture of precision instruments, experimental electronic equipment, and engine-propelled vehicles. All three are capable of filling state orders.

We enter the July 27 Truck Factory.

"Do you like the name of your factory?" I ask.

"Certainly," the representative of the revolutionary committee answers. "It is meant to dramatize the intervention of the workers on the superstructural front." *

---

* It was on the evening of July 27 that a propaganda team consisting of 30,000 workers and People's Liberation Army soldiers occupied the university and halted the violent confrontations between the rival student factions. Most of these men were withdrawn on July 30; only 300 remain today. The intervention was also due to the fact that, as I have already indicated, 300 students had taken over the university and were fighting pitched battles while the majority of the students had abandoned their studies. Between April and July the confrontations had been allowed to continue in the hope that the students would resolve their problems. But as the situa-

A new type of truck has been developed here; it has a very ingenious design and will be mass produced throughout the country. Right now it is still in the experimental stage. It is the product of a common effort by workers, students, and teachers studying and working together. The truck is in the courtyard outside the workshop and looks very functional. It was produced for teaching purposes, and thus illustrates the unity of scientific research and instruction, but large-scale production will begin soon. The factory is also engaged in the experimental application of various kinds of research on welding processes and in developing a new type of bus.

We enter the workshop of the Institute of Mechanics, which studies and plans the production of precision machine tools. The worker-representative of the workshop revolutionary committee has a long gray beard. He points out that no distinction is made between factory and university, or between the students and teachers on the one hand and the workers on the other.

"Were these machines here before?" I ask.

"Yes, but there were no students, workers, or peasants. Only experimental work was done here. We are now also producing for the state."

I see the grease-stained hands, the patched jackets, the workers' caps worn by the women.

"It used to be easy to tell the students from the teachers," says the worker, as though reading my thoughts. "Now it's impossible."

We enter into conversation with a young man beside a machine bearing a stamp indicating its foreign origin—"Cincinnati." He is sixteen, fresh from junior middle school. A friendly, bespectacled teacher standing next to him treats him like his own son. This young man went straight from school to the factory; we were to find out later what the collective thought of his work.

We meet a worker who completed his engineering studies at the university. He was a Red Guard but is now teaching, working, and studying. He wipes the oil off his fingers with a rag and cordially shakes hands with us. Not far away, two women workers who came

---

tion grew worse and serious injuries began to occur, the workers and soldiers, following Mao's directive on the role of the university, intervened on July 27 and re-established order and unity.

here for a two-year stay after finishing middle school are working side by side under the supervision of a professor who has taught at Tsinghua for the past ten years, and of an experienced woman worker who has just arrived from a metal plant to teach at the university.

We are told how students are selected for admission to the university. Those who have completed senior middle school must generally spend one to two years as apprentices in a factory or commune first. Workers and peasants selected by mass organizations, however, are credited with political experience and may enter the university immediately upon completing junior middle school. But nobody is regarded as "born red," and even working-class children generally spend some time working in the fields or a factory. Children from worker and peasant families acquire practical experience in the work place, and it is there that the decision is made as to whether they will go on with their studies and attend the technical institute or remain in the factory or commune.

The representative of the revolutionary committee shows us around the electronics department. An attractive woman with braided hair explains the operation of an electronic computer produced entirely with materials manufactured in China; it incorporates transistors, integrated circuits, analog integrated circuits, all produced locally.

This department is only a year old and exemplifies Mao's precept that creative study requires new, high-precision machines and should lead to the development of even better ones. This electronic equipment factory was planned and built by teachers, workers, and students working as a team. The old facilities were used to produce a new, technologically superior laboratory. The girl who is explaining all this points to two computers, an old one the size of a large closet, and another one of recent vintage hardly bigger than a typewriter. She adjusts the latter and we hear the sounds of "The East Is Red," exactly as it is being transmitted by the Chinese space satellite.

The university has its own experimental farm, also a year old. If the harvest is good, there will be a yield of 2,000 tons of rice for 8,000 mou* of cultivated land. All around us we notice, in addition

* There are six mou to the acre.

to the willows, cabbage fields cultivated by the students and teachers; and the university buildings that used to be "cradles of scholars" are now surrounded by 400 mou of rice land.

As we continue walking and chatting, I ask about the whereabouts of the ideologically "bankrupt" old president.

"He works in the July 27 Truck Factory."

Great surprise on my part.

"We have long discussions with him. We are trying to find out whether he intends to renounce his errors."

"And what does he say?"

"He says that we are wrecking Tsinghua and that he'll be around to witness our ruin. He says that his conduct was beyond reproach. Each time we part on this note, and he returns to the workshop to continue his research and other work."

After lunch we begin another three-hour segment of our "roundtable discussion," which will last eight hours in all.

This basic discussion of the Cultural Revolution has been organized by the Chinese with great intelligence and modesty. It enables us to obtain first-hand information from some of its leading participants: Lin Ping; the woman who was probably among the first Red Guards in China; the re-educated teachers. The university was visited three weeks ago by Maurice Couve de Murville and a Swiss correspondent. But no one before us has had access to so much information. And no one as yet has had the opportunity to meet re-educated Communist leaders like Lin Ping or other eminent professors of whom I will speak later on.

Another aspect of this roundtable discussion—and it is a constant feature of Chinese life—is the extreme casualness with which people here talk and discuss. They don't ever seem to get mixed up when they talk. They generally manage to express their thoughts effectively without resorting to notes, or occasionally with the help of a brief outline. They all seem to be born speakers and lecturers. This appears to be a general characteristic of the people.

As the red Peking sun is setting below the horizon, the re-educated teachers are given every opportunity to help us understand the enigma which leads Western skeptics like ourselves to ask: What is the meaning of an eminent professor proclaiming himself re-educated? What compels him, in addition to the study of Marx and Mao, to re-educate himself? Is he really sincere? It is impossible to give definitive answers to these questions, but it seems to me that the professors' own accounts are rather convincing.

The worker Liu resumes:

"I'll continue to explain what happened after our arrival on July 27. The majority of cadres had by then been re-educated and were part of the 'three-in-one' combination that runs the university. The revolutionary committee includes representatives of the army, workers from the Mao Tse-tung Thought Propaganda Team, and leaders of the revolutionary mass organizations. It also reflects three generations of cadres—old, middle-aged, and young.

"The propaganda team workers see to it that Mao's thought is fully respected. I was a worker in the big New China Steel Works. When I came here to participate in the task of running the university, I had to confront many problems and a sharp struggle. Our class enemies kept shouting that the working class is totally ignorant in matters pertaining to education and should get out of the university. Certain intellectuals said that although it is true that the working class should guide us politically, the professional aspect of the university must remain the domain of the intellectuals. It is clear that such a distinction nullifies the leading role of the working class. They wanted us to exercise nominal leadership stripped of all real authority. These are the facts.

"The question of power gave rise to a fierce struggle. The masses helped us organize wide-ranging debates between experts and non-experts, which helped the masses understand that the workers have created and must control all the sciences. The workers' reply to the mandarin-teachers was as follows: 'It is true that we are incapable of advancing the old system of education, but we are quite capable of furthering a proletarian approach to education which unites theory and practice.' We organized the students and university cadres into a vast movement of revolutionary criticism. When a teacher has to listen to a talk on politics—a subject about which he is profoundly ignorant—he usually falls asleep. When the talk is of professionalism, however, he is suddenly wide awake. When he is guided by the working class, he stays awake even when the talk is of politics, and he helps further revolutionary tasks.

"In running the university we are guided by three principles. (1) We help all those whose ideas conform to Mao's thought. (2) We help and re-educate all those who express ideas that do not conform to Mao's thought. (3) We organize the masses for struggle against those who oppose Mao's thought.

"We apply a mass line in running the university. We trust the intellectuals and rely on them. This approach is in keeping with Mao's principle: 'Let a hundred flowers bloom and a hundred schools of thought contend.' We encourage the intellectuals to express their opinions, to engage in discussion and criticism. This is how we succeeded in mobilizing the energies of the great majority of intellectuals. The work of these intellectuals furthers science and culture. Although the working class is in control of the university, it must also raise its own consciousness in the course of struggle, become an exemplary revolutionary force, and be receptive to the idea that it has much to learn from revolutionary intellectuals. If all these criteria are applied, the working class will be strengthened in the course of the struggle and succeed in smashing bourgeois domination of the university.

"Revolution in education means that we can be certain that *our descendants* will carry on the revolutionary cause and, consequently, that the 'three-in-one' combination will produce large numbers of teachers. This 'three-in-one' combination is made up of teachers, workers, and peasants from the factories and countryside who have acquired practical experience in the three great revolutionary movements, and of technical cadres from the factory research departments who are great assets to the university and are therefore warmly received by the workers, peasants, and intellectuals.

"Under the impact of the 'three-in-one' combination the number of teachers has risen considerably. This has enabled us to alter the traditional composition of the teaching staff and ensure the university's progress toward socialism. The teachers who have been corrupted by the revisionist line, the cultural mandarins who have separated theory and practice, must radically alter their conception of the world by serving the three great revolution movements. Whom does one serve? That is the question."

"But where are those teachers who were corrupted by the revisionist line?" I ask.

Sociology professor Shih Kuo-heng (he looks sixty-five, slender body, delicate features):

"Right here! I am one of those intellectuals of the old school, and I am also one of those teachers who was re-educated at the Tsinghua May 7 Cadre School in Kiangsi Province. I received my diploma here many years ago, at a time when the university was steeped in semifeudal conditions. I had studied sociology, and wrote books and articles in the hope of achieving great fame. It was my ambition to become a famous specialist. I studied in the United States and returned in 1948 to become a professor at Tsinghua.

"I had been deeply corrupted, first by feudalism and then by capitalism. After the Liberation I was unaware of my errors and shortcomings, and remained unaffected by Mao's thought. Under the influence of the revisionist line I helped further the conservative line in education, which means serving the bourgeoisie and not the proletariat, but I was not aware of doing this. The Cultural Revolution gave me a profound education. After the arrival of the propaganda team I began to realize that I was following the capitalist and revisionist road. If teachers are to serve the workers and peasants they must know how they live."

He looks very serene, nodding all the while as though approving his own words.

"At the experimental agriculture department of the university I received a very profound education. I am an intellectual who had separated himself from the masses as well as from the practice of proletarian politics. I had never engaged in manual work. In my agricultural work—why deny it?—I faced many difficulties and contradictions. I overcame all these obstacles, and this led to a thorough change in my ideological orientation.

"The principal work in the area where I was working consists in planting rice—the tiny seedlings have to be set into the earth and gathered when they have grown. Of course, I had never done this kind of work. I worked barefoot, with bare arms, under a scorching sun and sometimes in a driving rain. I reflected that in the course of my entire life—and I am no longer young—I had never paid attention to the physical fatigue suffered by human beings. I ate rice every day but did not know how it was produced. I reflected on this, and recalled a specific intellectual emotion I had experienced in the past.

"I used to have enormous admiration for a traditional Chinese painting depicting a peasant planting rice in the fields, wearing a large straw hat and a cover over his shoulders. I liked that painting a great deal, it afforded me intense pleasure, but I knew nothing of the reality it represented. As I worked in the rice fields in the rain or under the blazing sun I asked myself why I liked that painting so much. I admired it in a bourgeois manner. Now I have become very much like the man in the painting. I underwent a profound change, I was touched in my very soul. These memories move me deeply.

"My feelings were very different from those of the workers. How, then, could I *serve the people?* In the fields I had to carry heavy sheaves of rice to the threshing area. When I carried these loads on my shoulders I felt sharp shooting pains in my back and kidneys. Aware of my plight, the poor peasants gently showed me how to carry the sheaves and sometimes, out of pity, carried them for me. I was deeply affected by this token of solidarity on the part of the peasants. I was also led to reflect on another question.

"In the past I had frequently used the sedan chair of the old mandarins, whose weight rests entirely on the shoulders of the carriers. I insisted on using this means of transportation, I was totally unconcerned with the men who were carrying me, and I felt no desire whatever to stop using them. [General laughter.] And now, when it was my turn to carry a much lighter load, the peasants helped me generously. Education cannot be separated from transformation, says Mao, and I thus received a new kind of education. It is through the poor peasants that I came to understand exploitation. I also drew another parallel.

"Previously I used to believe that I was a great scholar, and I was very arrogant toward the workers, whom I despised. My re-education by the workers reminded me of an old book of mine. This work was based entirely on Western sociology and was an attempt, from a bourgeois point of view, to define the most effective methods for increasing workers' productivity and the pace of work in the factories. My book helped the capitalists exploit the workers. It was published in the United States and China. It was basically the success of this book that enabled me to study abroad. There was great appreciation of the manner in which I had treated the problem of organizing industrial production so as to increase productivity and the work pace—and, consequently, exploitation. My book contained basically bourgeois, revisionist theories. They were based on my sociological knowledge: I discussed the pace of work, bonuses and wage increases, and the need for cooperation between workers and employers."

Watching and listening to him, I begin to believe that physical fatigue has really changed him and given him great energy. He warms his nervous hands by clenching his glass of tea. The discussion seems to liberate him, he appears to view us as genuine discussion partners—in brief, he appears to be confessing himself. I feel only one doubt: how sincere is he? He continues:

"Whom does one serve? That, as I have said, is the question. The only way to transform bourgeois intellectuals is to integrate them with the masses. In my agricultural work I eventually came to feel happy, courageous, generous; I was among young people and experienced a profound inner upheaval. The comrades at Tsinghua tell me that I have changed a great deal. They used to call me 'old Shih'; now they say: 'Look how young old Shih has become.' [General laughter.] It is true that I have been rejuvenated, and I am now determined to support the Cultural Revolution to the end. An intellectual like myself, who has been exposed to the influence of the old society for so many years, obviously cannot resolve all his problems in a short span of time. But I know that this new kind of education opens up magnificent horizons."

The deputy second secretary of the party speaks again.

"The change in Shih results from Mao's 'May 7 Directive.' From a mere admirer of a painting, he came to resemble the man depicted in that painting. From a man who had had himself carried in sedan chairs, he became a carrier of sheaves of rice. This represents an enormous transition from one conception of the world to a radically different one. It shows that existence determines the course of knowledge, and that only the practice of revolution can transform the old ideology."

The worker Liu breaks in:

"As for the university people who preserved a bourgeois mentality, we criticize them continually and firmly."

"But where are these university people?"

"Right here," answers a small voice, and a burst of laughter greets this remark.

The worker continues:

"The oldest of these intellectuals are given an adequate salary. It is as though they had retired. They are free to study the works of Mao and engage in research or write critical works on historical matters. The famous architect Lien Su-chen, who used to teach here, began to study archeology and is no longer interested in the university. Patience! But those who are in good health and who wish to serve proletarian science and culture are given, in spite of the differences between us, every opportunity to continue working here."

The small voice is heard again:

"Right here."

The voice belongs to Professor Chien, a famous professor of dynamics.

"When I said that these bourgeois university teachers you were inquiring about are here, I was not joking. I am one of them. For forty years I taught dynamics in this university, where I was also a student. I received a bourgeois education here, and then went to the United States where I did research in the hope of achieving fame and becoming a prestigious bourgeois-type specialist. I returned to China in 1946 and have been at the university ever since.

"After 1948 I opposed the attempt to transform ideology, considering that there was nothing for me to transform. I used my professorial position to spread a spirit of derision and skepticism among the youth. Mao teaches us that we must unite theory and practice, but I maintained that theory is more important than practice."

The professor has a round face, smooth reddish skin, soft hair, and a mole under his left eye. He looks between sixty and sixty-five. The worker-representative of the propaganda team, who is sitting next to him, watches him obliquely through his tobacco smoke, and looks at him both ironically and affectionately. It is clear that there are very deep bonds between these two men.

"In encouraging the students to read and study, my only hope was that they would become scholars, engineers, specialists; I banked on pride and intellectual arrogance. I wanted them to follow my own example. When the president sanctioned bourgeois theories and the Soviet educational system, I became an instrument of his revisionist line. When the Cultural Revolution broke out my house was plastered with tatzupao. There were so many of them that they hid the door. Everybody at Tsinghua says that I am a hopeless case, that I am nothing but a university mandarin, a bourgeois reactionary. The Cultural Revolution, however, has made a profound impact on me. The workers' propaganda team was quite effective in educating me. The workers accomplished a twofold task: they guided the masses and criticized errors; and they effected a kind of mobilization of our inner resources so as to lead us to self-criticism. I was thus led to make my first self-criticism. My proletarian educators then sent me to work and be re-educated at the factory. Within the past two years I have worked side by side with the workers in three different factories where I introduced technical innovations and designed new machinery. I'll give you an example of the way I was re-educated."

He laughs, very pleased with himself. The worker looks at him affectionately.

"Once when I was working in a steel factory, a worker was scratching a number on some ingots and I thought that he was signing them. I thought that he was signing his name. It was a classical misunderstanding, of course, for obviously workers do not sign the products of their labor as I have always signed mine. Their situation is altogether different. My books were my products. I wrote books in order to acquire prestige, and signing them gave me intense pleasure. My personal prestige was enhanced and this, I thought, would enable me to work quietly and comfortably to the end of my days. This was an insignificant event. But the comparison between this 'worker's signature' and my own became a source of basic reflection on my part; it triggered a change in my conception of the world. I began to understand that I had done all my work for the purpose of gaining prestige."

The deputy first secretary:

"This apparently insignificant incident of the signature sparked a new awareness of two conflicting conceptions of the world."

The professor of dynamics resumes:

"With the help of my teacher Liu [the worker nods, and it is obvious to me that they work side by side] my factory work taught me that workers are in fact the proper teachers of professors. I have changed rather profoundly in the past two years. They still say that I am a hopeless case, but the gradual change I have undergone is such that I no longer feel that my situation is hopeless—I feel that I am a *comrade.*

"In the West they used to say that we intellectuals were finished, abandoned, driven into emptiness and inertia. That used to be my opinion too. That we had been destroyed as intellectuals. That we had been annihilated, like the great Western newspapers in China. But I assure you that the Cultural Revolution revived me in a very real and profound sense. I can truly say that a new political life began for me.

"I have really abandoned the old road and the old ideology. I must say that I am extremely interested in this link with the workers. I realize that it is a source of both scientific and moral enrichment. The worker Liu, who was my teacher-comrade, helped me a great deal in the factory. And the same is true of other colleagues of mine who were greatly aided by workers, peasants, and soldiers. These professors were thus enabled to continue with their scientific work. They helped design new machines, and established closer links with the masses to whom they had felt so superior in the past."

The worker Liu:

"I will now explain the line of socialist administration which we adopted at the university. The students must not only study literature, but also agriculture, and do military exercises and manual work. We must continue the revolutionary tradition of Yenan. We apply the educational principles of Chairman Mao. Education must reflect proletarian policies and be linked to production.

"Peking has ten universities, and in all of them education is being transformed under the impact of social practice. The blackboards now display the machines and plants that will be encountered in practical work. In our university workshops we must establish close links between social practice on the one hand, and research and production on the other. To this end we have taken the following steps:

"1. The arrival of the propaganda teams has led to the establishment of a university factory. We have workshops specializing in the design of new buses, in experimental electronics, in precision machine tools, and so on.

"2. We have set up research centers which have the task of reaching and surpassing the most advanced existing levels of scientific knowledge.

"3. We are engaged in agricultural work. The land not only provides us with an abundant yield, but also enables us to train agricultural technicians.

"4. We have specialized faculties whose research is applied locally. The hydraulics faculty, for instance, is located in San Min Sha on the Yellow River, where it conducts irrigation research. The architecture faculty is active on construction sites. If you ever visit the neighborhoods in Peking where new housing is going up, you will see students and teachers participating in construction work. Before this the students gained all their knowledge from books and years elapsed before they were able to design and supervise the construction of a building.

"5. We are organizing the work of the teachers to enable them to stay in factories and people's communes so they can carry on scientific research and make innovations; in this we implement the principle of 'quantity-quality-speed-economy.'

"6. We see to it that the teachers leave the university to carry on research in various sectors of society. We study the resulting experiments, innovations, and inventions. After our investigation we modify the courses in the light of the innovations or inventions suggested by the local workers, peasants, and soldiers, and then reincorporate them in the courses so that they may be elaborated upon and taught to the students.

"Culture is thus generalized and raised to a higher level. At the same time, we give a great impetus to industrial and agricultural production. We are also taking other steps."

"How are the students selected for admission to the university?" I ask.

"Mao teaches," answers the worker, "that students must be selected from among the workers, peasants, and soldiers who already have practical experience. They spend a few years at the university and then return to the factory or countryside. We have abolished the revisionist system under which the student must pass one examination to graduate from a middle school and another one to gain admission to a school of higher learning. The new method of university recruitment is as follows:

"1. The workers, peasants, and soldiers must themselves request admission to the university.

"2. The masses in their respective sectors determine who is to be selected.

"3. The local revolutionary committee ratifies the choice of the masses.

"4. The university verifies whether all conditions for admission have been met.

"The grading system has been abolished. A student who leaves the university does not receive a degree, but a certificate of university attendance which emphasizes the student's political qualities."

"How long are the courses? What is the age of admission?"

The worker:

"Following Mao's teaching on the importance of shortening the course of study, the duration of university study was reduced from seven to three years. The state provides for the student's material support at the university and pays all his or her expenses.

"One must be about twenty to be admitted to the university. Some young people entering the university have a senior middle school education, but they must also have spent at least two or three years in production work. Working-class veterans and poor peasants are admitted irrespective of prior schooling or age. The only requirement in their case is that they have practical experience. These workers and peasants come to the university to do scientific research and make innovations in the area of production. While at the university, these workers and peasants continue to be paid by the factory or commune which selected them for university study. This year 2,800 workers, peasants, and soldiers were enrolled.

As I have already said, they are distributed as follows: 45 percent workers, 40 percent peasants, 15 percent soldiers.

"The woman student-sailor, for instance, belongs to the People's Liberation Army. She completed middle school, went into the army, and was selected by her soldier-comrades as a student candidate. This is a concrete example of university selection. Those who do not come from working-class families are investigated as to their class origins and political conduct. As I have said, nobody is 'born red'—such an attitude would create a kind of privileged sector among the youth. We have admitted a few students from non-working-class families, but 90 percent of the students are clearly of working-class or peasant origin, or come from the army.

"The chief subject matter for these students is Marxism-Leninism and the relationship between theory and practice. The number of new intellectuals is growing rapidly. Before the Cultural Revolution 40 percent of the students came from non-working-class families—before Liberation this figure was 100 percent.

"The revolution in education is something new in the task we must accomplish. We have to deal with shortcomings and difficulties, as I have already indicated, but we hope to overcome them. Peking has more than fifty university centers, and before the Cultural Revolution there were 300,000 students. We have accomplished a good deal in two years."

"Who finances the universities? The state alone?"

"The state provides subsidies. In the future the universities will be administered autonomously, in keeping with the general precept of 'self-reliance.' *

---

* This principle was formulated by Mao Tse-tung during the War of Resistance against Japan. It was then applied to revolutionary wars and people's wars. Signifying above all that external aid plays a secondary role, it means that although all peoples must support each other's struggles, each country must wage its own struggle by accumulating first-hand experience, both positive and negative; by making an independent analysis of the problems of its own revolution; and by finding solutions that are relevant to its specific circumstances. In the absence of these preconditions the experience and aid of other countries are useless. The principle then became a pivot of the Cultural Revolution. It is applied not only to the individual, but also to the entire socioeconomic structure. The state, of course, helps the factories, communes, schools, local health services, etc., through subsidies, supplies, staffing, and techno-

"The logic of our system demands that the university do its utmost to meet its own financial needs, and that state subsidies play an ever diminishing role. The old universities give rise to centers of industrial and agricultural production, and new university centers originate in industrial centers capable of financing them."

Today: the spirit of the "pledge"

On leaving this university one has the impression of having passed from one era to another. And yet only fifty months have elapsed since that day on August 28, 1966, when Mao Tse-tung, dressed in sober army uniform and wearing a red armband, and Defense Minister Lin Piao met with one million young people in Tien An Men square. Today is October 29, 1970. The schools and universities have been reorganized. They have been infused with politics, with a revolutionary spirit. Those wondering about the state of mind of the young Chinese entering the university today should consider the following event.

At the end of August 1970 a few hundred students about to enroll in Tsinghua made a Long March from Tientsin to Peking. They walked for four days, pitching camp like a detachment of soldiers in order to dramatize the state of mind in which they were about to undertake their university studies.

When they arrived at Tien An Men square, where it had all started, one of them read the following "pledge":

"We students, workers, peasants, and soldiers place no value whatsoever on a career, we have no faith in past traditions or in the West. Inspired by the boldness of the revolution and the courage of new creation, we are determined to follow the line elaborated by the Anti-Japanese Imperialism University at Yenan and become revolutionaries. We will never allow ourselves to be corrupted by self-interest or the pursuit of famc. We have made a firm decision. In changing our occupations, our revolutionary consciousness re-

logical resources. But each local unit is urged to unify all mass initiatives, find ways of making autonomous use of all available resources, and become accustomed to solving its difficulties without relying passively on help from the state.

mains unchanged. In changing our environment, we remain workers. Summoned to a new task, we will continue to wage our fierce struggle as in the past."

To be a chronicler

We are very moved as we leave the university. In the car Lu, the interpreter, almost breaks into tears.

"I participated actively in the Cultural Revolution and in all the Red Guard rallies. I struggled with great determination. But I have never been so moved. What impressed me most [he is answering a question of mine] was the narrative of the party deputy secretary who was in Yenan. I did not think that it was possible to reach such a point, that that renegade Liu Shao-chi . . ."

The lids of his onyx-like eyes begin to redden. He is holding back his tears.

They have been very meticulous and kind in giving us access to first-hand data and knowledgeable informants, and in taking us into the very heart of the Cultural Revolution—the revolution in education. I recall what Marx said about the Paris Commune: "They are storming heaven."

And now? And now, I don't know. Here one can only be a chronicler, narrate, transmit the documents or testimonies gathered at first hand from the Chinese. Just relate what you saw and heard, I tell myself. Be modest.

In the hidebound West there has been no attempt to understand. But this is not only due to ignorance. It also reflects uncontrollable panic on the part of a hoary establishment. For the people of this country have overturned the ancient educational pyramid which dominates the superstructures of the world.

3
The May 7 Cadre School

The guerrilla war within

Under an intensely blue sky we leave Peking and travel through a vast open countryside, frequently encountering soldiers of the People's Liberation Army, red flags held high, on their way to help the peasants. There is a sense, in this landscape, of the feverish activity gripping China. We are heading for the May 7 Cadre School, a "reeducation" school for members of the party and state administration. Here, about thirty miles from the capital, we will spend the day with party cadres, in a school utterly unlike our party schools in the West.

It is the first time members of a Western Communist party have been permitted to visit such a school. I have the exciting feeling that this is a key point in our journey.

In the West, the popular belief is that the Chinese Communist Party has been totally destroyed, that Mao has reduced it to ashes, that he has eliminated its outstanding activists. This calumny persists even though Mao Tse-tung has repeated a thousand times that 95 percent of the party cadres are healthy elements. A few days suffice to see this mystification for what it is. Furthermore, the first sentence of the little red book clearly indicates Mao's basic political orientation. The objective of the Cultural Revolution is to prevent the formation of a "privileged bourgeois stratum" (see "On Khrushchev's Phoney Communism and Its Historical Lessons for the World"), a "new class" which would exploit the privileges—modest though they may be—of the official or the party staff worker.

Lenin's dictum, that a Communist leader is a "professional revolutionary," is being revived here, but in modified form: the Communist leader is, quite simply, a revolutionary leader. The point is to prevent his transformation into a professional bureaucrat.

In the article I cited above, Mao notes: "It is necessary to maintain the system of cadre participation in collective productive labor. The cadres of our party and state are ordinary workers and not overlords sitting on the backs of the people." And at another point he cites an old maxim: "A Chinese Communist leader is poorer than a poor peasant." The comrade who welcomed us to Shanghai wore a threadbare jacket; he seemed poorly clad for this cold weather and there was nothing to set him apart from any airport mechanic. The cadre doesn't enjoy a privileged economic position: economic favoritism, authoritarianism, arbitrary behavior, displays of arrogance by political leaders, careerism, have all been swept away by the Cultural Revolution and the development of "new cadres." Turning again to the article cited above, an article which dates back to July 1964, Mao writes of the cadres:

> In order to guarantee that our party and country do not change their color, we must not only have a correct line and correct policies, but must train and raise millions of successors who will carry on the cause of proletarian revolution. In the final analysis, the question of training successors for the revolutionary cause of the proletariat is one of whether or not there will be people who can carry on the Marxist-Leninist revolutionary cause started by the older generation of proletarian revolutionaries, whether or not we can successfully prevent the emergence of Khrushchev's revisionism in China. In short, it is an extremely important question, a matter of life and death for our party and our country. It will be a question of fundamental importance to the proletarian revolutionary cause for a hundred, a thousand, nay ten thousand years to come. Basing themselves on the changes in the Soviet Union, the imperialist prophets are pinning their hopes of "peaceful evolution" on the third or fourth generation of the Chinese party. We must shatter these imperialist prophecies. What are the requirements for worthy successors to the revolutionary cause of the proletariat? They must be genuine Marxist-Leninists and not revisionists like Khrushchev wearing the cloak of Marxism-Leninism. They must be revolutionaries who wholeheartedly serve the overwhelming majority of the people of China and of the whole world, and must not be like Khrushchev, who serves both the interests of the handful

> of members of the privileged bourgeois stratum in his own country and those of foreign imperialism and reaction. They must be proletarian statesmen, capable of uniting and working closely with the masses. They must know how to work with those who agree with them, but also with those who do not. They must especially watch out for opportunists and conspirators like Khrushchev and prevent such bad elements from usurping the leadership of the party and the state at any level. They must be models in applying the party's democratic centralism, and must master the method of leadership based on the principle of *from the masses, to the masses.* They must not be violent and despotic like Khrushchev; they must not make surprise attacks on comrades or act in an arbitrary and dictatorial fashion. They must be modest and prudent, and guard against arrogance and impetuosity. They must be imbued with the spirit of self-criticism and have the courage to correct the errors they may commit in their work. They must never cover up their errors as Khrushchev did, claiming all the credit for themselves and shifting all the blame on others.

A party with such cadres is certainly no fetishized party, no idolatrous cult with its priestly caste, its promotions "without regard for merit," and its consequent isolation from the masses.

Make no mistake about it: although in China one sees numerous portraits of Stalin displayed side by side with the great Marxists, Mao has totally eliminated any Stalinist conception of the party—whereas many Communist parties, formed just as Stalin was taking over the leadership of the Third International, were permanently cast in that mold.

For Mao, the break with Stalinism goes even deeper. As early as 1956 he analyzed the errors of Stalin and came to grips with the fundamental question of the relation between structures and superstructures in the socialist system. On December 29, 1956, directly following the events in Poland and Hungary, he published an article in *People's Daily,* presented as an account of a debate within the political bureau, which contained some very severe criticisms of Stalin. But that wasn't all it contained. Rereading the piece today, one discovers that it opened a debate over the structure of Soviet socialism—a debate which was abruptly terminated when the break with Khrushchev came, for at that point China initiated its polemical defense of Stalin. Moreover, the evaluation of Stalin tried to take account of the complexity of a historical situation, the long-term situation of the first socialist country; the Chinese refused to dismiss the problem as lightly as Khrushchev did. But the Chinese party, *throughout its history*, seems never to have been a vassal of Moscow; after the Second World War it rejected Stalin's proposed experiment of a united front with Chiang Kai-shek. It is a party which remained under arms up to the very moment of socialism's triumph: for Mao, "political power grows out of the barrel of a gun." Despite all the insinuations in the USSR and elsewhere regarding Mao's "return to Stalinism," the history of Chinese Communism seems the very antithesis of the Stalinist experience. "Stalin's methods of work"—Mao's style is evident here—

> were somewhat detrimental to the principle of democratic centralism in the Soviet Union. In many areas, Stalin seriously isolated himself from the masses and made subjective decisions on numerous important matters, thus committing grave errors. . . . How are these errors related to the socialist system in the Soviet Union? The Marxist-Leninist dialectic teaches us that any form of relations of production, and the superstructure that reflects them, pass through the stages of birth, development, and decay. When the development of the forces of production reaches a certain point, the old relations of production essentially cease to be sufficient. When the economic base reaches a certain stage of development, the old superstructure becomes essentially inadequate. At this point fundamental changes inevitably occur, and whomsoever stands in the way of these changes is cast aside by history. . . . Even when the basic system meets the real necessities, certain contradictions exist between the relations of production and the forces of production, between the superstructures and the economic base. . . . The system is of decisive importance, but the system is not, in itself, all-powerful. Once the proper system has been set up, the chief problem is applying it correctly, having a correct political line, correct methods, and a correct style of work.

In reading these lines, one might say that Mao Tse-tung was already outlining the Cultural Revolution—and this was almost immediately following the Twentieth Congress in 1956 and Khrushchev's blunt, impromptu critique of Stalin. The Cultural Revolution was obviously a challenge to the organizational structure of much of Communism today: primarily to that of the ruling Communist parties, and to the Communist Party of the USSR in particular. As far as we know, China didn't even come near the degree of deviation for which it denounced the Soviet Union. In China there was no consolidation of a "new class" in the sense meant by Milovan Djilas (in his book *The New Class*) in his analysis of the Yugoslav regime, which he accuses of having suppressed all diversity of thought, of having secured a monopoly on thought in pursuit of its own personal interests. It cannot be said that in China a class has been established at the proletariat's expense. For years members of the Chinese party have been participating regularly in manual labor. And since 1962, campaigns for rectification of errors have been quite widespread. Broad masses of people were mobilized by the Socialist Education Campaign.*

But how did the danger of the development of a party bureaucracy make itself known in China? How was the presence of "overlords sitting on the backs of the people" detected? What deviations, what germs of privilege, greed, and ambition among party leaders and state administrative cadres required the use of such a strong vaccine as soon as the first symptoms appeared? In his report to the Ninth Congress, Lin Piao stated: "Cadres must constantly

* The Socialist Education Campaign was launched in 1963–1964 to counter the rightist offensive. After the Great Leap Forward, the decade of the 1960s began with natural disasters that afflicted the entire country, the economic break with the USSR, China's obligation to pay off all its debts to the Soviet Union, etc. All this permitted the right to regain influence in the countryside. This campaign was a great movement which prefigured the Cultural Revolution, opposing Mao's line to that of Liu Shao-chi: its chief goal was to intensify the class struggle in the countryside (see below, on the Tachai brigade) and to return the initiative to socialist forces everywhere. (Liu Shao-chi later attempted to sidetrack this campaign by stripping it of its class content. He sent out his own work teams in an attempt to expel revolutionary cadres.) The political objectives of this movement, as defined by Chairman Mao, were as follows: "The main target of the present movement is those people who, even though they occupy leadership positions in the party, follow the capitalist road. . . . On the higher levels, there are antisocialist elements at work in the governing bodies of the communes, municipalities, districts, counties, and even on the provincial and central levels. . . . This is why we must rely on the working class, on the old, poor and lower-middle peasants, and on the revolutionary cadres; this is why we must focus on the class struggle and the struggle between the two roads, the socialist road and the capitalist road."

sweep away the dust of bureaucracy and must not fall into the bad habit of *acting like overlords.*" Back in February 1957, in his work "On the Correct Handling of Contradictions Among the People," Mao discussed the problem of those who hold political power in a socialist country, their standard of living, the wage differentials between a cadre and a worker, between a worker and a peasant. He stated that the wages of some workers and of certain officials were too high, and that the peasants were right to be discontented. At that time, Chinese wage policy was influenced by the Soviet model because of the way Chinese industry was organized, the centralization of factory management, and the method that had been chosen for industrializing the country. In the early 1960s it was not uncommon to encounter state administrators, party secretaries, and trade unionists who were exempt from all practical work and who received the equivalent of six times the pay of the ordinary worker.

In launching the slogan, "To rebel is justified," Mao is taking aim not only at political opportunists, but at any sort of bureaucracy. This slogan is complemented by another which is the very antithesis of the Stalinist conception of the party: "Constant vigilance is necessary if we wish to prevent the emergence of a new breed of overlords within the party."

An extraordinary day in a party school

A wooden gate bears the name of the school. We pass through it and the car drives into a small courtyard where a group of men and women are awaiting us, waving the little red book as a sign of welcome. The meeting begins without further ceremony in the great hall of the school. The floor is of packed earth; on the wall is Chairman Mao's "May 7 Directive," * in magnificent calligraphy, and many photographs of Mao.

---

* Chairman Mao's "May 7 Directive" (1966): "The People's Liberation Army should be a great school. Our soldiers should receive a political, military, and cultural education there. They must be able to participate in agricultural production and activities related to it; they must be able to manage small and medium-sized factories; they must be capable of making the products they need for their own sustenance and of trading them, through the state, at no profit to themselves. They must

We settle ourselves around the table and are immediately provided with cups of tea, watermelon seeds, and nuts. The representative of the school revolutionary committee, which is composed of re-educated students elected by the collective, immediately begins to speak:

---

be able to perform jobs at the base, to take an active part in socialist education in the factories and in the villages. Once they have developed a full socialist consciousness, they can lay the groundwork for new tasks at the base, in such a way that the army becomes an organic part of the life and needs of the masses. Further, they must fight for the cause of the Cultural Revolution and criticize the bourgeoisie whenever necessary. The army will thus be able to combine theoretical study with the practice of agricultural and industrial work, and with the political education of the masses. These different tasks must, of course, be coordinated; distinctions must be made between what is urgently necessary and what falls within the framework of a long-term policy. Each unit of the army must apply itself to one or two of these areas: agricultural work, industrial work, political work; it should not work in all three at the same time. Our army, millions strong, will thus fulfill an extremely important function.

"The workers will concentrate on industrial production, but will also educate themselves on the military, political, and cultural levels. They must also participate in the Socialist Education Movement and criticize the bourgeoisie. Conditions permitting, they should undertake agricultural production on the side, following the example of the workers in the oilfields at Taching.

"The peasants in the people's communes should concentrate on agricultural production (including the upkeep of forestland, stock breeding, fish culture, and related activities). Yet they must not neglect military training, political and cultural education. Where conditions permit, they must attempt to establish small factories. This also applies to the students who must primarily devote themselves to studying and at the same time acquire other types of knowledge. They must study not only cultural things, but industrial, agricultural, and military things. They must also criticize the bourgeoisie. The period of schooling must be shortened; education, too, must be revolutionized. Bourgeois intellectuals must no longer dominate our schools.

"Conditions permitting, workers in the commercial sector, employees of administrative services, party cadres, and members of the state administration should do the same.

"Going back to manual work at the base is an excellent opportunity for leaders in the highest positions to relearn everything. Except for the old, the sick, and the infirm, everyone should follow this road. Those who are designated to remain in leadership positions must also, when the time comes, go as a group to do manual work at the base."

"Before the school was built there was nothing here but an abandoned camp, a sort of uninhabited cemetery. We came here on November 7, 1968; we comprised over 1,400 political cadres from the Eastern District of Peking, which has more than 600,000 inhabitants." (Since the Cultural Revolution, Peking has been divided into twenty-six districts run by revolutionary committees, instead of the ninety districts which had previously existed under the control of a bureaucratic and administratively top-heavy organization.)

"We follow the teaching of the 'May 7 Directive': our cadres must 'participate in production, which at the same time gives them an opportunity to return to theoretical study . . .' "

The comrade reads us a few lines of the "Directive" from the posters on the wall: "Going back to manual work at the base is an excellent opportunity for leaders in the highest positions to relearn everything. Except for the old, the sick, and the infirm, everyone should follow this road. Those who are designated to remain in leadership positions must also, when the time comes, go as a group to do manual work at the base." He quotes again: "Conditions permitting, workers in the commercial sector, employees of administrative services, Party cadres, and members of the state administration, should do the same."

What do they take as their model? The representative defines it as follows:

"We draw our inspiration from the 'three-eight' style of work defined and taught by Mao.* The model is the People's Liberation Army; it is the style of the Anti-Japanese Imperialism University, the style of Yenan; a return to the absolute purity of our soldierly origins, opposing any form of bourgeoisification or hierarchization that would set China back on the capitalist road."

Mao's directives are addressed to the workers, to the peasants, to the students, to the intellectuals, to the soldiers themselves. It is often forgotten that it is among the soldiers that the Cultural Rev-

* The People's Liberation Army developed an excellent style of work in the course of the long years of revolutionary struggle. Mao defined this style in three phrases and eight characters. The three phrases are: a firm and correct political orientation; an industrious and simple style of work; a flexibility in strategy and tactics. As for the eight characters, they represent unity, alertness, seriousness, and enthusiasm.

olution was born: it began with a thoroughgoing remodeling of the army, with the soldiers going back to the people, becoming one with the people; and it was Yenan that was the point of departure for this movement. It is through the army that Mao's transformation of Chinese society, the Cultural Revolution, was begun. Imperialist propaganda proclaims that a military dictatorship governs China. But in reality the army was remodeled because it is the primary social unit in socialist society and must serve as an example to all. "A great school," says Mao, "capable of accomplishing great things not only in military action but also in agriculture and in the factories, side by side with the masses; capable of participating in the work of socialist education in the factories and the countryside. As a result, it is always in perfect unity with the people, always prepared to participate in the struggles of the Cultural Revolution, always prepared to criticize the bourgeoisie."

As Schickel writes (in *Grande Muraille, Grande Méthode*, to be published by Editions du Seuil), in the West, "army" (my quotes) is synonymous with "power" (my quotes): people often think of the function of the army—the defense of the state—in terms of the "Greek style" of 1967. By analogy, the assumption is that there was a power struggle in China and that Mao Tse-tung and Lin Piao were victorious thanks to their control of the army.

Another question seems relevant here: to what extent has the People's Liberation Army generated a "new class"? To what degree has this bureaucratic and hierarchical deviation provided the Cultural Revolution with one of its points of departure? Schickel writes:

> In the army itself, as among officials, artists, and writers, there had been a certain tendency toward isolation from the rest of the population. New directives were given: in addition to strictly military training, soldiers were to work in the fields and factories, so that the bond between them and the rest of the nation could be re-strengthened. It is at this point that the head of the general staff Lo Jui-ching was removed from office.

The "May 7 Directive" was written principally for the army: it was to go back to the plow, to the tools of work; soldiers were to merge themselves with the people. No more ranks: generals would share the life of the common soldier and participate in the most menial tasks.

In the May 7 Cadre School, this directive is posted on the wall. Originally meant for the army, it is at the same time a symbolic stage and goal of the Cultural Revolution.

To get on to the main topic of discussion, I ask about the social and political background of the "students."

For the most part, I am told, they are party staff and officials from the Eastern District of Peking. "Among them are old leaders who fought in the war against Japan and the war of liberation, activists of working-class and peasant origin. Then there are the so-called 'three-door cadres': out the 'door' of the family, into the door of the school, then through the door of the party organization. There are young instructors, middle school teachers, state administration employees, party staff workers, trade unionists. At present the school has 1,390 pupils. Already, however, 864 have finished their course and have returned to work, either in the Eastern District of Peking or in localities where there is a need for the political ability they have developed through the study of Mao Tse-tung's works and through the lessons of practical work. When they go back to their former place of employment, they are assigned new tasks, and they apply themselves to their work with such energy that a revolutionary leap is achieved in that sector and the dictatorship of the proletariat is consolidated there."

"Could you give us an example?"

"Certainly. A worker, seeing a political leader or trade-union cadre return to the factory after having gone through the school, says to himself: this leader is no bureaucrat. He does greasy, dirty jobs just the way we do; we are on an equal footing with cadres like him. Cadres coming out of the school often find themselves given administrative tasks which take the load off other officials. The most capable among them enter the governing bodies of other cities, of provinces, of industrial enterprises, of mines—for with administrative decentralization, all these depend on local management."

"Is it correct to say that in your school, you are training a new generation of cadres for the state administration and the party; a generation tempered by what I would call a sort of internal guerrilla war, a guerrilla war of the individual against himself, against his own weaknesses, his own egocentrism?"

The comrade smiles. "What you call the internal guerrilla war is the act of becoming conscious that the revolution must be made within oneself. We are guided by the four firsts: man should take primacy over weapons; political work over other work; ideological work over routine political work; and in ideological work, living ideas in people's minds over ideas in books. Many become lazy, take it easy, and the revolution becomes just a memory. But from the study of Mao's theory on carrying out the revolution, we learn that the old cadres shouldn't rest on their laurels, take advantage of their successes, and advance their careers. Rather, they should struggle to keep from being cut off from the masses, struggle against vanity, against greed; struggle to transform their world outlook; struggle to transform their conception of themselves; struggle to hammer out a revolutionary outlook."

"How did bureaucratic deviations manifest themselves in party cadres or high officials?"

"Let us take an example. Comrade Li had taken part in the revolutionary struggle since 1934; at that time he was barely fifteen years old. During the war he learned to read, and throughout the protracted fighting he always carried Mao's writings with him. Like the others, he led a rough life, slept in caves, ate what he found, risked his life in the War of Resistance. In short, he was completely dedicated to the revolution. When Liberation came in 1949, he went to Peking. It is a big city, he had a fine office, comfort, a happy family life to which he devoted much of his time. A certain lack of interest in politics crept into him, an indifference to the struggle of the masses. His thoughts turned to bettering his position and that of his family, to giving his children a good education so they, in turn, could make careers for themselves. His head was filled with projects, one more self-indulgent than the next. The revolution no longer occupied his thoughts and his revolutionary activity grew slack, deterred by the least obstacle—by ill health, fatigue, laziness."

"You mean he was a sort of pensioner of the older generation?"

"Yes, in a way. But here these 'pensioners' are rediscovering their revolutionary youth. Comrade Li came to the school, he rediscovered the revolutionary style of life, the style of Yenan; through his current political rejuvenation he is recapturing the youth of his earlier days.

"Take the case of the most arrogant intellectual cadres, intolerant of restrictions of any sort. Now, at the May 7 School, they till the soil, they work the land, they build houses, they organize our workshops. They have learned to struggle against the bourgeoisie, to expose the hazards of a return to the *capitalist road*."

The May 7 School gives practical lessons in living in close relations with the workers, the peasants, and the soldiers; in increasing one's dedication to the proletariat. Who is a *genuine Marxist* and who is a *phoney Marxist?* The test, says Mao, is the desire to work with the workers and peasants. Liu Shao-chi's influence had been greatest in the big cities, in the capital. Officials had been divorced from the masses; peasants had been treated with arrogance and contempt. Certain intellectuals had begun to wonder if it was really worth the trouble teaching peasants to write, if the most important thing wasn't for the peasants to learn to produce good harvests. Certain doctors and teachers couldn't bear the dirt and disease which afflict the humble people.

It seems to me that Mao wanted to prevent not only the formation of a class of bureaucrats, but "class formation" of any kind. Although people refer to the "bourgeoisie" (my quotes), it is obvious that the bourgeoisie as we know it in the West, as an economic power, no longer exists here. The problem is the crystallization of groups and tendencies, possibly giving rise to the formation of conflicting groups and a restoration of capitalism in another guise.

Two classes, two lines, locked in struggle. This is why, at the Tenth Plenary Session of the Eighth Congress of the Communist Party, Mao Tse-tung spoke of "the presence of contradictions, of classes and class struggles," and delivered the following warning: "The class struggle must never be abandoned or forgotten." He attacked "the tendency toward 'every man for himself' which was appearing among the bourgeoisie and in certain party leaders."

"Take another example," the representative continues. "Comrade Chen was head of the Ministry of Health in the Eastern District of Peking. When a peasant came in from the country she would disappear; she avoided all contact with him, for she had a horror of dirt. She is here. Since entering the school she has changed so much that she even lived with a peasant woman who had just given birth and was seriously ill. Not only did she give her injections and provide her with the necessary care, she even disposed of her excreta and washed her. And she nursed her like this for several nights.

"A school like this one is characterized by three elements: first, the style of Yenan; second, perfect unity with the masses; third, leading a simple life in the service of the revolutionary cause, fearing neither hardship nor death, giving a proletarian meaning even to such aesthetic categories as *beauty* and *ugliness, happiness* and *unhappiness, pleasure* and *pain.* These are concepts which have served a class, the bourgeois class. Those who are ugly are usually poor. Those who do the most menial tasks are *ugly* and *poor.* There are some activities—for example, the collection of garbage and excreta (translated by our interpreter as "waste material") which are allotted to an *inferior category of human beings.*

"In the spring of this year we organized teams of comrades from the school; they went into the Eastern District of Peking to collect garbage and drain the sewers with buckets and carts. When one does this sort of job, one loses any sort of bureaucratic attitude, any notion of hierarchy. It isn't easy, especially at first. The disgust, the shame at being recognized as a former leader, the fear that other people are talking about your errors—even the fear of disease—all that does exist. One woman, a professor of zoology, objected to the collection of excreta, saying that if a drop of water contains hundreds of microbes, there was no telling how many would be found in this filth. But an offensive must be launched against notions of dirt, ugliness, danger, fear of death, if one wants to make the revolution within oneself."

The comrade who is head of the revolutionary committee of the school must be about forty; he is handsome and vigorous-looking and he speaks fluently, glancing at his notes from time to time. Nearly the whole revolutionary committee (fifteen members) is seated around him. All are not members of the party. All have been elected by the students. The revolutionary committee runs the school, but it is pointed out to us that it is under the political direction of the party committee.

The comrade continues his account. With utter simplicity, he relates a story which made quite an impression on me.

"On his return from thc May 7 School, the deputy representative of the Eastern District of Peking [something like a deputy mayor] was put to work in the sanitation department of his district, picking up the dirt and garbage, and shouting 'Bring your garbage here,' as he went by—the classic cry of the garbageman. But he was ashamed, because everyone had known him—the important man who made speeches to crowds, who had power. Then he asked himself, 'Why can't I shout "Bring the crap here" as freely and naturally as the garbagemen do? Because I am accustomed to a comfortable life, because, in a way, the revisionist influence is eating away at me. If making the revolution were as simple as riding in a car, that would be great, everything would be easy. But I myself know that the opposite is true: otherwise, why would I be so afraid?' Thus, in analyzing himself, in detecting in himself the desire to become part of an upper class, he was able to overcome his distaste and shout with the others, 'Bring your garbage here.'

"In this school everyone leads a simple and industrious life. We all eat and sleep under the same conditions. We follow the three basic principles of training a soldier in the People's Liberation Army: unity, alertness, seriousness. Those who live here have brought about changes in their characters comparable to changes in the face of the earth. Strength of character becomes material strength. In Peking, in December 1968, it was bitterly cold. We pulled down part of the old Peking Wall . . ."

(Then these are the people, I say to myself, who dismantled a small section of the famous Wall.)

". . . in order to build 311 houses where people could live, and this in the record time of twenty-five days. The sandy, uncultivated soil became *good earth.* Nearly twenty-five acres were cleared and fertilized with the excreta [in China this is called nightsoil] we collected in the city. The work tanned our faces but our hearts became more revolutionary, our resolve firmer, and our health better.

"We are concerned with ensuring the political development of the school, but the concrete results of the work are also of great importance to us; we hold democratic meetings to evaluate the results of our activity, to estimate what the harvest will yield, to increase agricultural production, to devise plans for the workshops, central power station, and irrigation station. We have undertaken to form groups of the 'four-good workers'; these groups are composed of those who excel in four areas of work: ideological and political work, the 'three-eight' style of work, military training, and organization of daily life."

The comrade glances at me. While listening, I have devoured a whole bowl of nuts and seeds. He pauses a moment, then adds, as though in answer to unspoken questions:

"No, it isn't all simple. It is neither an idyll nor a game. In the beginning, some people thought they were lowering themselves by tilling the soil. But their study of the theory of permanent revolution taught them that all tasks are equally valuable. Liu Shao-chi regarded manual labor as a 'punishment.' Or else he ridiculed those who went 'to work in the fields in order to satisfy their own vanity.' According to him, party membership, the role of a political worker, should permit one to hope for an improved economic status, for a successful career. *Give up the pen for the spade? How awful!* That is the response of some. And they add mournfully, *To the pen, farewell!* They haven't yet grasped that the revolution must be carried forward unceasingly. If this way of thinking had triumphed, this school would have become nothing but an agricultural school, or an old-style party school, like Liu's and Peng Chen's . . ."

At this point I ask what this re-education consists of, and whether a little pressure isn't applied to the comrades who come to attend the May 7 School. Did the students come voluntarily or were they pushed into it?

Not at all, they tell me. Comrade Chen, the one who ran the Ministry of Health in the Eastern District of Peking, is seated on my left. She explains:

"You see, I applied four times before I was accepted . . ."

"Why such persistence when you didn't have, so to speak, a great propensity to mingle with the masses?"

She replies very calmly:

"That was just it . . . To be convinced of a thing in theory and to put it into practice are very different things. I needed practical experience."

Hesitations, fears, even suffering, are exorcized not by the sincerity of political commitment, but by the harshness of confrontation with reality. I really believe that in a way it is as difficult to be admitted to the May 7 School as it is to be chosen for a space flight. The admission procedure, moreover, is quite complicated.

"The application for admission is made through the revolutionary committee at the base level. It is passed on to the revolutionary committee of the sector which, after reviewing the request, relays it to the district revolutionary committee, which makes the final decision. Furthermore, even when employees of the various units have been admitted to the school, they can be recalled at any time if their services are needed."

"How long does the course last, and what does the comrade do on his return from the school?"

"The course lasts a minimum of one year . . . On his return, the comrade goes back to his former work unit, or else he may request a different assignment, or he may even be recommended for another position by the revolutionary committee."

We go to visit the fields, to meet the students working there. The zinc bucket factory, pride of the school, was constructed from scratch. In the small workshop men and women are making buckets, putting handles on them, and then stamping them with May 7 Cadre School in red ink.

I ask the factory manager: "What did you do before you came here?"

The manager, who had been one of the most important trade-union leaders in Peking, replies: "I was in charge of trade-union work."

Here is a woman worker, forty-five years old. Seated on the ground with a bucket between her legs, she hammers away. What was her former employment?

"I worked in the administration of the Eastern District."

And smiling, she returns to her work.

And so I meet a middle school teacher, a schoolmistress, an accountant. They all greet me cordially and answer my questions without a trace of embarrassment: "I did this or that," as if it were no more than a trivial biographical detail. At the main pumphouse —completely planned and constructed by the school—the comrade-director strikes me as surly, ill at ease.

He had worked in the Ministry of Finance of the Eastern District, as administrator of a deposit bank—the equivalent of a bank manager. He livens up only when he starts to explain to me how the irrigation pump works. This pump would normally have cost 5,000 yuan (about $2,000) but thanks to his work and that of the students, it cost only a few hundred.

It is noon. The students come to the kitchens, receive *ample* food, *the same for everyone,* and a bowlful of rice. They carry it off to their homes, for the school is actually a village, made up of small wooden houses. The head cook, his face flushed under his cap, seems so at home among his pots that I take him for a professional chef.

I ask him about it.

"No, I was head of the office of the National People's Congress for the Eastern District."

"What induced you to come here?"

"I spent my time sitting in my office [he was a real bureaucrat!], I gave orders, I didn't participate in production, I didn't study the works of Mao Tse-tung."

"You knew how to cook?"

"No, I learned here."

"That can't be easy."

"It isn't. But if you expect things to be easy, nothing goes right."

He introduces me to the other cooks, who are preparing the sausages. None of them had known how to cook, they learned at the school. All three had been teachers.

"In that case, the food can't be very good!"

"Taste it, and you will see," says the comrade-cook, taking offense. "Through hard work, we have learned to cook."

"Fine," I reply, "we will soon tell, since you have invited us to lunch at the school."

The central power station which serves the school is also the work of the students. Here is the head of the Ministry of Cereals and Oil-Bearing Crops for the Eastern District of Peking—he must have been a powerful person!—transformed into a worker at the station. Most courteously he explains its operation and potential to us. As we are leaving, we meet two soldiers on a motorcycle with a sidecar. They are so surprised to see us that they stop, mouths open. They are delegates of the People's Liberation Army, members of the revolutionary committee of the school. Their role here, they tell me when I ask, is to give all necessary assistance.

"Our first priority is to learn the style of Yenan from the army," the director tells us once more. "We are re-educating ourselves through the study of the thought of Mao Tse-tung."

"As for us," the soldier replies, "we learn from the school that we must make the revolution within ourselves." He adds: "The revolution must promote production, too; at the school, twenty-five acres of land are under cultivation."

We go to visit the infirmary. A young man and woman in white smocks wave the little red book in greeting. They seem very shy; they don't seem to know what to do with their hands.

The young man:

"I have studied medicine but I am not a doctor. I wanted to come here to remold my world outlook by working with the peasants . . . Then we will see if the collective of the school thinks I can continue my studies, or if I should do something else."

The young woman:

"I am a political cadre from the Ministry of Health of the Eastern District. The road of the 'May 7 Directive' is correct. I was very lucky to have been admitted to the school."

In neatly arranged glass jars, we see medicines made from herbal extracts. All these remedies were prepared here, with herbs gathered in the fields and on the mountainside. On the wall, botanical charts depict the plants, and, alongside, the treatment of the illness—headache, gastric inflammation, rheumatism—as prescribed by ancient tradition. The two young people are currently using acupuncture to treat rheumatism, arthritis, even colds.

The students built their houses themselves. I am told—I wouldn't have noticed it by myself—that the brick beds (*kang*) are made with great stones taken from the Peking Wall. The comrades show them to me, reminding me of that icy winter of 1968. I remember someone telling me that of the nine monumental gates of Peking, only six now remain. I gaze at the stones with a touch of sadness. I venture into a simple dwelling which serves as a dormitory for six women. Everything is in perfect order, the brightly colored padded blankets rolled up at the head of the beds. One of the women, her face beautiful and unlined, tells me her husband is a photographer in Peking. She has a child who goes to the kindergarten of the May 7 School. There is a nursery and a kindergarten for the students' young children.

"What did I do before? Cadre of the Communist Party, Eastern District."

She has an air of great serenity. The women appear to be great friends. They provide us with a lively commentary on our unexpected arrival. Married? Yes, and both schoolmistresses.

"My husband works in the city," says one of them; she must be about forty. "I have full-grown children. Only one is still in school."

"You don't mind being separated from your family?"

"No, no," they answer quickly. "We see each other every two weeks. And why don't you ask the men the same question? Mao says women hold up half of heaven and that 'true equality between the sexes' can come about only through the socialist transformation of society as a whole."

"The school's students," the leader of the revolutionary committee explains to us, "are 40 percent women, of all ages. We take this into consideration by assigning them to the least tiring tasks."

"And leaving their children, their homes—that doesn't pose problems for them?"

"No, and the same goes for all the other women."

They look at me in amazement, as if my conception of the family—which I have unconsciously brought with me—were extremely backward.

The school newspaper, which comes out regularly, is posted in the library. It is called the *Bulletin of the May 7 Fighters*. Beside it are other papers from other cadre schools, in Peking and other regions. The names are similar: all refer to "May 7." We go by car to tour the wide expanses of land, enriched, cultivated, and planted by the students. The students are divided up into seven brigades: five work in the fields, one cares for the vegetable gardens, one runs the school. It is the harvest season. The Number Four Brigade is winnowing the rice with the threshing machines. It is hard work. The women lift the sheaves and feed them to the machines.

"We also made this machine ourselves," the comrade tells me. "Where the threshing floor is now, there was nothing but a swamp before. The peasants didn't even cultivate this soil, it wasn't worth the effort. When we arrived, they were so glad to see us that they welcomed us into their homes; young couples even delayed their marriages in order to give up their beds to us."

The women, lined up all along the furrow, wave the little red book in greeting. Those who are digging stop for a moment, give their greeting, then carefully return the books to their pockets. We spend a little time with the other four brigades but there isn't time to talk with everybody. The garden is as exquisite as an embroidery; one section is called the "revolutionary garden" because the seeds planted there were a gift from the military brigade which worked with Mao in pioneering irrigation studies.

In the pigsty, a sturdy man with slicked-down hair is busy with his giant pigs.

"Before, I was a trade unionist," he tells us quickly, "a secretary in the Eastern District."

But immediately he goes on to tell us about his pigs. "A tremendous effort is being made to raise pigs; the brigade of the people's commune of Wang-Kisen-Se (Hopei), cited by Mao, gave the correct example of the proper ratio between grain production and pig-raising. In our sties we are raising 250 pigs; we have learned to treat their diseases, to assist sows in delivering their young—one doctor has become a veterinarian specializing in everything to do with pigs. In our school there are also 3,000 ducks and 500 chickens, so we get excellent organic fertilizers, too."

Not far from the vegetable garden is the kindergarten. There I encounter the little son of the comrade I met earlier, very cute, waving a small toy and displaying a huge badge with Mao's picture on it.

We visit the shoemaker, where a man and woman are repairing stacks of rubber and cloth sandals; they are putting rubber patches on them. I no longer inquire what they did before they came to the May 7 School. Behind their intent faces I can picture professorial chairs, government offices, banks, commercial offices—in short, these are all middle cadres of the party or state administration.

Our lunch with the revolutionary committee is informal and gay. I go on with my questions. I discover that these people are nearly all party and state administration leaders. The deputy representative of the school, whose face is as brown as a peasant's and who really looks like a farm worker, tells me:

"I am not a peasant; it's the sun which has 'cooked' me like this; I was the administrative representative for the Eastern District."

Another is a trade-union official; another, the manager of a local office of public education; yet another, a teacher, then a party leader, and so on. None of them is a peasant. From the peasants they have learned things they knew nothing about. The lunch is excellent. The head of the office of the National People's Congress has become a really first-rate cook. Can we tell him so? The official arrives in his apron. Congratulations are offered to him and to his assistants, the teachers. Everyone seems content.

"Good enough, I admit a high official and a professor can most certainly become cooks. Your meal [twelve dishes] is the best I've eaten yet in China."

And it's true. This strange fraternity, the unprecedented humanity which permeates this school—where does it come from? There has been a radical reversal of values, an essentially nonviolent revolution which has affected everyone in the same way. In the party, in the state administration, in the army, the Cultural Revolution has done away with all the values, grades, distinctions, insignia of rank, and formalities which recalled the past or which threatened to revive a capitalist mode of life in China. Careerism, egocentrism, any sort of elitism, have been eliminated. People have replaced these notions with new values representing an authentic political commitment; they have fought a relentless guerrilla war against themselves—a war which makes them stronger, better prepared, for the bitter struggle against the external enemy as well as against the insidious internal enemy.

One wonders: does the myth of *success*, as we know it in the West, have any meaning here? *Managers*, symbols of the all-powerful technology, are cultivating the very soil whose reclamation was made possible through their efforts. Besides, when such equality prevails, to take on greater responsibilities simply means giving more of oneself, leading a harder life, being more responsive to the masses. "It's easy," the cook had said, "but the easy thing isn't the correct thing."

After this plentiful meal, I get around to asking the representative of the revolutionary committee where he had worked before. Well! He is none other than the hero of the garbage collection story, the deputy director of finance and commerce for the Eastern District of Peking. Now I understand how he was able to describe the man's anguish so well. He is silent for a moment. Then he tells us about his internal ordeal.

"It was no joke. Collecting nightsoil in front of so many people who knew me—people I had refused to see, perhaps, or people I had been too hard on in imposing taxes and fines. The tradesmen came to watch me from the doorways of their shops and said: 'At heart he's a good fellow. He seemed so proud. And now he's like everyone else, he cleans the street, he collects trash, he calls out to people to put out their garbage cans.' This new idea they had of me—this unaccustomed admiration, this esteem—moved me deeply, I must admit."

I wonder about this relationship between man and nightsoil (which I heard given various names at the school: waste material, excrement, manure), and I see that it is a sort of test; essentially (beyond the practical uses of the nightsoil) it is a question of conquering the greatest of all petty-bourgeois loathings (I add: of conquering *my* greatest loathing).

Who are the "untouchables" in India but the people of the lowest caste, who are made to sweep the streets, pick up the garbage, clean the latrines, and so on? In Asia, where sewer systems are almost unknown, people tend to be divided into two classes: a lower class forever fated to clear the ground of the leavings of the upper class.

"If this school is a school for the middle cadres of the party and state administration," I ask, "are there May 7 schools for leaders on a higher level? For example, for university professors, diplomats, members of the Central Committee?"

"Certainly," the representative answers. "Peking University has a May 7 School for students and professors. The Ministry of Foreign Affairs has one, too. Even the members of the Central Committee go through a May 7 School. And the secretariat of the Central Committee has established a school. In his directive, Mao spoke of 'upper cadres.' There are numerous May 7 schools. In his report to the Ninth Congress Lin Piao called 'for the whole country to become a great school for the study of Mao Tse-tung's thought.' "

I am left alone for a moment in the great hall. Facing me is the "May 7 Directive" and the pictures of Mao. I am awaiting the start of a performance especially prepared by the students on the occasion of our visit. I open my travel diary and reread some notes on the May 7 schools.

Statistical interlude

Let's look at some figures. In the past two years a hundred or so May 7 schools have been established and they are found all over China (I was able to verify this personally). About 90,000 cadres—qualified, well qualified, and highly qualified—are attending these schools. In a single school you might find old cadres on the highest levels (university professors, important doctors, members of the Central Committee, secretaries of party committees) and middle cadres of the party and state administration. The method applied in these schools is the same for everyone—no methods A, B, or C, depending on the qualifications of the students, as one might think. The schools are differentiated only according to the body which created them and on which they depend; ultimately, however, they are unified under the direction of sections of the party's Central Committee and of the State Council. The May 7 cadre schools may be attached to the party administrative office, to a ministry, to a party school, to a large university, a party committee of a big city, or to a district party committee (which is the case here). The party is responsible for political direction but the management of the school is handled by the revolutionary committees. The schools may therefore be created by central bodies on the national, provincial, or municipal level. Thus, there is initiative coming from below; organization and direction from above. The revolutionary committee's role is to decide on requests for admission and to find useful work for the cadres.

The various schools—and I was able to verify this too—are interconnected. A doctor may be sent to a school created by the Central Committee with the assignment of organizing teams of "barefoot" doctors in the countryside. As far as I could make out, what differentiates one school from another is not the theoretical study, which is of course the same everywhere, but the type of practical activity which prevails there: reclamation of swampland, agricultural work in peasant communities, organization of sanitation services, industrial production, improved grain production, and so on.

A conference of delegates representing the 90,000 cadres was held in Peking, and the list of accomplishments presented there is an impressive one. Since their establishment, the cadres of the May 7 schools have produced 50,000 tons of cereal grains, 650,000 tons of cotton, 3,200,000 tons of oil-bearing crops; they have raised 24,000 pigs; they have built almost 5 million square feet of housing; they have constructed about 100 small factories. Ten thousand students have joined commune production teams or have joined Mao Tse-tung Thought Propaganda Teams. Many schools are self-sufficient in grain production. Others, which give their surplus to the state, obtain grain and cotton from those who have exceeded the targets set by the national program for agricultural development.

The May 7 School attached to the Ministry of Public Safety has particularly distinguished itself in the struggle to combat the desire for promotion—a bourgeois desire—by setting its students to work at especially hard tasks in order to discipline them both on the ideological level and in their work. The May 7 School attached to the party school of the Central Committee has supplied over five-hundred "barefoot" doctors who go to care for the peasants of the people's communes and to organize production teams. The May 7 School attached to the Central Committee administrative office has labored to drain a lake and to induce grains to grow in arid, mountainous land; the school is now self-sufficient in grain production, oil, various commodities, vegetables, and wool. The students at the May 7 School attached to the Federation of Chinese Trade Unions have become part of production teams; they are working and studying side by side with the peasants; they have struggled against selfishness and revisionism; they have assisted the advance units.

At the Peking conference of the one hundred May 7 schools, emphasis was put on strengthening the leadership role of the party, and the future tasks of the schools were discussed. The goal is to continue to intensify the mass movement through the living study and application of Mao Tse-tung's thought. To this end, the example of the People's Liberation Army must be followed: give precedence to proletarian politics; observe the "four firsts" * to the letter; apply the "three-eight" style of work; respect the "three democracies"; pursue the development of the "four-good workers."

In Peking, 60,000 persons had been employed in the offices of branches of the state administration. Personnel has now been reduced by 90 percent. The political and administrative apparatus has been streamlined to the point where there are now only 10,000 administrative officials. The other 50,000 have for the most part (80 percent) entered May 7 schools. In the only school I visited, 864 pupils had already completed the two-year course, and there are currently 1,394 pupils, making 2,258 cadres in all.

It is in Peking that Mao's injunction to "simplify the administrative structure" has been most strictly applied. Where there were ninety districts, there are now only twenty-six. Decentralization on an enormous scale has stimulated the migration of urban cadres to regions in the interior, where they are working in industrialization and in cultural and social services in the provincial towns and countryside.

* *The "four firsts."* This is a formula proposed by Lin Piao in 1960 to apply the thought of Mao Tse-tung to political work within the People's Liberation Army. The formula means: "In the relationship between human beings and weapons, the human factor must be given primacy—that is, the revolutionary consciousness of the soldiers, which represents the decisive factor in the revolutionary war. In the relationship between political work and other activities, political work must take precedence, for even in socialist society the class struggle exists, and thus if one's orientation is lost, all is lost. In the relationship between ideological work and other political activities, ideological work must come first. And in the relationship between 'living' [that is, human] ideas and those that are found in books, the 'living' ideas must take first place. In this way, political work doesn't become limited to its organizational, routine aspects, ideological work doesn't become reduced to an exercise in memory which has no meaning for the everyday reality of the class struggle, and we don't lose sight of the principal goal of a revolutionary transformation of our own world outlook." In 1964, following Mao Tse-tung's appeal to "Learn from the People's Liberation Army," the criterion of the "four firsts" was extended to all other spheres of activity. Its full implementation on a mass scale took place during the Cultural Revolution.

Elimination of a "lower class"

In this country, the largest in the world, clay and earth are being used to remodel the governing apparatus of state and party. The objective, however, is not to turn this apparatus into a ruling class and a separate corps of officials, but rather to make it a sort of collective guide, intimately linked with the masses. Joining the party out of career ambitions, status-seeking, class envy—all that is completely finished, and in its place is the hatred of all revolutionaries for the bourgeoisie. The concepts of *beauty* and *ugliness*, of *cleanliness* and *filth*, of *elegance* and *grossness*—all class concepts—are also undergoing a revolutionary change; these were concepts belonging to an upper class which apppropriated beauty and cleanliness to itself, while leaving the ugliness and dirt to others. These concepts are being replaced with the power of politics and criticism, with reflection on the transformation of theory into hard practice. I don't know if all those I saw will triumph in this internal guerrilla war, which is bound to be bitter and terrible. Undoubtedly some will fail, fall behind. Some will ultimately be defeated. But those who win out in this war will be men and women of incorruptible class consciousness, those Mao calls the "successors," destined to carry on the socialist revolution in China. They are the antithesis of the decadence shown by the class of political rulers in other socialist countries—taken by Mao as a "negative example," from which, according to his method, a positive lesson must be drawn. "The Communist Party is the core of leadership of the whole Chinese people; without this core, the cause of socialism cannot be victorious." This quotation from Mao is in the very beginning of the little red book, which is lying open before me on the schoolroom table. It raises the fundamental question: what, then, is the Cultural Revolution? Lin Piao responded in his "Report to the Ninth Congress" of April 1969: "The Great Proletarian Revolution is the broadest and most deepgoing movement for party consolidation in the history of our party." "Liu Shao-chi," says Lin Piao in the same speech,

> went on spreading such reactionary fallacies as the theory of "the dying out of the class struggle," the theory of "docile tools," the

> theory that "the masses are backward," the theory of "joining the party in order to climb up," the theory of "inner-party peace," and the theory of "merging private and public interests" (i.e., "losing a little to gain much"). . . . [Liu Shao-chi tried] to corrupt and disintegrate our party, so that the more party members "cultivated" themselves ["Self-Cultivation" was the subject of Liu Shao-chi's book], the more revisionist they would become and so that the Marxist-Leninist party would "evolve peacefully" into a revisionist party and the dictatorship of the proletariat into the dictatorship of the bourgeoisie.

Such was the revisionist line. In a sense, the May 7 Cadre School is a vanguard in the struggle against revisionism. It is necessary to "continue to run well the Mao Tse-tung Thought study classes of all types and, in the light of Chairman Mao's 'May 7 Directive' of 1966, truly turn the whole country into a great school of Mao Tse-tung Thought." The aim of the school is for party members to "really integrate theory with practice, maintain close ties with the masses, . . . always keep to the style of being modest, prudent, and free from arrogance and rashness and to the style of arduous struggle and plain living."

While the political significance of the school seems to grow before my very eyes, a trifling detail comes to mind, the echo of the words of some political leaders in another country: "What would you be without the party? A worker, a peasant; now you are somebody, member of such and such a governing body; therefore you owe obedience and gratitude to the party which has given you and continues to give you all that . . ."

Here, in contrast, with the help of the party, this bureaucratization is avoided; one goes down among the masses to learn to live like the peasant, the worker, in order to be a revolutionary.

The school theater and the "May 7 Directive" set to music

It is time. From the meeting hall where we had lunch we go back to the courtyard, bringing along our chairs and arranging them in two rows, as in a theater. We are going to see a show. Those who have already returned from work are grouped behind us. A crowd of women and children, many more than I had imagined, and men, dressed like poor peasants, are standing up or sitting on the long benches they have brought with them. They examine us with a great deal of curiosity. I feel their eyes upon me. We are the first visitors—and foreigners, as well—to have been taken on a tour of the school. The performance, with song and orchestra—flutes, tamborines, and Chinese mandolin; sharp, mewing sounds, bright colors under the red sun of midday—is enthusiastically applauded. The show is completely political. The performers are students of the school. We are amazed at how they have learned to sing, to dance, to turn gracefully with paper sunflowers, red flowers, and props made to look like agricultural tools. Bursting with enthusiasm, they sing the "May 7 Directive" set to music—word for word, thanks to that phonetic quality, peculiar to the Chinese language, which makes it possible for a political speech to be as moving as a beautiful Neapolitan song. "We follow the shining road of the 'May 7 Directive,'" they sing passionately, accompanied by flute and tamborine. Then up comes an old peasant. He relates the miseries of his past life, and I see that a young woman in the cast is really weeping, big tears running down her face. This was to be repeated when other peasants spoke, people of the village where the school was established who are coming to thank the brigade for helping them in the fields. "The renegade Liu Shao-chi belittled work in the fields," says the peasant, and all the students listen. Then there is the celebration of the harvest around the portrait of Mao, the song of the war against Japan, the song of the people's militia, and finally, Mao's speech of May 20, 1970: "A weak nation can defeat a strong, and a small nation can defeat a big. The people of a small country can certainly defeat aggression by a big country, if only they dare to rise and struggle, dare to take up arms and grasp in their own hands the destiny of their country. This is a law of history." Now they dance. And I think, as I have throughout the day, *of their internal guerrilla war.* But for the first time, seeing them dance as if in a ceremony duplicating thousands of others in China at this same moment, my emotions are stirred. I no longer think of them specifically, of the *re-educated cadres,* but rather of the entire people they represent. For the first time I have the sensation of glimpsing a tiny corner of the truth, of what the Chinese really are.

I see them as a vital people, carving out a new, unprecedented path of development in the heart of Asia—a path founded on the theory, proven by practice, that the superstructure and the structure must simultaneously be transformed in order to define the correct revolutionary relationship between them, to comprehend it in its continuous dynamic. They are a people who call on the rest of the world not to succumb to apathy; a people who condemn gradualism, revisionism, and integration; in short, a people standing thousands of miles away from our cities, waving a little red book, and demanding that we, too, make the revolution.

4

Treading Softly: Everyday Life in China

Our four suitcases are way too many. One-third of what we brought would have been enough since slacks, sweaters, and wool socks are all that can be worn. As it gets colder in Peking, we realize that the Chinese dress in a practical fashion: under their cotton outfits they wear knits and tights and they seem padded with wool. They dress warmly but from the inside to the outside. When the thermometer goes below freezing, they put on warm jackets or lined overcoats and wear sheepskin hats. We hermetically seal two of our suitcases, dragging them behind us like a dead weight, and complain vigorously if even our friends help us. "Three, four, ten outfits," Lu gently pokes fun at us as we put our clothes in the closet. And how can we possibly use all the medicine we've brought along on the "advice" of a European who told us to bring everything, even aspirin, or else we would have to get any medicine we needed at the hospital. We would like to throw some of these things away, but in China it is impossible to get rid of anything because the Chinese are so scrupulously honest and thrifty. If I pretend to forget my newspaper, an old issue of *Unità*, in a restaurant, or if I throw some papers in the wastebasket, I will find them carefully returned to my table. Yesterday a railroad employee ran after us for a good ten minutes and, out of breath, returned a half-empty box of matches we left in the train coming back from Tientsin. So we have to keep everything with us, like porters.

The honesty of the Chinese is shown in a thousand ways, to the point of becoming another dimension of life. We have become accustomed to doing small things like leaving drawers open, or leaving all our money on the table in our room, and never closing the door. Once I slammed the car door shut and instinctively started to lock it up, when a Western companion admonished me not to worry about it. He said that nothing was locked up in China and that the Chinese would not steal a pin.

The barber at the Hsin Chiao's barbershop also washes and dries women's hair, but the women can't get their hair set there. Foreign women have to set their own hair, with the use of a generous supply of curlers and hair dryers. Chinese women have pretty, straight, thick hair, shaped in the same way as the men. Young girls wear their hair in braids. Everyone's hair is washed with soap and water. Makeup doesn't exist. The soap in our bathroom has a rusty color and a smell of disinfectant. Everything is poor, clean, honest, basic.

As the days go by, we find ourselves changing bit by bit in scarcely perceptible ways. To send postcards, I have to glue the backs of the stamps (which don't have glue on them), using a paint brush. After fifteen minutes my hands are all smudged. I remember once making a scene at the main post office in Rome over one stamp that didn't stick. Now I feel completely different about it. Unconsciously, I have accepted the Chinese way of doing things, pitching in in my small way to alleviate the work of others. When I got sick, I saved all the empty medicine bottles and took them back to the hospital so they could be reused. I was thus participating in a general movement which tries to keep everything that is still usable, to be thrifty and to use all possible scraps. I realize that I no longer pay much attention to how I dress. Two holes have appeared in my already threadbare slacks. In Rome I would have thrown them out by now, but here I take them back to the laundry and mending service in the hotel (laundry and mending are always found together). They return the slacks with two circular patches sewn on in an extremely fine stitch, like an embroidery stitch. Cost: 30 fen, or about 12 cents, carefully written on a small note. Our room is full of these small notes on which everything extra is scrupulously accounted for, with an explanation of what is involved and with the absurdly low price beside it. People do not give tips, either; this is considered an insult.

The Chinese people emanate purity; they are men without sin as it were—using our categories. "They have a kind of purity which is characteristic of those devoid of all trace of vulgarity," Goffredo Parise wrote in *Espresso* (May 25, 1969).

> The physical and spiritual attributes of each and every Chinese you see here, wearing their humble mended garments and their black felt or cloth shoes, signify a kind of great inner lightness. Confronted by such a collective presence, Westerners (except peasants, the poor, and some rare exceptions) tend to feel awkward, stingy, and "slobbish," I'm sorry to say.

Here in China morality means giving precedence to politics and politics means sacrifice, courage, altruism, modesty, and thrift. After twenty days, we are plunged up to our necks in this sea of purity. Even those who denigrate China are shaken by this fact and have to admit that it exists. I keep telling myself that the experiment being conducted by the Chinese in the most astounding political laboratory in the world must be occurring under antiseptic conditions, with no threat of outside contagion. They are trying to transplant something into the hearts of several million people, and to overcome any body rejections that might occur from the transplant. Aren't the Chinese always talking about the "revolutionary red heart"? The world is full of germs, such as revisionism, the technocratic society, the consumer society, not to mention the Number One Enemy, imperialism. They must rely solely on themselves to avoid slipping into corruption and subjugation. But this is not to say that Chinese society is spartan or Jansenist, as some people say. China is a socialist society underpinned by Marxism-Leninism and the thought of Mao Tse-tung, even in the unwritten code of its strict morality.

The inner and outer elegance of the Chinese is so striking that it even affects such foreigners as Western diplomats, those thoroughbreds of the international bourgeoisie, some of whom try to model themselves on the Chinese and even compete with them. They re-educate themselves, as it were, the men by wearing simple sweaters and plaid shirts, the women by doing their shopping in slacks, helping the cook, and living simply. Now and again they go to Hong Kong, their biggest amusement, to buy wine and cheese, and back home they smell of camembert. We had dinner with some diplomats, including two young Englishmen. These young men are not the typical diplomats you might meet elsewhere around the world. The strict life in China has influenced them. No longer are they arrogant or haughty, but rather timid and cautious in their behavior, with an unparalleled modesty. They have been re-educated without knowing it, or rather, because they live here among the Chinese, they are trying to adapt themselves *to the Chinese tempo*, to the Chinese way of being and of behaving. They are also demonstratively pleasant and patient, now that the shoe is on the other foot after centuries of ruthless British domination in this Asian land and harsh English concessionary rule in cities such as Shanghai. If you want to stay in China, you have to treat the Chinese with the greatest respect, in a circumspect and courteous way you wouldn't use anywhere else. In any other country, if you were obliged to wait at the airport a full day to catch a plane, as happened to a diplomat yesterday, only to be told that the plane wasn't taking off anyway, you would return home furious and nerves on end. Here you would just be "a little tired" when you returned home, since you had remembered to bring some interesting books along to read during the extra time. Foreigners, diplomats, businessmen, and journalists are beginning to consider it a favor even to be allowed to stay in China, which indicates that they are *persona grata* here.

The diplomats are all very impressed by the political, rather than geographical, scope of our trip. They invite us to dinner in their "diplomatic ghetto"—for this is how their isolated quarters strike me. The wife of the English diplomat is wearing slacks, sneakers, a light sweater, and a jacket. One of our foreign service friends has on a red sweater, a plaid shirt, and his hair is unkempt. The Englishman is also wearing a shirt with a big checkered pattern, and a heavy out-of-shape jacket. No snobbery, no chic. Even the way foreign diplomacy is conducted is keyed to the situation.

What really strikes one is the way foreign observers admire the Chinese people, on a personal and aesthetic level, as they say. But the Chinese, in their relations with foreigners, are very detached and deal with them only on an official basis. Foreigners we met often complained that they felt *excluded* from the daily life of the Chinese. "We have never eaten with the Chinese at the same table," a young English diplomat from the British delegation told me. "You are lucky to be able to mix and travel with them, to get into their factories, communes, and to sit down to a meal with them."

Everyone envies us, in short, and perhaps they would give a lot to be able to do what we are doing. Diplomats and journalists in Peking try to analyze why the Chinese are so fascinating, some attributing it to the antiquity of their culture, others to Confucianism, and still others to the "religious nature of politics" in China, centered on the thought of Mao. The word "religious" keeps recurring. One day a diplomat called dialectical materialism "religious" and I told him that the two terms contradict one another. "Religion comes from the Latin *religio,*" I said, "and it relates man to the metaphysical, to an external force which transcends and dominates him. Dialectical materialism is just the opposite since it brings everything down to earth."

How could he keep confusing religion and the scientific method of dialectical materialism? This conversation was held with a Catholic diplomat, a long-time resident of Peking, a Westerner extremely knowledgeable about China. His "religious" interpretation of China can help us better understand our own terminology.

A Catholic diplomat's religious interpretation of China

"In my opinion, however antithetical China may be to religion, and given its atheism, the country still has two points in common with Christianity. Not early Christianity but that of the eleventh and twelfth centuries when the Church was the center of everything. In Europe, Germany, and France, the people built great stone cathedrals as a testimony to their faith. The only public entertainments were the mystery plays, like the revolutionary works which are a kind of religious theater here in China. God and the saints were always portrayed as austere and ascetic figures. Politics itself was religion.

"As for Chinese intellectuals, my feelings on the subject of their re-education and self-criticism are quite different from the conventional Western view. Those who really understand China realize that these experiences are not as painful as they are made out to be, but are rather a sort of liberation of the individual. Re-educating yourself means becoming part of the masses again and part of the mass religion. Inner freedom, happiness, and a sense of spirituality are achieved by being re-educated among the ordinary people, peasants and workers, since the ultimate humiliation in life is to be isolated from the masses. Chinese intellectuals will be able to consider themselves as such only if their people can benefit from the wealth which they themselves can give to others, only when their abilities are judged within the social context. The intellectual who wants the fatted calf to be killed in his honor when he is re-educated is less concerned with re-enacting the old parable than with the fact that his mental capabilities will go unused if he is cut off from the masses. The day when he is accepted again, like the prodigal son, is a day of reconciliation for him.

"You have heard of self-criticism. I have not had this happen to me, but I know that self-criticisms in China are made and then re-made many times over like a work of art. The man or woman who undergoes this experience has to be completely sincere because he or she has to speak out loud in public. This public loves this person and wants to redeem him, and it exposes his limitations, his weaknesses, and any hypocritical attitudes he may unknowingly have had. When the self-criticism has fully satisfied the masses, the person in question has achieved a sort of absolute sublimation of the self. You don't go through searing mental agony or anger during this experience, as is often alleged abroad, or if you do this is a minor aspect of the process. I have never visited a May 7 school, but I don't see any similarity between the people who come out of these schools and those who come out of concentration camps. Just the opposite in fact, the people who graduate from the May 7 schools are men and women of a new Long March, one accomplished inside themselves. The idea is to reclaim everyone and everything, and you will pass the 95 percent mark, as Mao said.

"How can anyone in the world be as virtuous as the Chinese? Let me make some comparisons. The Chinese people know neither jealousy, greed, nor egoism. They mend, they save, they find a use for the most insignificant scraps. They are serious and ponder what they do. Their old sense of trade, in which they are extremely clever and infinitely honest, is now entirely focused on the collectivity and no longer on the individual. Could as formidable an achievement as the Cultural Revolution have been accomplished by less than a people who are not only sensitive, upright, hardworking, and intelligent enough to debate philosophical points, but also passionately committed to politics?

"The industrial revolution in China is yet to come and when it does, it will change many aspects of life. But what counts is that it will have been accomplished by millions of people all working and sacrificing together, little by little, not for themselves but for their country. Industrial growth in China will be the opposite of what we have known in the West. Instead of being conducted by a managerial elite, it will be led by the masses.

"The only question is what new form the distribution of consumer goods will take when what is called technological progress and industrial growth occur. At present, Chinese society is egalitarian in nature in that the necessities of life reach everyone equally, or are so limited in number that everyone starts from the same point of departure. But what effect will the coming economic explosion have on the distribution of well-being among men? How can new disequilibriums be prevented from occurring? In brief, won't some people necessarily get there 'first,' according to a sort of objective law which also governs the economic principles behind an industrial boom?

"Something further needs to be said. The Chinese not only have complete confidence in their own revolutionary and socialist country, but are convinced of their absolute political superiority over the rest of the world, which is a kind of nationalism. But at the same time, they have a universal vision of the world that stresses, like Christianity, devotion and sacrifice for the sake of strangers. Not only for other Asians, Africans, and Latin Americans, but also for Western European and American whites, workers, farmers, and intellectuals. Mao is the only man in the world who has a political conception on the scale of the universe. Unlike the Russians, he has a sense of what the great currents are in the world, and his intuition has led to a strategic understanding of what moves the masses. He has the genius to capture their imagination, to make them enthusiastic, and to set high ideals for them, especially for the world's despairing young people whose passionate searching he seems to have foreseen. Don't you think that European young people need high ideals? Wouldn't you agree that American young people are going through a severe crisis because they lack an ideal and this is why they are abandoning themselves to drugs?"

Young Lu asked me once or twice, "Is it true that in the West young girls wear miniskirts and the boys wear long hair like women? Do a lot of them take drugs?"

"Yes, that's right. But maybe they would prefer other values. Did you know that many of them think they can learn a lot from China?"

"No, that can't be right," Lu answered, irritated. "A lot of these young people are just being used, as an objective instrument, to spread bourgeois ideology among the masses. Underneath their behavior lurks bourgeois ideology—like the Beatles, whose music makes young people hysterical."

I explained to Lu that a lot of young people are tormented by the consumer society. He looked at me questioningly. He kept quiet, but a question was on the tip of his tongue: "So why don't they make a revolution?"

"It's not that simplc," I wantcd to tcll him.

"And your daughter, does she wear a miniskirt too?"

"No, the style has just changed and she's wearing a maxiskirt."

"And you, do you wear a miniskirt?"

I burst out laughing. "No."

Lu was reassured. He admitted to me that before my arrival he had read my book, *Letters from Inside the Party*, in Italian, and found it very interesting.

To celebrate diplomatic relations between Italy and China: a game of ping-pong

Today, November 6, 1970, at 5 P.M., we learn that Italy and China have re-established diplomatic relations. Now that the People's Republic of China is twenty years old, our diplomatic turtle has finally reached its goal. We call to Lu by banging on his door, located about twenty yards from our room on the same corridor. We still have some whisky left from the trip, and we use it to toast *the friendship between the Chinese and the Italian people.* Then we raise our glasses to "proletarian internationalism" to remind ourselves of the importance of other things besides diplomatic events.

People's Daily dedicates its editorial of November 8 to the renewal of diplomatic relations between Italy and China and stresses China's policy on the question of diplomatic relations. Peking insists that one condition be met: the severance of ties with Taiwan. China has faithfully maintained its position on this issue ever since Mao's speech on foreign policy on the eve of Liberation. This position is repeated each time diplomatic relations are established with another country:

> We are ready to start negotiations with any foreign government to establish diplomatic relations. These relations will be founded on the principles of equality, mutual advantage, and mutual respect for each other's sovereignty and territorial integrity, on condition that the government in question be willing to sever its relations with the Chinese reactionaries, that it cease to plot with them and to help them, that it adopt a friendly attitude toward People's China, and that it be sincere and not hypocritical.

China has thus always been interested in re-establishing diplomatic relations with other countries. Its diplomatic strategy, I think, is currently inspired by the conviction that any break in the bloc led by the United States constitutes a success for China and a defeat for the United States. Of course, this does not at all mean that China confers some sort of diploma of democracy on a particular country by recognizing its government. China considers its principal enemy to be the United States and it does all it can to weaken that country's political position. Diplomatic recognition of Italy, I think, occurred in this context.

People in the factories, communes, and schools we visited expressed satisfaction with the news and hoped that it would help to strengthen the bonds between Italians and Chinese. Everyone we met was more or less familiar with the news, as it had been broadcast by radio even in the most far away corners of the country. We were often told that the recognition was a victory for the increasing international prestige of China and a testimony to the strength in struggle of the Italian people. What was meant by that?

China in 1970 has emerged from its diplomatic isolation, widening the breach of encirclement forced upon it. The triumphant Cultural Revolution, combined with the growing universal political consciousness of the peoples of the world, have broken the blockade. The success of the Cultural Revolution indicated the country's strength. On the crest of this movement, China now faces the world at full strength, with a solid home front, agricultural and industrial accomplishments, space conquests, and the atomic bomb. Now that its second revolution has in fact been completed, the country is dealing with its adversaries in their own backyards. These enemies are those who cry "Yellow Peril" and they are being fought on the very ground on which they chose to attack the Chinese when they tried to shock the world by playing on the threats of chaos, disintegration, military dictatorship, and famine on the mainland. The official world has been surprised by China's strength, while ordinary people have been fascinated by events in the country.

This prepared the groundwork for the present Chinese world initiative. In 1970, China established diplomatic relations with Canada (on October 15), Guinea (on October 20), Italy (on November 6), Ethiopia (on November 24), Chile (on December 15), and in 1971 with Kuwait. The countries which now recognize Peking number fifty-two. China established relations with half of these countries, most of them from the socialist camp, in 1950, next established relations with the Arab world, and then with Black Africa after the end of French colonial domination. During the Sino-Soviet dispute, these relations became very strained. Many African countries were influenced by Moscow's anti-Chinese propaganda and expelled their Chinese diplomatic missions, while others suspended diplomatic relations (Burundi, Ghana, Tunisia). French diplomatic recognition in 1964 was certainly a great victory, but at that date none of these countries had re-established relations with People's China, except South Yemen and the island of Mauritius.

The diplomatic victories which followed one another were crowned by the United Nations vote on November 20, 1971, when 51 percent of the member countries for the first time voted for the admission of the People's Republic of China and the expulsion of the representative from Taiwan. This event provoked a profound psychological shock in the world and the Chinese, we can say as personal witnesses, welcomed it with satisfaction, great calm, and with words they have repeated many times: "These victories represent the strength of China and the strength of a people who are united." As far as Italy's vote in the United Nations was concerned, the Chinese response to our asking what they thought of it was subtle and ironic: "Italy? At first we thought we were wrong, but it seems that Italy voted for both the Albanian motion and the Philippine motion, without showing preference for either . . ." Speaking of contradictions!

We celebrate Italy's diplomatic recognition of China at the new stadium in Peking, where a ping-pong tournament is being held between teams representing China and North Vietnam. Ping-pong and basketball are the most popular sports in China and the stadium is packed. It can also be used as an amphitheater, seating 18,000 people, and has a mechanized retractable central arena which can be converted into a skating rink. Two-thirds of the audience is composed of soldiers from the People's Liberation Army, dressed in greenish or faded green fatigues. Although they are passionate spectators, the people in the audience manage to preserve their dignity, not to overdo it, and not get overly excited. Those strong passions which in our countries go for football or cycling are in China reserved for politics. Watching the people in the stadium brings something else to mind. When Westerners think about people being regimented in China, they don't realize the degree to which the Chinese instinctively love politics, the confrontation of ideas, philosophical discourse, and cultural activities.

The Chinese teams win all the ping-pong matches, except for the women's tournament cup which is taken by the North Vietnamese. Practically the entire Political Bureau of the Chinese Communist Party is here, seated at the podium. Among those we recognize are, seated next to Chou En-lai, Chen Po-ta, Kang Sheng, Chiang Ching—Chairman Mao's wife—Chu Teh, Liu Po-cheng, and numerous others. Chou En-lai is speaking with Norodom Sihanouk, on his right. All the members of the Political Bureau, including Mao Tse-tung's wife, salute the crowd by waving the little red book. Mao's wife is in military dress, fatigues, slacks, and a cap clamped down to her ears. Lin Piao's wife is also wearing a uniform. You can't distinguish the men from the women by their clothing, or the leaders from the people. Mao Tse-tung's wife is wearing thick round glasses and wipes her face from time to time with a hot towel. She practically never smiles, but often politely turns to talk with Sihanouk's beautiful wife.

Do the wives of Chinese leaders play a determining role in political affairs? Certainly, but less in their capacity as wives, as one suspects is the case in the West, than as combatants from the days of the Long March and as members of leading party organizations. The first person to enter the warring front lines of the Cultural Revolution was a woman, Liu Shao-chi's wife. A Russian I met in Peking told me that Liu's wife was particularly seductive at the time she led the propaganda team into Tsinghua. "She looked thirty instead of fifty. She always wore dresses of antique silk, her skirt slit way up the side of her leg . . ." Mao's and Lin Piao's wives have responsible positions in the Political Bureau, and Chiang Ching practically raised the curtain on the first act of the Cultural Revolution by subjecting the theaters of Peking and Shanghai to revolutionary criticism. These women appear to be the feminine symbols of Chinese revolutionary life.

Crowds, markets, and retail prices

Peking has the air of a provincial capital, where each day seems like fair day or market day. Small shops and big department stores are open even on Sunday, and an uninterrupted wave of people, a continuous stream, runs along Ta Shalan, the street with a thousand shops. The crowd is quiet, poorly dressed to be sure, but far from "miserable." "Among the 600 million people in China," Mao Tse-tung said in 1956, "there is a lot of poverty and backwardness. This could be interpreted as a bad sign, but in fact it is a good thing. Poverty makes you want to change things, to act, to make a revolution." Twelve years have passed since this was said. China has resolved its number one problem of being able to feed its immense population of 750 million.

I watch the crowds going up and down the stairs in what we call "supermarkets," pressing together in the Hsitan covered market, or wherever they eat or buy clothes. The prices are decidedly low. I buy a brown linen woman's coat, lined, for 21.70 yuan (about $9.00). A big padded man's jacket costs 17 yuan. Felt shoes with rubber soles, like those worn by Lin Piao in photographs, are 2 yuan a pair. Leather ones cost 6 to 8 yuan. Precut material for an outfit in blue cotton costs 11.29 yuan; made up it comes to 17 yuan. A lined sheepskin jacket, 50 yuan. The famous Chinese silk, 2.8 yuan a yard. I go into a two-story department store where I see some girls trying on linen jackets which they are carefully smoothing down for a better fit as they stand in front of the mirror, laughing and acting coquettish. I ask them why they aren't buying silk and they say that it isn't practical in the winter but that they always wear silk in the summer.

The Hsitan covered market is a sort of Noah's ark, brimming over with live animals: rabbits, geese, chickens, small pigs, and fish. There are mountains of sausage, salted foods, lamb and pork flanks, pyramids of cabbage, apples, pears, bananas, persimmons, colored candies, and tea boxes balanced on top of each other. I learn the price of some of the food sold here. Per pound, lamb costs 71 fen; spaghetti 2 fen; chicken 73 fen; eggs 9 fen; cabbage 1 fen; apples 3 fen; tomatoes 14 fen; and soysauce 3 fen. I never see any kind of ration cards in the hands of the shoppers. The crowds are so large that small detachments of Red Guards have to monitor the streets. Over battery-run megaphones, they ask the passers-by not to overcrowd the streets, then pause and read passages from Chairman Mao's little red book.

Sunday in Peking is like any other day except that you meet families going for an afternoon walk in Tien An Men square. Roving photographers, heads buried under the black cloth of ancient cameras, take their pictures in front of the square's famous podium. The Chinese love to take pictures and to have themselves photographed, but they always include some political symbol in the picture. Even fiancés look at each other tenderly while holding Mao's little red book tightly in their hands or on their hearts. They don't have to do this, so they must enjoy it.

Since we have a camera and photographic equipment, we feel obliged to take some pictures. Our two interpreter friends offer their help and encourage us to take as many pictures as possible.

(We were even able to get pictures of the May 7 School in the port of Tientsin, and a picture of the river traffic on the Huang-pu at the Nanking Bridge, where the guards posed with us.) No one ever asked to check our film. If we didn't return home with rolls and rolls of film, it is because we felt awkward taking pictures and because we were often distracted by other things. We instinctively continued to use our old ways of recording our observations—eyes, speech, etc. When we left China, via Hong Kong, we told some television correspondents who had been waiting there for visas to go to China for a month that no one checked our film. They didn't believe us and insisted that no one could leave China without first having had his film developed and checked by the Chinese. Our experience proves just the opposite.*

When everyday Peking faces the excitement of a public parade and demonstration, the city unfurls like a rainbow and explodes into a thousand colors, like the blossoming of spring flowers. We are there on the day the city prepares solemnly and grandiosely to receive the president of the Islamic Republic of Pakistan, Yahya Khan, who is incidentally a good example of a reactionary. Early in the morning, children with yellow, red, and green paper flowers parade past. Enormous scarlet drums are perched on tricycles. Bands follow one another, interspersed with units from the People's Liberation Army. And women, and city people. Hundreds of red balloons rise up toward the sky from one end of Tien An Men square to the other. In front is a forest of red flags, like low clouds, clouds of fire. There are still more red flags on the gates, on lions, stair landings, and handrails.

The car in which we are riding makes its way with difficulty through the crowd. We skirt a detachment of young girls aged thirteen or fourteen from the Peking militia who are carrying semiautomatic rifles slung across their shoulders, their faces motionless and serious. There are a lot of these girls, with childlike faces, short pigtails, small caps, and big guns. The crowd, miles long, goes by in waves; the people wear Mao badges on their chests and carry more flags and gigantic pennants with huge ideograms on them. What strikes me is the ecstatic look on their faces, as though this is a festi-

* The policy of no checking has existed down to the present.—*Trans.*

val being held especially for them, as though they feel they are the main actors. The bands play, the people sing and wave their flowers and flags. I again have the extremely vivid impression that here is a people who are the living expression of their highest ideals. Red Guard units with their armbands, the younger Little Red Soldiers, children of all ages. All the colors and inventions of "pop art" are here, coming together in a panorama of unbridled fantasy, red flags stamped with gilded and painted characters designed by thousands of anonymous artists.

As we drive to the airport, we see thousands more red flags floating over the fields, brought by workers who are working on an irrigation project. These fields of red flags are now a new part of the vegetation in the Chinese countryside. They rise above the men and women bent over the land; when the day's work is done, they put them in their carts and file home in endless columns. Thus the symbol of the revolution, not only the Chinese one but the world revolution as well, as we are repeatedly told, rises from the midst of tools, sacks, and buckets.

"The final victory of a socialist country not only requires the efforts of the proletariat and the broad masses of the people at home," explained the article in *People's Daily* dedicated to the 100th anniversary of the Paris Commune, "but also involves the victory of the world revolution and the abolition of the system of exploitation of man by man over the whole globe, upon which all mankind will be emancipated."

"Preparations for a possible war," and "Who is afraid of whom?"

Day and night these same millions of Chinese dig holes and rip open entire streets to build underground anti-aircraft shelters for the population, which are also to serve as guerrilla bases. They dig methodically, patiently, and tenaciously like millions of termites. They do it openly, in sight and hearing of everyone. China has dug another world, an underground world, in the heart of its big cities and in the surrounding agricultural areas. "Preparations for a possible war are carried out in the interests of the people": the most widely read and discussed document in China these past months, giving rise to many interpretations, has been Mao's statement on May 20, 1970, in which he analyzes the international political situation.

> The danger of a new world war still exists, and the people of all countries must get prepared. But revolution is the main trend in the world today. . . .
>
> U.S. imperialism, which looks like a huge monster, is in essence a paper tiger, now in the throes of its deathbed struggle. In the world of today, who actually fears whom? It is not the Vietnamese people, the Laotian people, the Cambodian people, the Palestinian people, the Arab people, or the people of other countries who fear U.S. imperialism; it is U.S. imperialism which fears the people of the world.

5
The Chinese Experiment

Before we meet some factory workers

The Cultural Revolution is basically an implacable war on the values underlying the traditional division of labor, the type of leadership associated with it, and what was left in China of capitalist and later post-Stalinist industry. The struggle between Mao and Liu Shao-chi is, especially on the ideological level, a sharp and definitive battle whose outcome will determine the future of China itself.

Liu Shao-chi supported the classical model of capitalist accumulation, that adopted by the USSR. He considered utopian the idea that a country could escape obeying the laws of the industrial revolution. These laws, responsible for industrial growth in every other country, include the division of labor, of qualifications, and of tasks; specialization; and the establishment of a hierarchy whose top echelons are leaders in production and social life. At the top of the pyramid would be cadres and experts, socially set apart by higher salaries and therefore a higher standard of living (including homes, vacations, cars, and later perhaps special stores for food and consumer goods). The working masses would form the base of the pyramid. The greatest efficiency possible would be gotten from them by increases in salary, various incentives and bonuses, and by accelerating their pace of work.

After 1960, in "The Charter of the Anshan Iron and Steel Plant," Mao Tse-tung deliberately turned his back on all earlier types of industrialization. He proposed a new, revolutionary way for the transitional society: not only to destroy from the start "the legal basis of property relationships, but to try to establish a noncapitalist mode of production even during the first phase of socialist construction." * The Chinese Communists know that state ownership of the means of production will not in itself guarantee a socialist type of management, and that the decisive factor is the system of relations established inside a society. To the Chinese, Soviet society has already been proven a failure, since a caste of technocrats increasingly removed from the masses has arisen, men who lord it over the masses and act like new bosses, men who look down on the masses and stifle their initiative. According to Mao, free expression has to be given to the people's imagination and to their pride in producing. They should not be set against the experts but should be their equals, so that the ideological strength of the cadre and the worker's practicality and proverbial ingenuity works together. Recall Che Guevara's comment on his return from China: "The Chinese worker can do anything that any other worker in the world can do, and what is more, he can do what only a Chinese worker can do." Experts and simple workers in China are no longer set apart from one another now that philosophy and political texts are studied in the factory and are accompanied by continuous political and theoretical discussion.

Philosophy in the factory

Mao's general line on industrialization was formulated in 1958, the year of the Great Leap Forward ** and collectivization in the

* Lisa Foa, "*Al Ritorno da un Viaggio in Cina*" (*Home from a Trip to China*), *Giovane Critica*, Winter 1970–1971.

** *The Great Leap Forward.* Economic development in China was still uneven, even after the people's communes were created and industry was completely socialized. In some sectors there was a long tradition of socialist management, whereas in others the forces of production had just been liberated from the old economic systems. The industrial process was still shrouded with mystery in some regions, a problem which the Great Leap Forward particularly helped to solve. The Great Leap mobilized the masses and taught them how to do fundamental tasks themselves, following the example of the vanguard. As a result, the peasants became adapted to the industrial process and established a closer relationship with the working class. All mass initiatives which would improve and spur production were encouraged, even if

countryside: "The principles for building socialism are: the utmost use of everyone's efforts, continuous progress, with emphasis on quantity, quality, speed, and economy." "The most intelligent people are the humble people and the aristocrats are the most stupid," he wrote in a letter to the agricultural machinery factory in Tantung. What he meant was that China would have an inexhaustible supply of creative energy at its disposal if it knew how to liberate the masses from their awe of the cadre and their submissiveness to the new "aristocracy" of experts. In 1960, Mao rejected the form of Soviet industrial development as written up in "The Charter of the Magnitogorsk Steel Plant," in favor of another model represented in "The Charter of the Anshan Iron and Steel Plant." The principles emphasized in this latter essay were:

> Always put politics in command, reinforce the leading role of the party, launch vigorous mass movements, systematically promote the participation of cadres in productive work and of workers in management, revise any unreasonable rules, assure a close working relationship between cadres, workers, and experts, and energetically promote the technological revolution.

He also said, "Economics is the base, whereas politics is the concentrated expression of economics." In a class society no "economic organization" exists apart from the classes, and production is never separated from politics. So, Mao concluded, "political work is vitally important for our work in the economic field." When the Cultural Revolution began in 1966, the whole role of the leaders and cadres in China, starting with the basic unit of production, was

---

results weren't immediately forthcoming. This profound mass movement liberated the masses to the point where they are now confident in their own abilities. "Without political change, the productive forces in China are condemned to failure": the Great Leap Forward was launched by this one sentence from Mao.

On February 3, 1958, *People's Daily* criticized the opponents of the Great Leap, saying, "Comrades who see the present as a function of previous experiences and old regulations know only how to look backward. They don't realize that when the forces of production are liberated, the awakened masses can accomplish much more than previously thought possible. If they will examine a current case, they will see that such a case can be generalized. It has to be understood that our cause is a revolutionary one and that revolution is a leap. We are proletarian revolutionaries and not reformists."

called into question. Since then, the Chinese have refused to see the expert's role as a privileged and autonomous one and have refused to separate productive activity from manual labor.

One of the key points of the Cultural Revolution, and one of the Sixteen Points of August 1966, is: "Take firm hold of the revolution and stimulate production." This order was repeated incessantly for years and we heard it on the lips of all the workers and cadres we met. It explains why the Cultural Revolution did not result in economic disaster, as predicted by the West, although some stagnation did occur in certain important industrial sectors.

In fact, what happened was that the industrial revolution gained ground and production increased as the political revolution progressed. Everywhere we went the goals of the 1970 economic plan were exceeded or factories were ahead of schedule. Growth was 25 to 30 percent greater in 1970 than in 1968–1969, even though a split had developed among both cadres and workers, who had divided into two camps in the big factories of Shanghai and Tientsin, the two big industrial cities in China. But little by little the revisionism of Liu Shao-chi and his most famous forerunners (Kao Kang and Jao Shu-shih) * were denounced. Some of the slogans

* "Within the 1937 leadership group, Kao Kang and Jao Shu-shih were accused in the mid-1950s of organizing an independent state in Manchuria (perhaps with the support of the USSR). . . . The critical point in the history of the party organization occurred between 1954 and 1955 when the positions held by Kao Kang and Jao Shu-shih were eliminated and new party unity forged. . . . Kao Kang's suicide was made public in March 1955 . . ." (From *The China Reader*, vol. 3, "Communist China," Franz Schurmann and Orville Schell, eds.) Given the importance of these men—Kao Kang was then secretary of the Northeast Central Committee and chairman of the State Planning Commission—and the importance of the crisis which they precipitated, one which was injected into the very core of the subsequent struggle against Liu Shao-chi's line (Kao Kang was closely tied to the Soviets, and in 1949 he had signed an agreement for exchanges between the Soviet Union and the Northeast government, thereby creating mixed Soviet-Chinese enterprises), it is not strange that Liu Shao-chi's line continues to be referred to in China as the line "of his forerunners Kao Kang and Jao Shu-shih." We should also read what the well-known economist Roland Berger wrote in *China Now* (March-May 1971). He explains how the role played by Kao Kang in what he calls the "era of the managers" was fought throughout the years of the Cultural Revolution. In effect, "with the [Soviet] installations came Soviet advisors and their methods of factory organiza-

and statements used against them at this time were that revisionism is "giving the manager the power to decide," "the theory that the forces of production are all-powerful," "profits in command," "expertise in command," "bonuses in command," and "submission of the workers to the experts." The conflict in Chinese industry from 1960 to 1970 centered on the attempts of the revisionists to reintroduce capitalist organizational techniques into the industrial enterprises which they held like fortresses. Liu Shao-chi's line also included dependence on foreign countries for machinery and technical assistance, cooperation with other countries, and the entry of foreign capital. The latter would have slowed down the Chinese economy and would have made it dependent on capitalism and imperialism.

There was heated debate on these questions. Mao defended the position of eliminating any dependence on foreign countries from the start, of appealing to the people to be "self-reliant," and of promoting "mass initiative and eagerness" following the traumatic unilateral cancellation of Russian economic assistance. Soviet technicians were withdrawn in 1960, at a time when China had to cope with overwhelming difficulties. But as Mao says, good can come from bad. The Chinese humiliation made them determined never to be at the mercy of foreign countries again and to solve their own problems with their own resources. The conflict in Chinese industry lasted about twelve years, and was finally resolved in favor of the line which radically questioned the laws ruling industrial societies. The West reacts negatively, in an energetic and fanatical way, to the Cultural Revolution insofar as it feels the basis of its own society challenged by this movement. The legal basis of private property is questioned, as is the hierarchical nature of our societies. Thus the Chinese experiment, even if it is not yet fully verified, is of great importance.

To those in the West who are used to capitalist industry, Chinese factories come as a surprise and even appear disorderly at first sight. A few months before going to China, I visited the Canon factories in Japan, and I retained an image of women workers whose

---

tion. Work standards and regulations were often a literal transposition of those applied in analogous Soviet enterprises. . . ."

bodies seemed to meld into the machinery, as if they were part of the gears. They never looked up at the visiting foreigner as they nervously and quickly worked to fulfill their daily quotas. I remember the comment of some Japanese industrialists who visited the Italian Fiat factory in 1970: "You make good cars, but the work pace seems a little slow to us." Chinese factories are incredible places. Their large workshops are full of colorful tatzupao hanging from the ceiling to the floor. Some are glued to the wall, others are suspended by strings, and some are even put on the machines. The tatzupao are used in the factories to express opinions, to discuss political and philosophical matters, to protest any waste or errors, and to criticize small theft and negligence.

A worker may put his newspaper, *People's Daily*, beside his machine and look at it from time to time. Or he may have a photo of an actor in a revolutionary work, or a notepad to jot down some thoughts for a talk he is preparing. In China, a new person is being created, the worker who places politics first and releases his own creative energy by doing so. The worker's relationship with the expert is established on this basis, so that he is never reduced to an inferior position.

Later on I will write about a woman who works at the textile factory in Tientsin (2,000 workers) and who studies philosophy at the factory. She is not alone, as 127 other workers, the "philosophy brigade," study with her. She explained to me in detail what the terms *dialectic* and *contradiction* mean in Mao's writings. She also said, "According to Liu Shao-chi's line, we workers are naive to think that we are capable of studying philosophy, which is a science only intellectuals can master. Mao's line tells us that we all can study it to good advantage by applying theory to running our own factories." Textile Factory Number 2 exceeded the goals of its 1970 plan by the middle of the year and started on those for 1971. Women in Shanghai who formerly belonged to the subproletariat now build transistors in a small suburban factory. The machine tool factory in Shanghai, a city well known for its workers' university, has built precision machines whose quality matches or outstrips the highest world records.

Quantity, quality, speed, economy. How can these be measured, how can statistics on productivity be evaluated or reduced to a single factor? The Chinese themselves are wary of statistics, which can be "manipulated at will." The important thing is what you see when you go into a factory. The workers keep telling us: "We have been told that we can do little, that we are imbeciles with no expertise. But look at the technical problems we have solved and what we have made or invented. We have made machines which sell for half the price of foreign machines, and which are just as good and sometimes better."

The Chinese are trying to organize an alternative means of production to the model of capitalist accumulation in a country where the industrial revolution has not yet occurred and where Soviet-type management existed for a short time only. The system of one man at the top giving orders is being eliminated, whether he is the manager of a factory or the president of a university. The hierarchy of rank and skill is no longer valid in China, which means that unity between theory and practice as well as between technical and productive capacity can be achieved. This social experiment therefore cannot be called (as it often is in the West) a new type of religion, voluntarist egalitarianism, or a society motivated by faith.

The factories are now run by collective organizations—the revolutionary committees—which consists of a three-in-one combination of representatives from the revolutionary masses, revolutionary cadres, and the People's Liberation Army. Another three-in-one combination of young, middle-aged, and older cadres simultaneously participates in management. These new "red power" organizations have replaced the old management apparatus in every factory and administrative organization. Our investigation revealed that about 75 percent of the former apparatus has been replaced. Factory trade unions in part disappeared as a result of the intensity of the criticism. They were blamed for being instruments of Liu Shao-chi's economism, wage-oriented, and unpolitical. In some cases they were replaced by workers' councils, mass organizations which are in charge of reorganizing labor in the manner described earlier. This is not yet standardized throughout the country, but apparently it will soon be.

High salaries were one of the targets of the Cultural Revolution, since inequalities had developed. According to Roland Berger, writing in the *Society for Anglo-Chinese Understanding News*: "In the early 1960s, it was common to find leaders, secretaries of the party, who earned 300 yuan and more each month, and Peking Opera stars who earned as much as 3,000 yuan." In the ten factories I visited, salaries went from a low of 46 yuan to a high of 110–120 yuan. The salary ratio between worker and skilled technician is now 1:2.5 at the most.

Mao has said that

> high salaries must never be instituted for a small group of people. The discrepancy between the salaries of party, government, industry, and people's commune personnel on the one hand, and the masses of the people on the other hand, must decrease in a gradual and reasonable fashion. The personnel must not be encouraged to abuse its power or enjoy special privileges.

It is how to determine salary levels that is now being discussed. This is characteristic of the revolution going on in China. The Chinese seek to avoid any undue haste. Egalitarianism, for example, cannot be demagogically imposed from above but must be an experience consciously and politically shared by everyone, to give it a strong foundation. Later on, we will listen to the workers themselves on how this problem is handled where they work, in the factories and peasant communes. Discussions have led to the return of trade unions to the factories in the form of workers' councils, and they are responsible for restructuring the work process and instituting a new form of collective management.

Bonuses and material incentives have been eliminated in China, in contrast to Soviet policy which the Chinese press accuses of being responsible both for the chaos and confusion in Soviet industrial production and the "black market" in spare parts. Production in China has not suffered at all from its chosen path, but in fact has increased.

The goals of the state plan are set at higher organizational levels and implemented at the base level after discussions which, I am told, are rather cautious. In general, goals are fixed and then exceeded because of the creativity of the masses. The party committee had not yet been re-established in many of the factories we visited, but Communists are leading members of the revolutionary committees which are responsible for management. In other factories, the party committee was reorganized after a factory congress was convened.

Against a "new kind of barbarism"

From an industrial standpoint, China seems to present a successful alternative to our technological society. Some, including the Russians, claim that this is due to the fact that China has not yet become as highly industrialized as other countries. This allegation is easily countered. Now that China is realizing crucial technological achievements (such as the space satellite), it has chosen to socialize science and technology and to stress close collaboration between scientists and workers rich in practical experience. This does not reflect "poverty," but rather a specific type of economic progress.

As China enters the industrial age, it rejects the traditional model of capitalist accumulation, of the division of labor, and of disparity between industry and agriculture (with the former exploiting or at least taking priority over the latter). The Chinese refuse to worship "the golden calf," that is, the American model, the most powerful and prestigious in the industrialized world. The Chinese do not consider technology to be a fascinating sort of "forbidden fruit." Rather, they see in technology a *new kind of barbarism* reducing man to slavish dependence on the industrial machine and subjecting him to a class system of privileged and exploited, of segregation based on skill, of high and low salaries. This system destroys just what man needs the most: political consciousness. This —not aggression or war—is the challenge the Chinese face, and the future of the world depends on its success. If it fails, it will be a terrible disaster for the progressive peoples of the world, including the Soviet Union, and for mankind in general. China's challenge inspires such a fear that the United States, from its intervention in the Gulf of Tonkin to the invasion of Laos, continues to press ever closer to China's borders. Every Chinese, from the five-year-old child to the old man, knows that war threatens the country.

Anyone who accepts this analysis, or at least part of it, will have a less prejudiced outlook on Chinese workers and their factories. He or she will understand why the industrial accomplishments resulting from the unity of theory and practice, and from mutual cooperation between technicians and workers, are considered products of the Cultural Revolution—this applies to great feats, such as building the Nanking Bridge, as well as to more modest achievements, such as the construction of a crane from recycled scrap iron. Above all, this analysis leads to a clearer understanding, on a human and political level, of the atmosphere in Chinese factories and the almost unbelievable stories that come out of them: their only explanation is that a type of development radically different from our capitalist type has occurred.

Getting to Tientsin

It is not easy to get to Tientsin, China's second largest port after Shanghai. The city has shipyards, textile and automobile plants, and over one hundred electronics factories. The population is 4 million. "You don't actually enter Tientsin," some strangers at the Hsin Chiao Hotel tell us, watching us with curiosity as we depart. Our train leaves from the new Peking station (not built at the time of my 1954 trip) with its marble, its wide open spaces, its escalators, and an enormous crowd which we have to work our way through to get to the first class car, with its velvet and lace seats, reserved for us. We are alone in the compartment. The train goes about forty miles an hour. Chinese trains are slow so it takes about two-and-a-half hours to reach Tientsin, about sixty-two miles from Peking. We are free to gaze at the countryside, its rice paddies, its cotton and grain fields. Teams of peasants are at work and red flags are staked in the ground, blowing in the wind, like flags over trenches. Girls wearing thick jackets of padded cotton are returning home from the fields, spades slung across one shoulder and red flags on the other. There are quotations from Mao and his portrait on the peasants' houses, and characters as far as the eye can see, usually saying "Long live Chairman Mao." Even a small pagoda on the horizon has a huge portrait of Mao. Lu reads us an article from *People's Daily*. Lu and Chao never tire of reading and explaining things to us. If we fall asleep, they sigh. As soon as we wake up, they begin again. At any rate, everything is very interesting. Out the window we see thousands of people planting a river bed, hundreds of red flags and portraits of Mao on a knoll, and in the distance the setting red sun. Red flags are also staked in haystacks on higher land.

Lu keeps talking about Liu Shao-chi, that "renegade traitor, agent of the enemy." I interrupt him, "He *was* president of the Republic and he did hold that position for a long time."

"That's right," Lu answers, "and it was very difficult to discover what his plans really were. Years went by while he 'waved the red flag to oppose the red flag.' "

We go up to the seventh floor of a modern department store in Tientsin. You can find everything there. The prices of everyday food are very reasonable but are prohibitive for radios, televisions, cameras, and watches. From the top of the building we look across the entire city, the canals, the old neighborhoods and the new ones, and over toward the horizon, the sea. A crowd follows us, curious. The representative of the revolutionary committee accompanies us through the various departments in the store. Children wait for us outside, laughing and shy but full of curiosity about these two foreigners who are wandering through the streets of Tientsin.

Hoping Lu, Peace Street, is the main street. It is full of bicycles, and the cyclists wear white cotton gloves, something I don't remember seeing in Peking. There are brand-new buses in the streets and two-car trolley buses. Cars, buses, and trucks are manufactured in Tientsin. The car we are riding in seems unlike others we have used previously. It is a minicar, just out of the factory, and it still smells of paint. The seats are covered in plastic. The automobile factories in Tientsin are among the most modern in China.

We are alone in our hotel, an old hotel still furnished out of the past. It is comfortable and the service is perfect. The huge dining room is opened only for us. The tables are covered with immaculate tablecloths. Two comrades from the city's tourist agency join Lu and Chao and our little group gets ready to meet the workers of Tientsin.

Chinese watches do not go by Russian time

We are visiting a watch factory. This factory employs more than a thousand people, workers and other employees, and has eight workshops, two for repairs and machine tools, and six for manufacturing. At the beginning of the visit, the girls who assemble the watches show us a machine made by the workers after foreign technical assistance was withdrawn. In front of them is a Swiss Hauser machine, sullen like an old aristocrat. The equipment and the machine tools in the factory are still foreign, but the workers have made more than ninety improvements on them to increase their efficiency.

The pace of work is calm in the workshops, as it is elsewhere. There are a lot of *hsaiotzupao*, small handwritten posters encouraging thrifty and efficient work. Everything seems to be very simple, almost rudimentary. There is a big portrait of Mao in needlepoint. Another one is on the staircase. One worker has a plastic portrait of Mao on a small tripod near her magnifying glass. Another wears a red heart decorated with a portrait of Mao on her pocket.

A watch from this factory costs 120 yuan. The model, created during the Cultural Revolution, is called "East Wind." It is expensive, worth the monthly salary of a well-paid worker. A watch is considered a luxury compared to the essential needs of food and clothing. The representative of the revolutionary committee tells us the story of the brief and intense life of this factory. In 1958 it was called the May 1 Factory and was mass producing watches from a prototype developed in 1955. That was the time of the Great Leap Forward.

"After our factory was first set up," the representative of the revolutionary committee says, "Liu Shao-chi, China's Khrushchev, had Russian specialists brought in. We were happy with this at first. But they told us everything had to be redone and that we had to buy Kirov, that is, Russian, machines if we wanted to make good watches. Watches made with Kirov machines were so fat and of such poor quality that the expression 'You are as bad as a watch from the May 1 Factory' became proverbial. They were also called 'applause' watches: you clapped your hands and they stopped. Our mail was full of complaints. We had our own machine but the experts told us that we needed a machine to make the watchsprings with a wheel of special wood. After doing some research, we discovered that this wood could only be found in Sinkiang and that it came from a small, almost leafless tree. So we either had to wait a hundred years for the trees to grow or we had to import the wood from the Soviet Union, which our Russian specialists advised us to do. Liu Shao-chi accepted Russian advice like orders from the emperor and anyone who took issue was criticized at workers' meetings and sometimes even punished. Then in 1960 the Russians unilaterally broke off the assistance treaty. At first we were indignant. Then we realized that we had to rely entirely on our own forces, to improve the old and to build the new. We accomplished a lot after that. We got rid of the Kirov system and the cult of foreign machines and then completely reorganized the work according to our own needs. Workers and skilled technicians worked side by side to redraft the plans. This is how we produced the 'East Wind' watch, which is wound every forty-eight hours instead of every thirty hours and is as thin as a leaf, unlike the 'May 1' watch. But the important thing is that we ourselves conceived the project and that we have begun to improve the machines and design new ones. This would have been impossible with the Russians. They were the experts and we provided the labor force."

Our comrades show us three watches. The first dates from 1954 and is rather pretty. The second is the robust Russian watch and the third is the "East Wind" model, with the date of manufacture engraved in gold on the dial. They are very proud of this watch.

"What did you do before you became the representative of the revolutionary committee?" I ask this young man of about thirty who has been speaking to us and who serves as the manager of the factory.

He answers timidly, "I worked in the manager's office."

Everyone laughs. He must have had a very modest job, perhaps the office boy.

"And where is the manager now?"

"He is here. He joined the three-in-one combination after the criticism session. He became a revolutionary cadre. Revolutionary cadres have a lot of experience in running the factory and we need them. Now a good relationship exists between technicians and workers and rigid divisions have been eliminated, even if there is still a division of the work load. The atmosphere is one of frank co-operation. There are differences in political and technical level even among the workers, but these are differences among comrades. The important point about the management cadres is how they are linked to the mass of workers and how they allow the workers to use their initiative. The revolutionary committee runs the factory—under the direction of the party and through its Communist members. The Communists hold separate meetings. We are getting ready for a congress to elect the party branch at the factory. The former party committee was dissolved after having been criticized during the Cultural Revolution."

I ask, "Can you tell me the exact time?"

The comrade doesn't have a chance to answer me. A big pendulum clock in the window strikes twelve in notes from "The East Is Red."

Philosophy in the factory

> Marxist philosophy holds that the most important problem does not lie in understanding the laws of the objective world and thus being able to explain it, but in applying the knowledge of these laws actively to change the world. From the Marxist viewpoint, theory is important, and its importance is fully expressed in Lenin's statement, "Without revolutionary theory there can be no revolutionary movement." . . . The active function of knowledge manifests itself not only in the active leap from perceptual to rational knowledge, but—and this is more important—it must manifest itself in the leap from rational knowledge to revolutionary practice.
>
> —Mao Tse-tung, *On Practice*

Here we are at the meeting place. Tientsin Textile Factory Number 2, famous for its wool fabrics and for its study of philosophy. I have already read some articles translated from the Chinese press on workers who study philosophy. The articles were often hard to understand because they used a specialized language which I had difficulty grasping. This only increased my curiosity.

Going into the factory, I had a quote from Lenin in mind, the one from *Materialism and Empirio-Criticism* about Dietzgen, the German proletarian who Marx and Engels said had discovered "dialectical materialism all by himself" because he was a proletarian militant. "The graduated flunkeys," who "use their sham idealism to keep the people in ignorance [that is how Dietzgen looks upon the professors of philosophy]. As Lord God found his antipodes in the devil, so has the pious professor found his antagonist in the materialist." *

I thought about this as soon as the workers started to talk philosophy. Chinese workers repeat "Now I am studying philosophy" a thousand times over, as if to say, "I have fully and completely regained my dignity." These words make me pause and fill me with emotion. I think how vastly different this concept is from the Western Greco-humanist ideal of the "cultivated man" (even if this ideal includes an artisan spending his spare time in the study of philosophy). Another relationship between man and knowledge, between man and reality, exists here. The worker studies philosophy so that he can participate in political life more consciously.

I cannot fully measure the significance of what I see here, but I shall try in this section to give some explanation of it. Abandoning my role as simple chronicler, I will try to make some comparisons between my "Western" experiences and the objective, although incomplete, observations I have made here.

This requires my own participation because, as in any socialist political situation, it deals with the problem of the relationship between theory and practice. This relationship is the concrete problem brought into focus by "philosophy in the factory," and has nothing to do with the relationship between intellectuals and workers.

The phrase "philosophy in the factory," which contains two apparently incongruous terms, goes straight to the heart of the matter. The key concept in Marxist theoretical analysis developed dur-

* V. I. Lenin, *Materialism and Empirio-Criticism*, in *Collected Works*, vol. XIII (New York: 1927), p. 295.

ing the Cultural Revolution is the primacy of *politics* over *economics*, especially with respect to *social factors*. The study of philosophy in the factory is consequently one of the basic points of the Cultural Revolution, representing the first qualitative leap of the individual in the revolution of the superstructure. The "artistocratic" nature of philosophical speculation has disappeared; now it is a mass science. Through philosophy, the masses become actively politically involved, a process which is basic to the worldwide political work of building a socialist society.

The Chinese are trying to develop a long-range theoretical and political strategy, rather than to sort out their daily problems as such. This development must be watched closely. What is involved is a revolution of the *superstructure*, a revolution which is not subordinated to *social* and *economic* factors, but which determines their impact on society and anticipates the emergence of a new type of *structure* within the socialist society.

We are sitting around the revolutionary committee's table as our long discussion begins. A woman is seated to my right. I look at her closely. The interpreter introduces her as "an old Communist who will talk to you about studying philosophy." Comrade Tu, deputy representative of the revolutionary committee, speaks first, followed by Comrade Yang. The revolutionary committee was elected in February 1968.

After some introductory remarks, Yang goes to the heart of the subject by outlining the vicissitudes of the progress made by the factory. We learn that this is not just any factory. Mao became personally interested in it in 1956, visiting on January 12 to question the workers in the different workshops on their political studies. He concluded from this investigation that their ideological level was dangerously low. Workers were turning into robots, as in capitalist countries, and were an easy prey for revisionism. Mao suggested that a course on philosophy be set up, since the workers needed both to study theory and to apply it in practice. The director of the factory considered it to be a waste of time, and when the course was established in 1958, he sabotaged the program to the point where it became ineffective.

"After the victory of the Cultural Revolution," the worker continues, "the study of philosophy became possible for all workers.

The Ninth Congress of the Chinese Communist Party restored the study programs and the masses are using their initiative in applying the thought of Mao to the three movements: scientific experiment, class struggle, and production. Each of the 127 factory work groups includes a group of workers who study philosophy for an hour or two after work. The factory has taken on a philosophical air. Each group has its own room. As the intellectual development of the workers progresses, production increases and the workers' environment changes both objectively and subjectively. In January 1970, our production figures were up 10 percent over January 1969. The increase for July-September of this year was 27.55 percent over the same period last year."

The study of philosophy in the factory is not meant to encourage haphazard self-education. The party is being rebuilt into a qualitatively different institution than before. A party responsible for leading "worker-philosophers" cannot be a party of bureaucrats. The Cultural Revolution, far from weakening the party, made it transform itself profoundly. The Cultural Revolution was also in fact one of the main reasons for the introduction and the diffusion of philosophy in the factory. "Ideological revolution" and "the intervention of the proletariat in the realm of ideology" were the guiding principles used to revolutionize the state ideological apparatus, that is, the party.

The political and economic structure of the factory, work pace, salaries, and production plans

The party committee has not yet been elected, the worker explains to me. The struggle in the factory was hard, but the factory congress is to convene shortly. The revolutionary committee operates the factory and is composed of twenty-three members (revolutionary cadres, representatives of revolutionary mass organizations, soldiers from the People's Liberation Army), nine of whom are on the standing committee. Seven of the twenty-three meet separately and actually run the factory: they are party members. It thus cannot be said that the party has lost its leadership function. Even though the party committee has not yet been elected by the workers' congress, the cells have been re-established in the factory and the party members are now politically better qualified because of the rectification and reconstruction movement. This movement continues; it constantly creates new cadres, releases fresh energies among the workers, and corrects bureaucratic laziness and errors. The factory congress will be held soon. (In the courtyard of the factory I saw some big red posters which proclaimed, "Let us prepare for the congress.") The revisionist line entailed serious disturbances here too, but in general the cadres participated in the work of the factory: they have not gone to a May 7 Cadre School, but they have re-educated themselves with the workers in the factory itself.

"What happened to the trade union? Does it still exist?"

Besides the revolutionary committee, the workers' representative conference is one of the new organs of red power. It is elected by all the workers and has charge of the daily problems of the factory, the administrative and social problems; it works with the revolutionary committee. It and the workers' council have replaced the trade union, a tool of Liu Shao-chi's economist line. The responsibilities of the workers' council are greater than were those of the old trade union. It is in charge of work loads, the enterprise's social services, and job distribution. The revolutionary committee and the workers' council are freely elected by the workers. The first meets every two weeks, the second once a month. The revolutionary committee has a standing committee which meets when necessary and the 127 work groups hold their own assemblies. In sum, the party has the leading role, the revolutionary committee is responsible for management, and the workers' council is in charge of the revolutionary reorganization of work and acts as a control from the base level on the higher echelons. All the factory organizations function democratically.

To my query on the salary scale, piece-work wages, and incentive bonuses, the worker answers:

"We have eliminated piece-work wages and incentive bonuses. The salary scale has been reduced. The highest salary is 120 yuan, the lowest is 50 yuan. The difference between the pay of an engineer and that of a skilled technician is 40 yuan, 80 for the technician and 120 for the engineer. The average salary is 65 yuan. The struggle-criticism-transformation movement is still dealing with salaries, but it is a delicate problem. It is relatively simple in a commune which is collectively owned, but a factory is the property of all the people so salaries not only depend on the factory—textile in this case—but also on what the state leadership decides. The question of salaries is basic to the workers' lives so we have to be cautious. We are eliminating unjustified disparities in salary but we are keeping reasonable differences."

"What is unjustified?"

"For example, a 5 percent a month bonus, which has been abolished. These matters must be worked out in the struggle-criticism-transformation movement. After we discuss the problem with the workers, consider their advice, and study it further, we make our recommendations to state organizations, which make the final decision. At the moment, we are putting politics in command and we are abolishing unjustified salaries."

"Who decides the pace of work?"

"To avoid any confusion from the start because of the differences in our respective countries, remember that production goals in China are fixed by a state plan because this is a socialist system. The plan for the factory is drafted by the Ministry of Textile Industries and lasts for a year. Monthly work plans are drawn up at the factory itself by a production team from the revolutionary committee which includes technicians, workers, and administrators. This is how the pace of work is defined."

"An obvious aspect of capitalist exploitation is the pace of work, sometimes fixed to a tenth of a second. Even the total manufacturing time for a product is calculated."

"When we get a copy of the year's plan, we discuss it with the workers and then we prepare our own *internal plan* for the factory according to what we can accomplish. We do not automatically commit ourselves to follow our own plan 100 percent when we send it in for approval. Our estimates are based on a discussion of last year's production figures, our personal experiences, and our needs for machinery replacement and repairs, which will be presented to the revolutionary committee on the next level. The plan is thereby worked out in detail and everyone understands it better. If we try hard, we can exceed the goals of the plan by using our productive resources—but only on the initiative of the masses. Last year we produced from 165,000 to 175,000 yards of material each month. This year we are putting out about 200,000 yards a month, 40 percent of which is exported. And this is without using material incentives. In the Soviet Union and in Western socialist countries, production increases or decreases in relation to material incentives and production bonuses. Our workers also repair the old machinery in the factory, accomplishing real miracles."

"What about retirement and sick leave?"

"Older workers receive full sick leave and the young are paid half of their salary. Retirement pay comes to 75 percent of the worker's salary, if he has worked a minimum of fifteen years."

> There is an old Chinese saying, "How can you catch tiger cubs without entering the tiger's lair?" This saying holds true for man's practice and it also holds true for the theory of knowledge. There can be no knowledge apart from practice.
>
> —Mao Tse-tung, *On Practice*

Lin Tien-hsi, forty-six years old, is an old worker. Her face expresses vigor and commitment, which are not products of age. Looking at Chinese women, you can't help thinking about our standards of beauty and ugliness. By our standards, Chinese women are not pretty, but are even plain. No coquettishness, no make-up, short hair held by two barrettes, wearing pants and oversized jackets on their small bodies. But as you get to know them better, you discover they have another kind of beauty formed by intensity and passion. They are near you and yet far away, like light. They are attractive in a different way, not easily described in terms of our traditional models of beauty. Before I left Paris I heard a famous Parisian couturier quoted as saying, "It would be better to put women in uniforms, like Chinese women, so that they would have to come up with a personality and a brain, if they have one." The worker Lin's arms are crossed over her threadbare jacket as she begins to "speak bitterness," to tell the story of her life in the old society. The old society is an obsession with the Chinese, who recall only the agony of the past. The fear of the past was one of the factors which triggered the mass struggle against Liu Shao-chi, for the people were convinced, as Lin Piao explained in his report to the Ninth Congress, that the leader of the right wing of the party would restore capitalist domination in China.

The worker tells her story:

"I am a worker from the dyeing and weaving workshop in Factory Number 2. I have worked here since I was seventeen years old, when the factory was owned by the capitalists. My father died from an illness because he didn't have proper medical care, and my salary was supposed to support five people when it hardly provided enough to keep two alive. We had to eat bean curd and potatoes and we were always hungry. In the winter we had thin jackets and no blankets. Cold and hunger were with us everyday. I got up at four o'clock in the morning to go to the factory and I returned home after the sun went down. I was very afraid I would catch tuberculosis like others, which meant I would get fired. Workers had hernias and rheumatism in the joints but they hid their illnesses for fear of being laid off. Even if you stayed in the toilet too long, you could be out of a job. There was so much misery that no one dared to object. The police were tools of the bosses: the capitalists had an electric bell in the workshops which they rang to summon the guards to arrest the workers. They lived off of our flesh and blood. We lived like animals. The bosses ate chicken, duck, and fish, and they lived in big houses. We were the dregs of humanity, like human garbage.

"The Liberation in 1949 was like a step toward heaven for us workers. But the struggle between the two lines began soon afterward in the factory. The bourgeois right, still in power, sowed distrust among us, telling us that we would be worse off than before. I was so mad it made me sick but I couldn't fight back. All I knew to do was to say that yes, we were a lot better off. But we didn't have the theoretical knowledge we needed to formulate our criticisms. In June 1958, we organized our first team for the study of philosophy, under our old master Li Shih-an. We held classes in the evening because daytime classes were impossible. I realized that the study of philosophy wasn't as difficult as I thought, and I learned above all that philosophy is linked to human practice. In July 1958 Cha Ho-hai, a member of the Central Committee and a comrade from the proletarian headquarters, came to the factory. Kang

Sheng visited us on August 3, 1958. Both of them helped us organize philosophy courses for veteran workers. We learned a lot from their recommendations because we tended to confuse everything at the start. But our studies taught us that the study of philosophy helps you understand things better and to solve all kinds of problems, and that an understanding of philosophy would help us to become a force capable of changing society. Its study is not for study's sake but for the revolution and to develop class consciousness. Philosophy is participating in the class struggle on the level of production."

The worker opens her little red book to quote Mao on the subject of contradictions:

" 'Of the two contradictory aspects, one must be principal and the other secondary. The principal aspect is the one playing the leading role in the contradiction. The nature of a thing is determined mainly by the principal aspect of a contradiction, the aspect which has gained the dominant position.' After I understood what was meant by 'main contradiction,' I realized that there was a main contradiction in my workshop, which repaired the fabric-damage caused by the machine we were using. Aside from this problem, the machine worked well. We solved the problem by concentrating *solely on this problem*, and giving it our undivided attention. But after old contradictions are solved, new ones appear. Equilibrium is short-lived because situations are never static. By studying philosophy, we learned that we could have a *subjective initiative*, and that material force became in turn a spiritual force, capable of changing society. Goals and tasks were not enough. The problem is a problem of method, and it is this problem that must be solved. Otherwise there is no point in talking of tasks.

" 'If our task is to cross a river, we cannot cross it without a bridge or a boat. Unless the bridge or boat problem is solved, it is idle to speak of crossing the river.' "

The worker then selects another passage from the little red book, this time a beautiful quote:

" 'Let us be more concerned with the conditions of the life of the masses and let us pay more attention to our work methods.' "

Lin continues her philosophical discussion, touching on the theme of "one divides into two" and relating it to political struggle.

"The fundamental law of dialectical materialism," she says, "is that the unity of opposites is only temporary. Mao says the struggle bursts forth continuously: 'One divides into two.' * When Yang Hsien-chen, director of the Marxism-Leninism Institute and assistant director of the party school, claimed that it was possible to 're-unite two elements and make them one,' he made a frontal attack on philosophy. He tried to legitimize bourgeois philosophical theory, the very basis of the bourgeois idealist conception of the world. This theory of reconciliation basically *reduces two elements into one* because it reconciles the bourgeoisie and the proletariat, nullifying the class struggle. But the phrase 'one divides into two' brings out the antagonistic element in the contradiction. 'Reduce two to one' means that you view the contradiction as nonantagonistic. Therefore this concept effectively negates conflict, and in actual practice confuses us as to the nature of the class enemy, the nature of the bourgeoisie and class enemies. To Mao, the contradiction must be antagonistic.

"Bourgeois capitalism drank our blood. How can there be any confusion about it? It would be revisionism, capitulation, the restoration of capitalism. You cannot hide the contradiction between the working class and the bourgeoisie. What we have to do is *to di-*

* This phrase is a composite and popular expression of a fundamental concept of dialectical materialism, and consequently of Marxism. It is taken from a passage in Lenin's *Philosophical Notebooks* where he says: "The split of a single unit into two and the knowledge of its contradictory elements . . . is the essence . . . of the dialectic." Heated debate on this point broke out in China in July 1964 during a much larger campaign criticizing the cultural and ideological positions opposed to the thought of Mao, and Lin is talking about this debate. It dealt with the confrontation of the two political lines, diametrically opposed, in the highest echelons of the party. One of the lines stressed the need to make a much clearer distinction between the proletariat and the bourgeoisie and between socialism and revisionism. The other tried to erase both this distinction and open confrontation.

Today this phrase is used in political and ideological work and is applied in various situations. For example, it is used as a standard to judge behavior fairly, one's own or one's comrades', avoiding either totally positive or totally negative judgments. Also, the new organs of power created by the Cultural Revolution cannot be considered to be exempt from contradiction because they themselves are "divided into two," that is, the struggle between the two lines still goes on within them too.

vide one into two, struggle to divide, to liberate the working class from the bourgeoisie's grasp, from reactionary revisionism, so as to make the revolution.

"Liu Shao-chi's bourgeois headquarters made fun of the workers who studied philosophy. He sent us Yang Hsien-chen himself, an authority on philosophy. He visited the factory and scoffed at us. He told us sarcastically, 'But really, you're studying philosophy? What an idea, what a confusion! If all the workers studied philosophy what would we philosophers have left to do?' One of his colleagues, another academic careerist, questioned us and said that he noticed our studies were haphazard and poorly structured. They ordered us to disband two-thirds of our philosophy teams and shortened the time we needed for our studies by stepping up the pace of our jobs.

"We would have given in had we not been convinced that philosophy is a weapon of revolutionary struggle. Not having the time to study at the factory, we studied on vacation and at home. But now everything is different. The 'protracted war' to study philosophy has begun among the workers."

Personal reflections: the relationship between what I see and hear at the factory and the Marxist classics

> The XIth Thesis on Feuerbach proclaimed: "The philosophers have only interpreted the world in various ways; the point is to change it." This simple sentence seemed to promise a new philosophy, one which was no longer an *interpretation*, but rather a *transformation* of the world. Moreover, this is how it was read more than half a century later, by Labriola, and then following him by Gramsci, both of whom defined Marxism essentially as a new philosophy, a philosophy of praxis.
>
> —Louis Althusser, *Lenin and Philosophy**

In the course of our discussion, I notice that the little red book is

* Louis Althusser, *Lenin and Philosophy* (New York: Monthly Review Press, 1972), p. 36.—*Trans.*

read by the workers for its *philosophical* message. I would like to take our worker's story and write below it: "Dedicated to the bourgeois philosophers." But the Chinese situation is not the same as ours. At home people wouldn't care for such a statement and might be offended. It is not only a question of China and Mao, but of something else. Louis Althusser explains it this way:

> Academic philosophy cannot tolerate Lenin (or Marx for that matter) for two reasons, which are really one and the same. On the one hand, it cannot bear the idea that it might have something to learn from politics and from a politician. And on the other hand, it cannot bear the idea that philosophy might be the object of a theory, i.e. of an objective knowledge.*

Establishment philosophy dislikes the thought of Mao for the same reason, when it does not hide itself behind a deliberate ignorance of the contribution of Marxism to the theory of contradictions. Althusser describes the difference between academic philosophers and Marxist thinkers:

> Between Lenin and established philosophy there is a peculiarly intolerable connection: the connection in which the reigning philosophy is touched to the quick of what it represses: politics. . . . a theory of philosophy is essential to a really conscious and responsible *practice* of philosophy . . . Lenin happens to have been the first to say so. It also happens that he *could* say so only because he was a politician, and not just any politician, but a *proletarian leader.* That is why Lenin is intolerable to philosophical rumination.**

This comment also applies to Mao and to what bourgeois philosophers find unacceptable in his works. These philosophers make fun of his philosophical interpretations, clear as they may be, and accuse him of being simplistic; they claim that a "thinker" must render obscure what is clear. To understand their hostility, recall the words the worker quoted: "What would philosophers do if the workers started to study philosophy?" This is a key sentence.

Mao's philosophical method. Proceeding from the hold feudalism and idealism used to have on China, Mao says, in "On Contradiction":

---

* Ibid., p. 32.

** Ibid., pp. 34, 33.

> In China, there was the metaphysical thinking exemplified in the saying, "Heaven changeth not, likewise the Tao changeth not" and it was supported by the decadent feudal ruling classes for a long time. Mechanical materialism and vulgar evolutionism, which were imported from Europe in the last hundred years, are supported by the bourgeoisie.

Struggle has to replace age-old passivity. Revolutionary action must replace the philosophy of resignation. The battle between the philosophies of idealism and materialism is being fought to determine which one will be the dominant theory in the world. To Mao, philosophy is *one arm of the revolution.* Just what this means in the concrete context of the following ultra-Leninist sentence became clear to me for the first time. "The basic function of philosophical practice is to draw a *line of demarcation between true ideas and false ideas.*" And I grasped the truth of this notion in a factory, not in a lecture hall, among weavers who produce about 200,000 yards of fabric each month. As you act and struggle, draw a demarcation line between antagonistic classes. The struggle in China continues —the little red book is the weapon, philosophical practice the strategy. This is what the worker meant as she described her everyday experiences.

This discussion concerns not only China or "academic" bourgeois philosophers. I am particularly concerned with this point because of my own internal debate as a Western "Marxist intellectual." Workers and the mass of Westerners are not familiar with Marxist philosophical works, not even with the first volume of *Capital.* The great classical texts, basic to the socialist revolution, are closed up in the libraries, where professional philosophers of all philosophical viewpoints work on them. They are not accessible to the workers, whose ensuing intellectual poverty is much more serious than their material poverty since it makes them truly vulnerable. In an interview published in *Unità,* Louis Althusser says, in an apparently provocative way, that *Capital* is more accessible to workers than to others because of their class instinct. He is doing more than just criticizing university people. "It is not easy," he says, "to become a Marxist-Leninist philosopher. Like every 'intellectual,' a philosophy teacher is a petty bourgeois. When he opens his mouth, it is petty bourgeois ideology that speaks: its resources and ruses are infinite." *

Moreover, it is difficult to establish what the relationship is between theory and praxis and between culture and praxis in the West. These elements often seem in conflict with one another. Bourgeois society often tries to cover up its ugly nature by claiming to represent the latest in cultural progress, in innovation, in breakthroughs; it tries to hide behind the role played by academicism, the ivory tower of elitist culture.

Lenin understood this well. To him, Gorky was only a petty bourgeois intellectual. Gramsci also understood it. Both of them insisted on the need for intellectuals to achieve a "revolution" in their own ideas and to become "ideologists of the working class" (Lenin) or "organic intellectuals" (Gramsci). This "revolution" of ideas may occur here in China because the political revolution has been completed, feudalism has been eliminated, and socialism is being built on *all levels.* Re-educating intellectuals takes on a wider meaning in this new political context. But re-education cannot be considered an end in itself, isolated from the revolutionary forces in the world. There is a new, concrete, relationship between theory and praxis in China, one you can almost touch. It is evident in "philosophy in the factory," in Mao's language, and in what the Chinese worker-philosopher thinks the role of "intellectuals" should be.

The following quote from Althusser best sums up our discussion at the factory in Tientsin: "What is new in Marxism's contribution to philosophy is a *new practice of philosophy. Marxism is not a (new) philosophy of praxis, but a (new) practice of philosophy.*"** This new practice of philosophy moves slowly and runs into all sorts of difficulties, but it is vigorous and pervasive, especially among the working class. This is where the little red book fits in, the book we are supposed to laugh at. At first you are haunted by it, you see it everywhere. Then you realize that it is essential, that it brings philosophical reasoning and dialectical materialism to every Chinese. In this way the thought of Mao will live on in China even

* Ibid., p. 12.

** Ibid., p. 68.

after he dies. The alleged "cult of Mao" becomes an altogether secondary matter—it is the opposite of Stalinist and post-Stalinist dogmatism.

> Where do correct ideas come from? Do they drop from the skies? No. Are they innate in the mind? No. They come from social practice, and from it alone; they come from three kinds of social practice, the struggle for production, the class struggle, and scientific experiment.
>
> —Mao Tse-tung, *Where Do Correct Ideas Come From?*

Yang Tong-hua, another worker from the dyeing workshop at Textile Factory Number 2, explains what studying philosophy means to him: "I study philosophy in order to apply it to technical innovation. At the factory we didn't have the high-temperature fixing-baths which you need to prevent the material being dyed from stretching and losing its shape. We had always imported this equipment. The problem was this: were we going to ask the state to buy a foreign machine or did we dare to make one ourselves? It was a contradiction between two conceptions of the world. To rely on a foreign source is a metaphysical attitude—it is placing your trust in an *external cause.* Doing it yourself means developing the *internal cause.* The external cause is the condition whereas the internal cause is basic. To rely on external factors is to depend on something which will betray you, and to progress slowly and gradually is revisionism.

"Our group is made up of seven workers and we are responsible for more than fifty machines in the workshop which must be in good working order. The number of workers in our group is small and it is a heavy responsibility. But man is a living entity whereas we are working with what is inert so it has to bend to man's will. Under the leadership of the Communist Party, and as long as man exists, we can invent anything. It is necessary to liberate the intelligence, to dare to think, dare to act. The study of proletarian philosophy gives us this liberation. We have gotten the courage we need by studying the theoretical works of Mao, 'On Practice' and 'On Contradiction,' and by discovering the great truth that knowledge originates in practice. We visited other factories to see at first hand how fixing-baths are made. There was one which was more than twenty yards long and very complicated. In another factory we studied the parts of a machine dismantled for repairs. Applying the principle "One divides into two," we decided that the main contradiction that needed to be resolved was the problem of achieving a high enough temperature. None of us were engineers, but we started working on the project, building it with our own hands. Sometimes we ran into problems which couldn't be solved so we had to begin again. We didn't have enough steel to hold up the central section, so we used train rails. Who would have thought of that? Some people made fun of us and asked, 'How can chicken feathers fly? How can workers from the repair workshop make machines?' We answered by saying, 'If the working class can launch a satellite why can't we build a machine?' We didn't know principles of physics or anything about alternating currents. We made dozens of electrical circuits, and we made mistakes. But once we solved that problem, the machine was completed. It cost one-tenth of what an imported model would have cost, 10,000 yuan instead of 100,000. It also reaches higher temperatures, is lighter, simpler in design, and it is just as automated as the English and Italian machines."

"No," he answers my question, "we do not know how long it took to build it. You can't compare our experience with capitalist societies. This equipment is the fruit of our working-class consciousness. By raising our consciousness, we have increased productivity and our own capacities."

We walk through the workshops which are full of tatzupao and banners draped from one end of the room to the other like pennants. Nothing routine here. There is an air of invention everywhere, in the designs of the characters, in the colored poster paper. Many of the workers draw. For the factory congress, they took a blackboard and drew a woman worker in the midst of her studies. On another blackboard they drew the podium of the Ninth Party Congress in colored chalk. I see written on a tatzupao: "When you find it difficult to read the thought of Mao, try to get help from others. When there isn't as much work to do, take advantage of the free time to study philosophy. On the road, think about it. Before going to bed, read a little. In the morning, read a little more. After you have done some studying, write down your thoughts. And think through what you have learned about philosophy."

A veteran worker shows us the famous fixing-bath they made. He says that he is a member of a group of eighteen veteran workers who drew up the plans and machinery for a complete production cycle by studying philosophy. He sums up by saying, "I didn't get a university education and before the Liberation I didn't know how to read or write."

6

Port of the Dialectic

"No foreigner since the Cultural Revolution has visited the new port of Tientsin to talk with us and write about it. You are lucky," the representative of the revolutionary committee tells us. On his jacket he has a badge with Mao's portrait over a small ship, the badge of the Chinese sailors. A brisk wind blows through the port, making the banner flutter above the sailors' club. It reads, in English, "Workers of All Countries Unite." The club is comfortable and the restaurant menu has a choice of fifty dishes. Sailors can buy just about everything in a nearby two-floor department store—rare jade jewelry, china, rugs, even long blond silky wigs for 18 yuan—everything except the "female merchandise" that all other ports in the world offer sailors. To compensate, they can see films on revolutionary achievements and obtain the works of Mao free of charge. Even so, foreign sailors complain that this is poor compensation! To foreigners, China's morality appears strict, although the Chinese are not at all puritanical. But we must not forget they have made such a total break with the past, with the celebrated brothels of Tientsin, Canton, and Shanghai, that it is unthinkable today for a Chinese woman to have anything other than a political relationship with a foreign man.

The port of Tientsin—15,000 workers and employees—also represents the end of another traditional image of China, that of the *coolie*, the Chinese porter, doubled up under the iron handles of his ricksha. Our guides proudly but modestly show us that 80 percent of this port is now mechanized. This "salt port," which must have been like a hell in the past, now has machines to move the salt which replace 130 people working with shovels. Loading and unloading 330 tons of salt takes only one hour. During the Cultural

Revolution, the equipment was increased and then improved. The workers sometimes see boats and foreign crews from hostile, capitalist parts of the world, which has the effect of a horsewhip. (The representative of the revolutionary committee remarks, "The workers see the entire world through this port and they do everything they can to help the Chinese and the worldwide revolution.") Chinese dockers relate their verbal battles with the captains of arriving foreign ships who believe that unloading their boats will take twenty days. Forty-eight hours later they leave, completely dumbfounded. "There was one captain," a young longshoreman accompanying us says, "whose ship was full of merchandise to be unloaded. We told him that it would take us two weeks to do it, to which he replied, 'That's impossible. In a capitalist country it takes a month; as for you, if you finish in three weeks, I will give you my head as a souvenir.' This challenge enraged us workers. We gritted our teeth and unloaded the boat in ten days. Then we went to find the captain, not to get his head, but to make him admit he was wrong. And he admitted it."

So the dockers of Tientsin enjoy flabbergasting the captains of foreign ships that arrive "in Chinese waters" and giving the "sea dogs" who come from the outside an idea of *what the Chinese can do.* And the foreigners no longer react like one captain who arrived and, before unloading 2,500 tons of steel, telegraphed his company that it would take five days. He sent three more telegrams to say he would leave sooner than expected, and in the end he left at noon the day after he arrived and didn't have the time to send the final telegram. Everyone laughs when these sailors' stories of events after the Cultural Revolution are told.

The "philosophical" crane

We go to the pier to look at a floating crane on an iron barge. It can lift 165 tons, whereas it used to be able to lift only 85. I ask how this was achieved.

Before, when foreign boats arrived at Tientsin, the captains insisted that the port didn't have a crane powerful enough to unload their cargo. By studying the works of Mao on contradiction and on practice, and on internal and external causes, the workers of the machine repair workshop found a solution to the problem. To increase the lifting capacity of the crane, they had to enlarge the barge on which it rested. This was impossible, so what they did was to put two floating drums on each side of the barge—to us they look like two wings of a carcass, an old scrap heap, because the barge was built from the remains of a discarded tanker. They took steel from the tanker for the drums, which they made in the shop, and spent 360,000 yuan and eight months' work. For five months the workers ate and slept on the boat. The resulting "philosophical" crane was subsequently donated to the Ninth Congress. "Be self-reliant" is written across the barge, and under the red flag there is a smiling portrait of Chairman Mao.

"Hey!" we shout to the workers who are walking toward us on the pier, "even though we are old friends of China, we wouldn't have believed what you have done if we read it in a newspaper." The interpreter translates, talking against the wind. The workers stop a moment, perplexed, and then they all clap their hands in our direction. We have understood each other. It is not often that you have this feeling of closeness, of trust, between them and us. But here in the port we really feel what is meant by the word "comrades."

We eat lunch with the revolutionary committee in the captain's cabin, where beautiful, thick pearl-gray rugs with blue rosettes cover the floor. The bowls are made of fine china and on the wall is a delicate ceramic of China, with a poem dedicated to his country engraved in the middle. The meal is abundant, although Chinese food is never heavy. As we are being served, we get right into the subject which interests us most: how the revolutionary committee is elected in this port of 15,000 workers.

"Free expression by vote," as in the Paris Commune

"Our revolutionary committee," our comrade, the representative of the committee, tells us, "is a three-in-one combination and was founded in February 1968. It has also been in charge of the port since that date. There are thirty-three members on the committee:

fourteen are delegates from the revolutionary cadres, sixteen represent the revolutionary masses, and three come from the People's Liberation Army."

"But why these thirty-three and not thirty-three others? How are they chosen and what accounts for this distribution? Could you explain precisely how a revolutionary committee is elected?"

"In deciding how many delegates each of the three groups should send to the revolutionary committee, it was decided that the representatives from the revolutionary masses should comprise a majority; then come the cadres who are in production work with the workers, followed by a smaller number of delegates from the People's Liberation Army. The three soldiers we elect have already been elected by their unit, which is stationed near the port, and they continue to receive their pay from the army. They are generally sent here for only a short time; others, also elected, will take their places. There are twenty-six members of the Chinese Communist Party among the thirty-three members of the revolutionary committee in our port. The standing committee is made up of nine of the thirty-three.

"In February 1968 the masses held several meetings, including a general assembly which made a democratic preliminary assessment of likely candidates to propose for the revolutionary committee. As for the criteria involved in selection, the choice was first of all political and was made on the basis of the specific qualities Chairman Mao has defined as appropriate to 'the successors to the revolutionary cause.' The masses freely compared likely candidates according to these required qualities. Following this, a long list of names was drawn up. Then a preliminary classification of the names on the list was made according to how many people the revolutionary committee needed and how many delegates from each of the three groups—the workers, cadres, and the army—should be included. The overall number of people needed for the revolutionary committee was discussed. Finally, a committee was elected to prepare for the elections. It still required three meetings at the base level and three meetings with the top echelon, going back and forth, to reach the widest possible consensus on the list of candidates. The final list was given to the base-level organization to be discussed again, case by case. So the whole process of electing the revolutionary committee was the result of total and direct democracy. Elections were held on the final list. At the beginning the list of names was very long, but it got shorter and shorter as numerous discussions and straw votes gave people, both candidates and electors, a deeper appreciation of the role and responsibilities of the revolutionary committee. The members of the revolutionary committee are chosen in the most democratic fashion possible; they are the result of 'free expression by vote,' as is said of the Paris Commune."

"What do you mean by that?"

"I am referring to the statement of August 1966 by the Central Committee of the Chinese Communist Party where it is stated that a general voting system like that in the Paris Commune must be established."

I wonder if what was at a certain point in history relevant for the Commune, so exalted by Engels, can really be applied in this part of the world: the masses exercising revolutionary rights and duties, discussing candidacies, electing the members and leaders of their groups, criticizing the elected, and being responsible for replacing them.

I then ask if the party organizations are elected by all the workers, even if they are not members of the party.

"The masses have a role in the election of the members of party organizations, and nonmembers can also give opinions. The elections of Communists is not a private event which takes place inside the factory walls. On the contrary, what we are trying to do is to make the party live among the masses even during an electoral period."

"But before the Cultural Revolution, how were factory elections conducted?"

"Union and party leaders in the factory used to be appointed from above. Even if the candidates were good people, the masses were only allowed to endorse names chosen during top-echelon meetings, in the offices of the enterprise's directors or of party officials. Leaders were not required to do any manual work, which isolated them from the activity of the masses. Today it is different. Every member of the revolutionary committee works in the factory at least three days a week. And he can be dismissed or removed by the base."

"And the party?"

"The party has twenty-six members on the revolutionary committee. In February 1969, we started a rebuilding and consolidation movement in the party, and then we re-established the cells. In the fall of 1969 we held a congress to elect the party committee for the port of Tientsin."

"Can you tell me who is the representative of the party committee for the port?"

The comrade lowers his head modestly and allows that it is he.

"Can you give me an example of some of the mistakes made by the Communists who followed the capitalist road?"

"Here is an example. In the director's office the most influential of the eight managers, the general director of the port, was a veteran Communist who had participated in the war of liberation. He was put in charge of the port after the war and he made the mistake of gearing the work of the masses to material incentives: rewards for production, fast work schedules, and so on. He was severely attacked by the workers during the Cultural Revolution. Even the Red Guards, who arrived in the port by the thousands to give us revolutionary help, took part in criticizing him. After the masses criticized him, they helped in his re-education by involving him in the collective study of the works of Mao. He has since been elected to the standing committee of the port's revolutionary committee. The bourgeoisie in the West and the revisionists have asserted in their propaganda that we made a clean sweep here. But in fact only a handful of people were replaced—those excluded from the party were no more than 1 percent. They also stupidly asserted that we destroyed the Communist Party. Not only did the party gain new strength during the Cultural Revolution, but it never lost its leading role. The Communists were always in charge at the factory, through their representatives on the revolutionary committee. This Communist core constituted the leadership until a new factory congress could be convened."

"The ants who strip a bone clean bit by bit"

The "Tientsin" is a ship completely painted in white and still smelling of paint. Its copper shines brilliantly in the sun and it looks as if it is decked out and ready to sail, all 10,000 tons of it, for distant ports, the first of which will be Shanghai. Work on this ship was begun in April 1969 and it will probably be launched soon. Between 200 to 300 workers, out of the 3,000 who work at the shipyard, worked on it. Cargo ships of 4,000 tons used to be built in Tientsin but today ships of up to 10,000 tons are built. The shipyards in Shanghai used to make ships of 15,000 tons, compared to 18,000 tons today.

The "Tientsin" is almost entirely automated. It has a handsome bridge, an instrument room, and a radar screen with a detachable cover. The plans were worked out on the spot. Technicians and workers solved the most difficult problem together: how to build a vessel of 10,000 tons in a shipyard only equipped to build one of 5,000 tons.

"This problem demonstrates how dialectics was applied to the construction of a 10,000-ton cargo ship," says the shipyard's revolutionary committee representative, a tall man with a handsome smile. He has such an outgoing personality that I ask him straight off: "Have you always worked here in the port?"

"No, I came to the shipyard during the Cultural Revolution. Before that I worked in the People's Liberation Army. I am forty-four years old."

"Is the saying 'Political power grows out of the barrel of a gun' what your presence here means?"

"The People's Liberation Army must be among the people, like fish in water. It must mix with the masses and contribute as much as it can by 'putting politics in command.' At present our country needs to develop its shipbuilding industry, to build the many ships that make powerful merchant and naval fleets. This is our revolutionary duty and the army doesn't intend to shirk its responsibility."

I doubt that this man was ever a naval engineer, and maybe he was just an army officer and didn't even belong to the navy. But why be surprised at that? Perhaps the two soldiers we saw yesterday were peasants, the ones who were fast asleep on the two hay wagons they had finished loading, wearing unbuttoned army jackets, red insignia on the collars, their caps with the People's Liberation Army red star on them askew on their heads.

"My coming here coincided with the period of the most intense struggle between the two main lines," the soldier says. "One, that of Liu Shao-chi, asserted that 'with respect to the problem of ships, buying is preferable to building and leasing preferable to buying.' This line gave *carte blanche* to the Chinese revisionists and the capitalists in our country and abroad. The other line was to make our ships ourselves. The political struggle brought out another challenge: by tackling the demanding new production jobs and by overcoming the difference between engineers, technicians, and workers, we made our shipyard a unique place for drawing out energy and inventiveness, and for eliminating the gulf between those who conceive the projects and those who execute them. We created a special revolutionary committee to build the 'Tientsin,' elected by the 3,000 workers in the shipyard. The workers were given the principal role in the committee. The management of the shipyard thus no longer depends on the technicians but on the workers who work with them."

"Forward, plough through the seas, against wind and tide," is written on the ship's bridge beneath the ever present portrait of Mao Tse-tung.

"This is the way you look at it, right?" I ask, pointing to the portrait. "To proceed in spite of storms. Is this your philosophy of life?"

"It's that," the soldier says, "as well as something else: to change small things into big things by daring to act and daring to think.

"Do you know what we had to do to solve the contradictions between the length, the width, and the capacity of a shipyard which could only build 5,000-ton ships, to change it into a shipyard which could build 10,000-ton ships? We told ourselves that it didn't make any difference if the hull of the ship was too long, if the bow hung over the end of the building ways, or if the stern was in the water, and we didn't get excited at the idea that the hull would be too big. It would just make the work a little more inconvenient. But the key problem was the weight of the hull of a 10,000-ton cargo ship, which exceeded the weight the building ways could take by about 1,000 tons. We scientifically analyzed the building ways and we believed that we could distribute the pressure evenly on the ground by multiplying the number of supports under them. The problem was in fact solved in this way. Look, for example, at the way an awl falls. If it falls point down, it will go into the ground, but if it falls handle down, it won't go into the ground, even if its weight remains the same. This means that the more you reduce the surface area of an object, the more pressure will be concentrated. After we made detailed calculations, we put several stays under the hull to increase the surface area. We reinforced with cement the part of the ways which had to hold the most weight. The workers drew from their rich experience to do the scientific work, changing an unfavorable situation that kept us from advancing into a favorable one. Once the opposition between experts and workers was eliminated, the full talent and wisdom of the working class came into play. The plans for the hull were drawn up in two months, whereas before it would have taken one to two years. We only drew up nine blueprints, instead of the usual hundreds. We then solved the problem of the crane that could only lift forty-four tons by splitting the hull up into a hundred pieces which we assembled later, thereby overcoming its limited lifting capacity.

"We needed but couldn't obtain a big milling machine to fashion the propeller which was over 16.5 feet in diameter and weighed almost 15 tons. So we followed the *method of the ants who strip a bone clean bit by bit* to make the propeller, using a drilling machine with a diameter smaller than 8.5 inches equipped with a small tool holder. The ship is now almost ready. It will be launched in a few days. So you see that we applied the dialectic of Mao Tse-tung to build the cargo ship." The soldier opens the little red book and reads, " 'Those who are in a state of inferiority and are passive can take the initiative and achieve victory from those who hold the initiative and have a superiority of forces if, basing themselves on the actual situation, they utilize great subjective activity to create certain indispensable conditions.' "

"How many ships have you built in Tientsin?"

"This is the first. But they build six 10,000-ton ships a year in Shanghai, whereas before the Cultural Revolution they only built two a year. In the future we will have a powerful fleet to take to the sea like China has never had before."

"If you go to Shanghai soon," I say, "perhaps we will see each other there. Or perhaps you will be able to come to Naples one day and I will show you our port."

"We would come willingly, but we would rather see Genoa since we understand that the workers there got together and went on strike to help a Chinese boat in difficulty that the harbormaster refused to assist. We will not forget this act which showed courage and working-class fraternity."

When we arrived in Shanghai, we asked several times if the white "Tientsin," which we thought of as of a human being, was tied up yet on the Huang-pu. We visited the Shanghai Industrial Exposition and were amazed at the achievements and potential of the Chinese naval industry. We saw small models of 18,000- to 19,000-ton cargo ships, as well as models of two 15,000-ton oil tankers built in 1969, one in April and the other in October. The Chinese have also made progress in the field of large (3,300 horsepower) marine diesels. Visiting the Exposition and the port of Tientsin helped us to understand that as far as naval construction is concerned, China has set itself a goal totally unheard of in the past. In a few years, and this can be verified already, China will possess an important fleet in the Yellow Sea. In Shanghai we were able to reconfirm what our soldier friend in Tientsin told us. From 1949 to 1966 only two 10,000-ton ships were built, whereas from 1966 to 1970 six of the same tonnage were built, without increasing equipment or labor power.

Passenger service is also increasing. In a window in Shanghai we see the model of the passenger ferry "The East Is Red," which carries 364 passengers and runs on the Yangtze; it has carried Mao himself on two occasions. A 3,200-ton icebreaker is already in service, three months after work was begun on it. Underneath the model of an icebreaker with automatic controls—another achievement they are proud of in Shanghai—is an inscription, in English and French, which says that the ship was built in 134 days.

"The working class must lead in all things," says Mao

A specialist on China would have stopped talking about factories long ago, if he were writing instead of me. One of their books, which I have with me, says, "Again, the long line of factories they want to take me to. I object, but nothing can be done, and yet I know that nothing is more like one factory than another factory." Specialists are so horrified by factories that they shove the statistics and summary charts on the work places they visit to the backs of their books. They show no interest in the workers. But you cannot fundamentally understand what is going on without hearing what the workers have to say, and this is much more valuable than listening to officials. It is not by accident that a Western journalist who published a book in 1967 on his 1965 visit to China neglected to mention one thing: the signs which announced the coming of the Cultural Revolution. The difference between a specialist on China and an activist is shown by the fact that in factory after factory I discovered an extraordinary universe and the real actors in Chinese history. It is in the factories that you discover the differences among the workers, their hostilities, their violent struggles, their failures, and their victories. Above all, you can see how their "critical thinking" produces technical discoveries, and the source of their amazing inventiveness.

In the West we take technology for granted. In contrast, Chinese workers learn that the *products of technology* must be critically examined and that their technical achievements are not a return to the prehistoric but are the result of a critical ability resulting from practical experience. In the face of the inventions of the technologically advanced countries, the Chinese show no resignation or inferiority complex but carefully study these inventions, duplicate them, and, they say, sometimes improve on them. You can only understand what the future of industrialization is in China if you appreciate what this kind of technical invention at the mass level, accomplished by millions of people, means: today, a crane, but tomorrow, new and more difficult undertakings.

The factory which makes the blue cloth worn by the Chinese

If you are European, you probably imagine the Chinese as a people always dressed in blue, millions of them bundled up in blue cotton uniforms. It wasn't Mao, however, who invented the blue the Chinese wear, despite that impression back home. Blue cloth has traditionally been worn by the people; only the style has recently changed. The German geographer Georg Wegener visited China at the beginning of the last century and wrote in his book:

> And, finally, the indigo the Chinese use to dye their everyday clothing. Millions and millions of people wear this same blue-colored material in China, in all parts of the empire, so much so that a famous book on China is entitled *The Land of the Blue Gown.* A foreigner might unconsciously imagine the enormous Chinese mass to be an immense blue tide washing up against him on all sides.

The factory which dyes and prints fabrics in Tientsin—2,300 workers, mostly women—produces 328,000 yards of cloth a day, primarily but not exclusively blue. In the workshops, we saw some bolts of cotton being printed in fantastic designs, some of them abstract. The gay boubous (long tunics) of the Zambian and Tanzanian women are made here, the very ones I tried in vain to find in Lusaka and Dar es Salaam. Materials you see in Ceylon are also made here, the ones Ceylonese women use to make up their elegant saris. Batik, the famous Indonesian fabric, is found here in new designs painted by the Chinese. There are miles of fabric for the European taste which would make the couturiers of Paris, Rome, and London go mad. The fabric made in this factory is exported to thirty-four countries.

The designs are made by worker-artists in the factory and are then delicately engraved on copper cylinders, like those used for printing illustrated newspapers. Fabric prices are ridiculously low. A yard of blue fabric is 1.5 yuan. "For 5 yuan," the representative of the revolutionary committee says, "I can have the tailor make up an outfit like the one I'm wearing, which is tailormade."

Many women who own sewing machines buy blue outfits in their sizes at the big department stores and fit them at home. But there are also groups of women in some neighborhoods who work for the community by sewing clothing. "This work is *not private,* please notice, but is part of the commercial sector," we are told. (In fact, I saw many seamstresses whose stores were in the streets, particularly in Canton and Shanghai, a little like in Naples. They pedaled at a frenzied rate making blue outfits, but also sewed in other colors, which Chinese women wear in the summer.)

Much of the work in the Tientsin factory is mechanized in the workshops. They have invented a simple machine made out of scrap iron which does four operations in one and which was presented to the Ninth Congress, we are told. More than half of the quotas for the 1970 plan were filled during the first months and production is up 30 percent over the same period last year.

Salaries go from a low of 50 to 60 yuan to a high of 110 yuan per month. Piecework wages and bonuses have been eliminated here too.

What is the salaried worker's purchasing power in China, where, as we know, prices have been stable or almost so for the last ten years? I ask the women workers on the revolutionary committee about this. They, like most women around the world, seem to know more about prices than the men. When you ask a Chinese man a price, he mutters something, looks at his wife, and says that *she had better tell you.*

But these kinds of questions irritate the Chinese, since they are still in shock over Soviet allegations that "the Chinese feed two out of one bowl of rice." They become easily distrustful when this question is asked and it is something to get an answer. Usually they answer evasively or raise their shoulders as if to say, "Why are you so concerned about this question? Can't you see with your own eyes that people have enough to eat and that they are adequately clothed?" That is, when they don't add, "This is a socialist state and it would be wrong to compare it with your country."

With the help of our friends, however, we are able to work up an average family's budget to give an idea of purchasing power. A family of four—father, mother, and two children—spends thirty yuan per month on food, which generally consists of these everyday items: rice, bread, soup, fish or meat or eggs, and vegetables. Noodles and rice cost from fifteen to thirty or thirty-six fen a kilogram, depending on quality.

"How much rice and noodles can you buy," I ask, "and is there any type of rationing on these items?"

"Absolutely none," the women answer, irritated. "That is revisionist propaganda. At our food supplier's—everyone has the same supplier—you can buy as much rice and noodles as you need. The only thing is that you can't stock them, to prevent any sabotage of food supplies. This also stops the monopoly of any single supplier."

The best meat costs 1.60 yuan a kilo (a kilo is 2.2 pounds); fish costs 70 fen a kilo; eggs, sold by weight, cost 18 fen a kilo; a kilo of chicken is 1.40 yuan. For a full basket of tomatoes and vegetables you pay 10 fen. I found the same prices, with few exceptions, from one end of China to the other, from Tientsin to Peking to Canton. The workers feel that they earn enough money to cover their food and clothing needs, since food and clothing prices are low. They will tell you, however, that if you want to get a fuller picture of the standard of living and income levels in China, you have to take some other considerations into account. A Chinese family spends only 1 yuan a month on housing, water, and electricity. Medicine, hospital care, schools, and day-care centers are free. There is a day-care center at the factory, where most of the labor force is made up of women. After women have their babies they are entitled to 56 days off at full pay.

In the shop I meet a young and beautiful worker, whose face has fine features, in the process of making some new fabric designs. Next to her is a *People's Daily*, just off the press.

"Do you find the time to read?" I ask.

"When there is a lot of work, no. But when it lets up, yes. We never work at a fixed pace here as they do in Western factories," she answers in an ironic tone.

Tatzupao, "trenchant arm of the revolution"

The Peking Heavy Electrical Machinery Factory is located next to the Military Museum on a main street in the capital, one of the new streets bordered by fields of green cabbage, slender poplars, and kitchen gardens which come up almost to the sidewalks.

The leader of the revolutionary committee is called Chiu and the workers' representative on the committee is Li. Two other comrades join our meeting in the factory. One is a delegate from the revolutionary cadre and the other is in charge of the day-care center. These workers were elected to the revolutionary committee in this factory of 5,400 workers, including 1,500 women, one of the most modern in China. They are solid people and their faces are serene.

Li starts to talk. He is thirty years old and has a round dimpled face, big eyes, and heavy eyelids. The industrial expansion of the factory started in 1958 during the Great Leap Forward. It makes huge alternating and direct current generators, turbines, and steam-turbine generator systems of 3,000 to 25,000 kilowatts. Before the Cultural Revolution, it took six months to build a 25,000-kilowatt turbine, whereas now it only takes two. The price has also been reduced and each one now costs 1,350 million yuan. Trucks and gasoline-tank trucks are made and exported, mostly to Vietnam, with smaller numbers going to Albania, Zambia, Tanzania, and several other African, Asian, and Latin American countries. This type of truck is also used for railroad construction in Tanzania. Factory production goals for 1970 were completed by September and now (October) they are starting on the goals for 1971. "We have a boring machine from Czechoslovakia which cost 500,000 yuan and whose accuracy goes to 200/1000. [They tell me this so I will appreciate the high level of technical research being done in the factory.] Using this machine, we designed and made another machine which is more accurate and costs only 100,000 yuan. In 1960 we bought a boring mill from the USSR which measures 15 feet in diameter, but it was an old model and of poor quality and we didn't have access to spare parts after the Soviet technicians left, as you know. So we drew up the necessary plans to make a larger 16-foot-diameter boring mill, which was finished in 1970. It has only one arm, is of simpler design, and was built using the most modern techniques. Some of its parts are made of silicon. We made two other new machines, but they are still being tested. Most of the technical achievements in the factory occurred after the Cultural Revolution."

Like most Chinese factories, this one works three shifts around the clock, often including Sunday.

We visit the workers in both the steam-turbine and generator shops. As in the ten Chinese factories I have already visited, the "*Chi ta san fan*" movement is in full swing here, after having been recommenced in March of this year. It is based on Mao's order to

"Attack the counter-revolutionaries, struggle against misappropriations, theft, against speculation, extravagance, and wastefulness." I wonder how it is possible to be more frugal, thrifty, and honest than the people I see everywhere I go. To the Chinese these qualities, including dedication, the spirit of sacrifice, must be given unsparingly. In the assembly workshop—where there are many women and girls at work—you see a forest of tatzupao, each one measuring six feet by six feet, so many that you can't see anything else. Instead of passing through trees, we pass through inscriptions, colored designs, and multicolored festoons.

The discussion begins. A few of the women show me a simple machine to cover electrical cables that they made themselves "by combining old craft techniques and modern technical knowledge." Their work done, another group of women workers is writing its own tatzupao for the *Chi ta san fan* movement. It is entitled "A Strange Illness." It is the story of a young man who rarely comes to work. "The worker is not sick but sees the doctor constantly on the chance he might have some illness. In fact, his only illness is his laziness and his fear of the masses. He will not be cured by injections, only by the thought of Mao." This is what these young women workers think.

A huge inscription reads, "Let's Develop the *Chi ta san fan* Movement to the Utmost." "What does this mean?" I ask. "There is no trace of waste and what theft can occur here, among the workers?"

"It means that we must strengthen and heighten our class consciousness. There is a big difference between China and the USSR. In the Soviet Union, even the managers make arrangements with the workers to take important machinery parts out of the factory. There is a black market in certain spare parts. We don't want anything like that to happen in China. That is why we hide nothing and why we lead an open struggle against speculation and theft. To sum up, we are developing revolutionary consciousness, that of the honest worker oriented toward the collective, to the maximum. The worker affirms his honesty, which is born of mutual solidarity and common struggle, making the repression of laws and prisons unnecessary."

The following tatzupao gives an idea of the atmosphere in the factory:

> The worker Wang Ta-min stole machine parts to sell them in the market, and started to speculate to the detriment of the factory. This worker comes from a poor family and had to be politically re-educated to increase his class consciousness. We reformed him. Wang Ta-min came back among us and we welcomed him with open arms. In bourgeois society, a worker who steals something goes to jail, but in our socialist society he is re-educated.

I pick out a friendly looking worker at random and she tells me her name is Kan Li-kuang. I ask her about her background and I learn that she is an engineer and used to draw technical plans in the head office. Now it is her turn to work. Why? She answers my question calmly:

"After I got my degree and started work, I drew up plans for a machine part, but when it came around to actually building the machine I didn't know what to do. I was deeply humiliated by this. What good is it to make up a blueprint when you don't know how to build the machine? I am now acquiring some practical experience and learning that Mao's appeal to the technicians to learn from the workers is a brilliant idea. Before, I drew plans for complicated machinery that seemed perfect on my drawing board, but the dimensions were in fact inexact so the assembled models didn't work. I am now learning by working in production that our superstructure has to be changed and that bourgeois ideology has to be criticized in order to 'serve the people.' "

She has also written a tatzupao on what she thinks is unjust and doesn't conform to the thought of Mao. A worker suggests something to her. She listens to him as though he were her boss, as though the point of reference, as it were, for the dialectical processes going on in her mind were centered on this worker.

"I also wrote a small tatzupao," she says, "on a worker who stole a precision watch to sell it in the market and buy something else. I showed that this theft was not only in the worst interests of the collective but of the worker himself. This worker was also re-educated. He hasn't yet come back to the factory but I am convinced that he will soon be with us again."

On big yellow pieces of paper there are dozens of other tatzupao, which are blown out from the wall by the wafts of air from the machines. You would almost think it an exhibition of pop art. These tatzupao really seem to me like a popular expression of the "art and culture" of millions of people. A newly printed tatzupao dated October 18, 1970, reads:

> All false ideologies are poisonous weeds, monsters, and must be criticized. Ma Hu-wen, a worker, did indifferent work at the factory. He hadn't changed his view of the world. He had bourgeois ideas and was always thinking about enjoyment and pleasure. The workers in the shop criticized him to help him return to a proletarian world view.

I ask what this Ma Hu-wen, the pleasure-seeker, could possibly have done. They tell me that he avoided all political activities and spent his money solely on amusements.

The workers explain to us that each tatzupao is generally written by two or three workers and that writing these posters is a method of democratic intervention in the life of the factory, one which is never coercive and one by which everyone helps everyone else.

In the steam-turbine shop, my eyes rest on a thin young man. He is wearing glasses and his eyes are riveted to his machine. I stop and ask him some questions. I always choose the people I talk to in the factories on my own, both before and after my conversation with the leaders of the revolutionary committees. This goes for the cities and schools I visit as well.

"I obtained my engineering degree in dynamics from Tsinghua University. I came to this factory to be re-educated by the workers. Intellectuals who do not join forces with the workers cannot understand. There aren't many of us intellectuals here, but we are grateful to be able to enrich ourselves by learning from the workers."

"Will you be staying on here?"

"I am now getting the practical experience you have to have after you study theory," he says, "because this is the correct path to follow. The revolutionary committee will later decide where I will be assigned. All students who come to the shop to do production work are judged by the collective and their worker-teachers. They decide whether we will return to teaching, to the university, or if we should be sent elsewhere."

I meet another person who received his degree from the Industrial Institute of Talien (Dairen) and who has been doing production work since 1968. He says that, "Before the Cultural Revolution, we drew our plans closed-off in offices. We were little less than bureaucrats and had no contact with the masses since we followed the type of specialization advocated by Liu Shao-chi. Before 1968, this experiment could not have occurred in a factory. The new links being forged between workers and technicians, an experiment which I am now a part of, are opening up a new horizon of achievements for China. If the technicians had continued to draw their plans in their ivory towers, this would never have been possible."

Many of the factory's blackboards have colored designs on them. Many of the tatzupao talk about the study of philosophy. One of these criticizes Liu Shao-chi's view of life and his notion that there was no need for workers to study philosophy. In one that criticizes the theory of the end of the class struggle (which Liu Shao-chi agreed with, the workers tell me), I see for the first time a caricature of the former president of the People's Republic of China. Liu Shao-chi is drawn with a red nose, protruding teeth, hair on end, and a body which ends as a snake. His agent, Teng Hsiao-ping, is a small man who wears sunglasses like a spy and runs as fast as his legs can carry him as he tightly grasps a big black briefcase under his arm. A red quill pen (the symbol of revolutionary criticism) spears Liu Shao-chi, who screams, terrorstricken, and throws his arms up to the sky.

Another tatzupao brings up the problem of the structures and superstructures which must be changed.

"What are the superstructures that have to be completely changed?" I ask Chiu, the representative of the revolutionary committee.

"Government organizations. Politics, ideology, and culture. Art, education, and the press. Health. And the relations of production. The Communist Party, which is the core of leadership, and governmental organizations are under its direction. The revolution, every revolution, is destined to come to power, and state organizations are a center of power. The superstructures will disappear at the same time that the state disappears—all states."

Isn't the worker really referring to the debate, touched on at least by the qualified cadres here, which Marx and Lenin raised about the withering away of the socialist state and all its organizations, not only the repressive ones but the ideological ones as well?

In this factory, salaries range from 34 to 100 yuan. These are the lowest I have found. Bonuses and piecework have of course been eliminated. On the question of salaries, suggestions from the workers are at present being received and studied. They tell me why material incentives are not needed: when bonuses were used it took six months to produce the main turbine parts, but now, after the ideological revolution, the workers who work for socialist construction only take four months—with no extra incentives.

"We do not need bonuses," the representatives from the revolutionary committee say. "We workers share in the management of the factory in the three-in-one combination. We are building the factory politically and carrying forward the red flag of the Anshan Iron and Steel Plant."

"Why was the trade union eliminated?"

"The trade union followed the revisionist line, that of economism; it no longer exists in its former form. We now have Workers' Representative Conferences, which have taken the place of the trade union. The Workers' Representative Conference elects a standing committee, which is called the Workers' Council. A few days ago a delegation of Chinese workers went to Chile. In the group was a representative from the Workers' Representative Conference of Shanghai."

"What is the difference between the revolutionary committee and the factory congress?"

"The revolutionary committee is an organization of political power, while the factory congress is a mass organization. Both are under the direction of the party. We have already re-established the cells in the factory and a congress may be held anytime from now to the end of the year to elect the party committee. Among the twenty members of the revolutionary committee there are seven party members who constitute the core of Communists and who assure the leadership function of the party until the factory-wide congress takes place."

The workers' university at the factory, or how a worker-engineer is made

The Shanghai Machine Tool Factory, besides building precision grinding machines exported to thirty countries, also "makes" engineers. They are selected from the working class and study at the university in the factory. This factory is one of the most famous industrial organizations in China, and was cited by Mao in his directive of July 21, 1968:

> There must be higher education, especially in the form of polytechnical schools. But at the same time the length of time must be reduced, there must be a revolution in the field of education, hardships of studying must be lessened, proletarian politics must be put in command, and the example set by the Shanghai Machine Tool Factory must be followed. This means that the technical staff must come from the ranks of the workers. Students must be chosen from among the workers and peasants who have had practical experience. After they have studied for a few years, they should return to practice and to production.

The struggle to create a workers' university dates from the era of the Great Leap Forward when Mao personally visited the factory on July 8, 1957. Two hundred and ninety worker-engineers were trained at that time. But, according to the workers, the bourgeois specialists were opposed to this development and tried to prevent more worker-technicians from being trained, saying that "workers have big muscles but small brains." Of fifty workers chosen for the university in 1960, thirty-three were dismissed. The examiners, influenced by the revisionist line, wanted the workers to be able to speak and read foreign languages. The worker Ma Chi-chen objected that scholars in ancient China had made important inventions without knowing any foreign language. He held his ground and didn't give up. He went to night school simply to learn a foreign language. He learned how to draw plans, and when he asked for readmission to the university he was accepted. As for She Kunfu, a worker-engineer who received his degree from the workers' university, he also had found it very difficult to get into the school. Before he attended classes his job had consisted of cleaning the washrooms in the managers' offices. "Cleaning bathrooms is not drawing up plans," the managers sneered at him to discourage his eagerness to learn. Yet it was this worker who later made the first experiments on curved-surface-grinders.

We are now meeting with the worker-engineers, the representative of the factory party cell—who is also co-representative on the revolutionary committee of the workers' university—the worker-inventors of the Chinese grinding machines, and an intellectual, a woman, who studied at Moscow University. The atmosphere at the factory is extremely open. I don't believe I have ever before felt such a feeling of fraternity and rapport among the leaders and the members of a revolutionary committee or between workers and engineers.

The workers point out that the history of this factory is very special. Before Liberation it made pickaxes and plows. It belonged to the Americans, with *compradors* supplying most of the capital. The changes which occurred after Liberation have made this one of the model factories in China.

The secretary of the factory's party branch explains that worker-engineers are trained in four basic ways: (1) Some workers with long experience of production work are chosen to go to the university for a few years and then to return to factory work so that they can share the technical knowledge they have acquired; (2) other particularly gifted workers are sent to work in the technical workshops where plans are drawn up; (3) workers who have a great deal of practical experience are given management posts; and finally, (4) evening classes on technical studies are organized at the factory itself—the so-called amateur's university courses. These criteria were defended by the workers, although the program faced many difficulties between 1953 and 1958. And it was on this same basis that, after Mao's directive of July 21, 1968, discussions began on the creation of a real university center for machine tools.

When this factory of 6,000 metallurgical workers, one of China's pilot factories, decided to set up a university center, it submitted the proposal to the Shanghai industrial sector's revolutionary committee. Approval was given and the center was born. It now has fifty-two students, chosen from among the workers on the recommendation of each workshop, with the final decision made by the factory's revolutionary committee. The course lasts two years. The worker-students do nothing but study. They get the same salary as they did when they worked in production. There are twenty-nine teachers: some formerly taught in the factory's technical schools or at the University of Shanghai, and some are from the worker-technician cadres. Most of the teachers work at the factory. The university is run by a three-in-one combination of worker-technicians, evening-school teachers, and students. The expenses incurred in setting up and running the university are entirely underwritten by the factory. The university is a success and other such universities have been or are being established. Obviously only very big or relatively big factories can accommodate universities, but small factories can send their workers to study at the bigger factories' universities. In fact, some of the factory universities have more students than the university at the Shanghai Machine Tool Factory.

In spite of the successes in this field, the revolutionary committee points out to us that this initiative is still being tested. When they are more sure of the results they will expand the program and extend it to the country as a whole. If the hoped-for results are not achieved, the initiative may be revised or fundamentally changed. This is one of the characteristics of today's China: *all innovations must be tested in actual practice.*

Another extraordinary aspect of Chinese industry is that the workers do not hold advanced technology in awe or *venerate technology* as an inaccessible world whose laws are the preserve of specialists and whose conquest is reserved only for the highly industrialized countries.

Chinese workers study foreign products. They will tell you that they dismantle and reassemble foreign machines to improve on the original, not just to make a copy. Otherwise, they say, how could China have made so much progress encircled for many years by the profoundly hostile world of capitalist industry. Another noteworthy fact about the Shanghai Machine Tool Factory is that its workers know how to *re-invent* machines. Not only cranes, but large, highly automated precision machines. The factory produces curved-surface-grinders, flat-surface-grinders, and gear-making machines. We were assured that the quality of the machines made here is equal and at times better than elsewhere in the world.

This factory started from almost nothing and the stories my narrators relate are remarkable. In 1960, Chen Mei-fan, a worker in this factory who was then thirty years old, was sent to the international fair in Leipzig. He saw a grinding machine capable of burnishing steel by polishing the surface to the highest degree, much more than Chinese machines were then able to do. The Chinese worker stood in line with the other visitors to pick up the publicity pamphlet which described the machine and gave its specifications, but when he reached the head of the line he was told that no more pamphlets would be handed out. He didn't believe it and asked why they were unwilling to give him a pamphlet. He was told that, "Since you Chinese are technologically backward, giving you a prospectus is useless. You cannot have any use for the machine, and anyway, you cannot produce one. Such a machine is the result of the technology of a developed industrial country." Comrade Chen was so enraged by this that he grit his teeth. (I suddenly remember what the French students said in May 1968: "Be enraged.") Home in China, Chen told his comrades what had happened to him in Leipzig and proposed that they make a similar machine. They agreed, but when he submitted his shop's proposal to the factory's chief engineer, he made fun of Chen, saying that to make the machine it would take twenty years to acquire the technical knowledge and get the necessary equipment from the most advanced industrial countries in the world. Then he asked Chen if he knew any foreign languages. The worker said that he had only taken beginners' classes in a foreign language but that he was attending night school. The chief engineer "paternally" asked Chen to leave, suggesting that he go to night school for at least ten years and forget about the idea.

Chen was even more enraged after this and turned to the factory's party committee. This party committee, unlike those in other factories, had solid links with the working class and tried to help the shop workers. But the chief engineer refused to give the necessary equipment or gave it sparingly. Chen and his friends started to procure all the equipment they could personally get hold of, including discarded models. He worked day and night, after his shift, helped by other workers and technicians who were moved by his adversity and who were passionately interested in his work. When he couldn't get the equipment needed for the experiments, "Chen used his eyes, his ears, and his hands to do the experiments," the comrades tell us. "The surface of a grinding machine must be precise to the thousandth of a hair. But Chen didn't have the equipment to measure it so he used his finger to test the surface of the wheel." He worked on it for four and a half years and recorded about 3,000 failures.

While Chen was doing the experiments, we are told, a specialist from East Germany came to the factory. He claimed to have with him an instrument that could make the necessary measurements but he refused even to show it to Chen. One day the specialist went out and Chen, who had tried incessantly to convince him to show the precision instrument, took it apart to see how it was made. He was frightened by the complexity and intricacy of the mechanism so he reassembled it. The specialist found out when he came back. He denounced the worker to the chief engineer, who called Chen in and raked him over the coals, making him write out his own self-criticism. The worker "flew into a violent rage, as did a number of other comrades." In spite of the refusal of the chief engineer, they decided to make the instrument to measure the surface of the grinding machine, one that would "replace the work done by the workers with their five senses." They succeeded in doing so. Now the technique is being used in several factories and "it can even be learned by young girls of sixteen to eighteen years of age."

In certain respects the high-precision grinders produced by the Machine Tool Factory are the same ones Chen saw at the international fair in Leipzig, but in other respects they are superior—in degree of precision, for instance. A few years ago the machine was demonstrated at an international fair in Japan. Representatives from several capitalist countries asked for details of the manufacturing specifications. They were told that this machine was a discovery of the Chinese working class and that it was a secret. During the Cultural Revolution Chen was elected co-representative on the Shanghai Revolutionary Committee. He attended the Ninth Congress of the Chinese Communist Party as a workers' delegate.

The factory is presently in a period of important growth as far as production is concerned. In 1966 it produced 1,634 machine tools, the highest number for any year since Liberation. This year the plan forecasts a production of 2,300 much improved machines, but the comrades tell me that they think they will be able to produce 2,600 and maybe even more. As I mentioned, these are highly precise grinding machines, and they are presently exported to some thirty countries. The most important innovations in the making of these machines occurred during the Cultural Revolution when the inventive capacity of the workers came into full play. In this factory, bitter factionalism inside the party did not occur. It always followed Mao's line, and even after the Cultural Revolution the managerial group changed little. As far as the role of the intellectuals and the managers in the factory was concerned, the political struggle brought the engineers and the highly skilled staff closer to the working class. "In the factory there are three hundred intellectual cadres who graduated from the universities. Their re-education was particularly closely watched. They now all take turns doing production work, one-third of them work in the shops while the other two-thirds direct the technical work in the managerial offices." The comrade who is co-representative on the revolutionary committee explains to me that among these intellectuals, "there are very few who are bad, many who are comparatively good, and a few who are good. But all of them have a lot to learn from the workers."

As I said before, a woman engineer is attending this meeting. Her name is Tsao Wan and she appears to be about thirty years old. She tells us briefly about her intellectual background. She went to school, got her degree, and studied a foreign language for a year. Then she spent four years in Moscow where she became a doctor of mechanical engineering. She returned to her country in 1962. The workers criticized her later, pointing out that from 1962 to July 21, 1968, she had no relationship with the masses. (She lowers her head, embarrassed, as she says this.)

The workers said that she had book knowledge, that she had been influenced by the poisonous revisionist line, and that during all these years she had produced nothing. But during the Cultural Revolution she started to change her conception of life. She became involved in practical work beside the workers and she started to learn from the masses. Her comrades now have a relatively satisfactory opinion of her and they have elected her to the factory's revolutionary committee.

The struggle to raise class consciousness, even that of the intellectual cadres, was carried on in the factory. The main fault of these people was that they had forgotten the important point of serving the people. Various types of petty bourgeois ambition had to be combated as well. We were given the example of an electronics engineer who worked on more than sixty projects during the last ten years, none of which he finished. All he did was to increase his scientific knowledge to embellish his own prestige. At one point he was trying to build a small machine to make hair grow, insisting that an electrical apparatus of this nature did not exist anywhere in the world and that if he invented it he would become famous. Next he wanted to invent an electric mousetrap, since this did not exist either. He didn't succeed in either project. And all during this time, while he was an engineer in the grinding-machine shop, the workers were working day and night trying to improve production!

Intellectuals have been working with the workers since the directive of July 21, 1968. The atmosphere in the factory is one of total cooperation. I was told that the fundamental problem for the intellectuals was "whom to serve," the people and the revolution or their own prestige and profit? Those who follow the path of individualism serve no one. They are the main instruments of revisionism. The others are becoming proletarian revolutionary intellectuals who link their destinies with that of the working class.

The 13,500-ton hydraulic press, or how the foolish old man removed the mountains

Twenty-two miles from Shanghai I visit the 13,500-ton hydraulic press, as famous in China as the pyramids are in Egypt. The plans and construction for this press go back to the era of the Great Leap Forward in 1958. It is in the Shanghai Heavy Machinery Factory which has 12,000 workers. The press stands in a hangar as high as a cathedral and is itself 80 feet high, 26 feet wide, 120 feet long, and weighs 2,500 tons. It is "one-and-a-half times the size of a basketball court," my companions say. The compression capacity goes from 4,500 to 9,000 tons and can go up to a maximum of 13,500 tons. We see the white-hot steel ingot being flattened by the automatically controlled press, and the control panel shows us that the machine is using its full force of 13,500 tons. In the instrument room, you hear the muted wheezing of the compressor. I see many young people at work who appear to be students, wearing glasses and with smooth-chinned faces. They don't appear to be experts but are rather clumsy, like youngsters, as they move the white-hot bars of steel with iron rods.

"How many students do you have in the factory?"

"More than 500."

"Don't they disturb your work at times?"

"It doesn't make any difference. They have come to the factory to be re-educated by the workers and to plunge themselves into working life. The fact that production may be affected doesn't count. What is important is that they come out of the factory as true successors to the revolutionary cause."

"During the years of the Cultural Revolution a new shop was created to melt down the steel," the representative of the revolutionary committee, Chen Tsa-chen, tells me. "The furnace is a product of the Cultural Revolution. It was built in seven months and four days, 'a worldly miracle,' as the workers say. The manager and the engineers were hostile to the idea and said that they would stake their lives on the fact that we wouldn't be able to make it. When the shop was set up, on abandoned ground, we called the former manager to see it, showing him that we had accepted his challenge. The manager is now a manual worker, in keeping with Mao's belief in struggle-criticism-transformation, and he is being re-educated by the workers."

The struggle for the giant press was the first big struggle between the two lines for the industrialization of China, and occurred at the very time when the conflict first appeared. This was the era of the Great Leap Forward when Liu Shao-chi, as well as the Soviets, considered the project economic adventurism. The worker's story is very interesting because it allows you to see what the alternatives were based on.

"Producing the 13,500-ton hydraulic press was not only a technical battle; it was mainly a political battle because the two lines collided on this issue. Liu Shao-chi's men maintained that it was necessary to have a 11,000-ton press to build a 13,500 one, but the material conditions necessary to build it were lacking—equipment to make the parts, specialists, and necessary manufacturing experience. The workers criticized this revisionist resignation and said that Mao's directives had to be followed: We have to follow a road which no one has ever taken before and not do it haltingly. What we don't possess but the world has we must also obtain. The problems were immense. The base of the press bore down with a weight of 330 tons and we didn't have a crane capable of lifting it so that we could work underneath it.

"We read Mao's article on 'The Foolish Old Man Who Removed the Mountains'—he asked his children to dig away the mountains with pickaxes. The workers saw a mountain of steel in front of them, one which weighed 330 tons. They had the same kind of determination as the old man and they said they could flatten the mountain with their hands. The workers found forty-eight small jacks for raising trucks and used them to lift the piece of steel. Two worker-teachers worked each jack, surrounded by a group of workers. Other worker-teachers oversaw the whole operation. When the order to raise was given, the eighty-eight workers below lifted the block of steel in unison, and it was raised up an inch, then two, then three inches. As the mass rose, wooden wedges and then iron piles were put under it. It took two days and two nights to raise the slab of steel twenty feet. The 330 tons are like a mountain and the jacks are like ants which can lift mountains. We must be 'resolute and unafraid of sacrifice,' and 'surmount every difficulty to win victory,'" the worker concludes, quoting a phrase from Mao's article on the foolish old man in the little red book.

"After this success," he continues, "we made two pillars from recycled iron to put underneath the raised piece of steel. The mountain of steel was hoisted up. It took us four years of work in all: the giant functioned for the first time in 1962.

"The struggle started here long before the Cultural Revolution. There were several attempts at sabotage by agents of Liu Shao-chi who wanted to demonstrate that the objective conditions necessary to build the machine had not been joined. The steel which was being used to make the press was routed elsewhere. The construction crew was taken away. We were under continual pressure from the leaders on the party committee committed to the capitalist road. They exhorted us not to undertake such a 'hopeless task' since it was obviously impossible to build this hydraulic press. They said: 'We Chinese do not have this type of machine, only foreigners have it, and like it or not we are going to have to buy one from them.' 'Good,' we said, 'we don't have the prototype but we don't have a cult of foreigners either. And how did people make a 13,500-ton press the first time? Big things come out of small ones.' It is true that we didn't have a construction plan, only studies we had conducted throughout the country to learn how small and medium-sized presses work. Then we combined the best elements from all of them. The project was not to be the work of specialists alone, but of workers and revolutionary technicians as well—a matter which was resolved as we worked on the project. The particular method we followed is summed up in this sentence: 'Small pieces make big ones and short pieces make long ones.' "

Chen Tsa-chen accompanies us to the door of the factory. He cordially invites us to return.

"If we do, will we find another press, this time a 20,000-ton one?" I ask him.

"Yes," he says without boasting, "we are sure of it."

The key to understanding how the Chinese "read" the thought of Mao Tse-tung, and the story of the foolish old man and the "three constantly read articles"

The Chinese language comes as a big surprise to us Westerners, who consider ourselves so skilled in the use of words. In Chinese each word corresponds exactly to one object and one object only: an ant is an ant, a mountain is a mountain, and death is death. When the Chinese read a written passage, they see the language first as concrete and objective, afterwards as creative and as a generator of culture. From reading they must draw out their culture, take from it the knowledge they need to raise, enrich, and transform themselves. The Chinese never read mechanically. Just the opposite. Everything I observed on this subject makes me feel that the way the Chinese read is, culturally speaking, the richest way I know. Let us take an example.

The "Three Constantly Read Articles" by Mao do not take more than eleven short pages. They are entitled "Serve the People," "In Memory of Norman Bethune," and "The Foolish Old Man Who Removed the Mountains." The one who served the people was Chang Szu-teh, a soldier from the Guard Regiment of the Central Committee of the Chinese Communist Party. He took part in the Long March and in September 1944, as he was making charcoal, the charcoal kiln collapsed and killed him. "Though death befalls all men alike," concludes Mao, "it may be heavier than Mount Tai or lighter than a feather." This is an exaltation of the death of those who give their lives for others, expressed rationally, without pathos.

Doctor Norman Bethune was a well-known Canadian Communist who came to China in 1937 with a medical team. He had taken part in the Spanish Civil War and then came to China to work as a doctor in the revolutionary bases of the People's Army. He died in 1939 as a result of blood poisoning contracted during his work. Mao wrote that Bethune is an example of a true internationalist Communist, and in a few lines he poses the main theme of our age, the links between workers' struggles in capitalist countries and the struggles in the colonial and underdeveloped world. "Leninism teaches that the world revolution can only succeed if the proletariat of the capitalist countries supports the struggle for liberation of the colonial and semicolonial peoples. . . . Comrade Bethune put this Leninist line into practice. . . . Every Communist must learn this true Communist spirit from Comrade Bethune."

These two articles thus serve as a reminder of what the price of courage is, while they bring out, without dramatic effects, the meaning of a life and the value of a death dedicated to socialism and internationalism. In the parable about "The Foolish Old Man Who Removed the Mountains," Yu Kung, as he is called, is a kind of ancestor of today's revolutionaries. He is the rebel against the alleged divine edict, against the cosmic order and against its immutable laws. A kind of peasant Galileo, a people's Galileo, as it were.

This story was told by Mao Tse-tung in his concluding speech to the Seventh National Congress of the Chinese Communist Party on June 11, 1945. Yu Kung wanted to move two extremely high mountains because they were in his way. He and his sons decided to demolish them with pickaxes, a job which would be continued by those born in future generations:

> "When I die, my sons will carry on; when they die, there will be my grandsons, and then their sons and grandsons, and so on to infinity. High as they are, the mountains cannot grow any higher and with every bit we dig, they will be that much lower." . . . God was moved by this, and he sent down two angels who carried the mountains away on their backs. Today, two big mountains lie like a dead weight on the Chinese people. One is imperialism, the other is feudalism. The Chinese Communist Party has long made up its mind to dig them up. We must persevere and work unceasingly, and we too will touch God's heart. Our God is none other than the masses of the Chinese people.

The language of Mao in the little red book

The simplest approach to understanding the thought of Mao Tse-tung lies in understanding *how he uses the Chinese language.* Ignore the academic exercises of specialists and the fantasies of doctrinaires. In the West, Saussure and the structuralist geniuses have exposed the sinews of language, have dissected it so as to reconstitute it and return it to us within the framework of a system of intelligible laws. However, in China the language as used by Mao is not made to be reduced to a linguistic structure. It seeks above all to encourage knowledge, imagination, and creativity. Words have been "reinvented" to combat the erosion of meaning. Language thus has a great simplicity, and the sentences seem almost elementary: the language of Mao is the language of the Chinese people. Words have been emptied, deprived of all idealist embellishments, and *reinvested* with concrete meanings. Mao has invented a revolutionary language, one which makes words in the little red book always represent something concrete, something which thus becomes imagination, praxis, and, eventually, revolutionizes thought.* Westerners, mostly influenced by the Cartesian mode of thought—rigorous but forbidding to the imagination—can disastrously misunderstand the true meaning of the words Mao uses. "Bombard the headquarters" is a phrase which has been misinterpreted as a battle command, an order given to the artillery to fire. "Political power grows out of the barrel of a gun" has also been misconstrued in our part of the world to mean: get your hands on some rifles and start shooting. (This sentence of Mao's, moreover, has enormous theoretical and strategical implications based on a thorough understanding of the various divergences and differences in historical situations, which he has probably grasped better than any other Marxist.) These are only two examples; many more could be given. Let it suffice to recall one of Mao's most famous expressions: "Imperialism is a paper tiger" (transformed subsequently into: "The atomic bomb is a paper tiger," or "The dollar is a paper tiger"). In the West this phrase has been twisted and distorted and taken out of its original context. As elaborated by Mao, the phrase was a strategy for revolutionary struggle. It was used for the first time in 1946 to describe the alliance between the United States and the Kuomintang; it later took on a further meaning after a speech Mao gave to the Political Bureau of the Chinese Communist Party in Wuchang in December 1958. At this time, it was phrased in the language of class struggle:

> Just as there is not a single thing in the world without a dual nature (this is the law of the unity of opposites), so imperialism and all reactionaries have a dual nature—they are real tigers and paper tigers at the same time. . . . On the one hand, they were real tigers; they devoured people, devoured people by the millions and tens of millions. . . . But in the end they changed into paper tigers, dead tigers, bean-curd tigers. . . . Hence, imperialism and all reactionaries, looked at in essence, from a long-term point of view, from a strategic point of view must be seen for what they are—paper tigers. On this we should build our strategic thinking. On the other hand, they are also living tigers, iron tigers, real tigers which can devour people. On this we should build our tactical thinking.

* See Mao's essay "Oppose Stereotyped Party Writing," quoted in Chapter 16, *The Chinese Communist Party*, below.

Mao has employed the language spoken by over 700 million people. This really means that he will become immortal—not deified, not the object of a "cult" (ideas foreign to Mao's thought itself), precisely because thought survives the man who creates it. Thus the assumption that Chinese society will disintegrate after Mao's death is ignorant and stupid. The Chinese workers we met who make machines out of scrap iron are not Robinson Crusoes abandoned on a desert island. They have become inventors because they "think critically," an ability which has atrophied in the West; they *do not reject* those Western scientific and technological achievements which are helpful to their own continued progress. They are inventive in their work *because* they read the little red book politically. This does not mean that everyone is a great inventor. Doubtless many mistakes are made, results are inconclusive, and some good equipment manages to get damaged. But a new thought process has emerged from the simple act of reading in China, and reading draws out the greatest amount of individuality from the largest part of the collective, and stimulates creativity in production and technology, essential to the new China. This concept is difficult for us to understand. When Picasso invented cubism during World War I by working with pieces of colored paper because he lacked brushes and paint, thus creating his famous collages, we understood easily. But when a form of widespread popular imagination is born in China, one which expresses itself concretely in strange floating cranes, in giant hydraulic presses built from scratch based on Western technology (toward which they do not have a fatalistic attitude), in drilling machines, in 10,000-ton cargo ships on ways originally constructed to handle only 5,000-ton ships, we don't understand it. In Factory No. 22 in Tientsin, one of the tatzupao concludes with the appeal, "Produce philosophical ideas," epitomizing the constant need for liberating human creativity. And what are these tatzupao, if not a new form of collective literature, which everyone can use to learn to express and formulate ideas, and make them known to others? The tatzupao, "trenchant arm of the revolution," is another expression of the creative ability of the masses.

Those who first arrive in China could be taken aback by the way the little red book is waved as a sign of welcome. It is constantly being consulted during meetings, people are always quoting it—it almost seems an obsession. Sometimes you can no longer bear to hear the same sentences endlessly repeated, it makes you yawn. But as your awareness grows you begin to understand that the words from the little red book are not recited without feeling, and that the book is not a catechism written by a god-like Mao to be chanted mechanically. You soon discover that by reading the little red book you draw close to and start to understand a dialectical process. What you learn can be applied to what you do and how you act every day, in a way that is particularly significant to you and to you alone. And the way the little red book is read is anything but dogmatic. For example the story of Yu Kung applies to an infinite number of situations in the daily lives of everyone, having a different impact on each person, as I have been made aware in hundreds of opposing situations and different accounts.

The key to understanding the significance of the little red book in China, where almost everyone has a copy, lies in the meaning of the term *cultural* in relation to *revolution.* The German scholar Schickel has written: "The word for culture in Chinese is *wenhua. Wen* means *the written* in the highest sense of the word, the *written text. Hua* means 'to change, to become transformed, to evolve, to become something through what is written, to become a scholar.' " If culture is defined as change through the written word, then it is no surprise that contemporary Chinese civilization prizes the principle of pushing everyone to acquire *wen* and to undergo *hua,* regardless of what the person's origins might be or what this self-cultivation may bring. The fact that millions of copies of the famous pocket-sized *Quotations from Chairman Mao Tse-tung* have been printed in China is therefore important not only because Mao wrote it, but primarily because it enables and induces all Chinese to resort to written reasoning, vis-à-vis others as well as themselves.

There are 750 million copies of Mao's little red book in print in seventy languages all over the world (this figure was given on Peking Radio, January 2, 1969). There must be twice as many in China. The Chinese way of reading the little red book does not reflect an *amorphous mass phenomenon.* The thought of Mao makes the Chinese think about things in a new way, in an individual and original way, because everyone is obliged to formulate his ideas in the context of the primacy of politics, as he confronts objective reality and himself, thus making a "revolution" in both.

The little red book is also a unifying text since it enables everyone to use a common political language, one which transcends the ancient divisions of the various Chinese dialects throughout the country. (Even today these divisions persist: our interpreter from Canton needed a translator to make himself understood in Shanghai.) The little red book is thus the *unifying political work* for 750 million Chinese; they can read the same words with the same meanings and apply them not only to their political work, but also in order to have moral and collective rules: courage, devotion, thrift, and modesty.

The little red book gave the Red Guards who came to Peking from far north and south a common language. Generations of Anglo-Saxons (Englishmen and Americans) used a written text in a similar way, if you think about it: they learned how to read by reciting from the family Bible. In fact, the existence of the Bible, in many homes the only written word, enabled them to become the first to stamp out illiteracy. The omnipresence of the little red book in China perhaps makes more sense in this light. It encourages older people, who are illiterate and generally live in rural areas, to read and write their first characters. An eighty-year-old peasant woman we met in the New China commune, thirty miles outside Nanking, told us that she made a *tremendous effort*, with the help of some young people from the village, to learn to read and write the first sentence of the book, which is on the party.

Eighty percent of the Chinese people were illiterate before the socialist revolution, compared to less than 30 percent today. The kind of language needed to speak to the masses in an intelligible way had been a problem since the days of Yenan. Was the metaphysical language of the past to be used, that of the intellectual elite, the mandarins and self-complacent literary circles? Should it be the language of the scholar about whom Mao says ironically: "Without stepping outside his gate . . . [he] knows all the wide world's affairs"? Or would it be a language which would stress that:

> If you want to know a certain thing or a certain class of things directly, you must personally participate in the practical struggle to

> change reality, to change that thing or class of things, for only thus can you come into contact with them as phenomena; only through personal participation in the practical struggle to change reality can you uncover the essence of that thing or class of things and comprehend them.

The choice was obvious. It had to be a direct, elementary, political language, a language which would overcome the country's dialect divisions and linguistic barriers. Does this mean that the *Chinese language* was mutilated, rendered primitive and simple-minded? This could have happened, or has happened, depending on your point of view. Since I look at language from a political standpoint, a language which puts politics first is for me a language which is really in tune with man's development, carrying the sources of its own vitality and of its own cultural dynamism. While an old culture dissolves, a new one is being built ("there can be no creation without destruction"), and the little red book testifies to the fact that theory plays an important part in the elimination of an old culture in the course of a struggle which tests the very roots of language in the fire of debate. To the masses, the violent debates about theory unleashed during the Cultural Revolution focused on the use of political language, on what meanings would be attached to particular words in everyday practice. The slogan "Waving the red flag to oppose the red flag" is characteristic of this arduous battle which was often based on the meaning of political language. What Lenin wrote on the debate on theory in the socialist movement, and later the Communist movement, comes to mind. In *What Is to Be Done*, he called it the problem of "shades of meaning," and said that it was necessary to take a stand on this problem since "the fate of Russian Social Democracy for very many years to come may depend on the strengthening of one or another 'shade.' "

Art in China after the Cultural Revolution

Every revolution has been aroused by a destructive fury toward the past. This is more or less agreed by everyone. In creating a new culture, the past will be transcended as fast as men and women see their culture with new eyes and write their own history themselves. What new era has been built on the ruins of the old? What will emerge, superstructurally, from the political language of the masses in China? What novels, literature, music, film, sculpture, and painting? Although we can understand the function of a factory's revolutionary committee, we cannot predict what aspects and forms this part of the superstructure, which is called art, will assume in a revolutionized superstructure.*

Whatever the outcome, art in China is something very different from what you would expect. The professional artist, the individual destined for creation, has disappeared, just as the exclusive function of the manager no longer exists and the mandarinate of professors in the universities and medical schools has been eliminated. Artistic communication in China today is expressed by the individual working through the group and vice versa. Is the painter who climbs up to the top of a fifteen-foot ladder to paint a billboard at the gates of Hangchow, a billboard which depicts a soldier from the People's Liberation Army with a sack of wheat on his back, an artist? Can those who have taken photographs of Mao and Lin Piao standing on the Tien An Men square podium, and carefully painted them on the walls of peasant houses or in the Coppermine commune near Nanking (like the people who go to the Uffizi Gallery in Florence to copy Botticelli's *Spring*) be called artists? Are the workers in the Tientsin Watch Factory who did a huge needlepoint tapestry of a young Mao looming forth between the sea and the sky, his coat swept back by the wind, creators of fine tapestry,

* "By criticizing the old, the proletariat creates the new and by criticizing the old world, it establishes a new one. The weapon we use in this criticism is the proletarian conception of the world," Mao has stated. The "great revolutionary criticism" movement which emerged from this analysis was a crucial element in the Cultural Revolution, making criticism a product of the expression and practice of the masses. In fact, the consolidation and the penetration of a revolutionary line cannot be accomplished by administrative fiat or by simply changing leaders. Any attempts to make changes must be done by critically appraising the situation, which is the only way the new world can arise. Even in the artistic and cultural field, the masses are continually encouraged to sharpen their critical ability so that they can confront all problems and wage a *relentless struggle* against the old conceptions, which are incompatible with the socialist infrastructure and superstructure.

like Lurçat? Certainly not. And yet, the longer I am in China, the more I get a feel for what art is through what I see expressed in drawn and written forms. This includes those panels where Mao's handwriting has been copied almost to perfection in characters cut out of gold and silver paper and pasted on red material (representing hours and hours of work, done the way Roman artists used to work), along with paper flowers, and poppies and sunflowers, sometimes sculpted from wood or plaster and then painted.

The tatzupao combine writing and painting. Each one represents a creative effort on the part of its creator, an effort which one could call *art*. Sometimes the creators stay up nights writing, pasting, painting images and characters, presenting their ideas in the best form, the one most pleasing to the eye. You could say that they are artists, journalists, and writers all rolled up into one. Among all of the new art forms which are being born in China today, the tatzupao seem to me to have the potential of becoming mass art. This occurred to me less in the factories than when I saw tatzupao plastered on street walls for miles in the big cities like Shanghai. I am convinced that the "involvement" of hundreds of thousands of people in making these posters has an artistic value. I could artistically make an *aesthetic* comparison between the writing and the designs which went with it. Even if Mao's slogan stays the same, the final product is always the result of *individual* inspiration.

Isn't the theater as it is performed by the masses another form of aesthetic communication? The seven or eight revolutionary works are known by heart. They are sung and danced by millions of people, young and old. Everyone I saw in the Peking Heavy Machinery Factory day-care center, the May 7 Cadre School, the kindergarten in the Shanghai workers' district, Peng Pu, and in faraway communes, could imitate, either well or poorly, the songs and actions of Yang, the hero in *Tiger Mountain*, the dances from *Red Detachment of Women*, from *The White-Haired Girl* (which is now a ballet), and the ballads from the Shanghai opera, *On the Docks*.

What's more, people sometimes put their self-criticisms into verse, creating a sort of collective theater to express common feelings, to increase the importance of the self-criticism while keeping it in bounds and preventing the experience from being cruel for the people in question. At Tsinghua University, the deputy secretary of the party made his own self-criticism by reciting the self-criticism in verse of Comrade Wu Tien, who had been with him at the base area of Yenan. Wu Tien's self-criticism had been recited during a theatrical presentation for the peasants of a Kiangsi agricultural enterprise where Wu Tien had gone to re-educate himself by working in the fields. In this collective monologue, which apparently was very well received by the Kiangsi peasants and which is presently being given elsewhere, Wu Tien narrates his ups and downs and those of Tsinghua University.

> While wielding the scythe I reflect carefully.
> The experience of history cannot be forgotten.
> Thirty years ago I was in Yenan,
> I followed Chairman Mao, I followed the party.
> After Liberation, after returning to the city,
> I found no trace of the scythe or the shoulder pole.
> With his "six black theses," three of which refer to the party,
> Liu poisoned the cadres: it is an inexcusable crime.
> The president was fiercely ambitious, he considered himself
> the king of Tsinghua.
> He had made of Tsinghua a huge vat
> of revisionist hue.
> By following the president
> I took the path of error,
> I floundered in the revisionist swamp.
> We constructed buildings several stories high,
> we lived in Western houses.
> I got used to prestige, to privilege,
> I acted the bureaucrat and the patriarch.
> After more than ten years of "peaceful evolution"
> there wasn't a trace left of worker or peasant spirit.
> On July 27, Chairman Mao called on
> the working class to assume its leadership role, and
> I was brought back to the revolutionary line of Chairman Mao.
> Fearing neither the boiling sun nor calluses on my hands,
> neither shooting pains in the kidneys, nor sore legs,
> nor serpents' stings,
> full of energy and a strong determination to struggle,
> each stroke of the scythe is a forceful stroke against
> Liu Shao-chi: each stroke expels old ideas.

If you asked me what the Chinese do in their spare time, I would say that they put on revolutionary theatrical performances, play the parts of the heroes of the people, sing or play the music for these parts, draw and paint, write poetry on and compose music for Mao's directives. They are incredibly romantic and revolutionary. Millions of them are protagonists in their own lives. They embody what Chiang Ching, Mao's wife, said about art in a speech in 1966: "We must combine revolutionary realism with revolutionary romanticism in our creative work." This revolutionary realism is completely different from the "socialist realism" of the past.

The statuettes of Tientsin

In the late afternoon, after an exhausting day, we are finally given permission to visit a *real* art center, the Tientsin Academy of Fine Arts. We had expressed a desire to see the famous terra cotta figurines of Tientsin (*Ni jen*), but didn't think our request would be granted. These figurines were created by the artisan Chang during the nineteenth century. He modeled clay figures of well-known personnages from Chinese literature and mythology, as well as of the common people, then baked them and painted them. I had seen some of them in 1954 at the Summer Palace Museum. Pierre Loti says somewhere that figurines of Western soldiers were sold in Tientsin and surrounding areas after Allied troops passed through in 1900. Some of them had "ferocious expressions," but the French ones were friendly looking because of their yellow and brown silk mustaches. Some of the figurines even carried a Chinese child in their arms. The Tientsin Academy of Fine Arts was closed during the Cultural Revolution. Built during the fifties, it is a marble building with grand and high bay windows and a main entrance which solemnly opens into a garden surrounded by a peristyle. The architectural style is triumphal in the Stalinist manner. We enter the building on the ground floor, through a kind of service entrance, into a big square room which is in back of the main building. Ten or twelve artisan-artists are working in silence. The animation and the curiosity which accompanied our other visits are overwhelmed by the deafening silence. The artists continue to work, heads lowered.

"The statuettes of Tientsin used to represent emperors, dancers, and courtesans. Now they are ordinary common people," says the representative.

"Who are the artists?"

"They are artisans who formerly owned private art shops in Tientsin, students, sculptors, and art teachers."

"Why don't you want to show them to us?"

"Because we are in the process of experimenting with a new figurative art," the comrade says. "We have made an effort to do you a favor."

The sculptors work surrounded by an enormous crowd of natural-sized statues of men and women from the old China which clutter the icy cold room. Peasants pulling plows behind them "like oxen and horses," crushed under back-breaking pressure; peasants paying taxes to the landlords' stewards, half-dead in their rags; skeleton-like women with babies tightly clasped to their breasts; the landowner's feared overseer with a whip (real) in his hands, behind his back, and a cigarette (also real) hanging out of his mouth; Kuomintang soldiers torturing the peasants. The artists very cleverly and scrupulously copy the people from old photographs, digging into the soft brown clay with their small spatulas and knives. They put in despairing eyes of black and yellow, the only non-clay material to go into these sad-looking people from the old China. The same statues, only these are six to eight inches high, the traditional height for Chang figurines, are lined up on a long counter. They include present-day heroes, soldiers from the People's Liberation Army, workers, peasants, women soldiers, and Red Guards. The arrangement of both the big and small statues make complete tableaux. The history of China under feudalism. The exploitation of the peasants and the revolt against the landowners. The War of Resistance against Japan. Finally, the Cultural Revolution. I had seen some of the small terra cotta figurines last spring at an exhibition at the Guimet Museum in Paris presented by courtesy of the Chinese Embassy, but as they stand here all together, they give a totally different impression. A shot of energy flows from these huge human forms, half-alive, modeled from the soft clay of the earth.

Artistically, they resemble certain eighteenth-century Neapolitan nativity scenes and some of Gemito's sculptures of the Italian people, or, in a more general way, our Romantic, Neo-Classical, and Naturalist periods. The statues are a product of the *revolutionary romanticism* created by the Cultural Revolution. "Our work must show our arduous struggles and heroic sacrifices, but must also express revolutionary heroism and revolutionary optimism," Chiang Ching said in that same speech. Lin Piao wrote in the introduction to the report of this discussion:

> The last sixteen years have witnessed sharp class struggles on the cultural front . . . Which side will win is still unknown. The bourgeoisie will certainly take over the mantle of art and literature in China if the proletariat doesn't claim it first. This struggle is inevitable. It is here, in the domain of ideology, that the socialist revolution is extremely vast and profound.

The artists continue to model the docile human clay with their hands and their tools, eyes still lowered. The representative of the revolutionary committee is a soldier from the People's Liberation Army. The army seems to be a kind of guardian of ideology here. The revolutionary committee also includes seven or eight artists, artisans, and revolutionary teachers.

"Do you also do sculpture?" I ask the soldier.

"No, I study Mao's Yenan speeches on art and literature with the artists."

"What principles guide you in the artistic work here?"

"We follow the principle that revolutionary art and literature 'can and ought to be on a higher plane, more intense, more concentrated, more typical, nearer the ideal, and therefore more universal than actual everyday life,' " he says, quoting from a 1966 discussion of Mao's. "Reality isn't everything. We must not limit ourselves to real people and things."

Mao in fifteen colors

The Hangchow Silk Factory is located on the edge of a lake in the middle of some weeping willows; it produces silk tapestries with

Mao woven in them in fifteen colors. A new technique invented by the workers produces the tapestries. Using 56,000 perforated cards in an electronic process, 500 automatic machines weave the political portrait of China around the clock. Some of the designs reproduce exactly, from official photographs, Chinese and Marxist leaders, finely woven in multicolored silk. The workers have also reproduced the famous scene of Mao in Yenan after the Ninth Congress on a silk tapestry which measures five by seven feet.

"This is the first time the factory has made tapestries as large as this and in fifteen colors," Comrade Chen from the revolutionary committee tells me.

You can hear the fast hum of thousands of machines as the full beards of Marx and Engels, Lenin's small goatee and Mao's head crowned with a military cap appear. The factory also weaves events into tapestries, such as Mao making his May 20 speech, Mao in his bathrobe ready to take the famous swim in the Yangtze River, Mao and Lin Piao seated at a table with teacups on it, Mao writing his first tatzupao, "Bombard the Headquarters," Mao, Lin Piao, and Chou En-lai on the podium of Tien An Men square saluting the crowd with their arms raised, and Mao playing ping-pong. The factory also does Mao's poems, but not in color. The Nanking Bridge, scenes of Hangchow, and Tien An Men square are produced in bright colors. The factory has 1,700 workers who work three shifts, day and night, to fill orders from all over China.

"We are able to produce enough tapestries to satisfy all the demands of the workers, peasants, and soldiers. Everybody wants tapestries of Mao, of other Chinese leaders, and of socialist achievements. The new weaving process, first developed by the factory to make traditional tapestries for the old society, has been very well received by the masses. This factory used to do only scenes of emperors, dignitaries, dancers, and the favorites of the Court. And these tapestries were in black and white only."

Comrade Chen has gray hair, her shorts and her jacket are loose, and she has a cold and blows her nose. A humid breeze blows off the lake.

"We send tapestries all over the country," she continues. "Black and white tapestries cost 3 yuan—a little more for the twelve-inch-square size. Every worker has bought one for his home."

The most beautiful tapestries, multicolored and larger, are rolled up in elegant-looking bolts tied with red silk ribbons. They cost just over 6 or 7 yuan. All the shops in China carry them. We saw people gathered around the counters asking the clerk to show them. The clerk unrolls them. The people comment on the best way to put them up, then they choose one and buy it, according to their taste and which political scene they want to have at home to look at everyday. The really big tapestries (like the famous "Gobelins" French tapestries) are found in official reception rooms, in train stations, in offices of the revolutionary committees, and in hotels. There is a long silk wall hanging in our room in the Shanghai Hoping Hotel: a smiling Mao sits in a wicker armchair in front of the Summer Palace lake; he gazes at us as if to welcome us.

7

Another Model for Industrialization

If the masses are fully aroused, and proper arrangements are made, it is possible to carry on both the Cultural Revolution and production without one hampering the other . . .

—*Decision of the Central Committee of the Chinese Communist Party Concerning the Great Proletarian Cultural Revolution* (August 8, 1966)

The Central Committee of the Chinese Communist Party offers its congratulations to all the workers, to all the officers and soldiers of the People's Liberation Army, to the revolutionary cadres, the scientists, engineers, and technicians, and to the people's militia, who participated in the research and the realization of the launching of the satellite. . . . It hopes they will remain modest, avoid haughtiness and hastiness, that they will continue their research with conscientiousness and diligence, that they will work in perfect collaboration, will redouble their efforts to develop Chinese science and technology ever further . . .

—Message of the Central Committee on the launching of the second satellite, March 3, 1971

The Cultural Revolution is a strategy for economic development; it is not yet development itself. It is the taking-in-hand of the management of industry and the progress of technology by the workers, side by side with the technicians and scientists. Thus, between 1966 and 1969 (the year of the great industrial revival), everything was begun anew at the base and directives were enriched by the experience of the masses; but enormous material difficulties remained, preventing these from having their full effect. The thing that most astounds in China, as you move closer and closer to the problems of the country, is the vastness and the simultaneousness of the tasks undertaken by the working class. The working class carried through the Cultural Revolution, created the revolutionary committees, fought the rigidity of the party, rebuilt party organs by calling assemblies to elect them; it re-educated the cadres and educated the young; it kept industries running by bringing in a new kind of management; it reorganized production in such a way as to make workers and technicians collaborate, and restructured the division of labor; it achieved great industrial advances, technical conquests whose culmination, of course, was the launching of the satellite. All of this would have been impossible without a political and theoretical line that was constant—the line of Mao Tse-tung, which has been nourishing the Chinese masses for a half century. Mao has sometimes had to carry out tactical corrections, but the guiding ideas, from 1926 on, have been essentially the same: they are *ideas the Chinese know*, and they are the ideas which determined the Cultural Revolution after 1966.

To understand this mighty movement of technical innovation, one must think of it in three stages. The first was the Great Leap Forward, between 1958 and 1960, and was a desire to transform everything. Difficulties were underestimated, political and economic obstacles were serious, but the line was fundamentally correct. The second stage was that of the years 1964–1965: despite difficulties in running industries, technical plans were beginning to be carried to completion; the workers created prototypes, but often the prototypes could not be mass produced, production and marketing proving too expensive. The third stage, from 1966 to 1969, was the Cultural Revolution itself. The technical-innovation groups—technicians, workers, and cadres—took the prototypes and moved them from the stage of project to the stage of product, managing to cut down production costs. This success is presented as the outcome of a struggle between two camps: the originators of the projects, mostly workers, and "reactionary cadres." The workers win. The working class takes over the administration of enterprises, of the university, of the whole school system.

This did not happen without, here and there, a certain confusion. China is a huge crucible in which precious metals are being boiled to purge them of their impurities. The impurities themselves will be used, but first the nature of the new alloy must be discovered. The Chinese are themselves careful about sketching the new industrial model they are trying to create: first because they are modest; then because they realize that once the apparatus which put them in danger of falling into a traditional technological web has been destroyed, the new solution, the solution of liberated human energies, can only be created in day-to-day practice and with constant re-examination. They know the difficulties of a class struggle which fails to pause during the transitional period, which can destroy what it is creating if the danger of division is not constantly countered, if faith is not placed above all in the political commitment of the masses. Managers of enterprises, plunged back into production, did not undergo the trauma one can imagine they would undergo in our society if that happened to them; but—and this is understandable—one senses an unease in them, a tenseness. Indeed, the visitor who arrives in China has the impression of a fever in a mighty body. A revolution has taken place, ending in the defeat of millions of men. Can they willingly accept the role of defeated people? The re-education of the cadres has been almost 100 percent successful, but has this not cost the society an exaggerated political effort? And the revolutionary committees subject to recall, the compulsory work for their members—these will be inadequate to the task if there is not a healthy political climate in the factories, if the line is not steadily nourished by correct politics. Thus the tenseness I have spoken of.

Everything is founded upon an untiring development of man, on the slogan "politics in command"; on the twin aims: destroy the past and construct the future. When the construction phase is further along, many obstacles will have fallen; the essential transformation of the superstructure will have been achieved: The future will be different. In ten or fifteen years, the Cultural Revolution in the schools and universities will have produced a new generation of technicians shaped by a new ideology. Already political work and manual work are part of their studies, from the first days of their schooling. Already they see no qualitative difference between the technician and the worker.

The Chinese wish is, in a few dozen years, "to transform China into a modern industrial power which will have all that the foreign world has, plus that which does not yet exist." But industrialization is another "protracted war." The strategic line China has chosen for its industrial revolution contains several key principles which I will try to elucidate here by drawing on Taching, the example of industrialization singled out by Mao,* and on the most recent Chinese documents on the subject: "China's Road of Socialist Industrialization" (*Peking Review*, no. 43, 1969), drafted by the Peking Revolutionary Committee; "Simultaneously Develop Big and Small and Medium Enterprises" (*Peking Review*, no. 48, 1970), drafted by the Writing Group of the State Capital Construction Commission; "Vigorous Development of Small Industry" (*Peking Review*, no. 6, 1970), drafted by the Revolutionary Committee of Honan; and "The Road Forward for China's Socialist Agriculture (*Peking Review*, no. 7, 1970).

The basic principles of the Chinese strategy can be stated this way:

1. Politics is at the heart of everything, and political work is the core of all economic work. The only guarantee of socialist industrialization is if proletarian politics does not cease. Politics must be in command of industrial production. In his report to the Ninth Congress, Lin Piao said:

---

* Taching: A famous Chinese petroleum complex which is held up as an example to Chinese industry, as Tachai is held up to agriculture. Its development began in the Great Leap Forward and sprang from the principle of "self-reliance," and was hence in sharp opposition to the right-wing ideas of Liu Shao-chi. He wanted big industrial centers, heavily concentrated, tightly specialized, monopolistic. When oil was discovered, a few workers built the whole installation using whatever resources they had at hand. They refused to repeat the old industrial patterns of economic management in which industrial needs outweighed those of agriculture and gobbled up state investments. After the factory had been planned, families, mostly peasant, were brought in. Whereas families in town led largely parasitic lives, here they helped build houses on the rural model, and planned agricultural production according to the needs of the community. They are a living picture of the fusion of workers and peasants. From the start the schools followed the "half studies, half industrial or agricultural work" line. And the very management of the complex was a revolution along Cultural Revolutionary lines. All the top-level cadre did unskilled work, together with the unskilled workers. Taching has achieved the fusion of city and country, workers and peasants, intellectuals and manual workers, leadership and masses.

> Politics is the concentrated expression of economics. If we do fail to make revolution in the superstructures, fail to arouse the broad masses of the workers and peasants, fail to criticize the revisionist line, fail to expose the handful of renegades, the enemy agents, capitalist roaders in power, and counter-revolutionaries, and fail to consolidate the leadership of the proletariat, how can we further consolidate the socialist economic base and further develop the socialist productive forces.

2. The rapid industrialization China needs has been described by Mao in *On the Correct Handling of Contradictions Among the People* (February 1957). Here is where any analysis of Chinese industry must begin.

> In discussing our path to industrialization, I am here concerned principally with the relationship between the growth of heavy industry, light industry, and agriculture. It must be affirmed that heavy industry is the core of China's economic construction. At the same time, full attention must be paid to the development of agriculture and light industry.

In a land of 500 million peasants, it is impossible to do what Stalin did in Russia, which Mao specifically condemned: "Soviet agricultural policy has always been wrong: to catch the fish, the lake was dried out." China's strategy is a balanced development of industry and agriculture. It is "necessary to walk on two feet." China renounces the idea of collecting a surplus, a tithe, from the countryside—something Stalin considered a "historical necessity" (see his report to the Central Committee of July 1928) to achieve *socialist primitive accumulation*. Mao, on the other hand, said that the revolution triumphed thanks to the help of the peasants, and industrialization must count on their contribution to bring off victory.

In making "agriculture the foundation and industry the leading factor," the Chinese believe they have correctly resolved the great problem of the dictatorship of the proletariat: that of the relations between the two great classes of working people, workers and peasants, and the alliance between these two classes. The following is from the document drafted by the Peking Revolutionary Committee:

> There are two ways of developing heavy industry. One is to neglect light industry and agriculture. . . . The other, the one urged by Mao,

consists of paying greater attention to light industry and agriculture. When light industry and agriculture are developed, they will be able to satisfy the daily needs of the population. . . . With a developed agriculture, industry can be supplied with greater quantities of raw materials, and provided with markets for industrial products, especially those of heavy industry, which could then develop on a more solid base.

3. To progress rapidly, industrialization must develop large and small industry simultaneously: "The law of development of things is always from small to big and from lower to higher." The document on the development of large, small, and medium-sized industries, published at the end of 1970, begins with a quote from Mao:

> We must build up a number of large-scale modern enterprises step by step to form the mainstay of our industry, without which we shall not be able to turn our country into a strong modern industrial power within the coming decades. But the majority of our enterprises should not be built on such a scale; we should set up more small and medium enterprises and make full use of the industrial base left over from the old society, so as to effect the greatest economy and do more with less money.

Hence the creation of big industries, but linked to small and medium-sized ones. The Chinese believe big industries in isolation are like "bones without flesh," and cannot play their proper role or fully serve. The State Capital Construction Commission declared, in the same document:

> One of the major reasons Shanghai has developed its industry so fast, achieved such a high value of industrial output, and become China's top producer of complete sets of machinery, is that it unswervingly adheres to this principle of simultaneously developing big and small and medium enterprises, making the big ones the mainstay and building large numbers of the latter.
>
> Shanghai's machine-building industry is mainly one of small and medium plants. Thirty percent of the city's machine-building plants are bigger ones which produce the main machines and complete products. Forty percent turn out auxiliary machines and parts, and the remaining 30 percent take on odd jobs and tasks to meet the needs of the others' technological processes. Working in close coordination with each other, like a field army, regional army, and guerrillas, they form a powerful fighting force.

4. To industrialize quickly, China had to decentralize; and this made it possible to encourage initiative from the base, to give free rein to the ingenuity of the masses and to self-management by the communes and provinces: everywhere, small and medium-sized enterprises were born of local initiative, and they have kept much of their autonomy. "The localities should endeavor to build up independent industrial systems," Mao said. "Where conditions permit, coordination zones, and then provinces, should establish their own relatively independent and varied industrial systems." The development of heavy industry, now in full swing, follows its own strategic concept: "Sharpen our vigilance, defend our motherland," and "Be prepared for war, be prepared to deal with natural calamities."

In speaking of the document on industrialization, we could speak of *strategic decentralization*:

> Let each region, each province draft its plan in case of war; local administrations must create autonomous industrial systems. First the regions, then the provinces, must create industrial systems that are relatively independent, considering both the rational distribution of industry and its overall development. If American imperialism and social-imperialism impose war on our people, we will be ready with many industrial bases, big, small, solid, inextinguishable. We will be able to bear the war, wipe out the enemy, and win.

Let us not forget that China has an area of about 3.6 million square miles.

All over China we saw the construction of little steel mills, fertilizer factories, cement works, small food-processing plants, agricultural implement repair shops. We saw, everywhere, people prospecting for coal, oil, all on local initiative. Small enterprises exploit natural resources on the spot (refining sugarcane, for example) and save on transport. At Hangchow they found coal and gave the lie to the proverb "No coal south of the Yangtze." Provinces, communes create industries. The Chinese tell you that economic profit is certain, that transport costs are cut. The furthest and most underdeveloped regions are rendered useful by such small industries. The production of automobiles and of vehicles of all sorts began in twenty different places. The auto industry of Kiangsi began with some small workshops and has produced 500 trucks in very little time. In the autonomous regions, where transport used to be by animal, the technicians and workers conceived and constructed a new type of vehicle. The same was true in Chinghai, a region which not very long ago had exactly forty ancient foreign cars. Fertilizer and cement produced by small plants today represent one-third of the national production. Every commune produces several kinds of grain, so as to be independent in case of calamity or war. Alongside the people's communes we visited there had sprung up a whole series of industries which tied industry in with agriculture, reintegrated the two, and helped the mechanization of the farms. They told us in Shanghai that over 80 percent of Chinese districts have themselves created plants for the construction and repair of farm machinery. In twenty provinces they turn out tractors of different types, adapted to local needs. In many regions agricultural machines are constructed using local products: steel, cast iron, factory machinery, fuel, energy. With the increase in the number of drilling pumps in Hopei, the number of wells is two and a half times greater than the number of wells drilled before the Cultural Revolution.

5. Chinese industrialization does not tend toward centralization, but rather builds on the greatest possible development of the forces of production. The Chinese do not limit themselves to developing an essentially agricultural economy designed to meet the needs of 700 million people. They have launched their heavy industry and their light industry—a modern industrial operation whose efficiency we shall see demonstrated further on, with figures; and at the same time they have created a multitude of small and medium-sized industries which are beginning to mechanize the countryside. This industrialization is not centralized, not at all—even if the state obviously does coordinate local initiative and achievements. "One of the superiorities of socialism," Charles Bettelheim writes, "is its ability to follow a model of industrialization based on the greatest possible development of the forces of production." It seems to me that this is exactly what the Chinese are doing. Bettelheim continues:

> Centralized industrialization, using modern techniques, requires a high investment for each worker and thus does not permit giving

modern means of production to more than a minority. Otherwise stated: at the beginning of industrialization, you can get together material means to equip 10 or 15 percent of the population. This minority receives ultra-modern means of production, while the rest of the population continues to produce with inadequate instruments, especially in the agricultural sector.

Centralizing highly perfected means of production in the hands of a small minority of workers reproduces the capitalist mode of development; for capitalist development does not care about the development of the forces of production, but only about that of the enterprise or group of enterprises where the means of production are concentrated.

The liberation of the forces of production—the alternative—makes working-class creativity explode. At the base of this burst of ingenuity and originality is a confidence in the strength of the working class, a confidence that it cannot only create new machines, but improve the old, repair them, realize miracles in the thrifty use of them.

According to the economist Jack Gray:

> One of the essential characteristics of the economic thought of Mao is the importance he gives to the spirit of initiative . . . to the courage to "dare." In most enterprises where the Maoist line works, there is a person or a small group within the collective who thought up a new idea and persuaded the collective to adopt it after taking the risk of trying it himself. There can be no doubt that the Maoist perspective sees the spirit of initiative within the collective organization of industry as the key to rapid development; it is a basic of Maoist education.

We must again underline the difference between this and Soviet Stakhanovism. Stakhanov worked at unequaled speed and never lifted his eyes to look around at his comrades-in-work—or to look into the running of the enterprise, either. Individual devotion to his work, but a complete rupture with the collectivity. In China, on the contrary, individual work and collective work remain tightly intertwined.

The Chinese say Liu Shao-chi wanted to draw on the capitalist experience in managing enterprises, and above all on the management of monopolies; he believed that a link with highly developed countries was indispensable for a country that was underdeveloped, little industrialized. Mao replies that "China cannot follow the same path to develop its technology, cannot follow other countries at a snail's pace," nor depend financially and politically on them. What is to be done? "Rely on your own efforts." For the Chinese, this is the only way of escaping the characteristic evolution of societies born of the industrial revolution. In "China's Road of Socialist Industrialization" we read:

> Capitalist countries industrialized themselves by pillaging their colonies, imposing war reparations on defeated lands, and borrowing from other countries. Their industries are built on the bodies of millions of people.
>
> Social-imperialism openly begs investments from capitalist countries; and at the same time, under the banner of "economic integration" and "aid" it plunders wealth created by workers of other countries.
>
> Our country is socialist. It is guided by Marxism-Leninism and the thought of Mao Tse-tung. It cannot and does not want to resort to pillage to develop its industry. It will never permit neglect of the interests of the people, nor sell its people to develop industry. It is solely by counting on its own strength and on the creativity of the masses that our country will construct itself, with work, frugality, and sacrifice.
>
> To build socialism, a country must and can count on the labor of its people. Naturally, reciprocal aid, economic cooperation between friendly countries (one supplying the other with what it needs) are necessary. But the principle of the mutual respect of national sovereignties, or equality, of respect for the reciprocity of interests, must be adhered to. This cooperation can in no case replace the work of the people.

Transform and use all scrap and leftovers: industrialization needs everyone's effort, but it also needs the infinite re-employment of the existing potential. Technological renewal also means the maximum extension of the life of machines. Another political principle of industrial production is *total use.* When you look at the Chinese production system, you think of Lavoisier's axiom: "Nothing is destroyed, nothing is created." This principle applies to industry, in Chinese factories large and small. All industrial waste is scrupulously recovered and reused. "In making one product, resources are partially transformed into this product and the rest becomes 'waste,'" says an article in the *Peking Review* of February 5, 1971. It continues:

> The question is how to look at this "waste," from which point of view and with what attitude. From the metaphysical point of view, waste cannot be used and should be gotten rid of. On the contrary, the materialist dialectical view holds that what is waste and what is not waste are relative terms. There is nothing in the world which is absolute waste. "Waste" under one condition may be valuable under different ones. "Waste material" left from one product can become good material for another product. After being transformed and utilized, "waste material" can become a product or a useful material.

In a Canton commune, we saw the smoke of a lime furnace reclaimed to provide calcium carbonate, usable in pharmaceuticals and toothpaste manufacturing.

But we saw the most extraordinary example of this in a Canton paper plant which employs 300 workers. The recovery of waste is exemplary. Mao visited the plant in 1956, read the plant paper, and listened to the workers' proposals for re-using waste. I saw an unusual photo of Mao on his visit, in baggy pants belted at the waist and an open-necked shirt, talking with a worker near a machine. The paper factory adopted the principle "Participate in the revolution by observing the strictest rule of economy, wasting nothing where a technique of synthesis can be found." Another photo of Mao: he is pointing at a cart of garbage and talking to the workers. I am told that the paper mill manages to save 400 cubic meters of wood a year, and to make 200 more tons of paper with them. Further, by recycling the wood fiber and water used in making the paper, they obtain pine resin and sulphuric acid, which are then used in making synthetic fibers; and now they're thinking of extracting alcohol from liquid waste. At present the wood fiber is channeled underground to the place for recycling. Scraps of paper are immediately taken to a boiling vat which makes wrapping paper from them. The water used in papermaking is boiled too; with chemicals added, and purified, it makes vanilla powder! We were told that the workers have learned not only how to eliminate waste so as to avoid pollution, but how to make waste useful and beneficial.

The line the Chinese have chosen—a refusal of capitalist accumulation, of oppressive technology—may seem in contradiction with certain terrible pictures we have before our eyes: of men stripped to the waist, harnessed with straps, dragging huge tree trunks onto massive vehicles in Nanking. It may seem in contradiction with the scarcity of tractors, with the one-blade plows being pulled by buffaloes, with the manual irrigation of immense expanses, using water buckets hanging from yokes. But China did not choose its road by thinking of its underdevelopment. It was the choice of a young country, one that has already accomplished two socialist revolutions, one that has carried through the longest socialist revolution the world has known, one that is reaching a very advanced stage of economic construction. China is attacking the problem of the organization of work by calling forth a huge collective effort; it is its attempt to escape the contradictions and handicaps of the underdeveloped world, and especially to free itself from all dependence on the technically developed world. In terms of economics, a country of the Third World could not have made a better choice: its fundamental resource was human capital, and that is the one it is using. Economic cooperation—the line opposed to Mao—was leading straight to subordination. Relations with the socialist countries themselves were a negative experience. China verged on catastrophe after break with the USSR and the withdrawal of Soviet technicians. To follow any other path than the one outlined by Mao meant political defeat, throwing into question the whole revolutionary future of China. We would have seen the development of a class of technocrats, a new division between rich and poor. China's unity, its most precious possession and the fruit of a hard liberation struggle, would have broken down into a split between city and country.

China's economic power

Here are a few statistics which indicate the progress of China's science and technology.

Chinese technology is changing fast. Its successes in the atomic arena and in space are remarkable: hydrogen bomb (June 17, 1967); first launching of a satellite (April 24, 1970); second satellite, weighing almost 500 pounds (March 3, 1971). These accomplishments imply progress in physics, electronics, metallurgy, computers, precision instruments, automation, chemistry, and telecommunications. The simultaneous launching of satellites and the development of the economy show Khrushchev was wrong when he said that if they invested in space, the Chinese would "end up without a shirt."

Of course, we don't have all the facts we would need to evaluate the Chinese atomic program, or even the overall economic plan. But the figures on China's technical evolution are available. Chinese magazines print them; we were given some during our trip, at the Industrial Exhibition in Shanghai and at the Canton Trade Fair. So we can draw up a balance sheet, not definitive but impressive, on Chinese technical development. We shall also use some overall indicators, the first published, on Chinese economic development: we owe them to Edgar Snow's report on his conversation with Chou En-lai. Other figures come from the Scientific Research Office of the French Ministry of Industry.

Metallurgy

The withdrawal of Soviet technicians struck a hard blow to Chinese industry. Soviet aid had made it possible to build, in their entirety, 150 factories, including the Changchun Truck Factory and the Loyang Tractor Factory. A hundred and five others were planned. Chinese technicians and workers had to make superhuman efforts to keep up production; there were periods of stagnation and numberless other difficulties. The metallurgical industries suffered most, and their problems continued up until 1969.

The Chinese then developed a method for making a low-alloy steel, and made it into a very durable metal. This is the steel which went into the bridge at Nanking. The Chinese produced thirty times as much of it in 1969 as in 1965, and in 1970 they made over

20 million tons.* The modernization of techniques is continual. The metalworkers of Shanghai succeeded in building an automatic converter using injected pure oxygen which compares well with the best that other countries have produced. Oxygen-injection steel furnaces, rotary oxygen converters, powerful blast furnaces, rare metals: everywhere Chinese industry is progressing and modernizing its methods.**

Electrical construction

Great progress in the field of transformers. In Shanghai we saw a 125,000 kilowatt steam turbogenerator with a double water-cooling system, made in April 1968.

---

* Some people are not convinced that the actual figure of 20 million tons of steel constitutes a success in as much as steel production in 1959 was about 13 million tons. My response is that the figure must be judged within the general context of this entire chapter, and of the section on metallurgy in particular. It is not a question of absolute figures, but of the situation created by the withdrawal of Soviet technicians and equipment and by the enormous effort made to remedy the crisis that threatened as a result. This crisis did not involve industrial production alone, but also agricultural production, and it had to be faced by means of a general political process of restructuring the countryside—the people's communes—and with efforts not only to develop agricultural production, but to resolve the basic historical problem of food supply, of eliminating the differences between city and country. (For more details on this situation, see Appendix.) In such an *economic-political* context, it is justifiable to speak of *success* if, after the drop in steel production in 1965, the Chinese have succeeded in almost doubling 1959 production figures, that is to say, doubling production in comparison with a period when they were receiving aid from a "superpower" as hyperdeveloped and advanced as the USSR! The editorial in the January 1, 1972, *People's Daily* states that in 1971, 27 million tons of steel were produced.

**The continued development in this important sector was underlined in an editorial which appeared on New Years' Day 1972 and was reprinted in the *Peking Review* (no. 1, 1972). The editorial states: "The total output value of China's machine-building industry in 1971 rose 18 percent compared with 1970 and production of major products increased by big margins."

Mining and geology

Mines, too, have been equipped and modernized. Thousands of abandoned mines have been put back into service, new ones opened, new strikes exploited. Geological prospecting is widespread, with the masses aware and participating, which means that previously underdeveloped regions are being opened up to a new activity.*

Electronics, computers, precision tools

The electronic sector is one of those that is experiencing the biggest advances. By 1969, Shanghai had 120 electronics factories, Tientsin about 100. In October 1967, the Institute of Technology and Mathematics perfected the computer needed for atomic and space development. The competence of Chinese physicists is no longer in doubt.

In 1968, micro-electronics appeared. At the Shanghai exhibition we saw a giant electron microscope which enlarges 400,000 times. According to Chinese publications, the value of electronic production increased, depending on the sector, from 80 to 350 percent over the previous year. The electronics industry has made its appearance in Chinghai, Ninhsia, and Tibet. It is present almost everywhere. The massive manufacture of transistors made it possible to perfect industrial machines for the production of silicon monocrystals starting at the beginning of 1970. Since then, socialist cooperation has grown up between the big electronics industry, the "backbone," and the small industries. Many electronics factories have surpassed the national production plan; the Nanking plant, for example, had reached the year's objective at the end of the second quarter. An important effort has been made in the area of laboratory equipment: magnetic resonance and double-ray infrared apparatuses were completed in 1967. At the Canton fair, 90 percent

* The same editorial states that in 1971 "the country's coal output rose 8 percent over that of 1970, production costs were cut and a number of new shafts built."

of the 875 scientific instruments on view were of recent construction.

Mechanical construction

Great progress in shipbuilding was also achieved between 1968 and 1970: freighters of 18,000 to 19,000 tons, two tankers of 15,000 tons in October 1969, six freighters of 10,000 tons launched at a Tientsin construction yard designed for no more than 5,000-ton ships. A 3,200-ton icebreaker was built at Shanghai. Great progress, also, in diesels.

In Shanghai we saw a precision machine tool built during the Cultural Revolution by workers who had previously worked in a cigarette factory (60 percent of them women). An electronically controlled boring mill. An electronic radial drill. A loom operating with compressed air. These machines, built in 1969 and 1970, were in the Shanghai Industrial Exhibition in 1970.

Automobiles and railways

There were some remarkable prototypes exhibited in Shanghai. One was a 32-ton dump truck made with the collaboration of a hundred small factories (imported trucks used to go no higher than 27 tons). Another was the "Shanghai" car, a convertible which resembles a Mercedes and goes up to 95 miles an hour. Still another was the "Shanghai" bus, whose seats can be taken out "to make it into an ambulance in time of war," our guide told us. Speed: 80 miles an hour. But auto production is held in check; all the stress is on public transport.

Auto production is still insufficient. Over twenty provinces participate in this area, turning out prototypes of trucks and cars. There are also new accomplishments in locomotives and electric trains are already in service. A train built in Shanghai is already running on the Hangchow-Shanghai line.

Chemical industry

There has been important progress in fertilizers, in organic chemistry, in pharmaceuticals. Edgar Snow says that the annual fertilizer production is 14 million tons and that it rose greatly between 1969 and 1970. China needs 30 to 35 million tons, and hopes to reach this goal in 1975.

China makes almost all its own antibiotics; experimental production is on a level with the most advanced countries.

Petroleum

For the first time, China is able to meet the needs of its economy, its national defense, its science, and its technology in this area. In 1970 (according to Snow's interview with Chou) China passed the 20-million-ton mark. Production is climbing in the petroleum refineries, and the state plan has been surpassed in gasoline, kerosene, fuel oil, asphalt, etc. The oil industry is exploiting new oil strikes. Crude oil production was up 34 percent in 1970 over the previous year. Over 130 new petroleum products were displayed at the Canton Fair.

Textiles

China is self-sufficient in cotton, wool, and silk. It is the world's leading producer of cotton goods and exports large quanties of them.

Bridges and roads

The Nanking Bridge (road and rail): over four miles long, almost 1 mile of it over the Yangtze. This is the most important achievement in the field, and it was finished in October 1968. A 2,300-foot bridge crosses the Pearl River at Canton. Three other bridges have been built: the road bridge at Liuchou, 2,000 feet long, in reinforced concrete; a railway bridge over the Chang in Anhui, 950 feet long and built in eight months in 1969; and a 4,000-foot road bridge over the Hsinyi in Kiangsu, completed in October 1969.

Neither inflation nor debt: price stability

China has solved the ageless problem of hunger that still haunts the underdeveloped world. From one end of the land to the other, towns, communes, the smallest agglomerations are rich with foodstuffs, fruits, vegetables; prices are absolutely stable, tied to the stability of wages. The population has what it needs to nourish it.

The price of finished products is based on the constant value of the yuan, which was fixed in 1953 (at 2.40 yuan to the dollar) and has not varied since. Domestic prices are stable; some have even dropped. China has no debt, internal or external. All foodstuffs cost less than in any other country.

Bettelheim writes: "A proletarian practice characterizes China in its market relations: it has as its constant preoccupation a financial rigor made of steady or declining prices, and the improvement of the standard of living of the masses through the reduction of the prices of mass-consumed products. This is no fetishism; it springs from respect for the masses' work, respect for their rights."

However, per-capita income in China is still one of the lowest in the world, for a population which, despite its massive use of contraceptives, Snow puts at 800 million. Sihanouk confirms the 800-million figure, though the official one is 700 million.

The direction of Chinese agriculture

After nine years of good harvests, and thanks to fertilizers and irrigation, China produced 240 million tons of grain in 1970—a record. It has reserves of 40 million tons. But China still imports grains, Chou told Snow. This is because "wheat is cheaper than rice on the world market, so it is advantageous for China to exchange some rice for wheat and other products."

For the first time in their history, Hopei, Honan, and Shantung, provinces with a total population of 150 million, are self-sufficient in food.*

Agricultural machinery

The total value of farm machinery in the country went up 22 percent in 1970 over the first half of 1969. The production of the main types of farm machinery increased. Two times as many tractors were produced in the first seven months of 1970 as in all of 1966. China now makes more than a thousand different models of agricultural machinery, or three hundred more than in 1966.

Total value of industrial production in 1970

According to Chou En-lai's statements, industrial production in 1970 can be placed at $90 billion. This figure does not include anything but industry and transportation—not, for example, services. Agriculture accounts for 25 percent of the total value of industry, transport, and agriculture, so Chinese production in these three areas was about $120 billion in 1970.

The overall picture: "Ready if there is war"

In 1967, at the time of the reorganization of industry, the reform of the industrial structure, the "revolution and production" committees, new ideas began circulating among the masses. The overthrow of some old values, the discouragement of others, the audacity of still others, were such that factories often found themselves paralyzed. Sometimes this happened when they had both to transform and to produce. The political struggle, whether acute or limited to serious confrontations, the interruptions of work, also

* In 1971, according to the same editorial quoted above, wheat production reached 246 million tons.

caused bad production tieups. Thus it seems that total production in 1967 was 5 to 10 percent behind 1966 (Chou En-lai said this in a speech in February 1968). In 1968, as we have seen, all production was reorganized and industrial development was tied in with agriculture. The first half of 1969 showed the first positive balance sheets. In 1970, China had a solid domestic situation, a general upturn, and political stabilization. In industry, successes amazed the world, which was awaiting catastrophe. In agriculture, after nine straight years of progress China has harvested the largest crops in its history. Despite the stagnation of 1967–1968, key years of the Cultural Revolution, the objectives of the 1966–1970 Five-Year Plan have been reached, and even surpassed. The success of the Five-Year Plan, indeed its more-than-success, have now been officially announced by the Chinese authorities. "We can say," Chou En-lai told Snow in that interview, "that gains, both in the political consolidation of the leading group and in revolutionary progress, have far outweighed losses." So the Cultural Revolution was a success, not just politically but economically.

Under these conditions, does China feel ready to face a war, if American imperialism and the regime in Saigon continue their aggression? Chou En-lai's trip to Hanoi on March 5, 1971, takes on a clear meaning in this context. It shows that China's economic development after the Cultural Revolution goes hand in hand with a commitment to the fraternal peoples under attack in the Indochinese peninsula. As Chou En-lai said:

> For the past few years China's people have been engaged in a great and profound Proletarian Cultural Revolution, directed in person by Mao. . . . The thinking of our people has been deeply transformed, and a revolutionary dynamic is seen at work everywhere. Our country has victoriously carried out its Third Five-Year Plan for the development of the national economy. Agriculture has had good harvests for nine consecutive years. Industrial production is in full expansion. The dictatorship of the proletariat is stronger and more powerful than ever. Our great leader, Chairman Mao, teaches us the noble spirit of proletarian internationalism. . . . He has said that 700 million Chinese are the strongest ally of the Vietnamese people, and the vast territory of China their surest rear area. This is an essential, firm, and unchangeable principle of our people and of our government, it is the

> principle which guides the acts of all Chinese. Your struggle is our struggle, your difficulties are ours, and your victories are our victories.

And on March 13, 1971, the news of the retreat of Saigon's troops from the Laotian territory into which they had penetrated showed how seriously American imperialism and its acolytes in Southeast Asia take the new China that has come out of the Cultural Revolution.

8

Nanking Has a Very Long Bridge

We are traveling from Peking to Nanking in a very old Ilyushin which dates from the Second World War and which gets off the ground solely because of the adroitness of the Chinese pilot: joints strain almost to the breaking point, and it cuts the air with a concert of squeals. The passenger cabin is no longer pressurized and I begin to feel a sharp pain in the eardrums; so do all the passengers, and we chew and yawn to counteract the difference in pressure. A soldier holds his head in pain and rocks it from side to side. A Japanese family from the Japanese trade commission in Peking is traveling with us: father, mother, and two children. The smallest, chubby and gregarious, comes over and speaks to me in French.

"Do you want to play?" I ask him.

"Yes, but what games do you know?"

"You don't play with the Chinese children?"

"I'd like to, but . . ."

"They don't want to?"

"The People's Militia come and say, 'Go away, don't play with him.' "

"How long have you been living in Peking?"

"Two years."

"Are you sad?"

"Yes, because the Chinese children are good at games, but they never want to play with me."

We and the Japanese family check into a hotel which sits in the middle of a very big park. We have a bedroom and a living room. Everything is arranged with infinite care, but as always the hotel seems deserted, or inhabited by invisible guests. Nanking, which I visited in 1954, is unrecognizable. Full of boulevards, now tree-lined and asphalted, the city is resplendent with light, far from the dark nights of Peking. The city has developed impetuously, the revolutionary committee leaders explain to us in their "simple presentation"—the introductory remarks to every Chinese discussion. Industrial production in Nanking, from Liberation to 1969, has multiplied by sixty. This city, which has 2,600 years behind it, was a parasite before the Revolution; a city where everything was imported, *even matches*, where they used to say that the cars came from ten thousand lands, and where they called oil, machinery, and electrical appliances by foreign names. Now Nanking is living an industrial boom. The corrupt former capital of China has become a great industrial city. The symbol of this development—and that of all of China, not just of Nanking—appears in the conversation of every Chinese; it is represented on thermos bottles and photographed for postcards, woven into Hangchow silks and imprinted on teacups and doormats, designed on bedcovers and printed on bedsheets. It is the *Nanking Bridge*, the technical challenge met by China, a bridge which crosses the Yangtze, straight as a sword, over a length of more than four miles.

Because of the harnessing of the mighty Yangtze, the countryside around Nanking has had good harvests for eight years, and production—two harvests of rice a year and one of wheat—reaches fifteen tons a hectare. This is the highest production in all China. And the Nanking educational boom has been extraordinary too: there are 21 faculties and institutes, over 200 middle schools, and 500 primary schools. And the city is the seat of the revolutionary committee of Kiangsu, a province which has 45 million inhabitants, almost the population of Italy.

Two days from now we will have dinner with one of the leaders of this revolutionary committee. For the moment we begin a voyage across the fields that the Yangtze, as its whim dictates, can render extremely fertile or extremely arid. We are heading for the Coppermine commune, which overlooks an inlet of the river. There the rice harvest has begun. Our car is a historic Zim, the very one Mao used when he came to Nanking in 1963 to conduct an investigation which has remained famous. The driver is the same, too, with his head as round as an apple, and he is only the more modest because he is known as "Mao's driver." "It was a great honor for me. I am a worker, and after the Liberation I became a driver . . ." He wipes his brow as he speaks, and seems to be moved by the memory. In the street people stop to see who the black Zim is carrying. They must be disappointed.

The sight of the streets in the morning is overwhelming: they are congested with carts loaded with tree trunks and pulled by eight people, four on each side, like draft animals, ropes in hand, backs bare, bent in two. Dozens and dozens of human teams—women as well as men—haul great carts of sacks, containers, boxes, furniture. They weave their way among modern trucks and buses. "The streets of Sian," wrote Curzio Malaparte in *Io in Russia e in Cina*, "were crisscrossed without pause, during the day, by long columns of horse-men gripping the shafts of their carts full of bricks, iron rods for the reinforced concrete works, lime, beams, boards, by human livestock under bamboo yokes weighed down by two baskets of bricks."

"China still has to walk a hard road," our friends say, sensing our stupefaction. "Did you think that everything was resolved? You would be mistaken to think that, and we want you to see what our country still lacks, despite its achievements."

Again I turn to look at the crowd in the streets. Many of these men—workmen, masons, workhorses, human beasts of burden—are representatives of the Chinese people who participate in the great revolutionary struggle, and are absolutely equal to the others in ardor and in building China. I say to myself that if the external image is shattering, the *inner cause* is what is important in determining the route China will follow. We see this in each of these men and in the revolutionary committee leader we are to meet the following night.

Coppermine: the struggle between two lines among the peasants

The people's commune called Coppermine covers 42,000 mou (7,000 acres) from the Yangtze to the mountains. Its 28,300 members are divided into 16 brigades and 205 production teams. Irrigation, which was carried out as soon as the collectivization of land had been undertaken, is finally protecting the commune against the old curse of drought if it does not rain, flood if it does. After eight years of good crops, the results this year have been exceptional. Wheat and rice production has reached a half a ton per mou, which has enabled the commune to sell 8,300 tons to the state—a figure which is equal to its total production in 1962. It was also able to build up its reserves of cereal grains: 3,000 tons were stored in granaries, "in case of war and in case of calamity."

The standing committee of the revolutionary committee greets us in its reception room. The peasants seem friendly and alert, and there are three women among them. They look like heroes in a sort of peasant Western. They tell us how they dug two canals from the Yangtze to irrigate their land—each was six miles long—and how the network of small canals is almost one hundred miles long. They established seventeen irrigation centers and eleven reservoirs for times of drought. During the Cultural Revolution, and especially since 1967, they have dug up 7 million cubic feet of earth, as much as in the sixteen previous years.

"This," said Comrade Ling, "is how our land became a land of good harvests, even in times of drought or flood. During the same period, we cut into the mountains to create 14,000 mou of terraces, and we transformed 60,000 mou of swamp into rice paddies. In doing this, we struggled not only against nature, but against class enemies. The old landowner—that is what we call those who have kept the old mentality, even when they no longer own the land—said to us: 'You will change mountainous country into rice fields when the sun rises in the west.' He meant that it was impossible. We tore fields from the mountain during winter; in summer we were too busy. The mountain was hard as marble, and we were forced to use picks. Our hands and feet were bleeding, but Mao's saying—'Each commune is a battlefield'—was enough to keep us going. If our cuts were small, we looked after them ourselves. And even if they were more serious, we didn't think of the pain."

"When did the commune have its most intense period of development?"

"The commune was founded in 1958 and developed during the Cultural Revolution years, joining with a network of small industries which enlarged and multiplied its possibilities. There is a farm machinery repair shop, a factory for refining oils and another for grain products, including Chinese pasta and noodles. There are others for stonecutting, lime-making, and brick-baking. Now there is also a hospital. Irrigation, the treatment of grain and of waste are semimechanized. The commune has had important successes in the homes: over 70 percent of the houses have electricity and 90 percent have a radio. The commune has its own broadcasting station, with several hundred loudspeakers through which we can immediately communicate to our members each directive from Mao and from the Central Committee."

"So your work is ideological too?"

"If we have made many changes," said Comrade Ling, "the greatest is in the ideology of men. We have followed in every detail the example of the Tachai brigade—by caring little for suffering, death, sacrifice, and by relying only on our own strength, exactly like that brigade, pointed to by Mao. To give you an idea, one of our production teams was working on a tiny island in the Yangtze when the river, which was in flood, suddenly threatened to submerge them. More than a thousand members of the commune got together to form a dike; this human dike held, and the peasants who were fighting the flood managed to turn it aside. Then, on this land, we planted rice, and the harvest was better than in 1968. We are not just working for China, but to increase the possibilities of world revolution. We have decided to contribute more and more to the success of the Chinese and world revolutions by carrying the red flag and deepening our study of the thought of Mao Tse-tung."

I don't think that the Chinese once forgot, on our visits to factories or communes, north or south, to draw the close link of interdependence between the Chinese and world revolutions.

Information in the Chinese countryside

We visit the commune's radio station, equipped with receivers and transmitters. It also has its own editorial office for the distribution of articles, directives from the revolutionary committee, and information to the peasants on the life of the commune.

"The voice of the Central Committee comes to us immediately, every day," says Comrade Ling, "and we also receive news on the weather so we can warn the peasants. The masses like the loudspeakers and we have hundreds of them spread through the countryside. Our broadcasts are devoted to reading and explaining the Central Committee directives, the main newspaper articles, and foreign news—especially the heroic struggle of the Vietnamese and Indochinese peoples against American aggression, but also all the struggles going on around the world against American imperialism and the capitalist bourgeoisie. Our broadcasts try to make everyone aware that we must be ready to bear the risk of a war."

The two young women who operate the station tell us that another type of program is made up of directives from the revolutionary committee of the commune, and of news of successes and failures in the commune's experiences, of the harvest situation, and of dangers of natural disaster. No peasant is isolated; the radio lets the members of the commune know what is happening quickly so they can talk it over the same night. It also plays revolutionary hymns and popular songs, and gives sports news and general information. I ask if it also broadcast the proceedings of the Ninth Congress.

"Yes, we certainly did."

"And the speech Mao Tse-tung made to the Congress?"

"We broadcast long excerpts."

"And the constitutional charter of the new National People's Congress, which is being prepared?"

"We are starting to do so."

These dry facts open up a whole new subject. In the West we are told that news is broadcast in China to a limited circle, that it is reserved for a "ruling elite." What we learned in the commune proves that this is false. I recall, for example, that the last Peking correspondent for *Unità* told me that the report *On the Correct Handling of Contradictions Among the People* was not made available to the foreign public until some time after its drafting—the Chairman himself wanting to do some last-minute polishing and correcting. But while our correspondent was waiting for this text, he noticed that the loudspeakers in the countryside were broadcasting it, and had been for a long time. He also noticed that certain phrases had disappeared in the final version. Personally, I was able to see that the "secret or exclusive" facts, such as information on the progress of the economic plan, which we don't get at all in the West, are widely known to the people of China. That this information isn't given to foreigners is another matter. In China, "leaks" do not exist.

I came to realize that the information system in the countryside relies mainly on the radio stations. In 1964, figures reaching the West told of 6.7 million radios and loudspeakers and 11,975 transmitting stations. These figures must have tripled since, especially during the Cultural Revolution. The bulk of the news is broadcast by radio, and it is the instrument Mao's "proletarian headquarters" has always been able to count on. In all the country areas I went to, I saw loudspeakers hanging from posts broadcasting to peasants at work in the fields. If I did not know what they were saying, the fault lay with my lack of Chinese. But what I could understand was that the news of the reopening of diplomatic relations between China and Italy was broadcast everywhere, first by the ordinary radio network and then, as in Coppermine, by all the local stations.

The whole village, and especially the hundreds of children (I don't think the Pill has had much effect in the countryside) comes out to see us. They follow us in a procession, they touch us to see if we react the same way as they do and if we are made from the same stuff, and they want to be photographed with us at every turn. Old peasant women standing in doorways applaud us. Some have hung out the red flag for our visit; others wave the little red book: the harshness of working-class life gives way to peasant demonstrativeness. We enter the commune bookstore, full of Mao's works, Mao badges, Mao photographs.

"Before the Cultural Revolution," one of the woman comrades says, "if a peasant wanted to buy one of the works of Mao he had to go to town, which wasn't easy. Now he can buy them here for a few pennies."

The people of the village have a whole series of shops at their disposal: fabric stores, houseware stores, a bazaar with three thousand items, a carpentry shop, and a bamboo basket-making shop which does beautiful work. The barber and his sons are perched on the doorstep of their shop. There is also a hospital (we will discuss it further in the chapter on medicine), which the peasants are very proud of, and where medical professors from the big cities come to operate. "We don't have to go to Nanking anymore," the women say, "we have everything here." The commune's theater shows the same revolutionary films that are shown all over China. (In even further removed brigades which do not yet have electricity, the projector is run by the tricycles I saw at the Shanghai Industrial Exhibition: pedaling replaces other electric sources.) The commune even has a little "hotel" with two rooms containing bunks covered with red bedspreads, where we are invited to rest if we are tired. The people are poor in dress, their clothes patched, unbelievably patched, with unmatching pieces of cloth neatly sewn together, almost like a harlequin costume. Many children are barefoot. "The standard of living isn't very high here," the leaders tell me, "but as the commune grows . . ." The primacy of politics, in this commune, means that the peasants have given everything they could for the Chinese and world revolution, thinking only later of themselves. And indeed, you can *breathe* the heroic atmosphere. Everyone is determined to do his or her best, whatever the activity. The hog-breeder of the Starlight production brigade proudly tells us that his hog production has almost doubled that proposed in the plan.

After the meal—a peasant feast that goes on and on, and brings burps of satisfaction from our fellow eaters—we go out into the sun to chat. During the Cultural Revolution, the pay system was changed, following the example of the Tachai brigade. Every month each peasant evaluates in money the value of the work he has done; the production team then evaluates the total income, in money and in goods, and divides it among its members. Beyond this, families may cultivate small plots of land: vegetable patches are neatly laid out in back or in front of the peasants' houses. Poor peasants are allowed to sell their surplus from these plots to the commune. These tracts never make up more than 5 percent of the area of the commune. The major farm machinery is supplied by the production team, but peasants buy their own small tools.

How to earn your Chinese Communist Party card at the age of 73

After looking over Coppermine from one end to the other, we attend a small meeting of peasants especially called for us by the revolutionary committee. Here we find the aged Comrade Yang. She is 73, and everyone has told us about her. She is famous in her way: she is the first peasant to have received her party card this year. Head covered with a black scarf, face terribly wrinkled, she has a red-plastic shoulder bag in which she carries her *Quotations from Chairman Mao Tse-tung.*

This old peasant woman begins to tell us her story, a story of all the bitterness of the class struggle between poor peasants and landowners. Between 1966 and 1968, thousands of stories of this kind were presented as lessons to the "successors of the revolution" among the poorest peasants, helping the young realize just how deep is the abyss between them and the hated past. Having heard the horrors of the old society recounted, and the human sacrifices the old knew described, the young feel proud to be "successors to the revolutionary cause."

"My name is Yang Man-kun," the peasant woman says. "Before the Liberation I lived under exploiting landlords who rented me three mou. The harvest from this land was not enough to pay the rent. One day when I was pregnant, during an icy winter, I had to go out to find grass to eat. I gave birth on the mountain, and the baby died of cold. Returning home, I left traces of blood along the trail."

The old woman is crying quietly now, and the young peasant women watch her with tears in their eyes.

"Our life was misery. We did not even have the right to medical treatment when we were sick. The village head said no, we were fine, and we had to work. One day my daughter was sick and I secretly took her to the doctor. Somebody told on us, told the village head we had gone to the doctor, and he was waiting for us when we got back to our shack. We were so frightened that we took the medicines and hid in another house; but he found us, pulled us out, and beat us with a rod. We were in perfectly good health, he said.

My daughter and I fought back, and we were arrested. Since I had no money to pay the rent on the plot, the village head sent me to be a domestic in the landlord's luxurious house, and there I was assigned the worst tasks. I was illiterate, I couldn't go to school. For us, for peasants like us, it wasn't simply a matter of lacking education, we lacked even bread. When the Japanese invaders arrived, they burned my house. Nobody looked after me . . ."

The peasant goes on with the recital of her calvary. She has put the little red book on the table, and now and then she places her hand on it, like old women in Italy with their missals. She must have told this horrible story dozens of times, but everyone listens as if it was the first.

"After the Liberation, Mao saved us from suffering. Our life changed. But the renegade, the traitor to the working class, Liu Shao-chi, that devil, could have plunged us back into the hell we had known. I must say that our class consciousness was not very high. Once they organized a study group for old people, and I thought of joining to get an easier life, to get credit. Later, we took a course on Mao's thought, to recall our past life to us, our sufferings, and to define our future tasks. And I found myself making a revolution in my own ideology. I took part in the great criticism of the renegade Liu Shao-chi. I worked with my hands, dug out the mountain, and carried on my shoulders the rocks I had knocked out with the pick. I was tired, yes, and I would often have liked to rest, or give up. But at night I could not sleep, I was thinking that this desire to rest reflected the individualistic egotism of Liu Shao-chi. So back I went the next day, digging at the earth like the young people. In 1970, to increase production, I prepared fertilizers, digging in the mud of swamps, barefoot in the water. The other peasants wanted me to quit: they said I'd get sick, the cold on my feet would kill me. But I replied, like Mao, that to die for the people had the weight of Mount Tai, and to die for the imperialists the weight of a feather. This year I have become a member of the Chinese Communist Party, and not to be a *bureaucrat,* no, but to serve the revolution. To my last breath I will follow Mao. As long as my eyes are good, I will read Mao. As long as I can hear, I will listen to the directives of Mao. In the evening, when there is a new directive from the Chairman, I dance. I am still illiterate, but I am beginning to be able to read a few sentences. I have a teacher who draws the characters of a quotation from Mao for me, and I carry them around to learn what they mean. I study even as I cook, and it makes me forget to salt the water sometimes, or to drain the rice. My husband asked me: 'Why don't you sleep?' I replied: 'We can do without sleep, but we have to study the thought of Mao.' We both began trying to learn the first quotation in the little red book. But my husband could never remember the second sentence. 'Fine,' he said, 'I won't disturb you anymore when you are studying Mao's thought.'

"I was supposed to participate in a revolutionary criticism group, but my husband was very ill. He cried, he didn't want me to leave him. I finally persuaded him to let me go, telling him that in the old society we could certainly not have lived to be seventy, we owed that to Mao. My comrades wanted me to stay beside my sick husband. I answered: 'The death of my husband would be less important than the activity of the revolutionary criticism group. If my husband dies, the collective will be able to do everything necessary for him.' When I got back to the house my husband could no longer speak. The next day he was dead. There, that is my life, but of course there were a lot of mistakes in the way I told it."

She begins to laugh, to chase away her pain, perhaps, or to avoid betraying her sadness at the memory of the death of her husband. "Mao's driver" watches her, his mouth open; the party official nods; the peasants are tight-faced with emotion.

The student in the bushes

After the old comrade, a young student begins to speak. She is twenty-two, a graduate of a senior middle school, and her name is Sou Kuei-ta. Responding to the call of Mao, she arrived to join the commune brigade on January 22, 1969, in order to share in manual work in the countryside. Her story is that of a revolution lived to the point of physical martyrdom.

"I too," she says, "was imbued with the ideology of Liu Shao-chi, because for twelve years I had attended schools which fed my egotistical ambitions—to go to a university, to become famous. In these schools we didn't participate in the manual work of the countryside, and I would never have been able to carry the slightest load on my shoulders. I underestimated the peasants, I thought they were dirty. With an ideology of that kind, how could I have been a promoter of the proletarian cause? The call of Mao was clear. So I came and plunged into the revolutionary cauldron of the peasant world. The first day I helped transport mud from the swamps. My shoulders ached, and the next day I asked the production brigade to allow me a day of rest. Another morning, when the comrades came to wake me, I pretended I didn't hear them, I didn't get up. I began saying that my health wasn't up to this kind of life. But, not without repugnance, I continued to participate in the work of the brigade. My peasant comrades understood and set up a course in Mao's thought for me: old peasants told me of the atrocities of their pasts, and I was particularly moved by the story of the woman whose eight children died from hunger and sickness. This contrast between the past and the present heightened my class-consciousness and gave me strength. I understood that Mao sends youth among the peasants to test their revolutionary strength. I began carrying loads with more courage; a thousand times, in planting rice, I would have liked to have rested, but I could not help thinking that others would have to do the work if I did not. The head of the brigade explained to me that the revolution is not an easy job. One day I injured my leg while cutting grass, but I told myself I had to go on because others had died for the revolutionary cause. The peasants face the hardest tasks, the harshest work, with courage and humility. And us? Are we not human beings like them? I was climbing the mountain, and it was extremely difficult. To go on, I thought of Yang, the hero of *Taking Tiger Mountain by Strategy.* I fell, I hurt myself; my trouser leg was in rags. But I made it to the top. Now the task was to complete the job by carrying a load of wood back down. I didn't think I could make it, but, remembering Mao, I resolved I would have no more fear, not even of death. And I came back down into the valley with the wood. But I do not want to seem conceited . . ."

While I listen to her reveal without pity her weaknesses, with a sort of destructive passion and a face that is near ecstasy, transported and triumphant, I begin to feel unbearable pain shoot through my ear. Even when the old comrade was speaking my left ear had hurt, and the pain seemed to go through my brain from one ear to the other. I press my left hand against my head, trying to warm the ear. The pain is so great that I am tempted to lie down on the bench I am sitting on, but that would be a sign of weakness and I would be ashamed. As the young student talks of the tests to which she had been put and of her resurrection as a revolutionary, I feel my left ear revolt more and more and half my head turn to lead. Listening to the tale of a march against cowardice, the petty pains of my ear seem to put me on a low rung in the scale of human courage. On a page of my notebook I write a note to my husband: "I feel sick. Please, thank them and let's go." Chao notices—he notices everything.

"What is wrong?"

"I have a bad pain in my left ear."

"You are red in the face; you must have a fever."

Return to Nanking

The next morning I am in the Nanking hospital in the office of Dr. Chen, an ear, nose, and throat specialist whose diagnosis is an inflammation of the middle ear: the ear is very enlarged and has become infected from a cold I had had. The doctor explains that it all—all except the cold—comes from the lack of pressurization in the Ilyushin, and that the eardrum, though much battered by the variations in pressure, does not seem to have burst. She is very efficient and precise, her face finely featured like a miniature, intelligence shining forth, but severe and modest. She examines me, gives me a strong analgesic, puts drops in my ear, and finally administers a strong dose of an antibiotic. In twenty-four hours my temperature is down to 98.6°, and I'm feeling quite a bit less down and out.

Chao and Lu have come to keep me company. They are seated at my bedside and Chao has read me the article in *People's Daily* on the death of General de Gaulle. The story fills two-thirds of the front page, and includes the handwritten message from Mao to the General's widow, as well as Chou En-lai's message. The Chinese are profoundly faithful in friendship. Their homage to de Gaulle—an exceptional honor for a head of state of a capitalist country—is meant as an expression of gratitude to a man who shook the American yoke by defending the independence of his country and by recognizing China. I recall the salon of the Elysée in 1965, the press conference, the emotion around the world. And Chao tells me they called *from Peking* for news of me. They insist that I take care of my health, as if my health were something important, and that I don't move until I have recovered.

Another morning: I get up today to go and look at the Nanking Bridge, the epic of the Cultural Revolution in its struggle between two lines, the triumph of collective management of technology. The bridge is a perfect piece of work: it stands out against the blue and placid river like a steel skyscraper. It has two levels and trains puff across, Mao's face on the sides of the locomotives. I am happy to be up again, and I think that the *internal cause* has triumphed in me, even if I am still a little hard of hearing.

The Nanking Bridge is the Eiffel Tower of China. It is a shrine, so miraculous is the technical achievement it represents. Groups of schoolchildren continually come here; peasants and workers from all regions arrive by the trainloads to visit it, admire it, discuss it. At night it is lit up by a myriad of lamps and spotlights aimed at its enormous steel silhouette, bringing out its metallic blues, phosphorescent, while the Yangtze reflects its splendor.

If you want to know the length of the Nanking Bridge, tell yourself that at one end is Peking, and at the other the peoples of Asia, Africa, and Latin America. This is the idea, essentially political, that Chinese schoolchildren learn about the Nanking Bridge, which reaches the Third World by spanning not just the Yangtze, but whole hostile continents.

Technical information on the bridge is supplied by a soldier of the People's Liberation Army, which is in charge of the administration which oversees the structure. Impossible, as always, to know his rank. As always, one would guess a cook's helper, and he might be a general. From a boat of the Chinese inland fleet we watch as we pass under one of the arches—there are ten, each over 500 feet long. We then visit the bridge. There are two levels, one for trains, the other for trucks, cars, and pedestrians. The first level extends for a total of over four miles, the second over two. On the first, two trains can travel at the same time in opposite directions: on the second, four big trucks side by side. The all-steel superstructure is held up by nine piles of earth, each with a surface bigger than a basketball court. Under its ten arches can pass ships as big as 10,000 tons. Rising from it are four enormous towers, 225 feet high. I will give just one more indication of the proportions of the structure: the characters composing the phrase "Long Live Chairman Mao" each cover almost 700 square feet.

"But before that, how did you cross the river?"

"By ferries, which took more than two hours to take a train across. Now a train takes three minutes. The bridge is the communications link between north and south China."

"You planned and built this structure on your own, you say. But at the same time you speak of a struggle between two lines in connection with the bridge. What do you mean by that?"

"Capitalists and revisionists spread a lot of falsehoods about the Cultural Revolution and missed a good chance to understand China," the soldier says. "The struggle between two lines did indeed exist: the bridge was planned in 1958 and construction did not start until 1960. During those two years there were difficult discussions, including ones within the party structures themselves. The political struggle centered around three possibilities: (1) Should this bridge be built according to the principle of quantity, quality, speed, economy? (2) Should we rely only on our own strength, or should we depend on foreign help? (3) Should we rely primarily on technical specialists, or on the mobilization of the masses?"

The soldier-comrade raises his cap, thinks a moment, then continues:

"It was the struggle between two classes, two roads, two lines. That of Chairman Mao triumphed, and the bridge is the result of the fusion of the efforts of cadres, technicians, and workers; it proves that even in this difficult sector, China does not need foreign aid."

"Comrade-soldier, how do you see the political situation in China?"

"The Cultural Revolution is no more than the final explosion in a struggle that has been going on for a long time, not just among the leaders of the country, but among the workers. It will go on for a very long time yet. In the first phase the struggle managed to unmask a handful of men who had seized power and had tried to take China along the capitalist road. The struggle continues; it must be carried on. It is a class struggle that goes on under the dictatorship of the proletariat."

"How long is the Nanking Bridge?"

He catches the allusion and laughs. We take our pictures together, in a friendly spirit. This meeting confirms my impression that the army is above all political.

In the evening, the comrade from the Nanking Revolutionary Committee comes to dine with us at our hotel. Partly because I still have a slight fever, I speak with a polemical freedom about Stalin.

"For the workers' movement," I say, "the 'Stalin question' is not closed." And I add: "The concrete history of the Chinese Communist Party is an objectively anti-Stalinist history [I'm thinking of Yalta, of the cutting of the world into two blocs, of zones of influence]. You didn't put down your arms when Stalin asked you to."

"And you, why did you do so?" somebody gently asks me.

But this conversation, in which no one really takes up the polemic with me, will be the subject of another chapter.*

---

* On the delicate question of the relations between China and the USSR—in matters of *aid, specialists,* and *Sino-Soviet trade*—see the "Letter of the Central Committee of the CPC of February 29, 1964, to the Central Committee of the CPSU," in Appendix.

9

A Billion Peasant Hands

The struggle between two lines and the Cultural Revolution in the countryside

The Cultural Revolution developed much more slowly in the cities than in the countryside. The peasants at the communes we visited did not tell of great political upheavals. It can even be said that the Cultural Revolution in the cities depended upon the favorable economic and political situation of the countryside, or in those places where the communes had continued to develop. Throughout the toughest months of the struggle, cities like Shanghai—11 million inhabitants in the urban and surrounding rural areas—continued to be supplied with food by the people's communes. What would have happened if the peasants' contribution to the Cultural Revolution had collapsed, if there had been nothing to eat, for example? But Mao had already ensured several fundamental historical developments, the first of which was the creation of these communes which the Soviets called, at the time, the "collectivization of misery." Between 1959 and 1961, after the launching of the Great Leap Forward, lack of preparation, natural calamities, and the Soviet attitude paved the way for some sort of crisis in food supplies. So in 1961 material incentives were reintroduced, private plots were again given to the peasants, and a small amount of private trade in agricultural produce was encouraged. But the recovery which took place in the countryside in the next two years did not convince Mao. He perhaps even feared that this type of social development might undermine the foundations of Chinese strategy, different from Soviet strategy, and disrupt the balance between the development of the cities and that of the countryside. The advance toward collectivization in the countryside was firmly resumed and the aid which industry must give to agriculture strongly endorsed. An article published in *People's Daily* in the spring of 1970 by the Honan Revolutionary Committee discusses how local industry must maintain the correct road in the service of agriculture, and says:

> An essential condition for approaching the question of the relationship between the cities and the countryside correctly is the alliance between the workers and the peasants. China has lived through two periods. During the first, that alliance was based on the agrarian revolution. During the second, it was based on the collectivization of agriculture. This collectivization has made enormous progress with the coming of agricultural cooperation and the creation of the people's communes. Today the poor and lower-middle peasants have an urgent need to mechanize agriculture and are asking industry to provide them with a greater quantity of modern machines and equipment. To put itself at the service of agriculture, to help it, industry must not only speed up development, but must also consolidate the alliance between workers and peasants.

In another document, this one published in *Red Flag* at the beginning of 1970 under the title "The Road of Chinese Agriculture," every turn of the struggle between the two lines in the countryside is described, turns in a struggle which is still going on and which has opposed Mao Tse-tung and Liu Shao-chi.* During the *agrarian reform movement*, when alliances should have been being made

* Liu Shao-chi's line—called *san tzu yi pao*—became clear in 1960 and 1961 when, on the pretext that China was going through economic difficulties, he tried to reverse the situation in the countryside by destroying the bases of collectivization. Pretending to "stimulate" the forces of production, he tried to push his line, whose many points were: (1) Increase individual quotas. (2) Reorganize production on the basis of the family: the harvest still belonged to the collectivity, but any surplus was given to the families, and the families had to make up any losses. This policy undermined collectivization by very quickly creating a differentiation in the countryside. Families which had more plentiful manpower became rich, the poorest peasants went further into debt. (3) Develop free markets where the peasants themselves can sell their surplus production or the results of their quotas, thus encouraging capitalist aspirations in the peasants and promoting speculation. (4) Form small enterprises which assume profits and losses.

among the poor peasants and the agricultural laborers, Liu Shao-chi was seeking support among the rich peasants. When Mao forcefully encouraged the *agricultural cooperation movement*—mutual aid and cooperation among agricultural producers—he wanted the alliance to rest on the poor peasants and on the middle and lower strata of the rural population. But Liu Shao-chi believed in "Mechanization first, cooperatives afterward," and that "Cooperatives are a false, dangerous, and utopian conception of agricultural socialism." The Chinese say he blocked the formation of new cooperatives and reduced the number of existing ones. Mao's great battle against Liu's conceptions in agriculture reversed the trends that were preventing the transformation of Chinese agriculture in a socialist direction: "In 1958," says the article in *Red Flag*, "people's communes were created by the fusion of cooperatives, and *three levels of property* were recognized." The strength of the communes lay in the production teams. During this new phase, collective ownership in the countryside grew and moved to higher levels, while the combination of all the following elements was achieved: industry, agriculture, retail business, education, and military training—as well as stock-breeding, forestry, marginal labor, and fishing. All this gave a great push to Chinese agricultural production and to the whole rural economy. The fine crops of the years that followed testified to the superiority of the people's communes.

The direction Mao gave to the Cultural Revolution made the immense Chinese countryside—over 60 percent of party cardholders are of peasant origin—into an indispensable support for the success of this Cultural Revolution and for the measures it has determined will weaken, or wipe out, the differences between city and countryside, industry and agriculture.

The role of the peasants in the Cultural Revolution and in the building of socialism is brought home in this observation of Mao's: "We have a rural population of more than 500 million people, so that the situation of our peasants is very much a determining factor in the development of our economy and in the consolidation of the powers of the state."

The Cultural Revolution is a confirmation of the huge choice China has made. Unlike the Stalinist revolution, the Cultural Revolution constantly draws upon the purest Marxist tradition, on the words of Marx, who was the first to focus clearly on the essence of city-country relations: "The bourgeoisie has subjected the country to the rule of the towns," he wrote in the *Communist Manifesto.* He arrived at this conclusion after the analysis developed in the *German Ideology:*

> The greatest division of material and mental labor is the separation of town and country. . . . The antagonism of town and country . . . is the most crass expression of the subjection of the individual under the division of labor, under a definite activity forced upon him—a subjection which makes one man into a restricted town-animal, the other into a restricted country-animal, and daily creates anew the conflict between their interests. . . . The abolition of the antagonism between town and country is one of the first conditions of a communal life. . . . The separation of town and country can also be understood as the separation of capital and landed property, as the beginning of the existence and development of capital independent of landed property.

The Cultural Revolution does not leave the countryside a subordinate role. It doesn't extract a tithe from agriculture, and it doesn't make the peasants into a new "glebe," or make of them a "reservoir of reaction." It has chosen constant decentralization of the cities over megalopoli, over giant industrial centers where technology and "intelligence" have triumphed, so as not to leave behind the enormity of the land that is China, a land which until just a few decades ago was buried under feudalism. The Cultural Revolution reunites the city and the countryside by the mechanization of the latter, by small and medium-sized industries which depend on large ones, by the selection of peasants' sons for schools, by peasant teachers, by the restructuring of the university, and by the decentralization of medicine.

During the Cultural Revolution Mao created a link which he considered indissoluble between intellectuals of all sorts—teachers, professors, scholars, doctors—and the peasant population, beside whom these intellectuals are sent to work. And a considerable portion of this intellectual cadre will stay in the countryside, too, so that a reversal of the rural exodus which characterizes our "developed" world will take place in China. A trip through the Chinese countryside, a visit to the people's communes, gives the visitor a chance to see that tensions which one still senses in the cities and which in all likelihood still have their critical aspects, are quite different in the countryside. It is a basic conviction in the countryside that the immense peasant population is crucial to the success of the road being followed by China.

The good earth

> Apart from their other characteristics, the outstanding thing about China's 600 million people is that they are "poor and blank." This may seem a bad thing, but in reality it is a good thing. Poverty gives rise to the desire for change, the desire for action, and the desire for revolution.
>
> —Mao Tse-tung

The representative of the standing committee of the Nanking Municipal Revolutionary Committee, Chen, says to us: "Excuse me for not seeing you to the train tomorrow morning, but I'm going to work in the fields. It's the harvest season, there's a lot to be done, and we leave at dawn." From the window of the Nanking-Shanghai train I watch the countryside unroll before me like a painting. Cotton fields, as if snow-covered, bundles lined up like sentinels, and each one with a red flag stuck in it. On the navigable canals, fishermen's black junks, and transport junks with huge loads of wood, which men and women move along by pushing on long poles. Lands swallowed up by water, where the fishermen work, legs and feet constantly in water. I think to myself, Comrade Chen is here somewhere. Two young girls gather up the pieces of coal the locomotive has dropped along the side of the track as it chugs clouds of smoke over the fields. The Chinese waste nothing. They use everything, parsimoniously, and the two young girls follow the track, baskets on their arms, until I lose them from view. In the fields they sow wheat after harvesting rice, which itself gives two crops. When do the Chinese sleep? When they should be sleeping, they are studying the thought of Mao Tse-tung.

In China they tell you that "Something seen with your eyes is worth a hundred questions asked." This is true for the Chinese countryside, a magic lantern offering ever new visions, in the north, in the center, in the south. An immense peasant vitality, a numberless presence, at once physical and political, which confronts you unceasingly, from the flags to the slogans. And this: almost everything is done with the hands, a billion Chinese peasant hands, liberating energy to handle the plow, to pick, to cut away mountains, to canalize watercourses, to build dikes, to dig canals, to cultivate gardens where there were only swamps, to breed animals, to build houses, factories, and tractor-making shops, to create schools and hospitals. Nothing makes you dizzy in China as much as the spectacle of this peasant population (as many people as there are in all Europe) in continual movement in the fields.

Take the countryside around Canton. Its spectacle not only goes beyond what you know, but almost beyond what you can imagine. An unending and ardent digging at the ground by thousands of peasants—men, but mostly women. Fields like gardens, geometrically perfect, with triangles, squares, parallelograms of greenness, separated by small canals, where the peasants wet their feet as they take water and rhythmically sprinkle it on the sprouts and plants with pails or watering-cans, or with old barrels or cans. In addition to the irrigation canals, there is the morning and evening watering of the plantings. The fields are full, like city squares or streets. Teams of hundreds of women, bent over the fields, gather up sheaves of rice. Others, by the hundreds, carry them away in two huge bundles on opposite ends of a carrying pole. Others are planting the new rice plants in the water with the same speed, the same precision, with which a weaver traverses the warp of a tapestry. Other teams clean the rice. The paddies are covered with piles of yellow grain. The roads are full of people courageously transporting logs, pulling carts, carrying sacks or other mighty burdens on shoulder poles. And always water, a sort of lake-land. On it all, tens of thousands of mechanized transport vehicles, incalculable numbers of bicycles, people going to work on them, transporting goods with them, riding them in twos and threes.

From rafts on every pond barefoot men are fishing with nets for large fish which they will take to the brigade or commune marketplace. We also see schoolgirls of primary and middle school levels who have come with their red flags to help in the fields after their morning lessons are over. Blade plows pulled by buffalo, and small modern plows, the small kind we saw at the Shanghai exhibition. Old and new together, but more old than new. The constant thing is this population, in motion like a hive. It does not stop picking, sowing, watering, cultivating. The four seasons do not seem to make sense anymore, nor do they coincide with the gestations and births of the land. One harvests in one field, sows in the next. There are three harvests, two of rice and one of wheat. There should soon be four, with three of rice, in obedience to the tenacious will of the peasants of the communes of southern China. You can see that here we are at the apotheosis of mass action, of a frenetic tenacity which recognizes no obstacles, and we also have here the key to why there is so much food in China, so much fruit, vegetables, meat, and fish for the cities. Also, the harshness of the work doesn't seem to lead to a fearful rearguard, much as an army is not afraid to march. Men and women, young and old, stay in the fields. Grandmothers, even very aged ones, look after the children or keep an eye on the chickens and the family pig. The youngest children carry buckets of water on ropes held by two of them, and empty them in the irrigation canals. Every strength is used at its own level and however possible. You might say that there is no rest for anyone, but it would be truer to say that no one is considered useless in this great Chinese assault on heaven. In the south, tradition considers the women as strong as the men. They do the same work. It takes your breath away to see these slim silhouettes trotting barefoot with two mountains of straw balanced on the ends of carrying poles slung across their shoulders, carry water, or pump it. But was it not Mao who wrote: "With the rise of the peasant movement, the women in many places have now begun to organize rural women's associations; the opportunity has come for them to lift up their heads, and the authority of the husband is getting shakier every day."

"In agriculture, learn from Tachai"

It was in 1964 that Mao launched an appeal that rang from one end of China to the other. Just as Comrade Yang is the conqueror of the unconquerable, just as the "foolish old man who moved mountains" is the hero of the impossible, the Tachai brigade is the model of all revolutionary politics in the countryside, a model which will defeat the errors of Liu Shao-chi as well as natural adversities. *The Exemplary Story of Tachai* has been recounted to the Chinese peasants millions of times, by voice and by radio. Its bibliography has hundreds of articles, which continue to appear not only in the vast network of the regional press, in *People's Daily*, and in *Red Flag*, but also in all the publications China distributes around the world in foreign languages. An inexhaustible subject, as is the whole peasant question. If China has nine years of steadily better harvests behind it (and this year is a "record" one), it is partly because the Chinese peasants have learned from their modest comrades of the Tachai brigade what a revolution of the superstructure is, and have decided, so to speak, that in agriculture "impossible" belongs to metaphysics. They have defeated the egotism and the avarice which were at the root of exploitation in the countryside. They have opened their minds to the socialist generosity of collective management, wherein all is shared. They have counted days of work by work-points which a peasant grants himself once a month, after a group discussion with the whole brigade. This is the greatest imaginable political maturity.

Two million peasants have made the trip to the village of the Tachai brigade, perched in the loess mountains, in a thankless region of the province of Shansi. They have made this visit as one goes to some prodigious spectacle. The slogan "Learn from Tachai" is now the prologue to an epic in China. It is the guide for the "500 million members of people's communes who draw their inspiration from Tachai," as a special issue of *New China* (October 1970) said. The story of Tachai is another example of Mao's political pragmatism. The Chairman studied Tachai as an example which had come from the base and which could be the germ of development for all of peasant China. He analyzed it, he approved it, and he generalized it. This is what the peasants explain to you. I did not visit Tachai, but the fact that every peasant speaks of it in this way, with awe, is significant. The photos of the peasants of this brigade aren't as widespread as those of Lin Piao, but they are widespread. Tachai represents the victory in the struggle between two lines. The triumph of Mao's way of socialist management in the countryside;

the consolidation of the collective economy; the application of the principle of socialist sharing in the commune through a new system of payment based on the ideological consciousness of the commune members, according to which each peasant assigns himself at a meeting, as I said, "points" deriving from his activity as he examines it before the others. Beyond this, Tachai is a summary of the revolutionary line of a party which refuses to allow itself to become bourgeois or to be attacked by revisionism. In fact, the party cell at Tachai symbolizes the spearhead of the struggle against Liu Shao-chi. This exemplary behavior of a party organ indirectly testifies—I have already said it—to the fact that the troubles within the party, and its subsequent restructuring, were not impossible tests in the far countryside, as they were in the cities. The Communists of the countryside solidly maintained Chairman Mao's line and kept up a good level of socialist consciousness. This is so true that a large portion of the management cadres of the communes remained the same, even after the birth of the revolutionary committees and the installation of the three-in-one combinations at the head of each commune.

How an old peasant from Evergreen sees Tachai

In the Evergreen commune we ate with an old peasant, Su Chin-tun, sixty-two years old, and his three daughters (one a member of the party cell), who prepared Chinese wonton in a spicy sauce for us. The house is paneled in wood, on the bed are colored mats and goatskins. There is a set of mirrors and two fine pieces of colored metal furniture. There are flowers in the windows and on the wall a faded calendar showing two elegantly dressed women beside a nude woman, truly nude. This is the only *nonpolitical* picture I saw in China. The production team that the peasant belongs to includes 82 families; 212 families work 513 mou.

"Have you heard about the Tachai brigade?"

"Indeed," the peasant replies. "I also wrote a tatzupao against Liu Shao-chi, and I pasted it up in the village. Liu would have brought back the division between rich and poor in the countryside. For the old people today there are five guarantees: food, clothing, a house, medical care, and burial. Who had that in the past?"

"But what did you write in your tatzupao? And did you really write it yourself?"

"Only partly. My daughters helped me. I wrote that Liu wanted to revive the principle of working the land for gain and not for the revolution. This principle would have corrupted the peasants and would have again formed a class of exploiters and a class of exploited people. The Red Guards came here, to the village, and they carried out great criticisms and helped us understand. We spoke a great deal of the Tachai brigade then."

"Can you tell me the story of the Tachai brigade?"

"The story of Tachai?" the peasant asks with astonishment, as if one could not fail to know it. "It is a bitter story. It begins in 1952, when Chairman Mao, after completing the agrarian reform, gave the order to transform the cooperatives into mutual-aid groups. The brigade asked the leaders of the district for permission to turn themselves into a cooperative. But the leaders at first said no, for they were influenced by the renegade enemy of the people, Liu Shao-chi. In 1953 they agreed, but insisted that the cooperative be reduced to just thirty families, and not include all forty-nine who belonged to the village and desperately wanted to join the cooperative. But Tachai's revolutionary and anti-revisionist spirit was growing steadily.

"In the period of reorganization, between 1959 and 1961, after the birth of the people's communes, Tachai was the first to move out on the socialist road in the countryside. Even during the years of natural disasters, Tachai managed to increase its production. But the attack of 'China's Khrushchev' and his disciples fell upon Tachai, and a 'work team' was sent there, supposedly to introduce the Socialist Education Movement into the brigade. This team made an inquiry and concluded that the Tachai brigade was a brigade of mediocre farmers who had exaggerated their harvests during the drought period. A third-rate brigade, they said!" Here he hit the table with his bony hand. "They also said that people lived poorly at Tachai and that their system of management was bad because it emphasized political consciousness instead of quotas and material incentives. But Tachai persisted in its path: *being self-*

reliant, avoiding falling back on the state for aid, living with parsimony and frugality, developing production, and helping the world socialist revolution. Tachai put politics in command. And though the Liu Shao-chi group renewed their attacks in 1964, the Cultural Revolution years dealt a death blow to the enemies of the socialist road in the countryside."

"You have a great deal of admiration for Tachai, I can see. Is it just its political ability you admire?"

"No, not just its political ability, for politics and production, revolution and production, go together. The people of Tachai worked under terrible conditions. They had no modern farm equipment, they had no collective funds, they had a few plows, hoes, picks, shovels, baskets—that's all they had. Still they turned their out-of-the-way village into a model village. They scraped the mountain to replant it with trees, and now it is a fine green. They didn't have enough grain, but now they can sell grain to the state. They didn't have water, and they tamed and channeled the mountain torrents. They didn't have enough fertilizer, and they used the mud of the swamps. They didn't have houses, and they built houses; they didn't have schools, and they built them too. All this on a mountain, in an eagle's nest . . ."

"But have you been to Tachai?"

"Yes, I visited it in 1969. But what I have said can be said without having visited."

"Here, in your brigade, are you doing something which resembles what they did at Tachai?"

"We too, when Liberation came, had nothing, not even eyes to cry with. A hundred huts of mud and earth. This land belonged to a single landlord, and there was one rich peasant. We participated in the movement for cooperatives, and in the movement for the founding of the people's communes. Politically, we followed a correct course. We built 334 new little houses, we created an irrigation system, and where there was only 1 mechanical well before, now every house has one. Before there was just 1 bicycle in the village; now there are 134 bicycles and 82 radios. In this house we have 2 bicycles and a radio. The house was built in 1964. Production went up one-third in the past two years alone. Then came the 'barefoot doctors' and their clinic. I fell sick in 1967, and if it had not been for Mao's doctors, I wouldn't have gotten care here in the country and I'd be dead.

"Lin Piao teaches that 'If you do not understand the suffering of the old society, you cannot understand the class struggle, or the revolution.' The old society kept the peasant under the yoke. We had to go beyond the Great Wall to cultivate something, then carry the grain to the town on our backs to sell it. If we had followed Liu Shao-chi's way, we would be back in the old society. We old peasants must transmit the hatred of the past to the new generations, the hatred of revisionism and the love of the uninterrupted revolution. When the Red Guards came here, I recounted our past tribulations to them, because the young people must know. I told them that in 1948, when this region was liberated, we peasants finally took political power, and when you have political power, all is possible. The struggle against Liu Shao-chi was also a struggle for political power and we were determined to fight together, we old people and the Red Guards."

He places his hand on his Mao badge, his thin beard trembles, his eyes are wet and he murmurs: "Never, in my heart, will my love for the Chairman decrease." Then he goes into another room and brings back a photograph of his youngest son, a member of the People's Liberation Army serving in the navy. This is a great honor for this peasant family.

> On a blank sheet of paper free from any mark, the freshest and most beautiful characters can be written, the freshest and most beautiful pictures can be painted.
>
> —Mao Tse-tung

The woman who receives us in the Evergreen commune is a member of its revolutionary committee's standing committee. She was a simple peasant before the Revolution, and only after 1949 did she study in night classes. Her name is Wan Shen-yin. She has one of the most important jobs on this commune thirty miles from Peking. She is solid, calm, and she explains with great clarity whatever is under discussion, without notes. Beside her is a young man wearing the armband of the Red Guards. This is a pilot commune in some aspects. It sells 110,000 tons of vegetables to the state each year, twice what it gave before the Cultural Revolution, and 4,000 tons of fruit a year, which is 120 times what this land used to produce. It has 1,300 enormous greenhouses as well as fruit trees; it raises 100,000 pigs, 20,000 ducks. More: it has a central hospital, 12 health centers, and in each of the 137 production teams there are, on the average, 2 "barefoot doctors." Seventeen schools make up the commune's education system, including 2 middle schools. In these schools control is *in the hands of the poor peasants.* The commune is inhabited by 9,000 families, which means 40,000 people cultivating 40,000 mou of land. They are broken down into 12 production brigades and 137 production teams.

Mechanization has made much progress in this commune. There are 5,000 mechanical wells, and 98 percent of the land area is irrigated by canals dug by the peasants. They have a common fund for the purchase of equipment, and at the moment own 44 trucks, 20 large tractors, and 60 smaller ones.

"The difference in the revolutionary spirit of the masses," says Comrade Wan, "is so great today, after the Cultural Revolution, that it can be compared to the difference between the period before the Revolution of 1949 and socialism."

No one else has made such an unequivocal statement. But like all women, this one wants to go to the root of things. I think of the quotation from Mao that says, "Women hold up half of heaven."

"Can you tell me something about how you adopted the new work-point system for the peasants' work day, and how these work-points are 'self-assigned' in public meetings?"

"The old theory of work-points was much criticized by the commune members. We used to have long discussions every day about points and who should get them. After the Cultural Revolution we learned that you cultivate the land for the revolution, following the example of Tachai, and not for points. So now we assign points once a month. Each of us says how many points he or she thinks they deserve on the objective basis of the work done. We discuss this once every three months. This produces a deep change in the human being. [Before there was a sort of reward for Stakhanovism, with overtime to increase earnings and extreme speeds to obtain more and more points.] Back then, if we cultivated a mou of land we obtained ten points. But people worked much harder to earn twice this, paying little attention to the quality of the work. The important thing was points, that is, money. We realized that this form of piecework (which took no account of the quality of work and which was only an effort to get points) meant nothing and was causing the retreat of peasant ideology. We learned a lot from the People's Liberation Army. Before, when it was time to work, the bell rang and people were late. Now, even before the bell rings they have already been studying Mao's thought for an hour. And when the bell rings at the end of work, they don't leave the fields without checking whether they have finished what they went out to do. Briefly, they like the collective cause. We've just cultivated 10,000 mou of wheat. To harvest it used to take two weeks, but this year it only took one week, because revolutionary ideology prodded the peasants and made them think of their homeland and of the world. In the past when we had to go back to the fields at night, the members of the commune refused. Now even these sacrifices are made, and, as I said, the work has improved."

The woman looks at us as she speaks, without a note. Everything seems clear in her beautiful and proud head. Two pins pull her hair behind her neck, and under her cotton summer jacket she is wearing a colored pullover, as they all do; hers is orange.

A new pay system

The evaluating of work has thus totally changed across the Chinese countryside, following Tachai. Norms have gone, large differences of pay have been abolished, the principle "to each according to his work" has been better applied, and an enormous push has been given to democracy at the base. This is how, as I understand it, they have arrived at a system of payment in which points are assigned, during a public discussion, with the peasant himself judging his own contribution in work. The calculation is not based on the basic work day, which would have the effect of stimulating the peasants to work but the flaw of differentiating among them according to their strength, their age, their technical level, the number of people in their families, and would favor quantity more than quality. Now the calculation is based on the *effective* work day, which means, in effect, that we guarantee work, and that work-points are given according to the behavior of each person, a method that is simple and just. Weak or strong, all that matters is whether one is able to work. This is how the effective work day is assigned. With the exception of a few women who are occupied at home and whom we consider are in a special situation, we count all effective work days, taking out only necessary rest periods. Once the effective work day has been established, we make checks periodically, and estimates, just as we calculate work-points." *

In case of emergency

The commune leader takes up her story again, speaking with pride:

"On August 29, 1969, hail fell. There were hailstones as big as hen's eggs and the fruit trees were destroyed. Faced with this disaster, people organized. They decided not to be afraid of sacrificing themselves, to be courageous, and they gave battle for three days and three nights. They replanted 10,000 mou of land. They were aided by the People's Liberation Army, which sent detachments from other communes, and by the Peking Revolutionary Committee. We managed to recoup what would, without this effort, have been an irreparable disaster. The fields are once again covered with green. Our struggle to transform nature, guided by the thought of Mao, which helps us to be determined in everything we do, was victorious."

> In the countryside, it is up to the poor and lower-middle peasants, that is to say, the surest allies of the working class, to *take control of the schools.*
>
> —Mao Tse-tung

The old peasant lifts his head and sees us on the doorstep of his primary school class. He stops speaking to the pupils, astounded.

---

* "Management Should Be Based on the Ideological Consciousness of Commune Members," *Economic Studies* (*Chingchi Yenchiu*), no. 3, 1966.

The schoolchildren open their eyes wide at these events (amusing foreign faces passing by right under their noses) and draw in their breath as if we were lions on the doorstep. The comrade peasant-teacher has a big cabbage on his desk, and a bunch of orange carrots. He is in the midst of giving his agriculture lesson to the ten-year-olds. The brigade has fifteen primary school classes, with a total of six hundred children. In this class, forty children fill the seats. Next to the peasant, at a mechanical piano, sits a girl with braids. When the teacher has finished talking, the pupils sing revolutionary songs and she accompanies them.

The peasant has a face cooked by the sun. He wears large, patched, out-of-shape shoes. He is entirely bald with just a white hair or two on his head.

"We're sorry to bother you," we say. "But we would like to know how the peasants run the school. Do they find teaching difficult?"

"The poor peasants, following the directive of Mao, took over the operation of the school, along with the revolutionary cadre and teachers and the pupils. But the revolution in education did not happen in a day. Before, people said: 'I teach—you cultivate the field.' It was an old habit which we had to break so as to be able to do both. When we peasants began teaching, we were ridiculed. Liu Shao-chi's men said: 'Poor peasants running the schools will change nothing, sooner or later things will be as they were.' Or again: 'Teaching children how to raise pigs is a fine cultural innovation—what good will it do them?' Others were openly contemptuous of us: 'The poor peasants have no education. What can they teach?' Others thought they were born red: 'I was born in a family of poor peasants. Every day I am with them. I am as one with them. What more teaching from peasants do I need?' So we were moving around 'between four walls' as the saying goes in our area, and we got no results."

"But what did poor peasants like you think of the schools as they were before?"

"We criticized the schools. What kind of men were they forming? The children of poor peasants could not pass their examinations and had to stop their studies before their end. The examinations to enter the senior level were hard. The schools were very far away and the peasants could not reach them in a day. Once a poor peasant said: 'In our brigade there are twenty-eight families and of these twenty-eight families, only three peasants have gotten their middle-school diplomas. We went to see who they were. One was the son of poor peasants, but the other two were children of our only family of rich peasants.' So the question was, who finds the school's doors open to him? And then peasant children didn't have the time to learn their lessons because they worked at home as well and they often ended up too tired to go back to class. The priority was given to grades; never to the concrete aspect of studies, never to their political character. All the children thought about was marks. What power did we have, peasants like us, in the cultural field? The truth is that before the Cultural Revolution we had none.

"The 'March 7 Directive' from Chairman Mao spoke clearly and told us poor peasants that we should take the schools in hand. It was no simple task, as I said. We had to adopt tough measures, to act decisively. We had to abolish the system of a single authority, the school principal, and support the innovation of creating a revolutionary education committee, composed of poor peasants, revolutionary teachers, and revolutionary students. We did this, and we even reduced the length of middle-school studies from six to four years, divided into two two-year cycles. The first revolution in education—which gave us the benefit of the experiences I have just been speaking about—took place in the Teng Sha Ho commune in Chin-hsin district, and Chairman Mao made it widely known in the countryside. And, you know, it wasn't so difficult! The main thing was our class consciousness, our conviction that the teaching that had been dominated by the old system had to be radically transformed. Before Liberation, I was illiterate. Then I studied at night school, mostly during the winter when there was no work in the fields. I came here in 1968, answering the call Mao made on March 7, and I began setting up the new school run by the peasants."

"How does your lesson go, the one you are teaching now?"

"This is how: I tell the children what the agricultural processes are, from the birth of the seed up to the harvest. I also speak of possible calamities, from frosts to parasites, everything. But I don't limit my lesson to that. I take the students out into the fields and give practical lessons. And I go into the houses of my students to see what the social conditions are, to find out how they live, and I also work on re-educating teachers."

"But what is your basic political work?"

"We tell them how much the poor peasants suffered under the old society and why we hate that society. And we find out from them the history of their own families and that of the whole village. With the children we reconstruct the past, the present, we speak of the present happiness and the tasks which await us in the future. This we call 'lessons in class struggle.' The comrades who are in the people's militia in the commune are sent here to teach about military questions, as we peasants teach about agriculture. The commune workers give lessons on agricultural mechanics, the brigade accountant teaches mathematics, health officials teach hygiene. The teachers have overthrown their own ideology and are now helping us to organize the proletarian revolution in education. Many of our brigade schools are self-supporting—they don't need any aid from the state."

On the blackboard I see a cabbage, drawn in its various stages of development. The peasant notices that I notice.

"We explain what makes a cabbage grow, what fertilizers are needed, and so on."

The schoolmistress who is helping the peasant teach draws very beautiful Chinese characters above each stage of the cabbage's development, and the comrade-peasant indicates them with a bamboo pointer.

Then the mistress writes out the "May 7 Directive," and the children read it in unison, helped by a romanization written over the characters.

This young schoolmistress seems no more than nineteen, but she is twenty-six. She too questions the children, alternating with the peasant:

"In earlier times, class enemies exploited the people. Can we get along with them now?"

Two children want to answer and raise their hands. One is chosen.

"No. One day a class enemy wanted to take me out to eat and

drink. I did not accept, remembering the sufferings he had inflicted on my comrades in the old society."

Another child adds:

"Once my mother wanted me to sing and dance before a landlord. I refused. My mother got mad. When we were back in the house, I said to my mother: 'How can you make me dance and sing to amuse a class enemy who has exploited the people, and who exploited you too? You are not a logical woman.' "

Another question:

"Should we work for the revolution, or for well-being and money; to transform one's way of thinking, or for the material incentives of Liu Shao-chi?"

Three hands go up. A little girl recounts:

"I lost my Chairman Mao badge one time, the most beautiful one I had, and I cried at home. My father wanted to give me money, to buy me toys and cakes to cheer me up. But I said to him: 'No, Papa, I'm crying because of an idealistic reason and you want to give me material things, like Liu Shao-chi, that would corrupt me."

The old peasant squeezes our hands. He is very moved by the replies of his pupils, the successors to the revolutionary cause, who all applaud as we leave. Then they sing a passage from the Peking opera, *The Red Lantern.*

I ask the other teachers:

"How do you evaluate their work? With grades?"

"We used to give grades in school, but not now. When an exercise has been done well, the teacher draws a small red flag in the student's notebook and writes 'Loyalty to Chairman Mao.' When the exercise is poor, he writes the quotation from Mao: 'Be determined, courageous, and try to attain victory.' "

They tell me that after completing junior middle school, the children return to the fields to work for a couple of years. No one is "born red." Even the children of peasants must constantly transform their conception of the world. Then, all together, the peasants elect the children who are most worthy of going to the university, so that socialist society in its entirety may develop.

"How did you elect the school's revolutionary committee?"

"The revolutionary committee is elected by an assembly at the rank-and-file level. After an open debate, each member of the commune writes on a slip of paper who he wants as representative on the school revolutionary committee. Then comes the vote. At the end the outgoing revolutionary committee examines the results and approves them. In the present school revolutionary committee, three out of the five members are members of the party."

In other classes, we hear lessons in mathematics designed to calculate dosages of fertilizer, and lessons in reading where the students read some news items and articles from *People's Daily*. The textbooks I pick up are recent, printed since the Cultural Revolution, in 1969–1970. I am told that the old books were very complicated, sometimes abstract, and above all that they did not put the politics of the dictatorship of the proletariat first. The book I am looking at lists in its table of contents an excerpt from the speech of Lin Piao to the Ninth Congress and a quotation from Mao on the university at Yenan.

"In literature, what do they read?"

"They read poems written by Mao Tse-tung. In studying these poems, they learn the words, the style, and the political content."

"Could you have one read?"

"Gladly."

And the children, after the teacher explains to them what they are to do, recite in a chorus:

> Under high skies and fleecy clouds,
> We, watching wild geese dissolving south,
> Agreed that he who fails to reach the Great Wall could hardly
> be the hero;
> Reckoning up, already we had come twenty thousand li!
>
> On the high summit of Mount Liupan
> Our banners freely wave in the western breeze.
> Ready this day the long tassel in our hands.
> When shall we truss up that gray dragon? *

Many of the children are wearing triangular insignia on their arms, with "Little Red Guard" written on them, and a number.

* From *The Poems of Mao Tse-tung,* translated and annotated by Wong Mau (Hong Kong: Eastern Horizon Press, 1966).—*Trans.*

Two-thirds of the children are *Little Red Guards.* This is not an organization; it is a recognition for political work and study.

The tea brigade at Dragon Well: how revenues are divided up

We are drinking a light tea, clear as water. It is the tea of Dragon Well, a brigade of a commune on the lake west of Hangchow. In the depths of the cup tiny leaves, pale green and oblong, are revived as the water opens them up. This most famous of Chinese teas is unlike any tea we know. It is the most *anti*-tea that I have ever drunk. It has a very light aroma of freshly cut grass, like a living plant that has been plunged into boiling water. The countryside around this tea brigade is perfumed by the tea plants, which are bushes, and the tea flowers look like orange blossoms.

"Do you notice the air is perfumed?" I ask Chao, and I take his picture as he smells a flower.

"You photograph me like a capitalist!" Chao cries, irritated.

There are certain nuances of language I must pay attention to, I tell myself again. Try to understand that in old China, it was said of an intellectual that he *gave off a perfume.* You must also be careful about other nuances concerning good and bad smells, or when you praise someone because you find him handsome, or even very handsome, while another appears to you ugly. Men are distinguished by other qualities, as is often explained to us.

The green landscape of round bushes in meticulous lines, climbing up to the Hangchow hills, is the best-known Chinese countryside, a thousand times represented in the ancient tapestries. We are with Nei Chien-hu, a member of the revolutionary committee which directs the production brigade, in the former landowners' "club," a very solemn and refined place with an inlaid-mahogany table and massive chairs whose backs are inlaid with pink porphyry. On the second floor a gallery runs around an interior space with mysterious rooms opening onto it (for the courtesans of yesteryear?), but the Chinese do not answer our question, saying simply that the rooms serve to dry the tea, that is all.

"China," the comrade tells us, "is the first country in the world to have invented tea as a beverage by abandoning it as a medicine. What you are drinking is the spring tea of Dragon Well, the best of the three crops—spring, summer, and fall—we harvest each year. Life was not easy for the peasants under the plantation owners, who owned 80 percent of the land here. I was a poor peasant, like 95 percent of us. There are 200 families in the brigade, 3,200 people, and we have all been through the same hard past. In the day we worked for the landlord and at night we cut wood to survive. The annual income for a family then was less than 200 yuan a year; today it is 1,093 yuan. Tea production used to be very small (under five pounds per mou); we had no money for fertilizer, and if a peasant owned a few tea plants they were as thin as chicken bones. They were also exposed to every calamity, especially parasites, and there were no remedies. The landlord held us responsible for all this and hurled insults at us: 'You peasants, your hearts aren't pure, that's why heaven sent insects. So now, pray to be delivered; pray with the fervor you put into the greatest offerings to the gods.' We conducted processions through the tea plantations with statuettes and votive offerings. We didn't know that the parasites lived the life cycle of the plant, that after that they dropped to the ground and the plants blossomed anew. But when the plants flowered again, the owner, who knew this and exploited our ignorance and superstition, had us make another procession and give new offerings to thank heaven for the end of the calamity. When the second generation of parasites arrived we didn't know what to do, and in our desperation we cut the plants down, the ones that belonged to us, and sold them as wood in exchange for a little corn flour. Then Mao's People's Liberation Army arrived, and that is how, in 1949, we acquired our first technical knowledge of cultivation. The People's Liberation Army gave us fungicides which killed the parasites. The population then felt a great anger about the fraud the landlords had been commiting against the peasants for generations, and we destroyed all the statuettes and gods."

"How much do you produce now?"

"Before the Liberation we produced less than five pounds of tea per mou. By 1952, with help of the mutual-aid group and with technical aid—fungicides and fertilizers—given us by the state, we had already reached 120 pounds. In the years after 1958, after the founding of the people's commune, we reached 218 pounds. Increases continued, and last year we produced 300 pounds per mou. Before the Liberation we were uneducated, we were all illiterate. The only school in the village took twenty pupils, all sons or nephews of landowners. In this group there was only one village child. Now we have a primary and a middle school, and all the children can go there. Eight students from our brigade are at the university. We also have night courses, political and cultural, to study the thought of Mao Tse-tung. The consciousness of the masses has increased tremendously. Our production brigade has had important successes, but by comparison with the Tachai production brigade we still fall short in many things. We have largely mechanized the growing of tea. After the harvest, it is dried twice. Before, we had to use the wood we gathered in the mountains. Now we have electrical power. The only tea that needs hand work is the Dragon Well which you are drinking, for it is more delicate."

"How do you split up income in the brigade?"

"First you must remember that our brigade is in direct contact with the state, unlike the commune; this is true only for tea. The production plan is decided by agreement between the brigade and the organs of the state. We deliver 220,000 pounds to the state, and surpass the plan each year."

"What is the division of income among the peasants?"

"After selling the tea produced for the state, each peasant family may keep the amount it needs for its own use, and the price of this is deducted from its remuneration. From the payment received through the sale to the state, we first take off the 7 percent tax due the state itself, then 15 percent for agricultural expenses and 13 percent for the reserve fund. The remaining 35 percent is shared among the peasants."

"How?"

"After each harvest, the peasants of the brigade gather to discuss their own work, guided by the principle 'to each according to his work.' Each grants himself a certain number of daily 'points' as he himself judges his work, with a maximum of ten per day. Collective discussion helps in defining the daily mark earned by each person, using these three criteria: political behavior, attitude toward work, the quantity and the quality of the work. Ten points a day correspond to 1.75 yuan per person. With an average of five points—though in fact the average is much higher—each peasant is assured of a yuan a day. This is how the incomes of the 250 families are decided upon: by public discussion by the work teams of the brigade. Everybody in the family works—even small children can participate in tea production, which is an easy kind of work. So can old people. And further, electricity, schooling, and housing are free. Compared with the past, we peasants have touched heaven with our fingers. The commune's common fund has grown considerably. This year we have 400,000 yuan in hand, despite all the money we spent on mechanization, school-building, an implement repair shop, and irrigation. We don't store the tea, because that changes its taste."

"Are there students who come to work here with you, to be re-educated?"

"Many, about a hundred right now. They aren't paid, naturally. They eat with the peasants and listen to the tales the peasants tell them of their past life, which is an excellent re-education. When they eat with a peasant family, they pay the family the amount they would have paid to eat at the university. But the poor peasants give them the best food, often offering meat, which means that the payment becomes almost symbolic. Tea-harvesting is a technique. At first a student can only pick three or four ounces a day, but with practice he can collect two or three pounds a day. To learn to pick tea takes a year of practice; to learn to treat it takes four or five."

We leave the perfumed countryside of the Dragon Well brigade and go down the slopes toward Hangchow, dining on the edge of the lake in a popular restaurant which was once for tourists and is now filled with soldiers, workers, and families. For five, drinking a bottle of Chinese vodka, three bottles of beer, and eating six dishes (fish, crayfish, bamboo shoots, meat, roast chicken, and soup), we spent a total of five yuan. Sitting by the restaurant's huge windows over the lake we watch families eating, quietly, for a few pennies. Indeed, day-to-day life costs nothing.

We next take the traditional boat trip on the lake, island to island in a slow craft that a woman pushes with a long oar, helped in friendly fashion by the Chinese accompanying us. The sky is gray and rainy, but the lake gives off a soft charm nevertheless. It brings peace. They point out to us the villa that was once Chiang Kai-shek's, with its green roof. Our Chinese companions say to us: "Formerly only the great mandarins, the rich lords, and famous people came here. Now Hangchow belongs to all the people." In the gardens, we try to find a four-leaf clover in a little clover patch. I find one, and Lu finds two. I ask him: "So you believe in luck?" He answers: "It's just for fun."

But we keep our four-leaf clovers very carefully in our pocketbooks. As I understand it, the luck Lu hopes for from his clover is to become a member of the party. He greatly wishes it. But the test of practical struggle is hard, he tells me, the test of revolutionary capacity is high. For an intellectual, it requires many tests.

From Hangchow, we return to Shanghai on the new double-decker train, twelve coaches, maximum safe speed 80 miles an hour. The train is green and white. Inside, big two-place seats with a lever, as in planes, to lower the back. A first-class ticket for 135 miles costs five yuan. Second class, three yuan. From one end of the coach to the other you can find works by Mao, and the radio broadcasts revolutionary songs. The exquisite tea we are served of course comes from Dragon Well. The train is elegant, silent, comfortable for a long trip, heated in winter and air-conditioned in summer. It was built in Shanghai, but is still in a test stage and will not roll on the northern and northeastern lines for several months. A soldier from the railway militia arrives. He wants to greet us in the coach—where we have found ourselves, as always, alone—and begins chatting with our interpreters as if he has known them for years. This always impresses us, for it denotes a new relation between people. They talk like old friends, and we learn they have just met.

How the communes are industrializing

> She was right. The terrifying breath of winter was already starting to blow. We were surrounded by woods, but there was nowhere to gather fuel. Although excavators were digging peat out of the bogs all around us, none of it was sold to the local inhabitants; but if you were one of the bosses or ranked among the boss class—teachers, doctors, factory workers—

> then you got a lorryload. The local people in Tal'novo were not supposed to be given fuel, and it was no use asking for it. The chairman of the collective farm walked around the village looking at people earnestly or innocently and talking about everything under the sun except fuel. After all, he had his own supply. Winter didn't worry him.
>
> —Alexander Solzhenitsyn, *Matryona's House**

The New China commune, north of Canton in "flower county," is exemplary for the political climate you breathe there, a sort of counterpoint to the quotation from Solzhenitsyn on the Russian countryside. The leaders of the revolutionary committee are among the gayest and most likeable people we have met. But what is important here is the method of industrialization this commune has followed since 1958. Indeed, any one who wishes to understand something about China must start with this consideration: each commune creates bit by bit the base for industrialization, which allows one to foresee, ten or twenty years from now, a decentralized industrial development, a network of small and medium-sized factories reaching into the furthest localities.

Let us take a look at the New China commune. It cultivates 85,000 mou, of which 75,000 are irrigated and 58,000 are planted with rice. This by itself would not be much. What *is* important is that this commune, organized in 1958, has set up seven factories and twelve agricultural enterprises (for treating pork, bamboo, nuts, edible oils, and several other products of the earth). The factories build and repair agricultural machines, make lime, bricks, paper, treat sugarcane, and are connected to a stone quarry, etc. They have built, *being self-reliant*, three reservoirs which hold 35 million cubic feet of water. They have dug a forty-mile irrigation canal, created an artificial lake, built a dam with a new system of pneumatic locks, and set up seventy-three electrified irrigation pump centers. The dam was finished last year, during the Cultural Revolution, after two years and 600,000 man-days of work. Before, it would have taken six years.

In the area of mechanized agriculture, the commune has bought or built 68 new tractors, 120 rice-planting machines, 354 seeding

* In *Stories and Prose Poems*, translated by Michael Glenny (New York: Farrar, Straus, and Giroux, 1971).—*Trans.*

machines, and 1,000 harvesters. High- and low-tension lines go everywhere. Then they have built 4,000 new dwellings. The health system serves every brigade, and the hospital has had its equipment entirely replaced. Each production brigade—there are 31, divided into 326 production teams—has its own primary school and middle school. The commune also has a senior middle school. The income of each commune member has gone up. We are told that the relationships between the state, the collectivity, and the individual are positive. Before the Cultural Revolution the commune had to buy rice from the state: now, with irrigation assured, there are no more droughts and crops have increased to the point where the commune sells 8,700 tons of grain to the state. In the commune, peasant families (there are 13,000 of them, for a total of 61,500 people) have bought 14,000 bicycles and 2,000 sewing machines. More than 80 percent of the families have electricity and 80 percent have money in an account. The commune's income is divided in this way: 20 to 27 percent to the construction fund, 8 to 10 percent to the common-interest fund, and 10 to 11 percent in agricultural tax to the state (a tax which varies according to region).

"Now what we have to do," Comrade Tien Sun-ken says, "is develop grain-growing and hog-raising. Mao said: 'A pig is like a chemical fertilizer factory.' Between pigs and grain, therefore, there is a dialectical relationship: the more pigs there are, the more grain there will be, and vice-versa."

He laughs when he sees that his definition amuses us, and goes on offering us the nuts the commune produces and the bananas that grow in the fertile, sunny land of Kwangtung.

The leaders of the revolutionary committee of the commune are young (the comrade who is speaking is thirty and the other, Khao Tu-yen, is twenty-eight). Both were already leaders of the party and the commune, jobs they have kept while they worked to *revolutionize* their conception of the world. They played a key role in the Cultural Revolution.

"What is your judgment on Liu Shao-chi's policy in the countryside?" I ask Tien. "I'd like to get a better, more concrete, idea of how his line developed."

"During the Cultural Revolution our criticism pointed out these evils: Liu's line exalted the ownership of individual plots and the free market. It determined production on the basis of families and on quantity. This meant that a family with a big labor force, one which had money and was well equipped, could build up many work-points, while a small family that was poor got less. For example, before the creation of the communes, a family had to give a certain amount for a mou of land, let's say 500 yuan a year, and it grew what it wanted on it. If it produced a lot, it earned more than a family that produced less. And it could use the extra that it earned however it wished. It could sell its surplus to the market when the going price was greater than that offered by the state or when it found buyers who needed its products. Thus a division between rich and poor peasants—capitalism in the countryside—was being reintroduced. We criticized the 'freedoms' put forward by Liu Shao-chi: freedom to borrow on credit and to lend with interest; freedom to buy and sell land; freedom to hire agricultural workers; freedom of the market. The criticisms, made by poor and lower-middle peasants, raised peasant consciousness.

"But perhaps we should say that behind the attack on Liu Shao-chi, there were earlier incidents: in 1958, Khrushchev was already attacking the people's communes as something that was bypassed by history, something that only communalized misery. And he said that the people's militia we had built up in the countryside was nothing but a bunch of extra mouths to feed. Then the Soviet revisionists broke their contracts by cutting off deliveries, and at the same time we suffered some great natural setbacks. At the same time, the USSR ordered us to pay back the money it had lent us. We paid it back. But we were in grave economic difficulties. Then some bourgeois elements within our party, led by Liu Shao-chi, tried to stir up a storm and attacked the people's communes, saying they were a bad thing. They said the communes had been created too quickly, prematurely. In 1959 an enlarged meeting of the Political Bureau was held and the right-opportunist tendency of Liu Shao-chi was criticized. The tendency was corrected, but its ideological influence persisted. Of course, some rich peasants were in favor of a revisionist line, but the poor and lower-middle peasants' battle against them grew stronger each day. The struggle between two roads, two lines, two classes in the countryside grew. It didn't happen in the same way as in the cities, of course. Each struggle has its own characteristics, and Mao's 'The people's commune is good' campaign had been consolidating strength for all those years. So we can say that Mao's line always had supremacy. It is also the reason why production has increased from year to year in the countryside and why a Socialist Education Movement has sprung up. Yes, Liu Shao-chi had a certain class base in the country (landowners, rich peasants, reactionaries of all kinds), but they were all swept away as the Cultural Revolution advanced. And if my explanation satisfies you, could I take you and show you now? Seeing is always a lot better than talking."

We get into the tourist agency's little bus, on whose doors is printed in indelible ink, "Imperialism and all reactionaries are paper tigers." We begin our trip through the *industrial achievements* of the commune.

"This region was very poor," the comrade says, pointing to the surrounding countryside, "because they could never solve the problem of water. Nowadays it is easy to irrigate the land. With that help, and with the help of fertilizers (we are just now planting a plant which itself serves as a fertilizer), we are trying a new way of planting rice three times a year. Now we obtain from 1,700 to 2,000 pounds per mou in three harvests, but we want to get over 2,000 pounds. And in a year without calamities, we have experimentally established that you can really plant rice three times a year by this method, by planting the first two plantings as early as possible so as to have time to plant a third. For the moment this is merely in its beginning stages, for to plant a third time we need much more manpower and fertilizer."

Our first visit is to the *irrigation reservoir*, which we reach by crossing the Canton-Peking rail line. It is three-quarters of a square mile in size and forty-three miles long. Its capacity: 6.5 million cubic yards of water. It can irrigate, but it also has fish hatcheries which produce 11,000 pounds of fish a year. The fish sometimes weigh as much as 66 pounds. The reservoir stretches out like a blue lake at the base of the hills. The peasants have dug canals on the hillside which collect the water that used to cause them such woe and have channeled it into the reservoir.

A bit further on we see the dam, with its rubber floodgates.

"We used to make dams of wood, but they were far too expensive. We've found a system of dam-building which uses a pneumatic casing that stands up and puffs out like a wall and becomes as solid as the wooden gates were. Thanks to this reservoir and to the dam, we can now irrigate 30,000 mou of land."

A few miles further on, we come to the lime factory, which employs 130 worker-peasants. In this region lime is a necessary soil stabilizer and you have to put in 110 pounds per mou each year. Before, it was bought; now the peasants make it. With lime the rice grows better, each grain of the plant is fuller, and fertilizers fertilize more.

Around us we keep hearing explosions. These are the charges used to break the rock in the quarry not far away. The lime furnace was built by the workers and peasants the year before. Some wanted to buy insulating bricks from Canton, but that would have cost 70,000 yuan, so they made them themselves. The furnace is very simple, tall like a medieval tower. The stone is placed on top and the lime is collected at the bottom. They manage to turn out 25,000 tons of lime a year. They tell us that the rocks used to be carried up to the top of the tower on a man's back, but now an elevator throws them into the furnace. They're building a new chemical plant. It will produce, by purifying residues, a carbonate of lime which will be used in making medicine.

We move on to the quarry, which opens like a toothless mouth in the earth. Down in its depths they are setting off the dynamite charges we heard. The quarry is partly mechanized too, with buckets which move the gray stone swiftly to the top. The workers are all peasants, and among them are many women, working at the hard task of shoveling the stone that has been ripped from the earth and loading it into the little wagons. Further on we can see scattered over the commune dozens of brickworks. Each brigade has its own brickworks, something which made the intensive building of houses possible.

We continue to talk with our friends, and summarize our impressions this way:

"We come into a commune and expect to find rice and wheat fields and that is all. Then we come upon a factory that makes bricks, and that is fine. Then we find a lake, and we are surprised, but all is still well; then the dam, and it is becoming exceptional;

then the stone quarry and we are amazed. Then when we arrive in front of the furnace that extracts lime and lime carbonate, we don't know what to think. We say: 'Too much!' "

Our peasant comrades find this very funny. They say:

"But you haven't seen the tractor factories yet, nor the fertilizer factories. Nor the schools." In conclusion: "Have you any criticisms or suggestions?"

In a poor peasant's house in Hsin Tsun New Village

We and our friends are about to pay a call on Comrade Chen, and then to visit one of the peasant families in his production team. This particular team has forty-two families. There are innumerable children, and the lines of women carrying loads on their shoulder poles are astounded at the sight of us. We go into a peasant house where the head of the family welcomes us. With him are his wife, his five children, and his aged mother. His children attend the primary and middle schools, and his oldest daughter is waiting, now that she has finished junior middle school, for the group decision on whether she should be sent to senior middle school after a period of work in the fields. The little girl is very beautiful. She has two heavy braids which fall to her shoulders and she tells us that she would very much like to continue studying. The peasant house is entirely made of red bricks, uncovered inside. There are benches along the walls, a small wooden table, and two low chairs which we pull up into a circle to talk. We are able to admire a sewing machine, a bicycle, a table with glasses and china on it. At the end of the room are two large brick boxes covered with planks. They have something going on inside them, and strange noises come out. The peasants say there are rabbits in them. On the walls of the house I count twenty-two portraits of Mao, big, small, and tiny, on calendars or in other illustrations. Plus eight badges on the chests of the occupants.

"Our life is extraordinarily happy today because of Mao and the Chinese Communist Party. We had never had a real house before, it was always being destroyed by the floods. My mother had eight children, but only two of us survived. My two other brothers died of hunger and sickness. The Japanese aggressors blockaded our village and we were reduced to total poverty. So that we could survive, our mother crossed the blockade lines to get us a few sweet potatoes. But she was seen, arrested, and placed in a concentration camp. Before the Liberation, of a harvest of 450 pounds per mou we had to give 350 to the landlord. Why was our life so unhappy? Because we did not hold political power. In 1968 we built this house, and with the income from our work (our family can count on three workers, my wife, my eldest daughter, and myself, for my mother at 70 is too old) we were able to buy a bicycle, a sewing machine, and furniture. For the first time in our lives we eat all we want, we have clothes, and the children can go to school, though I am illiterate."

"Who built your house?"

The peasant, seated on his bench, moved because his family's eyes are fixed on him wondering what he will say, answers me very forcefully:

"We built it with our own hands. We were our own architects" —as he speaks he strikes one of his callused hands against the other—"me, the other poor peasants, we built all our houses. I helped the others, and when it was my turn, the others helped me."

When we arrived, in fact, I had noticed that this village was all built of new red brick, all of the forty-two families' houses. But I had not imagined that the architects of these square, well-designed houses, with their big yards, had been the peasants themselves.

"What is your family's income, with its three workers?"

"Each month our family may receive 130 yuan or more. In a year, this makes 1,600 yuan. The computing of our work is done twice a year, in summer and at the end of the year, according to the principle 'to each according to his work.' Ten points count for one yuan and twenty fen. Me, for example, I earn 10 points less 0.2, my wife 9.2, and my daughter 8.5 points. The total is given on the basis of the estimate we ourselves make of our work. There are days, today for example, when my wife does not work, other days when my daughter does not work."

We are leaving the village and I am still admiring these houses built by the peasants. We have our picture taken with the old grandmother who was a prisoner of the Japanese and who is now living a new life, the youngest children, the whole family and their friends.

"But who are the architects of these houses?"

Everyone laughs.

"Here are the architects," and they show the palms of their hands, proudly, as the peasant had, slapping them one against the other like paddles.

After we leave our friends at the New China commune, my husband says to me: "Twice I've had an urge to stay in China: once at the Shanghai Machine Tool Factory, and now in that commune."

"Well then, get out and stay," Tien says, and he opens the door of the car.

They are absolutely serious. But my husband hesitates. He has said something which goes, perhaps, beyond his real intentions.

"Fine then, goodbye and we'll see you soon," our comrades say, and they close the door again, courteously.

Liam O'Flaherty, as he was leaving the Soviet Union in the 1920s, wrote:

> When I crossed the frontier, I felt a kind of dejection and isolation. It was as if I had lost the battle in which I was to earn my honor, a battle in which I could, at the very least, have died trying to conquer a higher human dignity. It was as if I was fleeing beyond the enemy lines to vegetate in peace, to degenerate. In the train, almost everyone was a bourgeois tourist, and the keenness with which they hurled themselves at the dinner table repelled me. I felt the absence of simple poverty, of zeal, of seriousness, of the vitality ever awake and overwhelming in those fanatic builders of a new world. I was fleeing the battlefield, yet I didn't want to stay. I fled without shame, happy in my baseness, like a second Horace.

We, however, felt a profound desire to come back. We too are on a battlefield, *our own,* and of course we don't want to run away from it. And even if the struggle here is not the same, and if for fear of being superficial and of forcing things we hesitate to make comparisons, we can sense that our struggle is both directly and indirectly linked to the struggle of the Chinese Communists.

10

Medicine in China

My interest in doctors grew while I was in China. I don't understand very much about medicine from a scientific standpoint, but I come from a world where the medical problem, socially, appears insoluble wherever one turns. After I had my inflammation of the ear in Nanking I consulted several physicians between Nanking and Shanghai. My recovery was quite quick (fifteen days). The diagnosis was correct. The treatment was both Western and Chinese traditional: antibiotics and penicillin (made in China), as well as drops extracted from plants for my nose and my ailing ear. They kept telling me: "You see, in an illness, the *internal cause* is more decisive than medicine."

The woman doctor in Nanking who saw me and examined me at the hospital when I had a fever had hands as light as butterflies. She touched my head, which was in pain, and my ear without hurting me in the least. I see her freshly washed blouse, all patched together, so big that you would have said it belonged to her older brother, sleeves rolled up, the tails floating above her little feet in velvet shoes. Blue veins beat in her temples. Her face is pensive. She seems to me beautiful and self-assured. When I ask her: "Will I see you again tomorrow?" she answers, "I don't think so. I have to leave the city to do my tour with the barefoot doctors' team."

In Shanghai, in the big hospital in Nanking Street where I go for another examination, Professor Lu Yi, ear, nose, and throat specialist, takes my illness more seriously than the woman doctor because the fever has persisted and I can hardly hear anything with my left ear. He intensifies the treatment, makes meticulous notes on his chart, evaluates the present illness and its possible results. Then he concludes that in seven days I will be better. I say to him: "You won't be here tomorrow, I believe?"

"How do you know that?" he asks.

"I know that all of you work alternately in the hospital and in the rural communes."

"Yes, exactly," he responds good-humoredly. And, seeing a certain perplexity in my eyes, he adds: "Perhaps it is a little difficult for you to understand, but we learn a great deal from this practical experience among the peasants in the countryside."

He gives me a pill to take, and goes into the next room to fetch a glass of water.

"See," Chao says to me as the doctor walks away, "before the Cultural Revolution it was unthinkable that a great Chinese professor would himself go to fetch water."

"And who will replace you tomorrow?" I ask the professor, who also inspires confidence and calm in me.

"Someone like me," he replies, denying the privileged place I gave him by my question.

Indeed, I never saw him again, nor the woman doctor from Nanking. But every day, going to the hospital for injections (so lightly done that after a slight massage I could not feel whether the needle had been given or not), I meet other doctors. A woman, elderly and maternal, who attentively follows the professor's prescriptions, and a solidly built doctor who reads *People's Daily* regularly and wants to practice *acupuncture* on my husband, who has pains in his back as a result of a discal hernia operation in Italy. Alberto refuses. There follows a small scene. Our friends are perplexed and perhaps a little offended.

"If you are afraid, you shouldn't be," Lu says. "Look, I put five, ten needles into myself and still I feel nothing."

He gets up and holds out his arms like St. Sebastian. But the expression "If you are afraid" (indeed, aren't these Western Communists perhaps made of softer stuff than us?) has provoked in my husband a reaction of pride. He exaggerates, saying each person treats his illnesses as he sees fit, each country has its own therapy, that he has already been operated on, that what he needs is not acupuncture but vitamin C. They give him the vitamin and do not pursue the matter further. When we see the acupuncture specialist again, he greets us coldly, convinced of my husband's lack of courage and of our lack of confidence in traditional Chinese medicine. So I say: "Excuse me, but could I not be treated for my ear with acupuncture?"

"No, you have an infection, which is not the same thing. Your husband's case is different. There it is rheumatism, and acupuncture has excellent effects on rheumatism."

From the day that the "acupuncture question" arises, a slight chill exists between our Shanghai guides and ourselves. Acupuncture separates us.

Later, we ask for a meeting with a group of doctors and surgeons at a Shanghai hospital. The meeting is quickly arranged at the Huashan Hospital, which is under Shanghai Medical Institute No. 1. It is a 600-bed hospital, where 700 people work—doctors, technicians, nurses, and administrators, as well as the workers of the propaganda team and soldiers on the revolutionary committee.

Before we all go into this hospital for our discussion with the staff, I should point out that "the intervention of the proletariat in ideology" has transformed medicine as much as the university. In 1965, Mao violently attacked the Ministry of Health, calling it the "Ministry of the Health of the City-Dweller." "What does health protection mean?" asked the Chairman. "The expression becomes jibberish if it leaves 350 million peasants aside." He concluded that of the 500 million peasants, 350 million had no direct means of benefiting from health protection and medical care in their country areas. For millennia, the Chinese say, the exploiting classes have made medicine a piece of private property. Mao's directive was severe: "Center medical and health work in the rural regions; move its center out of the cities." This was a revolutionary step of huge importance. It rested on these points: (1) On the revolutionary transformation of the medical profession; (2) on a medical mass movement which will give birth among doctors, as well as among soldiers and workers, to proponents of a new health system for all; (3) on a decentralized structure which involves the training of thousands of barefoot doctors and the creation of thousands of medical centers, health centers, small hospitals, in the countryside and in the mountains, in the furthest zones; (4) on exalting the traditional

Chinese methods and treatments—acupuncture and herbal medicine—which are followed and administered by millions of men, not just graduate doctors but also barefoot doctors and soldiers of the People's Liberation Army, at the same time that the study of Western medicine increases, so that it can be integrated with Chinese medicine without dominating or replacing it. The "struggle between two lines in medicine," as the Chinese call it, seeks to conquer the "Liu Shao-chi orientation" that was limiting operations to the cities. You can see that Mao's medicine is already well along by simply looking in the windows of the pharmacies in the cities. Everywhere that traditional medicines are sold (they are generally sold in their own stores and Western medicines in theirs) there is a pink plastic model of a naked figure, a foot or so high, its body covered with finely drawn lines and figures. These are the acupuncture points, and you can buy a text which explains the numbers and the related medical prescriptions. The doll costs so little, about five yuan, that anyone can afford one. Next to the doll is a plastic ear: in the ear alone there are some thirty points at which the needles can be inserted to cure diverse afflictions. I found the "celluloid man" in each school, even in primary schools. And the funny ear, dotted with figures, was in the medical kit hung proudly around the necks of the middle-school children we met from Shanghai to Canton—next to their cotton batting and their instrument holders. "What are you doing?" I would ask them. "I'm learning simple medical facts," the student would reply, noting that acupuncture was sometimes used on city patients, but more often in the countryside. "We're going to try to be useful even if there is a war." The students carry around their toy-like plastic ears, their medical books in among the others in their bags. But it is no game. In schools I found whole herb gardens kept by the teachers and their students; children of ten or more can collect and dry herbs to draw simple medicaments from them. On balconies and terraces in front of schools, like the geraniums in the south of Italy, are medicinal plants. The barefoot doctors' movement teaches the Chinese from primary school on up how to give medicine to the masses, how to treat each other and even themselves.

China has 200,000 doctors and specialists, according to our criteria. Around this core—which Mao felt insufficient and ill-suited—

there developed during the Cultural Revolution years a "barefoot medicine" which could arrive at any time and be dispensed by anyone, soldiers, mothers, schoolchildren.

Conversations with Huashan Hospital doctors

The principal people at this meeting: Professor Yang, an old doctor of 73 who is a well-known dermatologist; Dr. Ling, specialist in Chinese medicine; Lu, a female employee; Comrade Hsuan, member of the hospital's revolutionary committee; Comrade Chen, another woman employee; surgeon Wan; Dr. Lin, professor of internal medicine; Liu Sun-tuan, a soldier-comrade of the People's Liberation Army propaganda team; and, finally, Lin Yang-chen, a worker on the hospital's Mao Tse-tung Thought Propaganda Team.

Lin, the worker, speaks first:

"This hospital has a history which goes back more than sixty years. It was built by a group of American Protestants and basically served the capitalists and the landowners. After the Liberation, the hospital grew a great deal and now it is twice its former size."

We are gathered outside a cottage, all of carved mahogany, in a garden full of plants, dwarf pines, rushes, flowers in Chinese vases, and numberless lakes with little pagodas and wooden bridges. We are told that this dream garden was built by a capitalist whose daughter had tuberculosis. Now it belongs to the hospital and the sick. The worker continues:

"The revisionist line of Liu Shao-chi had disturbed the revolutionary line of Mao in the hospital. The doctors, too, showed signs of bourgeois ideology. In October 1968, with the arrival of the workers' propaganda team and the People's Liberation Army, the Cultural Revolution entered the hospitals and radically transformed medicine. Doctors, guided by the thought of Mao Tse-tung, tried to change their view of the world. They underwent a profound inner transformation. They applied Mao's principal directive: move the center of health from the cities to the countryside. We sent seven teams of doctors into the countryside; except for those who were sick or weak, all the doctors in the hospital went into the countryside two or three times, in turn. They were re-educated by the peasants, the soldiers, the workers. Their class consciousness changed, and they began to be able to believe in the cause expressed in the words 'serve the people wholeheartedly.' The doctors and the professors will speak to you about this experience themselves. On another front, we achieved important medical successes in this hospital by applying Mao's philosophical thought. We pursued and explored medical practice and scientific research with a new drive. That is all I have to say in introduction."

Professor Yang Kuo-lien speaks. He is very old. His bushy beard is entirely white, and his black tunic, a sign of his profession, is frayed under his shirt.

"I lived a half a century in the old society, where I was one of the intellectuals," the professor says. "After the Liberation, I followed Liu Shao-chi's revisionist line in the area of health. I worked at the faculty of dermatology, where I had set up ten research groups. I concentrated my efforts in this theoretical field, but, separated from practice, it was a vain kind of research. I made an enormous effort to collect scientific materials, to write articles in important journals, to augment my personal prestige and that of the group. Many were the specialists who did not put proletarian politics in the front of their lives, and who practiced medicine in the great cities without thinking that there could be a role for us to play in the countryside. All our research was aimed at making us physicians of renown in the great cities. Mao, on the contrary, teaches that one must serve the poor peasants, the workers, and most of all those peasants who totally lack doctors. For years we did not follow Mao's line. Before the Cultural Revolution, we were unaware of the weaknesses in our behavior, even ethically. But in studying the thought of Mao we realized that we had been following a revisionist line. Take my case. I was a member of the party for ten years, but for me that had no meaning other than that everything was as it should be. That is why, after the Cultural Revolution, I asked to go to be re-educated among the workers and peasants. In October 1968 the work team entered the hospital (the workers have an enormous sense of abnegation and sacrifice) and they greatly helped me to re-educate myself. They gave me the chance to participate in the work of a medical team in Kiangsi province, in a region where we had to climb mountains to reach the sick. 'You are old, you cannot go so high,' they told me. But if we really intended to move the center of health to the countryside, specialists like me had to be able to go to the aid of the peasants where they most needed it."

The old professor's hands move across the cover of the tea pot. They tremble, they pause and warm themselves, they stop trembling. I am extremely moved in seeing this, and I take notes with my head lowered. The professor watches us timidly through his thin eyeglasses as if to observe whether our reactions are as strong as the emotion which makes him tell his life before us.

"The poor peasants told me of the life they lived in the old society, the changes they have known since then, and how they love Mao. They profoundly re-educated me and changed my class position. Working in the countryside was for me a chance to renew myself. But I wanted to do something else, because I am a member of the Communist Party. So I decided that I should fear no difficulty and go to the most far-removed areas of the mountains. Once I and some others climbed on foot more than 3,000 feet, a walk of twelve miles. The road was extremely rough. Few could follow it. There were moments when I felt I couldn't go another stcp. Then I thought about the 'foolish old man who moved mountains' and I kept climbing forward along the rocks. There were four of us. The three others were young. One preceded me, the other stuck by my side, the third, a fat man, followed me, fearing I would fall. But when we went down the mountain again I went as fast as the others. Those two months in the mountains made me stronger, made my desire for work increase, and rooted out the traces of bourgeois ideology in me. I can say that I have become younger. As Mao says in his poem, 'Though we cross countless mountains, we are not yet old/and the view is only more beautiful.' I learned Marxism-Leninism not from books but from direct contact with the peasants. Two months later I did the same work in the province of Honan. My companions wanted me to stay in Shanghai to rest, but I told them that I had no business fearing difficulties or fatigue. Some told me: 'You are over 70; retire.' I replied: 'I cannot retire as long as the class struggle goes on and the task of socialist construction still weighs on us.' As a party member, I must fight in the front lines; as a doctor, I must put all my effort into surpassing the world level in medicine. I still have an uninterrupted revolution to carry out in my own life, in my mind, following Mao's thought."

Comrade Lin speaks. He is about thirty-five, with a high forehead, black silky hair cut fairly short, a well-proportioned face with large features.

"I am a specialist in internal medicine. In the fall of 1968 I went into the countryside to learn from the poor peasants. Once our team stopped in a village where there was a woman who was considered incurable. The family was already preparing for the funeral. I decided I had to pay a call on this woman too. I examined her closely and I realized that she had a generalized arthritis; she had not been treated in time and she had swelled up. I asked her family, 'Why didn't you ever take her to a doctor?' Her husband told me angrily that they had taken the sick woman on a stretcher to a city hospital four years before, that this had cost them much money, but that the hospital had told them she was *incurable*. Back in her village, the woman took the medicine prescribed for her but the sickness worsened steadily. I learned from her husband that the doctor in question belonged to the same hospital as I did. When I returned, I looked through the files and found that the doctor who had made the incorrect diagnosis was me." Here he lowered his head like a guilty man. "I was tremendously upset and full of self-contempt. *Whom do we serve?* Mao asked. I was confronted with a very important series of problems. I had always replied to that question in the following way: We live in a socialist society. It is therefore clear that we serve the workers, the peasants, and the soldiers. For a young person like me, the important thing is to raise the level of medicine to serve the people. But the story of this sick woman taught me many things. I was medically prepared to cure the sick, but I lacked a just ideology. That was why I had examined the woman superficially and had been unable, not only to make a just diagnosis, but even to prevent her from becoming so sick that she was now almost dead. When I considered all this, I knew I had condemned her. This is how I came to understand that even in a socialist society the mighty question 'Whom do we serve?' must continually be asked. I returned to the countryside and again took up my work with the barefoot doctors; I had, at all costs, to cure this woman. The treatments I gave her were for me the beginning of a struggle to see the world differently. Each day I went to her house, I devoted all my attention to her, I observed her unceasingly; I adopted different treatments and mixed Chinese and Western medicine. After two months, the sick woman's health improved, she was able to get up, to take her first steps, and at length she could do a few light tasks."

The professor's lips are trembling. He is tense. His eyes are fixed on the table, as if he were at confession before us.

"After I changed my ideology, I cured twenty patients who had been considered 'incurable.' In truth, I believe it was the poor peasants who cured me of my ideological sickness, and not I who cured the peasants. If intellectuals do not pay attention to their own conceptions of the world, and seek to change them, they may possess a very high scientific level, but they are not in a position to serve the people."

Now it is the surgeon, Comrade Wan, who speaks. He is thirty, solid as an oak, has a bull neck and is rather fat for a Chinese.

"I am a surgeon. From 1967 to 1969 I worked in the countryside, first in a province in the south of Hopei, then in Honan. During these two years I acquired a rich experience which, at the beginning, was difficult for me too. I wasn't used to the work I was doing and I was losing weight and having piercing pains in the liver. The comrades who examined me told me my liver was hard as a rock and they feared cancer. They told me to go back to Shanghai. But I didn't want to leave the peasants and I stayed. Then they *ordered* me to go back to Shanghai for a medical examination. I could not refuse, but I was unhappy about it. 'If I have cancer, I want to give what time I have left to the peasants. If it is no more than an inflammation, I will come back here as soon as I am better.' Obviously I only had an inflammation, not cancer. I felt weak, I did not have the strength to get out of bed. Perhaps it was merely egotism, a mark of my inability to endure the test I had volunteered for. I read the story of Norman Bethune, the Canadian doctor who died for the Chinese fighters from an infection he contracted while giving treatment. I thought that thousands of men had died for the red flag. Then I had the strength to get out of my bed. Though I had not totally recovered, I wanted to return to the countryside and continue with the creative study of the work of Mao, through practice. The hospital organization didn't want me to, but they finally agreed and I returned to my region. From there I went to the autonomous territories and to the province of Honan with the second medical team. I had barely begun to try to apply the directive which said that health care had to move from the cities to the countryside, so I decided to go all the way."

He lowers his huge head. A gilded Mao badge shines on his chest; he rubs his head with one hand as if it hurt.

"The peasants made me understand what the old society was. My liver ailment disappeared. I now liked this region and I did not want to return to Shanghai. Sickness, I thought, can destroy the weak, but it cannot easily destroy a man whose will is reinforced by the thought of Mao Tse-tung. Then I came back to Shanghai for a new type of work. But this experience was decisive for me: we must integrate with the peasants, workers, and soldiers, for our whole lives."

Dr. Ling intervenes. He is a specialist in Chinese medicine, tall, lean, easygoing.

"In 1968, 10,000 worker-doctors were sent from Shanghai into the rural zones. The campaign for the decentralization of medicine had begun in 1960, and the ten districts of the Shanghai municipality had 3,900 worker-doctors working with the production brigades in the countryside. In 1961, there was the revisionist attack. All the medical centers were dismantled and there were only 300 worker-doctors left. After the 1965 directive, the districts of Shanghai, in cooperation with the traveling medical teams, sent out 4,500 doctors to train contingents of barefoot doctors. By 1968, we had trained 10,000 barefoot doctors. And the number we now have is 29,000. These new workers in the health field are at the service of the production brigades in the countryside in a proportion of about two worker-doctors to a brigade."

Now our discussion begins. We present ten questions for the doctors to respond to. Here they are; I think it is useful to list them in one place:

1. What type of hierarchy exists in the hospital? Are the chief surgeon and the ward leaders elected or appointed? How is this done?

2. How is popular control exercised in the health institution? Are the patients allowed a say?

3. How is preventative medicine carried out, especially in the matter of illnesses characteristic of a particular type of factory work?

4. Do medical students do their medical internships at the university?

5. Is research done solely in the institutes, or is it also done outside, in the countryside?

6. What links exist between the great scientists and the ordinary doctors?

7. What is the fusion of Chinese medicine and Western medicine? In this framework, what is the importance of acupuncture and the use of medicines extracted from plants?

8. What research has been carried out in new medicines?

9. What is the medical function of the barefoot doctors?

10. What contraceptive methods are used for birth control?

The doctors take turns answering our questions. I will summarize their answers without giving names:

"A revolutionary committee runs the hospital and each ward has its own revolutionary committee. Since the reconstruction of the party organization, which took place during the past year, the party is in charge of the hospital's political direction, while administrative matters are handled by the revolutionary committee. The various administrative decisions are approved by the leadership after it has been elected according to the democratic election principle of the Paris Commune. [This is a reference to a system of general elections, like that of the Paris Commune.] Here there is no trace left of the former hierarchy. There was one before the Cultural Revolution, but it was a senseless hierarchy, and we destroyed it. There was a hospital chief and a committee of hospital administrators composed of professors and specialists, men who had not transformed their conception of the world."

"Where is the old director of the hospital now?"

"He works as an ordinary doctor in the hospital. The comrades from the People's Liberation Army work in administrative work too. The administration here is thus the three-in-one combination, the organ of power defined by Mao's proletarian line. Specialists and professors, in rotation, are invited to work in the three great revolutionary movements to transform their conception of the world, as far as this is possible at the hospital.

"Control by the masses is necessary for the good administration of the hospital. The patients are the best judges of this, but they are not allowed to participate in the elections because they are only here temporarily. However, they can set up groups to study Mao's thought, in which patients and doctors study and work together and reflect on measures which might improve work at the hospital. The revolutionary committee has created a special team which collects the criticisms and opinions of the patients on the operation of the hospital and on the abilities and political spirits of the doctors.

"In the matter of preventive medicine to protect the health of the working class, we should tell you about our safety network, which is made up of worker-doctors who go to work in particular enterprises. They come from this hospital or from others, and they form part of the factory's health team, working together with the workers, not only to care for them if they are sick, but also to do something more important, to prevent their illnesses. These doctors live in the factories and study what the most frequent illnesses are. They examine the results of their inquiries. They analyze them. Then preventive measures are taken. Such a function cannot be carried out by these doctors in an office. They have to live in the factory. For example, in a chemical factory harmful fumes circulate during production. The doctor who has the practical experience of living in this factory knows exactly what must be done to eliminate toxic gases. And in being there, he can measure exactly to what degree the gas has been made harmless.

"Another way to work at preventive medicine is not only to improve plant equipment, but to reduce work speeds that can cause accidents. Thanks to the medical prevention network, set up in the factories by the doctors themselves, the number of sick people, as well as the number of industrial accidents, have declined. The victims of work injuries are all brought to this hospital. We can say that they are fewer as a result of this surveillance by the worker-doctors.

"On the internships of the medical students, our hospital is under the Shanghai Medical Institute No. 1 and the students come here to get the general rudiments. That isn't enough, though, and the students are also sent into the factories and into the countryside to deepen their knowledge. Even though they are still very young, practice makes them more thorough and accurate in making diagnoses. Medical students do a type of medical internship we call 'open instruction.' In a hospital it is difficult for a student to learn much about the most frequent kinds of sickness, those which hit most people and which can be cured in a clinic. So it is out there that they can make use of their abilities to deal with the commonest and simplest ailments.

"Medical research itself does not take place only in laboratories. It is also done in the units at the base. At the hospital here, we can conduct good research. But the directors of medical institutes also go out to the clinics at the base and collect hundreds of case histories of all kinds so as to know what medical research should study. They learn the most valuable lessons from this.

"As for the relations between scientists—'the luminaries of science,' as you call them—and ordinary doctors, nurses, and hospital personnel, they are relations of comradeship. The doctor and the nurse have relations of equality; the only difference is their experience, which is not the same. Even scientists are not considered precious specimens to be kept locked in laboratories or operating rooms: their science belongs to the people, and it is through these bonds with others, through collaboration with them, that it is enriched. Medical research, which is very important to us, is a question of spreading tasks around and not one of a subdivision between great doctors and lesser ones. All are working for the same objective: the revolution. In the area of salaries, too, we are in the middle of a struggle-criticism-transformation movement attempting to limit the differences in salaries, to lessen the distances between the various qualifications, even if these are obviously not going to disappear entirely. And this process of restructuring salaries is going on throughout the whole country.

"The fusion of Western and Chinese medicine is a shining idea of Mao's, one which we follow with great success. Both Western and Chinese medical treatments have both extremely positive aspects and insufficiencies. Chinese traditional treatments, for example, have made their contribution to the history of Chinese medicine, but in some respects they are not scientific. Western medicine developed as a modern science, but it has its metaphysical aspects too. Dialectical materialism and metaphysics have always been in bitter conflict in medicine. Our bourgeois medical authorities, working from their metaphysical viewpoint, considered their medical experiments and writings as absolute and unchanging truths. Often they diagnosed illnesses as *incurable.* Dialectical materialism teaches us that everything is in movement and transformation. Human knowledge and its potential for transforming what seems incurable are constantly developing. That is why we say that there are *no illnesses that are absolutely incurable.*

"Not even cancer?" I ask.

"Not even cancer. Precisely. Diseases like cancer will be cured when we learn the natural laws they obey, as has happened with other diseases throughout the history of medicine. The principle we follow is the one taught by Mao: 'The movement of transformation in the world of objective reality is without end, and hence man is never done learning the truth in practice.'

"As we examine the human body, we consider that it is always a unity of opposites. Its various parts are united, one to the others: they are in opposition and at the same time depend on each other; they are linked and act upon each other. A pathological change in one part of the body can affect the organs of the other parts, or the whole body. The condition of the body in its entirety can modify the course of local pathological changes. It is only in dialectically examining the relations between the parts and the whole in all their aspects, and in regulating them, that we can know the disease and cure it.

"Take, for example, the healing of fractures. By Western methods, the limb is enclosed in a cast to wait for the bones to merge again. The arm can't move, and sometimes it takes three or even six months of absolute immobility. By the time the bone has set, the articulation of the arm has often become stiff. Here is one of the limits of Western treatment. In the Chinese method, we put little wooden splints on the limb to fix the bone after setting it back in position, and we make sure that movement can begin as soon as the bone has set. It is a question of resolving the contradiction between stability and movement. Since we did not previously use X-rays, we did not know, in traditional medicine, exactly how the bone had broken and that was a drawback. In short, those who use one type of method treat only the fracture and neglect articulation and the overall body. Others do not limit their interest to the beneficial aspect of immobility for setting a bone, but also note the drawbacks of a healing method that prevents the simultaneous reassertion of the bone's solidity and the functioning of the whole limb. This is just an example. What is the conclusion? That in dealing with fractures, the doctor-workers of China use what is positive in Western medicine and what is positive in traditional Chinese medicine and immobilize the fracture with splints. This results in the unity of opposites, of the 'passive' and the 'active,' the part and the whole."

"What do Chinese physicians think of Professor Christian Barnard's research into heart transplants?"

"We have read various articles on this subject. From the technical point of view, what Dr. Barnard does is not difficult. But the method is not efficient because it is very difficult to find a healthy heart in a person who is biologically dead. We could say many things about the possibilities of transplanting an organ from one human being to another, but to do Dr. Barnard's operation you need a living heart—he therefore took the heart of a person who was not dead. Our law (since a heart can begin beating again after a twenty-minute arrest) forbids such a removal."

They all laugh ironically.

"The participants in transplants, whether as donors or receivers of organs, are black men or mulattoes," I say. The doctors know this very well and the old doctor of seventy-three shakes his head in disapproval.

"Now let us talk about acupuncture. It is an old tradition of medical science, not just in China but the world over, as anyone who has studied it thoroughly knows. When we say that Liu Shao-chi wanted to introduce a revisionist line in the health field, we mean that he claimed that traditional Chinese methods had no scientific value. Even before the Revolution, acupuncture had been almost completely eliminated by the reactionaries of the Kuomintang. Following Mao's call to dig deep into the immense heritage of traditional Chinese medicine, we studied acupuncture, and we obtained good results with it. The People's Liberation Army has treated deaf-mutes with it. Even paralysis has been treated with it, and we have obtained improvements here too. You would be interested in visiting one of these centers.

"You asked if we have manufactured new medicines. We have developed a new type of antibiotic for the treatment of burns, the one that you saw at the Shanghai Industrial Exhibition. We concentrated our research on the part of the burn which secretes green pus, and from there we developed a new type of antibiotic which eliminates this pus. It was in a little factory in Fukien which is under the university's auspices that this antibiotic was invented. It has yielded extraordinary results, in particular on a woman with 90 percent of her body burned.

"We have also had important results applying our scientific methods of production to modern drug production, and in perfecting the traditional Chinese pharmacology. Here again, new medicines were developed from plants. We now have, at an extremely low price, a new drug which is very good for toxic dyspepsia, one of the most common diseases among children. Doctors from the pediatrics department visited hospitals and research centers in the most distant regions, the furthest provinces, to learn from local experiences. They collected two hundred local recipes for treating this disease. By applying modern scientific knowledge and methods, and examining and analyzing various plants, they were able to find a few plants which were more efficient than the polymyxin antibiotics, and they made liquid or powder extracts from them. These plants are very easy to find, the medicines we make from them are very cheap, and they don't have negative side effects."

"And what about research against cancer? In every medical center I have seen people studying plants and preparing local recipes for medicines that are tried in the treatment of cancer. I have the feeling you are following a path that has already yielded some results in America with vinicristine and vinblastine, both made from plant extracts. I believe that you say that nature is a great whole, that we grow up eating plants, and that it is possible to find the approach to a cure by investigating both the external world and the internal world."

"For cancer, too," the doctors reply, "one of the research paths we follow is precisely that one, tied to the experiments with plants that are carried on in hundreds of localities. In this sense the traditional Chinese pharmacology offers a precious base.

"You asked another question, about birth control. Our party and our state attach a great importance to this question. This work is done in different areas: (1) There is, first of all, the work of ideological education, based on a political propaganda which can convince people of the importance of this aspect of life, so that the masses can become conscious of this necessity in the building of socialism. We do not impose anything on anyone. But we do return often to the work of discussing the importance of birth control. We give courses and deliver talks. In each factory or commune production team, there is a group which has the task of discussing this topic and there are doctors who are able to give all the necessary explanations of contraceptive methods. (2) We have developed all the necessary contraceptive products—the Pill, as you say. Also, for a long time now all the operations associated with abortion have been legalized. But we try, in this field, to go deeper into the problem. For example, doctors and workers in medical manufacturing establishments are now doing research on a new contraceptive product for women which does not have negative side effects like those found, from what we are told, in other countries.

"When, as doctors, we go into the countryside and we go into the houses of the peasants and their families, we explain what the situation is. It is then easier for the peasants to have confidence and to accept advice from a doctor. This is another fundamental duty of the barefoot doctor: the doctors who work in the countryside often perform abortions on peasant women who do not wish to have children—in their own houses when it cannot be done in the local medical center.

"Let us talk more about the barefoot doctors. One of our main jobs is to train barefoot doctors, and we help the people's communes create a basic health system. Doctor Ling gave you a whole series of important statistics on this. These doctors are trained by us in the following way: Each commune production team must have a certain number of barefoot doctors—one, two, or more. They don't stop working in the commune, they simply divide their time between medicine and the soil. They are also the living proof that the doctor's work is not totally apart from other people's. They are usually about twenty-five years old, and they generally come from poor peasant families. They earn 250 to 300 yuan a year, 100 from their agricultural work, the rest in fees from the commune. The salary level of the barefoot doctor is that of a manual worker in the countryside. These young people are trained in quick and simple courses. They can now treat the less serious diseases, which means that the peasant who catches one of these can stay in his village and be treated. The same is true for operations when the commune has its own hospital: these can be done by the surgeons who give their help in the countryside, aided by the barefoot doctors. Barefoot doctors also make plant medicines. More than a thousand types of plants are collected in some communes to help cure the sick of such things as constipation, burns, stomach aches, diarrhea, etc. This marks a huge saving for the country and is a form of direct health aid to the peasants. Though health care is entirely free in China, the commune itself has a great economic advantage if its pharmacies can offer medicines which are there because the barefoot doctors made them. Antibiotics are usually needed for intestinal infections, but in one commune they found a plant on the mountainside. Boiling and drinking the mixture cured some forms of acute intestinal infection. Thanks to all this work by the barefoot doctors, we have a basic health system, for where universities take years to produce a doctor, we take only a few months to train a barefoot doctor, who will then begin learning from practical experience."

We go with the whole group of hospital people who have been talking to us to visit several wards. On the door of each is hung a blackboard with the inscription, "Welcome to our Italian friends." The wards are simple and poor. Not only is there no trace of luxury, but the equipment consists of what is needed to practice good medicine and nothing more. In the paralytics' ward, we see many young people. A boy who has lost the use of his lower limbs—he is an intellectual who went to the countryside to work—has just gotten up and takes his first steps in front of us. There is another who was injured "on the northeastern front." He too gets up, hopping with a crutch. Then he brandishes his little red book and cries, "Mao *chuhsi wansui.*" For many patients the *internal cause is deci-*

sive, a doctor explains to me. To treat paralysis, they use acupuncture as well as Western medicine. In the surgical department, our friend Wan takes us near the bed of a worker who could well have been declared "incurable": he has nine serious injuries, his body is 30 percent burned, and he has a cerebral blood tumor. The doctors worked for six months on this human body, which was nothing but a wound. Now they can say they have cured him. On his night-table, the worker has a small plaster bust of Mao, the little red book, a can of milk, and some bananas.

In another surgical department, this one for children, there is a child who had a tumor on his arm as large as the head of a foetus—they show us a photograph. Previously they would have amputated his arm. But what would a worker's son have done with only one arm? "We cut away the diseased part and re-attached the arm. The arm is shorter, but it still performs all its functions." They ask us to check this by shaking hands with the child, who shakes our hands and says, "I am very grateful to Mao and his doctors." They show us photos of four children treated in the same way, one arm shorter than the other.

"We are able to re-attach hands higher up when they have been severed. When one peasant lost a part of his forearm, we attached his hand at the mid-point of the forearm. It is in the field of grafting limbs that we have had the most notable successes. Not only can we attach completely severed arms, but also fingers cut off by a thresher, legs severed by a train, arms ensnared in cables, and hands severed by punches. One particular example is a finger graft which requires operations on a very high technical level. We can also save a limb that has been partially severed for forty-eight hours, or one that has been totally severed for twenty-four, if the severed limb is kept in ice. Recently our hospital took care of a patient whose arm had been severed for twenty-four hours. During the trip here the arm was kept in a sack of ice, and we continued to keep it at a low temperature and to feed it locally throughout the treatment. After three days the arm began to move more and more, and the operation was a success."

The doctors gracefully accompany us to the door. All of them, except the old man, have strong and well-structured heads. This is a first-class team, an excellent school. The worker says:

"Now that diplomatic relations are re-established between Italy and China, perhaps there will be a better exchange of information between us, an exchange of experiences between Western and Chinese medicine."

I reply: "Yes. In Italy there is a great interest in acupuncture."

Then I ask the young comrade-worker: "What did you do before you came to the hospital with the propaganda team? Where did you come from?"

"I was in a typographical shop," he says. "We printed books for the primary schools."

The doctors stand in a row and wave goodbye to us, their little red books in their hands. The seventy-three-year-old professor is in the middle. His long and trembling hands shake the little book, his eyes glimmer behind his glasses, and he seems unsteady on his feet. "I became younger," he had said. But how was he before? I can make no comparison. I wave and forget to take a picture, so moved am I. In the car I say to my friend Chao: "For me, it is sometimes painful to hear people criticize their past behavior as the old professor did."

"It is not difficult for them," Chao tells me, "even in front of foreign friends. At first, no doubt, this self-criticism was difficult. For a doctor, confessing his weaknesses and lacks before younger colleagues used to be unthinkable, even more painful than speaking to strangers. Now it is different. They speak of themselves naturally. Their hearts have opened."

Grafted fingers in a hospital in the countryside

To see a hospital rise in the middle of fields is something new for me. The doctor is Comrade Lu, dressed very soberly, a scarf around her neck; she has thin elegant hands. The hospital has twenty beds and thirty doctors in different specialties. This is the health center that directs the health teams for the commune's 326 brigades. In 1962, this hospital, born with the commune in 1958, was almost abandoned because the doctors, following the revisionist line, felt that it was useless to care for the peasants in the countryside. They felt it was just as easy for the peasants to go into town to be treated.

"But later the doctors changed their conception of the world," the doctor says. "About one hundred barefoot doctors have been trained, and for the first time since the Cultural Revolution we have an operating room in this commune. The thing that is extraordinary for the poor peasants is that we can now do operations here which were formerly reserved for the great clinics in the cities—operations like the resectioning of a stomach, the grafting of a limb."

A peasant who is seated at the end of a bench lifts his hand; his fingers are twisted and brown like cigars.

"My hand was cut by an electric mower and my fingers fell to the ground," the peasant says. "I went to the center to get them to stop the bleeding. The new doctors from the town went to look for my fingers on the ground. They found them and put them on ice. Then they did a long and delicate operation and re-attached them. If the accident had happened to me in the old society, I would never have gotten my fingers back. If I have them today it is because of the good leadership of Mao and the Communist Party."

"I worked in a coal mine in the old society," another says. "I saw hundreds of comrades leave the mine dead because no one looked after them. Look—I have one leg shorter than the other because I fell under a sledge hammer in the mine and no one did anything for me."

He gets up and we can see that one leg is shorter than the other.

The peasant whose four fingers were re-attached shows us that he can move them; he moves his hand in front of our amazed eyes.

Now a young girl of about twenty arrives. Everyone greets her with affection and the peasants watch her with pride. She is wearing a braid which slaps against her back as she moves lightly, her step a dancing one. She once had a club foot.

"She was operated on here too," the doctor says. "The operation to lengthen the tendons was successful, and now she can carry a load of up to fifty pounds on her shoulders."

"In this country," the peasant says, "operations like the one I had and the one she had never took place before in anything but the big city hospitals. None of us ever thought they would happen in the countryside. All that is due to the thought of Mao Tse-tung."

What the peasant has said can help explain a certain type of typically Chinese formulation, often the object of glib Western skepticism. When the Chinese say, for example, that they have managed to remove a hundred-pound tumor in a case considered incurable using only rudimentary equipment but guided by the thought of Mao Tse-tung; when they say they have operated on a thirty-three pound tapeworm cyst on a mountain in Tibet, three miles up, amid snow—you have to understand this kind of language. These are not miracles from Lourdes.

What does the expression *due to the thought of Mao Tse-tung* mean? Here it means due to the decentralization of medicine, which brought doctors to the most remote places, which made them test their skills, using every means they could find, using rudimentary equipment, on the high plateaus, in the border regions, on islands, in order to try to cure people who had been considered lost, who had been considered *incurable*. Indeed, the doctors who form the base of this enormous decentralization are like doctors on a front in a war, trying to save lives that have been condemned. Nothing is less miraculous.

The hospital of the Canton commune has a research service dealing with medicines extracted from plants. Following Mao's call, the manufacture of traditional medicines received a great boost, and they are not expensive. The doctor explains:

"Medicinal plants can be kept anywhere and can be prepared on the spot. They are very widespread and constitute a medico-pharmaceutical reserve that is indestructible, even in war. It must not be forgotten that in medicine we must prepare to act in the interest of the people in case of war or natural catastrophe."

Medicines cost almost nothing: 5 or 10 fen for something to fight the flu, hemorrhage, inflammation from appendicitis, etc. In this hospital center, the research service is going forward with experiments in curing cancer with plants. In a huge herbarium I see potted plants that look absolutely ordinary, while they perhaps contain the extraordinary property of being able to conquer the "plague" of the modern world.

We visit the operating room, brand new and the best looking one I've seen—even compared to those of the great hospitals in Nanking and Shanghai. It has a radiology service, a blood bank, and resuscitation equipment. I think that the terrible thing for all the peasant populations of the world (the underdeveloped two-thirds of our world) is to feel that medical care and operations are a luxury which require, among other things, leaving home and taking a long trip to the city. Now, in China, they are trying to do the opposite. The dental office, with its chair and its shining chrome, makes me think of the weekly wait our peasants in Italy have for the village tooth-puller. In years past, when did you see a doctor in the Chinese countryside? Now they're all there, even the great professors. Naturally, they don't all come together, but each in his turn, as they explained to us at the Shanghai hospital. And the big thing is that the center of health is truly beginning to move from the cities to the countryside.

"Our first emancipation is socialist power," the peasant who heads the revolutionary committee says. "But the second is collective medicine, medicine in the countryside, barefoot medicine."

Our last stop is the storage area for medical supplies, full of boxes of dried plants. A violent perfume escapes them, a heavy odor that is both bitter and sweet. From this warehouse we go to the laboratory where the plant-based medicines are made. Herbs, roots, tufts of vegetable matter, and dried insects are handed to families in packets with precise instructions on the side as to boiling time and dosage.

In the acupuncture center they specialize in the treatment of infantile paralyses.

The hospital at Coppermine commune

It is a very poor hospital, but the peasants are very proud of it. There are already two or three barefoot doctors for each production brigade, and a group of doctors and nurses treats patients at the center itself. One can now come here for many operations, whereas it used to be necessary to make the trip to Nanking. The hospital has thirty beds and twenty-four people who work full time.

They show us the patients' rooms, with their shaky beds, their frayed bedcovers, and their poor tables, without any shame at all. It is a world of poverty, but everything is extremely clean. The operating room resembles one in an army hospital at the front, and the instruments seem rudimentary. They hope, as improvements become increasingly possible, to buy new medical and health equipment. Everyone is proud of what they have managed to do already, things that would have been impossible two years ago. Coppermine commune has two hundred production brigades which the barefoot doctors aid.

How barefoot doctors are trained

In the traveling center of the Evergreen commune fifty miles from Peking we are met by a young girl of nineteen who is both a barefoot doctor and a pharmacist. Her name is Kuo Yi-hsia. Her face is round and she has high Mongol cheekbones. She explains with passion how medicines are made, how much the peasants like "their old medicine," and how they set up the health center.

"It was created following Mao's 1965 directive about moving the medical profession from the cities to the countryside," she says. "The first core of barefoot doctors was formed in 1966, sons of poor peasants, boys of sixteen or seventeen. They had little education, had been to primary or middle school at the most. For three years, at night and in winter when there was no agricultural work, we studied under the doctors who had come from the cities. The first year we did theory; during the second and the third years we got the center together and began getting involved in practice. We worked on disease prevention, we distributed hygenic information and prophylactics. Beside that, we can treat the simplest sicknesses. We have cured peasants' sons, women, and old peasant women." She tells the story of a three-year-old child with a pulmonary infection which was treated and cured at the center. I think of that half-paralyzed old woman who was sent away from the big hospital as "incurable."

The young girl becomes enthusiastic. She says that Mao's thought makes it possible to overcome any laziness, that it is a will to courage and altruism. She tells us the story of her relations with her patients, imitating the gestures of the patients: she suffers, she is afraid, she doubts, then she gains confidence and there's recovery. Barefoot doctors at the commune cured a man of sixty who had arthritis in his legs and a woman with high blood pressure.

"Our center has thirty-six barefoot doctors, two for each brigade, and we are split into two teams of eighteen. The first team is only women, aged nineteen to thirty, who also act as midwives and distribute contraceptive information. Women are more listened-to than men on the birth control question. There are fourteen men. We go to the homes of the sick, because there are only so many beds at the center, and we cover long distances, going miles and miles on foot for as much as six days at a time, as long as there is sickness to deal with. We climb mountains to find the plants for medication, and we are now able to make the medicines ourselves and to take them to the peasants, just as we take ourselves to them and to their children.

"There is no barefoot doctor who works only at medicine. Everyone works fifteen days in the medical center and fifteen days on the land of the commune, in order to prevent any form of revisionism in them. There are only thirty-six of us for eight thousand people and that is not enough. At present we are organizing nine courses, and the center receives important specialists from the Peking hospitals' work team. We have shortened the courses in the hospital and we are giving accelerated courses in the countryside. So we keep on studying theory, while always tying it to practice. We learn of war by waging war. To increase our knowledge of acupuncture, we do experiments on ourselves."

While the young peasant-doctor speaks, all the women in the center—some with children in their arms, some pregnant—gather around her. The only one missing has just given birth to a very beautiful child and is still resting on the mat in the dispensary.

"We give out information on birth control," the young woman says, reading my thoughts. "It is information which is closely tied to ideology. We take prescriptions to the families and give them injections against conception. Nowadays the youngest couples have two or three children at the most."

"Who decides who will be the barefoot doctors in the commune?"

"The poor and lower-middle peasants elect someone from their production team. They say whom they prefer. Then there is a general consultation of all the brigade members, and finally the revolutionary committee of the commune chooses the final list. The list is then resubmitted to the assembly of all the peasants in the brigades."

The People's Liberation Army and the treatment of deafness by acupuncture

I saw muteness give up its secret and deaf children jumble their first words, all thanks to the intense exploration of new treatments by acupuncture. This is the kind of news which, when reported by Hsinhua in French and English, is received incredulously in the West, even though acupuncture rests on scientific foundations thousands of years old.

What is acupuncture in scientific terms? In the West, doctors consider it a three-thousand-year-old form of therapy from which came the modern treatment for pain by blocking nervous tissues by anaesthetic. For the Chinese it is more than that. It is linked to a very old tradition and to vast experience. Today, it is used in China on a wide scale. Here again the important thing is the mass line.

The scene: Deaf-Mute School No. 3 in Peking.

The actors: soldiers of the People's Liberation Army.

The patients: deaf-mute children.

I think that my report of these hours spent among little deaf-mutes will at least help Western doctors understand that the Chinese are not boasting but are reporting on a scientific field of knowledge. Also, it will help show (through the mass use of acupuncture by soldiers of the army) that all types of medical hierarchy have been abolished in China for good. Finally, I think this is the first account of this kind of episode written from direct observation.

We enter a small wing of the center at ground level (straw chairs, oilcloth table covering, poor but clean) and meet our hosts: Tang Shun-shan, soldier, head of the People's Liberation Army propaganda team; Wan Che-kuei, a woman teacher who belongs to the revolutionary committee; and Yen Nai-sha, a Red Guard who has just learned to speak at the school.

Medically, the school treats the deaf and the mute by acupuncture. We are told that after one year, 315 of 328 pupils can hear, 280 can shout "Long live Chairman Mao," and 180 can sing "The East Is Red" and recite other sentences and phrases from the works of Mao.

"The soldiers' and workers' propaganda team," Tang Shun-shan tells us, "came into the school in 1968 and liberated it from the old leadership which had been in control for ten years. With the brigade came a group of doctors who began to practice acupuncture at the school—formerly the young deaf-mutes had had to go the hospital to be treated."

I ask which doctor first tried this method.

"It was not a doctor," Tang replies, "but a male nurse from the People's Liberation Army, in the Shenyang Command. You see, in China whenever anything was impossible, we used to say that it couldn't be done *unless the mute speak.* Attempting to cure muteness by acupuncture was forbidden because it meant touching the 'yamen' point, 'the door of muteness,' situated at the back of the neck. Here too we had a struggle between two lines and two classes. The Ministry of Public Health, following the revisionist line of Liu Shao-chi, had consistently rejected acupuncture (which belongs to the richest heritage of old Chinese medicine), calling it a handicraft, nonscientific. Or else acupuncture had become a form of scholasticism, with more than a thousand needle points which were taught, along with the different uses of the needles, in a year-long course. The students went away stuffed with book knowledge: their minds were befogged and they were afraid to touch sick people. Also, the great doctors had a servile attitude about Western treatment methods and some would not use acupuncture, feeling it was provincial."

Tang Shun-shan goes on:

"We of the People's Liberation Army had studied acupuncture in the hope of treating the illnesses of the people, especially the peasants. The soldiers of Shenyang Command began studying traditional Chinese acupuncture with the doctors. We cut down the number of puncture points, we pushed the needles in more deeply and stimulated them more actively in order to increase the effect of the massage later. Where needles used to be inserted in great numbers and left for half an hour, we plunged in a single needle much deeper and drew it out quickly. We were trying to find the *principal contradiction*, applying Mao Tse-tung's teaching: 'In the study of any complex process, there exist two or more contradictions, and we must try to find the principal contradiction. Once this one is found, all problems are easily resolved.' The soldiers began trying acupuncture methods on themselves. Nurse Chao Po-yu proposed to find the yamen point on his own body, to touch the center of hearing and speech. It had always been said that the shallow penetration of the needle at the yamen point was useless, while a deep penetration would kill the patient. The soldier-comrade plunged the needle in just over an inch, hesitated, continued, was afraid. He felt his cheeks and his neck swell, his throat grow hot, his body shaken as if by an electric current. He thought he was going to become mute or die. But he made his decision, the soldier explains, when he remembered Mao's words: 'Arm yourself with resolution, do not flee sacrifice,' and 'When there is struggle, there is sacrifice.' He gathered up his courage—what he was doing could serve the people—and plunged the needle all the way in under his ear, finding the yamen point. After that, teams of soldiers went into the countryside to set up new centers of treatment. In February 1968 the soldiers' and workers' propaganda team entered this School No. 3 in Peking and began using the acupuncture treatment on deaf-mute children. But first we tried it on ourselves.

"We had hundreds of needle punctures in our own bodies. The needle, penetrating to the yamen point, often made our faces swell up so that we could not open our mouths to eat. But we realized that we had without doubt found the precise point for curing deafness. It was not until I was sure of my tests on myself that I began treating the children by acupuncture. We must undergo pain, but not impose any on our students. In the early part of 1969 I saw my first cures. Then we took the cured children into seventy rural districts and the peasants and soldiers who saw these children, once totally mute, speak, were so moved they sometimes cried. Our propaganda team at the school is composed of eight comrades, only two of them doctors; the others are four young soldiers and two teachers. After a year of work 95 percent of the students in the school can hear, and 90 percent can say a few sentences."

The once deaf-mute Red Guard speaks. She is still breaking the chains of her muteness and speaks in a whistling murmur, with difficulty. But she succeeds in saying distinctly:

"Today, Italian friends, you have come to our school. . . . Above all, I greet you by saying: 'Long live Chairman Mao.' "

This little girl with short braids, red in the face, and moved by the effort, takes her little red book and reads us a thought of Mao in a rough rush of words through a throat that used to be silent. Then she adds, spelling it out softly:

"My name is Yen Nai-sha. I am sixteen. When I was two I was a deaf-mute. Liu Shao-chi followed a revisionist line in medicine and the great hospitals were not at the service of the poor peasants, the workers, the soldiers, and their children. Mao sent the soldiers of the People's Liberation Army to cure deafness and muteness. After a year of treatment I can hear, and I can shout: 'Long live Chairman Mao.' "

We go with the young Red Guard, the soldier, and the teacher into the room where the deaf-mutes study and practice. The children all have little red books on their desks, and they place their hands on them. Their eyes are still those of wild animals, but they are no longer incurable. Their little eyes open wide, they get up, they applaud. One of the teachers approaches a little girl with a round face and long curved eyelashes, ten or a bit older, and proceeds to give us a practical demonstration of acupuncture. Without fear, the child crosses her arms on her desk, places her head on them, showing first her right ear, then her left. The teacher picks up a box, takes out a tube, and takes a long needle out of it. She quickly puts a bit of cotton behind the ear, then inserts half the needle at the yamen point. The child is quiet as a lamb and does not protest. She simply closes her eyes a little as if she were sleeping. There is only a slight pinkness behind the ear. Then the child quietly turns her head, and the teacher inserts the needle behind the other ear. "It is like a small electric shock," the teacher explains. The child remains with her head on her arms, looking at us, her braids held by red rubber bands, a Mao badge on her blouse, the little red book beside her. Finally she murmurs: "Goodbye, Italian aunt and uncle."

"The secret of healing," the teacher says, "is not only in finding the yamen point. Above all, we must create an army of medical personnel (first of all the 'barefoot doctors') to practice acupuncture on a large scale. Just try to remember that at Anshan, for example, they have a 'housewives' medical brigade; thirty-six women who have learned acupuncture and who have even cured cardiac cases considered incurable. The fact that acupuncture has been made available on a large scale is what has made many cures possible. In fact, we have found in our experiments that for deafness and muteness, the frequency of acupuncture—once or twice a day for each child—is decisive. It is unthinkable that a doctor in a big hospital could treat a child more than once in a while. In the beginning the child only starts to articulate, and it takes another year before he or she picks up many words. This is the most difficult period."

We go into another class. Three children, screaming, fight to pronounce a sentence written on the blackboard. When a guttural doesn't come out of the throat of a child, the teacher stops him and makes him repeat it. She points with a long bamboo stick at the Chinese characters written in chalk, under which romanized characters are written to help with pronunciation.

We go to look at an exhibition of photographs of the school. It shows many acupuncture "martyrs," soldiers of the People's Liberation Army standing in front of mirrors trying to puncture the backs of their necks. Some have deformed faces like the carvings in the fountains of Rome. Then we see pictures of the first teams of barefoot doctors, trained by the soldiers, going to treat the peasants.

We go into a hall where there are several rows of battered chairs lined up against the wall. The deaf-mute children are going to give a performance for us. They enter in groups, running and waving their little red books. They sing, "Hello, Italian friends, you are always welcome here." Then they move forward in a group, the little ones in front and four slightly older ones on the side accompanying the singing with drums, an accordion, and a Chinese harp. They all plunge into a song which goes: "The iron tree blossoms and the mutes speak."

Their faces are strained with the effort. The syllables explode and sometimes disintegrate in their atrophied throats. Others, however, come naturally. The guttural cries are strident. The will of these children, their mastery of themselves, their absolute determination, push them to articulate sentences, sometimes in formless sounds, sometimes in clear words. I realize that they do not feel inferior in front of us, only proud to show us what they can do. They dance with grace to "The East Is Red," carrying yellow paper sunflowers in their hands. Then, following the musical accompaniment, they sing sentences that are becoming more and more complex: "We solemnly acclaim the 'May 20 Directive.'" Then, still untired, they sing: "Be determined, fear no sacrifice, surmount all difficulties." Their eyes shine like mirrors. They are liberating themselves from their infirmity.

"The children in this show are from ten to fifteen years old," the teacher says. "They have been in treatment for a year and before coming here they were totally mute. They are all worker and peasant children. Research by the doctors showed that deafness and muteness are illnesses which, in the children of the poor, often go back to lung infections, badly treated colds, fevers, meningitis, or earaches. One peasant child of five who could not consult a doctor when he had bronchial pneumonia became deaf. Now he has totally recovered his speech and his hearing. It is clear that when muteness or deafness have causes of this kind, we quickly reach complete recovery."

It must be stressed that acupuncture rests on a traditional medical science, which is a science and not magic. Let it also be pointed out to Western doctors who are sarcastic about acupuncture that alongside the scientific aspect, there is another, which is the extraordinary human relationship which springs up between the patient and the soldier or the barefoot doctor in this mass therapy. What can one say to those who mock the acupuncture of the yamen point by these soldiers? No, Mao is no physician; no more are the soldiers. But in fact, besides offering the Chinese people the rediscovery of a renowned practice, these soldiers and barefoot doctors are presenting them with a moral behavior, a medical ethic, on a mass scale, that helps make it possible to bear sickness: courage, generosity, and absolute devotion of the carers to the cared-for.

The *political climate* in School No. 3 (which is a very sanctuary of human devotion) helps deaf-mute children start their lives again, helps them develop confidence in themselves, pulls from them the act of will necessary for them to speak their first syllables. Just before my departure for China, I saw Roland Neam's film *Mandy* on French television. It is a pathetic story of a deaf-mute child who is the victim of the lack of affection of her bourgeois parents, and who is cured at last by a simple doctor who liberates her from her loneliness. When, at the end, the little girl manages to say "Mommy," millions of French television-viewers must have cried. This happens in our countries, where we are inspired by the idea that one human doctor can exist among the thousands of merchants of health. Why then turn up our noses at the same quality in barefoot doctors who emerge from the masses and have no diplomas in medicine?

"In the West," I say to the teacher, "there is a hierarchy of values among doctors, bureaucratic and political values, with the 'mandarin,' the egotist, interested in profit and often incompetent, at the summit."

She says simply: "It's the result of the dictatorship of the bourgeoisie, and of retaining the privileges of a small caste of health exploiters, with their expensive clinics, their expensive hospitals, their expensive medications. Capitalism has no organic interest in caring for human beings."

And indeed, in the West the relations between patient and doctor are generally commercial ones. The patient is alienated by a medical hierarchy and ideology and by his resignation before the inevitable, before death. It would be too easy to let the responsibility fall on a lack of professional conscience among doctors, many of whom understand, in fact, that the root of the evil is in the backward society we live in and in the medical education they are given. Everybody calls for a new health system, but what lies at the root of the problem is the capitalist system.

I quote a letter Malaparte wrote me from China in 1957 on the love the Chinese bear the humans they care for. Malaparte had fallen sick at Chungking and was taken to Hankow and then to Peking. He was in Chinese hospitals for three months:

> It seems that in Hong Kong the English, the Americans, and the Chiang Kai-shek Chinese talked a lot about my case. They say that I asked for it, that now I'll have to learn to have confidence in People's China, that if you fall sick in China you're dead, there are no hospitals, public hygiene is neglected, etc. My dear Antonietta, I wish all the hospitals in Italy were as modern and well equipped as Chinese hospitals. At Urumchi in Sinkiang, beyond Tibet, I saw an all-new hospital complex which was twice as big as the Niguarda [in Milan], and Urumchi is still just a pioneer town in the Chinese Wild West of Sinkiang. Attached to the hospital is a great medical and surgical university, very well equipped, an institute of clinical and biochemical research, etc. All this not six miles from Milan, but at the foot of Mount Pamir, in the Turkestan steppes, in a town where people—Kazaks, Turks, Kirghiz, Uigurs—move around on horseback. Ultra-modern hospitals, I've seen them everywhere, in Kiangsu, in Shensi, in Szechwan, etc. My sickness will have turned out not to have been simply a painful thing. It will let me speak of public health in People's China not from hearsay, but from experience.

The soldier with the red-starred cap who displays that simple familiarity that circumspect people suddenly have when they realize there is a community of ideas between them and us, waves to us and the group of children.

"Mao's works are like the sun," the deaf-mute children call like a flight of gulls. They add: "Come visit us again, dear Italian uncle and aunt."

Medicine as mass work

Our long conversations with the doctors and patients of the Shanghai hospital and our visits to the communes and the acupuncture center for the deaf do not clarify all aspects of medicine in China, not even the one that is perhaps most interesting, the relation between practice and research. Naturally, I cannot bring a "specialist's" judgment to bear on this or that treatment or operation, but it nevertheless seems to me that in seeing what has been done and what continues to be done we learn one of the main aspects of the "Chinese approach." It is that, in this land of 500 million peasants, what is being attempted is a generalization of knowledge which not only does not harm research, but in fact constitutes the widest and most solid base possible for research to build on. In a certain sense, it is a *compulsory route* for China to follow. But it is also a *new route* for all of humanity. We can smile at the barefoot doctors and their "techniques." But the realities cannot be denied—these doctors are extending the practice of preventive medicine to the furthest reaches of China, and are actually *taking care* of the peasants, which is in itself a mighty result to have achieved in the light of what has been done in other countries. And the barefoot doctors, as they accumulate experience and refine their knowledge, gradually become real doctors, able, as the Chinese say, to draw on all that is best in Chinese medicine, including acupuncture, and all that is best in Western medicine. The same thought occurs to me regarding the doctors who go out from the hospitals or research centers to work in the countryside. Not only do they bring the peasants physical proof of the egalitarian spirit of Chinese society, but they learn to know life, to know the people they are there to care for, and in their own world.

Will this method last? I do not know. But I have the clear impression that this horizontal development creates the conditions which will let China achieve surprising results in a vertical sense. In the same way, the Chinese development of nuclear techniques cannot be dissociated from the work of generalizing technical knowledge among the people. In any case, this mass medical effort can only raise the level of China's medicine.

11

Introduction to Shanghai

"Socialism is a marvelous thing; a pity it doesn't work"—so one of our comrades, bemoaning the failings of the USSR, once remarked whimsically. In Shanghai, socialism works. It keeps things running smoothly in a city which, including its suburban areas, numbers 11 million people, the largest port in China and one of the biggest in the world, without anyone getting the least personal profit out of it.

For a bird's-eye view of Shanghai, we go to the top of a skyscraper built in the old days by the Americans. We are shown the site of the British embassy and the triangular garden which once exhibited the famous sign, "No Chinese or dogs admitted." Rising in the distance among the other skyscrapers is the Cathay Hotel, where I had stayed in 1954.

"Shanghai once had as many townhouses as Hong Kong," murmurs Yang, a comrade from Shanghai. "They were all built by Englishmen and Americans who came to our shores. For them Shanghai proved to be a promised land: in a few years they had made a fortune. The proprietor of the Hoping Hotel [the sumptuous townhouse in which we are staying] came to Shanghai with one suitcase to his name and without a penny in his pocket. At the end of a few years . . ."

From the top of the skyscraper, Yang points out the small tributary of the Huang-pu, on whose banks opium dens once stood.

"A starving Chinese, out of work, would make his way there; he would be induced to smoke and then, once he was well drugged, he would be thrown into a sack; when he came to he would find himself on another continent, sold as a servant, hardly any different from the old black slave trade. He would sell ties, work as a cook on a ship or as a servant in the home of some rich person in New York or London."

But Yang only knows the half of it; he is, I think, only dimly aware of what went on in the West—that people would say, "He has a Chinese cook" to indicate someone of high status, or that the Chinese who worked for whites were the butt of a sly sort of ridicule, a shoddy collection of anecdotes and jokes.

"And there," says Yang, indicating what is now the site of the Sailor's Club, "was the English court, which tried and sentenced the Chinese according to its own laws and imprisoned them in its own dungeons."

Shanghai in the old days was Sodom and Gomorrah: its 800 brothels made it the largest bordello in the world; it was a haven for receivers of stolen goods, black marketeers, international criminals, procurers; it was a city famous for its obscene diversions. Yet it was here that the struggle for a "human" condition began; here, in 1927, that the workers suffered a terrible defeat when Chiang Kai-shek, in yet another violation of the treaty of alliance, gave the order to *exterminate the Reds.* I am shown the little yellow villa on the Huang-pu whence the generalissimo, disguised as a fisherman, escaped in 1949 on a junk while the People's Liberation Army surrounded the city and while the Americans waited offshore to put this last remnant of imperialism in safekeeping on Formosa.

In Shanghai everyone has a fighting past. For the first time, Chao speaks of himself, of his childhood in Shanghai, and of his mother, a Communist militant whose job was to transport arms to the soldiers of the People's Liberation Army and who was captured and savagely murdered by the Kuomintang. "She was a heroine," he adds modestly.

Shanghai has always been decisive in determining China's destiny and even today, in a sense, it clinched the victory of the Cultural Revolution when its 1.2 million workers (the working class of Shanghai, not counting transportation and service employees) became the architects of the Shanghai commune and its revolutionary committee.

Shanghai-Calcutta: understanding China

With the panorama of Shanghai spread out before us, a prophetic remark by Lenin comes to mind: "The world revolution will pass by way of Shanghai and Calcutta." Perfectly true, but in Shanghai it has already come to pass—in Calcutta, not yet. Today, Shanghai and Calcutta are, in a way, the alpha and omega of an alphabet which can deliver us from the illiteracy of our Eurocentrism and enable us to understand Asia, and hence China. One has to have known the other Asia—the smell of India, with its blend of foulness and incense, the eyes filled with horror, the sickening decay—in order to understand China. I remember India as a country inhabited by a shadowy people, bereft of light, living in darkness, groping their way. In India, little children, their hollow eyes ringed with purplish circles, cling to your legs like leeches, brandishing their sores and stumps. They are hardened beggars. Hordes of lepers, blind men, and cripples imprison you in a circle of tainted flesh, rapacity, mystical neurosis, squalid devotion. They sleep on the ground, spread out over the vast reaches of the city of Calcutta. They die, on the average, at the age of twenty-seven. I remember Benares—the impassive holy men covered with dust, and a cataleptic people, afflicted with every imaginable disease, lying along the steps that descend to the Ganges, waiting for death; and the blazing funeral pyres, the sacred cows that go in and out of the temples; and the Parsee cemeteries on whose towers the vultures feed on rotting corpses, letting a shred of flesh fall on the unwary passer-by as they take to the air. All this must be remembered, I think, if one is really to understand the strength of China, to understand what cities like Shanghai—once as tragic as Calcutta—started from. Gandhi was received in India as the prophet of a population of believers he wanted to deliver from their misery. He failed, and yet even today the mere mention of his name will rally the Indian people. For the Chinese—and this is how the "cult of Mao" can be explained—the Chairman is the messiah who came to liberate the people. But contrary to any metaphysical expectation, he liberated them by leading them, weapons in hand—"political power grows out of the barrel of a gun"—through the longest revolution in history, from victory to victory, the most recent of which, the Cultural Revolution, is not the last but only the first in a long series of further revolutions.

Mao's prestige would be unimaginable for a Western head of state. But what's so shocking about that? The forms in which his thought is disseminated are, to be sure, contrary to our own custom, but why shouldn't other forms exist? Furthermore, what, in essence, is this "cult"? It doesn't consist simply of reverence for a finished work (nobody would be shocked by this in the case of Nehru, or Gandhi), but of an attempt to propagate Marxism-Leninism so the masses can make it their own—which they must do if they are to advance toward socialism. In my country, this cult is identified with Stalinism. But in fact it is something utterly different. The act of arming the masses with ideology is the very antithesis of the Stalinist praxis: whereas quotations from Stalin were used by the state apparatus in the ideological repression of the masses, Mao's thought teaches them that "to rebel is justified," and gives them the freedom to express themselves even if they make mistakes. The contrast between the amorphous, resigned masses of India, and this China, bursting with floods of human energy, makes it possible to understand not only the superiority of socialism, which goes without saying, but the transformation of the people; the metamorphosis, as in Shanghai, of the dregs of humanity into an immense political vanguard. What must be clearly understood is that this revolution is founded on an ideological revolution set in motion by the masses' appropriation of Marxism-Leninism, of Mao's thought. This "cult" is nothing other than the continuous practical application of revolutionary theory.

The life of the Huang-pu

From our windows we watch the river traffic on the Huang-pu. It is a vast artery, where all sorts of craft come and go—ships of 10,000 tons, twin-sailed junks, small craft, and little boats piloted by women who have put Mao's portrait, instead of a saint's, at the helm. At night we are awakened by blasts of the foghorn, its long, mysterious sound penetrating the blue velvet curtains. The panorama of the Huang-pu is reminiscent of the Thames and its docks, especially in foggy weather when the harbor master's watchtower tolls the hours like Big Ben—except that it strikes up "The East Is Red." Or again, it might be compared to the port of Amsterdam, with its miles of quays and canals. A trip down the Huang-pu is all we need to get an accurate picture of the physical layout of Shanghai. The harbor master has put a fast speedboat at our disposal and we take a three-hour excursion toward the confluence of the river with the Yangtze. We don't get as far as the Yangtze, for the river port goes on for fifty miles until it meets the sea, but we do get a taste of the teeming life of the river, with the great factories of Shanghai lining its banks—factories which seem small, seen from the inside, as compared with their external dimensions—the forest of smokestacks along the banks, the unbroken walls of sheds. Steering part way along the forty miles of quays and anchorages, we see large buoys dotting the river, which is a quarter of a mile wide and almost thirty feet deep at this point. The captain tells us about the river, providing the vital statistics we need to appreciate the industrial power of Shanghai. It is about seventeen miles from the urban center to the Yangtze, fifty-six from the Yangtze to the sea. At the confluence of the Huang-pu, the Yangtze is over nine miles wide, a vast port of entry and embarkation, through which an average of thirty foreign ships pass each day. There is an almost infinite number of sailboats and, most of all, of transport vessels: barges by the dozen, often drawn by motorboats, coming in from the communes with food supplies for the city and leaving the city laden with machinery needed by the communes. This is a mode of transportation particularly well suited to this area, which abounds in navigable canals that run like streets from the outlying areas toward Shanghai. The small craft, their maroon sails reinforced with long, lightweight bamboo rods, go at a great rate when the wind comes up, outstripped only by the fast speedboats of the navy. On the banks beyond the naval yards and factories rise the lofty outlines of the great cold-storage warehouses, where the big ships come to unload fish and other perishable goods. This is perhaps the greatest river port in the world.

The Hoping Hotel: the cloistered world of the foreigners

At six in the morning, whatever the weather, even if it's rainy or foggy, we are awakened by legions of Shanghai citizens singing on their way to work, or by troops of schoolchildren, with a drum and a portrait of Mao leading the procession. The harbor master's big clock chimes the hours, and many a night I lie awake counting them, brooding over the political fever which transports this city and disturbs my rest. In the bustling crowd, some people gather in a circle around a child doing acrobatic gymnastic tricks; others hold discussions in front of the tatzupao. Crowds of people wherever you look. A world in a state of perpetual effervescence. And the most striking contrast in Shanghai is between these throngs of people, filling up every bit of available space, and the emptiness of the hotels. The Hoping, in a superb location overlooking the Huang-pu, is deserted: a tree without leaves. Countless salons plunged in darkness, carpets on which no one sets foot, armchairs in which no one sits, endless corridors lit by small yellow lamps. A musty smell. Workers are repainting the rooms in one wing; perhaps they are getting ready to reopen it. Now that the revolution within the revolution has triumphed, I say to myself, perhaps China will resume face-to-face communication with the world—it has never stopped communicating with it politically—and will once again open its doors to the foreign universe.

It is cold in the hotel, but before we know it the heat comes on. Everything seems catered exclusively for our convenience. In the semicircular dining salon on the top floor, its bay windows opening on an extraordinary view of Shanghai, from one bank of the Huang-pu to the other, we see only four people: two at one table, two at another. They eat their meals in silence, barely glancing at us. Foreigners, like us; even greater strangers than we are, perhaps. Once we catch a glimpse of the obsequious Japanese gentleman from the commercial delegation in Peking, but we immediately lose him again in the dark labyrinths of the hotel. The brightest lamps are placed near the statue of Mao, reminding me of what a Parisian friend told me: "At night in the hotel, when I didn't feel like staying cooped up in the room and I wanted a bit more reading light, I went to sit on the pedestal of a statue of Mao."

My memories take me back to Shanghai in 1954, to its townhouses full of foreigners, where sumptuous receptions were given. I was staying then, as I've said, at the Cathay Hotel. I take another look at it; it seems closed. At the time I had handsome accommodations on the fifteenth floor; every evening I found a flower on my table, its stem wrapped in silver paper, ready to wear as a corsage. *The Bicycle Thief* was playing at the movies; foreign magazines and newspapers were prominently displayed on the stands. One evening there was a reception at the hotel that was so extravagant that I wrote in my journal:

> The hotel salon, resplendent with crystal, silver, and flowers, glitters like a great glass bell-jar suspended in the sky of Shanghai; from the outside, one can see the lights sparkling through the enormous bay windows, their heavy drapes drawn aside. In the salon, where Indians, Burmese, Japanese, Mongols, and Pakistanis rub shoulders, there are many Chinese women, which is nothing unusual, but they are different from these we've seen up to now, for these are the women of Shanghai: the most attractive, the most stately and graceful, in all China. They are wearing their afternoon or evening clothes: long, slim, form-fitting tunics, their only hint of coquetry a slit on the side, open to the knee, revealing the supple curve of the leg. Their gowns are of black or dark-red velvet or of silks with designs of flowers, dragons, landscapes traced in gold thread. All the dresses are cut the same; the side slit lends them a touch of lightness and style. Their faces, touched with white powder, seem to emphasize their cool, unfathomable expressions. Their hair, silky and heavy, rolled into a "page-boy" style or caught in a net, smoothly frames their faces; now and then the soft colors of a flower bloom behind an ear, making a superb contrast with the blackness of the hair.

Such ostentation is unimaginable today, in the China of the Cultural Revolution.

That skyscraper hadn't been to my taste, and I had written at the time:

> I am staying in a skyscraper which the English pompously baptized the Cathay Hotel; it is an architectural horror, but not the least of them in a city whose style has repeatedly been desecrated by the for-

eign rulers—each of whom had a replica of his own "home" built there. In these spacious rooms, with the thick green carpet and soft, roomy, salmon-pink couches, it is easy to see why the white man clung so tenaciously to the proposition that his presence was indispensable in a China that offered him—at the price of the sweat of millions of slaves—such sybaritic comforts. . . . The colonizer became very attached to this Chinese earth, and to minimize the risk of losing it, since he was superstitious, he took important precautionary measures, among them the elimination of the unlucky number thirteen wherever it appeared. And so the Cathay Hotel has no thirteenth floor, no room thirteen, no number thirteen in the cloakroom. A Chinese comrade said to me: "As you see, getting rid of the number thirteen didn't do the trick."

How Shanghai has changed! I remember the Huang-pu as I described it then, "covered with dilapidated junks or sampans jammed together under the bridges waiting for the signal to pass, like cars at a stop light." Today, as I've tried to show, the Huang-pu has become one of the world's best equipped and most modern ports. The gay lights of the townhouses have been extinguished; those of the work places, of the factories, and, above all, of the countryside, have been set ablaze. There is no longer anything in Shanghai which even remotely resembles the past.

Today the hotels are "ghettos for foreigners," and we seize every chance we get to mingle with the crowd, to share the everyday lives of the people. We had dinner at the Canton Restaurant on Nanking Road—a very fancy restaurant, Yang says, where a Chinese formerly wasn't permitted unless he was wearing European dress, and, in the evening, a dinner jacket. A double staircase of carved wood leads up to the high-windowed, mahogany-paneled dining rooms which today are frequented by the proletarians of Shanghai, alone or with their families. We are the object of eager curiosity—mingled, however, with a touch of superiority and amusement. The other diners want to see how we manage eating with chopsticks, and they laugh softly among themselves when I twice drop tiny shrimp, scarcely bigger than a bean, on my dress. Eating in a restaurant among Chinese families is like floating in a sea of gaiety, and the sense of isolation we had felt in the townhouse—the tables have really turned for a foreigner in Shanghai—is dispelled by the warmth of this crowd. In this restaurant, whose prices were formerly scaled to a clientele of millionaires, the meal for five cost us only five yuan: the most expensive dishes were the shrimp—1.80 yuan—and the fish in sauce—80 fen—and besides the main course we had bamboo shoots, cooked vegetables, soup with thin slices of pork meat and fat, a cup of tea, and two bottles of beer. The restaurants are organized as rationally as the factories: neither the customers nor the waiters have any time to waste, and everyone seems to be perfectly comfortable with a pace that we at home would find harrowing. These restaurants on Nanking Road, as well as the rows and rows of shops that line the thoroughfare, make it easy to see why the white man should have become so attached to his "superiority," to his civilizing role, in a Shanghai which harbored the temples of his dissolute morals and his power. He could kill, rob, and rape with impunity. And if the slaves rebelled the civilizer called on his race-brothers to send forth battleships and bombers to teach the Chinese their lesson, to teach them the very elementary lesson that *the presence of the white man is indispensable.* Surrounded by this throng of people, it is easy to imagine the theories the white man formed about the Chinese. "They aren't like us," they said of these people, of whom they understood nothing except that they had excellent tea and old porcelain which could be exported cheaply. "They aren't like us," echoed their mistresses and wives, watching as the coolie bent his back and agonizingly dragged the ricksha in which madame, under a white parasol, was going for her drive down the Bund or along Nanking Road. "They aren't like us," they said solemnly of the Chinese women who bore their babies with no help other than an old woman to cut the umbilical cord with a stone or bite it off with her teeth. Nor did they fail to voice their doubts about whether maternal love even existed among these wretches, who would often as not remain dry-eyed before the corpses of their children. The white man was convinced that the best these people—with their 4,000-year-old history—were capable of doing was polishing his boots, ironing his silk shirts, serving him his meals with silent discretion and the utmost speed. In addition to his activities as banker, industrialist, and exporter, the white man owned brothels and opium dens. In the brothels he offered Chinese women to his guests from abroad, and in the opium dens he gave

Chinese men something to make them forget that their women were being made into whores. Then he concluded: "'There's no doubt about it, they're not like us! Chinese blood runs twice as slowly as the blood of whites."

The history of Shanghai is the history of revolts and repressions, breaking like ocean waves, one after the other, over this immense city—until the day when a mightier wave swept away the filth of the black marketeers and cleansed the city. The colonizer was driven out, and all his commercial dealings went with him. All along the Bund he had founded his financial institutions, his banks, building them as if he expected to be there forever. Lofty, massive, austere edifices made of granite and marble, they proudly displayed their titles and functions on their façades: Hong Kong and Shanghai Banking Corporation, Banque d'Indochine, Bank of England, Bank of America, China Merchant Steam Navigation Company. When I last saw them, in 1954, the signs were still up but their windows were shut, their doors bolted, each barricaded entrance like the empty socket of the Cyclops' eye.

Today the signs on the banks have disappeared: the buildings, unrecognizable, now furnish lodgings, office space—they even house a revolutionary committee. On the Bund stands the villa of a great English textile manufacturer. I haven't paid it a return visit, but back in 1954 I sat in the garden which surrounds it, later recording my impressions in my journal:

> I basked in the sun on the white-columned court of the Georgian-style villa and for a moment I considered the sense of well-being a colonizer must have felt. Comfortably ensconced in a soft armchair, I looked at the blue and white Ming vases, filled with roses, scattered over the terrace in imitation of our lowly flower pots; before me, on a table of crystal and wrought iron, ancient green porcelain cups, precious antique pieces that had once waited to be filled with fragrant tea. In the background, in the English-style garden with its silken lawns, a Venus de Milo, a Winged Victory, and marble copies of other famous Greek statues did homage to the white man. How good and gentle the sun is in the villa of this manufacturer! How dirty and wretched the sun that filtered down on the marketplace of Shanghai . . .

How Shanghai has changed, even compared with 1954! The city

overflows with efficiency, dynamism, and raw labor power. The old districts are clean and make quite a creditable showing; the new districts, like those of Peng-Pu, now comprise a vast new suburb built on the ruins of the huts that stood there, sunk in mud or filth, in the old days. The brightest lights in Shanghai are not the lights of the townhouses or streets, for electricity is used primarily for the factories. The most radiant object I've seen was the surface of the polisher in the Shanghai Machine Tool Factory, so bright we could see our faces reflected in it like a mirror.

The streets of Shanghai

In contrast to Peking, all the stores of Shanghai are well stocked and one can spend hours window-shopping in Nanking Road, once the site of the most luxurious shops—like Via Condotti and Via Veneto in Rome, the Champs-Elysées in Paris, and Fifth Avenue in New York—the ones no Chinese used to be able to enter, like the restaurant, unless he was dressed European style. In Nanking Road there is a large store which sells nothing but pictures of Mao, badges, tapestries, calendars, and greeting cards citing Mao's thoughts. They must have at least fifty badges there, in various styles, designs, and sizes, but I am unable to find the one I'm looking for—white porcelain, printed with a color picture of the young Mao, very handsome and romantic, with soft locks of hair falling over his brow. Lu had had one, he told me, but he had given it as a present to his brother-in-law. The only gifts the Chinese exchange are these Mao badges, and the only things I can offer them, as comrades, without giving offense, are those which commemorate political events or refer to Mao's thought. And so we get up the nerve to present two silk banners to Lu and Chao, who are somewhat hesitant about accepting them. One depicts Mao walking with Lin Piao. On the other, Mao is seen in a white robe on board a boat, preparing for his swim across the Yangtze River. Reprinted beneath the picture are the lines the Chairman wrote after the crossing, in 1956:

> Heedless of boisterous winds and buffeting waves.
> Better this seemed than leisurely pacing home courtyards.

Today I have indeed obtained my release.
The Master had said on the river bank:
"Thus do all things flow away." *

There is a throng of people choosing badges in this "Mao department." I have noticed, in fact, that a change of badge constitutes the only frivolity in Chinese dress. They have badges for every taste: solid-colored badges—red, white, sky-blue—or multicolored ones; badges for sailors, soldiers, students, and workers; badges less than an inch in diameter and badges as large as four inches wide. An English diplomat who collects them is said to have tracked down 800 varieties; a Russian diplomat claims to possess 200,000 of them. There is a crowd around the counters, mostly young people. Nobody forces them to buy. They make their selections with such care, and are so certain of what they want, that there is no doubt that they are here out of their own free choice. What does this badge symbolize to them? A bond, I think, a commitment to their revolutionary future. There is a "Mao" on a little white plastic disc, with a red light which blinks on and off and a "Serve the people" inscribed in the Chairman's hand. It costs 35 fen, and after careful consideration an old worker buys one; Lu, in turn, buys two—one for himself, the other for a gift. In Apulia, the peasants hang pictures of Giuseppe Di Vittorio, Communist trade-union leader, in their homes, just as people do here with Mao's picture; it is the only common parallel I can think of. After the liberation of Italy, Togliatti had wanted pictures of the martyrs of the Italian Resistance to be displayed like pictures of saints.

At the photographic display counter, a whole set of pictures of young soldiers and Red Guards: A girl, her eyes riveted on Mao, the little red book clasped to her breast. A betrothed pair, their right hands holding Mao's little book, their left hands joined affectionately. Just as young honeymooners in our part of the world have their photographs taken in front of the Tower of Pisa or St. Peter's or Niagara Falls, so the Chinese have their pictures taken against a backdrop of Tien An Men square during the May Day demonstration, or the Nanking Bridge or, most often, a picture of

* From *Ten More Poems of Mao Tse-tung* (Hong Kong: Eastern Horizon Press, 1967).—*Trans.*

Mao. Who compels them to do so? No one at all, I remind myself again. Millions have themselves photographed this way, by the photographers in town or by small country photographers, with retouching, Rudolph Valentino-style—features sharply defined, hair cropped close, judicious shading, eyes glittering.

Many of the window displays show a great deal of imagination—the confectionery shops, the fabric stores, the children's clothing and toy stores. But the windows of the Chinese drugstores are what fascinate me most of all, for here are the medicinal herbs of the traditional pharmacology and the acupuncture model. The shoe stores offer a great variety of wares (leather shoes cost 8 yuan, a little more if they are fur-lined). Models of machine tools of all sizes are on display, an admiring crowd always in front of them. There are typewriters too—3,000 Chinese characters!—which no one can afford to buy. There are also shops selling shiny, chrome-trimmed bicycles (their price has been cut in half in the last four years, from 200 to 100 yuan). At 34 Nanking Road, in a bookstore called "The Class Struggle Continues," one can buy all of Mao's works and most of Marx, Engels, and Lenin. Only one title by Stalin: *Foundations of Leninism.* This is the little-red-book shop. A foreigner receives complimentary copies of Mao's works, the Chairman's thoughts, Chinese magazines and newspapers, at his hotel, but each citizen, in the city as well as in the communes, must pay out of his own pocket for the works which interest him: so, reading them really has to be a matter of choice.

In experiencing the intense, direct quality of this way of life, a taste for simple pleasures returns, and this is also part of the small-scale metamorphosis experienced by the foreigner in China. A film, a revolutionary play, or a visit to the zoo becomes a major event in one's day. I went to the Shanghai Zoo with an enthusiasm I hadn't felt since childhood. At first I had refused ("The zoo? I want to see the Chinese!") but now here we are, striding along in the rain, wending our way down the green paths, moving from cage to cage. We are captivated by a seal who, for the reward of a few fish, balances on his nose the ball thrown to him by the keeper. Two tigers from northeast China, as big as horses, look painted, their white, black, and yellow stripes, glassy eyes, and great whiskers are so perfectly defined. New to me are the Himalayan panthers, their black-rimmed eyes and white cheeks like a dancer's make-up . . . and they are herbivores. We go about the zoo with a band of schoolchildren at our heels. They are interested not in the tigers or the panthers or the clever seal, but in *us*. If we had been in a cage with a little sign I'm sure they wouldn't have been at all surprised. From time to time they hide behind trees to laugh at us more uninhibitedly, then they resume trotting along behind us, ten steps away, never too close. They are obviously sorry to see us leave and they turn back disappointed to the zoo.

There is no better proof that the past is dead than the fact that we are such a curiosity for the people of Shanghai. The young people and children are seeing these white bipeds, these ex-colonialists, for the first time since this city was practically closed to foreigners. So it is difficult to *get anywhere*. No sooner do we enter a store than people rush in to see what interests us, and when we leave they join the group waiting outside, enlarging it so that the walk turns into a procession. The curiosity we arouse remains courteous, however, with no sign of contempt or hostility, proof of the politeness the Chinese exhibit toward those they don't regard as enemies. A whole people is invested with the nobility and refinement of manners that we at home associate with a "great gentleman."

Commanders without ranks

In China it is very difficult to categorize a person according to his appearance, for our standards, ranks, dress codes, and attitudes no longer apply. It took us some time to realize that our friend in Peking—the one at the Hsin Chiao Hotel who had helped us deal with a thousand boring details—was a man of some importance, as evidenced by the fact that when we had wanted to make a change in the itinerary it was he who had done the telephoning and he who made the final decisions. During the official dinner we were given in Peking, he sat in a place of honor at the table. He always helped us carry our bags, and yet he must have been a highly qualified administrator who hadn't wanted his identity to be known to us. Through casual conversation we are becoming aware that our friend Chao must have more important duties than those of an ordinary staff member of the tourist agency. The representative of the Nanking Revolutionary Committee said to us as we left: "I can't come to the station tomorrow morning; I have to leave at dawn to go work on the rice harvest." Imagine the mayor of Rome, New York, Leningrad, or Prague telling you such a thing! With each step we notice that any hierarchical or bureaucratic mentality has disappeared. Just as ranks have been eliminated in the army, so no outward symbol or protocol distinguishes the party leader from the plainest citizen; in fact, the comrade who seems to us to be the most modestly dressed invariably turns out to be the *one in charge.* "Modesty helps one to go forward, whereas conceit makes one lag behind," says Mao. But there is something else here, too: a new way of looking at life. We have the feeling that here, unlike in certain hierarchies or general staffs in our Eurocentric societies, it is up to the very person who performs the highest functions to earn the esteem, the sympathy, or even the friendship of the masses.

Instruction without boredom: the interpreters

Sometimes the discussions go on for eight or ten hours with hardly a break for a meal. The people we talk with are indefatigable; they show a constant desire to compare ideas, to enrich their knowledge. In this respect they resemble French intellectuals, except that the Chinese are always coming back to the concrete, whereas the French are capable of reducing everything, even love, to abstractions. After seven hours of translating Lu's eyes are red with fatigue, but he says he just has a cold: "I'm not at all tired, I am only sorry to have translated so badly." Lu has gone several times to work in the countryside and also to the *People's Daily* printshop, where he learned the linotypist's trade: "But that was no hardship." Is being an interpreter a hardship? "Not at all," he quickly replies, "it is instructive, one learns a great deal."

In China, discussions are never brief—but they are never boring, either. Even when the speakers use phrases that are familiar to us, they illustrate them with concrete instances that put them in a new light. One is reminded of what Confucius said of himself: "Become a man of perfect virtue and instruct without boring."

Sometimes our friends the interpreter-guides express this universal zeal in a personal and deeply touching way, with us the object of their solicitude. "Not to have a correct political point of view is like having no soul," says Yang to emphasize the importance of acquiring a good political line, and he turns to us, in his much-patched coat and shapeless little green cap, with an expectant look on his face.

When we left Hangchow, Comrade Hsiu, who had been our companion for two days—he was a real walking encyclopedia and he had thought of simply everything, even of bringing bread to feed the goldfish in West Lake—stayed on the platform to wait for the train to leave. Young Comrade Hsiu, with his close-cropped hair, his little spectacles, his small maroon plastic bag imprinted with "Serve the people," thin and childish as a schoolboy, waving to us from the platform. We tried to express how deeply grateful we were to him for being so nice, so discreet, such a perfect guide, but he stood there, with his little bag, his velvet slippers, his white socks, smiling and only half satisfied. Then we told him that it was in China, while visiting the tea brigade, that we had truly come to understand the commune. At that, his face lit up. The train left and Hsiu remained there, frail and invincible, waving his arms at us until the very last moment, until the train had disappeared.

Those who would like to travel around China without an interpreter forget that if you don't understand Chinese, you are a sort of deaf-mute. The interpreter is the bridge between you and the vast outside world. Today, when I waited vainly for two hours for our guides to appear, I nearly went mad with anxiety. Where to go? Whom to speak with, and how? None of the few foreigners we have met here can believe that a "jewel" of an Italian-speaking interpreter really exists; all the writers, from Moravia to Parise, say that they never encountered such a person and that, furthermore, the tourist agency assigned interpreters as it saw fit, changing them constantly from city to city so that, as Parise said, "No sooner had one had the time to get attached to an interpreter than the next day, he was gone." We, in contrast, have now become a fairly close-knit group, surviving discomfort, impatience, petty annoyances, irregularities, urgent demands, and polite refusals. We feel ourselves gradually becoming deeply attached to one another, and when Lu's voice—"It's me, Lu"—answers at the other end of the line, no matter when we phone him, we feel a sort of affection and admiration which is not so much for the individual as it is for a way of living, of working, of "serving the people." When we leave or arrive in a city, passports in hand, they are the ones who have to fill out the police forms at the station (foreigners usually can't travel in any Chinese city without a permit issued by the police), they are the ones who get us the reading material which interests us, and, in response to a multitude of questions, provide us with fairly exhaustive explanations. They are the ones who reserve seats at the theater and, when we have had enough of the hotel, walk with us in the streets and take us to the popular restaurants or stores. It is perfectly obvious that this is in no way the "prison" some travelers have spoken of. It is true, of course, that sometimes one feels like Gulliver when that child of the eighteenth century arrived in the country of the giants: they overwhelmed him with kind attentions, passing him from hand to hand to get a closer look at this queer thing. We can go out alone as much as we like, but in general we don't.

When a Chinese is your friend, his good will knows no bounds. I lost the four-leaf clover I had found in a meadow in Hangchow. I had been keeping it in my notebook and the hotel waiter had brushed it away. Simply because I regretted the mishap, I told Lu I was vexed at having lost it. Whereupon they made another search, and when I returned in the evening I found it waiting for me like a gift on the small glass table in the salon.

The tatzupao of Shanghai: the freedom of the masses as proletarian democracy

We never tire of looking out the window at the river and the boats flashing through the water, their passage marked by two wings of white foam. Under the sun the river brightens, turns blue; in the distance we can see red flags and catch a glimpse of their inscriptions. But the continual stream of people which flows through the Bund and Nanking Road seems even more vital than the river. A hundred times, in early morning or evening, I have watched them putting up tatzupao on the walls which line the river banks. As each new tatzupao appears I hurry down to get it translated. These wall newspapers not only have writing, they also have sketches or color pictures which illustrate and summarize political events, or popular likenesses of friends or enemies. Shanghai is one big people's political art show. Only by traveling through this city—the largest industrial city in China—and seeing the tens of thousands of tatzupao which decorate its walls, from the center of town to the remotest suburb, can one judge the magnitude of the political passion that inspires its working class, a working class which is earthy, tough, and unpretentious.

Before I left home, an Italian comrade had said to me: "I would like to know if the Chinese are still so formal. When you meet, all this bowing to one another makes it impossible to break the ice." I can only reply that now we are simply thankful when they don't regard us with complete indifference, as has happened on occasion—at Textile Factory No. 17, for example. Even as friends of China, our political status is dubious: to put it bluntly, we are labeled "revisionists."

Before me a group of railway workers, making a careful job of it, has just finished pasting up a tatzupao with the heading: "Can the work of getting rid of the stale and taking in the fresh ever be finished once and for all?" The tatzupao explains the dialectical relation between old and new. "What is new today may become old tomorrow. This applies to everything, even to the task of inner-party rectification. Rectification is intended to give the party a correct leadership role. But this work of rectification can never be finished for good." And the tatzupao ends by reflecting on what Mao has said about the necessity for many more cultural revolutions.

Here is another poster whose heading is displayed in large characters: "Commentary on the theory of eating much and talking little." Then comes the text:

> In the old society it was said that the people should eat and shut up. This was a way of keeping the people from expressing their rebellious feelings against bourgeois society. But the Communist Party teaches that one eats to live, one doesn't live to eat. It also teaches that the people have to talk in order to make the revolution. If the people

don't speak up, if the people don't express themselves, they won't make the revolution.

The tatzupao deal with all sorts of events, from philosophical debates to political issues to theatrical works. Witness this critique of a play which was performed during the Cultural Revolution:

> In this work it was maintained that everything is going wrong in China. Is this true? Those who wrote it haven't been using their eyes and they have forgotten what life was like in the old society. What was Shanghai then? Compared to the tyranny we labored under in the past, today we have entered a period of happiness in our lives. The point of the play is to disparage everything we have accomplished and it obscures the fact that today the people of Shanghai are content, for they have embarked on a new road. And everything these people have done they owe to the Communist Party, to the dictatorship of the proletariat, to Chairman Mao.

This very day, November 2, a new tatzupao headed, "Can this really be idiocy?" draws our attention to the following tale:

> A young worker coming to the university out of middle school had no prior knowledge of what philosophy was, but through practice he worked out the following criteria: first, to learn philosophy proletarian class feeling is necessary; second, after some study Mao's works must be put into practice; third, the key question in philosophical studies is the application of philosophy to action. But this young worker studying philosophy heard a certain person say that his studies were idiotic. So, following the example of Mao's investigations, he undertook to analyze the situation so he could discover the truth about this fellow. In this way he learned that he was one of those who came to work late and left early. In analyzing the behavior of this man who had reproached him with being afflicted with *philosophical idiocy*, the worker further discovered that his critic hankered after good food and more comfortable lodgings, and finally that he fraternized with bourgeois elements. Starting from a class point of view, he thus discovered that it was not for nothing that this fellow had talked about idiocy, and he unmasked him to the movement.

Under the heading, "Take philosophy out of the philosophers' books so that it may become a keen weapon in the hands of the masses," another tatzupao explains, in a closely argued presentation, that two don't make one, and that to say the opposite is to display bourgeois idealism. It is signed, "Shanghai Electrical Factory No. 14."

In the morning, from the window we see groups forming in front of the new tatzupao to read and comment on them. Shanghai is overflowing with political fervor. Before going to work you go to put your tatzupao on the wall or to read the new ones, just as in our country you read the morning papers. This, however, is in no way a passive proceeding, but a matter of active participation, discussion, and criticism, which continues until it's time for work and people go streaming off to their jobs. The posters of individual citizens—small ones, no bigger than the page of a notebook—make a checkerboard pattern on the walls. Whole walls are reserved for them so that the larger posters won't overwhelm the smaller ones. Each of these expresses opinions and gives advice on all sorts of problems: the quality of goods sold at a certain store; the slow repair work on a pair of shoes or a watch; the cleanliness of the streets, etc. I am witness to a fantastic, almost absolute freedom of expression, a degree of individual participation in public life which is practically unknown in our country. I think of the "written questions" concerning poor mail service, a village without electricity, an impassable road, etc., which we in Italy, as deputies, present to the ministers to demand that the necessary measures be taken. I think of the quantities of letters which almost no one answers and which end up in the archives, abandoned to future generations of rats. The individual remonstrances of the Chinese resemble our parliamentary interpellations, but with this difference: theirs get results. The whole district reads and evaluates them, and I'm sure the district representatives waste no time in doing what is necessary. In any case, discussion of problems is open to everyone.

Here is an example of a small poster signed by a woman and posted next to a shoe store: "I came here and they told me it would take a week to repair the shoe. I went to another store and they repaired it right away. Is this a good way of serving the people?" A man who had taken his watch to be repaired is dissatisfied, and he puts it down in black and white: "I took a watch to be repaired and they told me that nothing could be done to fix it. I went to another store and they repaired the watch in two days. How do you explain that?" And he too concludes by wondering if this store is really serving the people. In another poster, the occupant of a building asks his neighbors to help him solve various problems, such as inadequate house lighting and needed street repairs.

As a result of these criticisms the masses are taking an increasingly active role in building people's power at the base of society. Even the revolutionary organs themselves are open to censure, confirming the extent to which the Cultural Revolution has made it possible for the people to recover the initiative vis-à-vis the bureaucratic apparatus.

In reading these small posters by ordinary citizens, you come to the realization that Mao Tse-tung's thought has accustomed an entire people to reasoning in accordance with the laws of a class logic which is inseparable from action. Thus the Maoist philosophy is nourished by the thought and creativity which accompany it. What is striking—and this point must be stressed—is the *absolute freedom* of each person to express himself, to say what is wrong, what is in contradiction with the life of a socialist state, without the least concern for hierarchy. Here, moreover, is the practical embodiment of the difference between this democracy and the Stalinist regime, which was an apparatus that set itself above the masses. The Cultural Revolution—and one gets a clearer sense of this in Shanghai than anywhere else—is a transformation of the superstructures which even revolutionizes the way people think. An immense mass meeting in which millions of workers, cadres, peasants, seek, through discussion, to determine the best course of action. An immense exercise in mental gymnastics, of several years' duration, which struggles to separate true from false, good from bad. The expression *dictatorship of the proletariat* comes to mind: completely distorted by the Stalinist praxis, in China it is rediscovering its true meaning. "What the Chinese Revolution reminds us is that the dictatorship of the proletariat is nothing other than proletarian democracy," writes Bettelheim. Which implies the broadest democracy for the popular masses, for the proletariat, and for the classes which fight at its side—for the overwhelming majority of the population. This freedom of mass participation and expression, including the *freedom to make mistakes,* harks back to one of Mao's basic axioms: The masses must learn how to liberate themselves through their own efforts, by drawing the lessons of experience. This dictum is one of the dominant motifs of the account of the Cultural Revolution in Shanghai which appears in the next chapter.

12

Report on the Cultural Revolution in Shanghai

A hundred years ago, Marx said of the Paris Commune: "Whatever . . . its fate at Paris, it will make *le tour du monde*." . . .

The historical experience of the Paris Commune tells us that to be victorious in the proletarian revolution and the dictatorship of the proletariat it is imperative to rely on the revolutionary enthusiasm of the masses in their millions and give full play to their great power as the makers of history. Lenin said: "The autocracy cannot be abolished without the revolutionary action of class-conscious millions, without a great surge of mass heroism, readiness and ability on their part to 'storm heaven.'" . . .

The mainstream of the revolutionary mass movement is always good and always conforms to the development of society. In the mass movement various trends of thought exert their influence, various factions emerge, and various kinds of people take part. This is only natural. Nothing on earth is absolutely pure. Through their practice in struggle and repeated comparison, the broad masses of the people will eventually distinguish between what is correct and what is erroneous . . .*

The official version of the Cultural Revolution in Shanghai

This account of the Cultural Revolution was given to us by Huang, a representative of the Shanghai Revolutionary Commit-

* From "Long Live the Victory of the Dictatorship of the Proletariat!—In Commemoration of the Centenary of the Paris Commune," an editorial which appeared in *People's Daily, Red Flag,* and *Liberation Army Daily* on March 18, 1971.

tee. It is the first time since the Cultural Revolution that Chinese leaders have released such a report for publication by Communist friends from abroad, so I think it is to our advantage to transcribe it as faithfully as possible. I believe it can supply a key to understanding the Cultural Revolution: it describes the whole process of development, the bitter and complex struggle, through which the pro-Maoist forces transformed themselves from a minority into a majority. Moreover, it emphasizes that the working class (and not just the Red Guards) was not only in the vanguard, but was decisive—a development which emerges as a new and vital factor when compared to the first Chinese Revolution. This account also makes it possible to recognize this mass debate as the most powerful movement of mass democracy in history; to evaluate the decisive role of the army; to define the nature of the struggle between the two lines; and, finally, to discern, through the vicissitudes in this industrial metropolis, the origins of the capitalist counterattack in a China ruled by the dictatorship of the proletariat.

The presentation lasted five hours. My personal observations are put in brackets; the few interruptions or interjections we made are in parentheses. Although this text is practically a word-for-word transcription, it may contain some minor inaccuracies. The subheadings are my own.

Comrade Huang's report

First of all, let me introduce you to Shanghai because this will make it easier for you to understand the reasons behind the Cultural Revolution in this city. For one hundred years Shanghai was an imperialist stronghold in the design for the dismemberment of China: the beachhead of foreign colonialism. But at the same time Shanghai was always a powerful force because of its working class—the most concentrated, the most militant, in China. Shanghai was the birthplace of the Communist Party and the site of its first congress. For fifty years, a head-on struggle raged between the bourgeoisie and the working class of Shanghai, and what was at stake was the victory of the proletariat and the defeat of the bourgeoisie, or vice versa. The bourgeoisie of Shanghai, trained in the school of the English, Japanese, and American imperialists, was extremely cunning, resourceful, and devious. But the struggle against this type of bourgeoisie gave the working class strength and endurance, turning it into a clear-thinking, well-disciplined force, ready for anything. Thus the working class of Shanghai, because of the anti-imperialist and anti-"comprador" struggle it waged directly at the point of the largest industrial concentration in China, has a greater wealth of experience than the others.

Although with the liberation of China in 1949, capitalist power was overthrown in Shanghai, the class struggle never ceased; it continued without pause under the dictatorship of the proletariat. But this struggle was different from the Anti-Japanese War of Resistance, from the struggle waged in the south and north of China, for in the earlier period the enemies of the proletariat were clearly recognizable and were confronted in armed struggle. After Liberation, however, the enemies disguised themselves and weren't so easy to identify. They had undercover agents within the Chinese Communist Party itself: revisionists, renegades, and traitors to the working class who took the capitalist road; irredeemable and incorrigible elements. This is why the struggle and the characteristics it displayed were so very different from those of the past. For seventeen years, from 1949 to 1966, Chairman Mao's line was supreme in Shanghai. This may seem incomprehensible to you in view of the kind of battle that developed. But in that period the leader here, the first secretary of the party in Shanghai, was Ko Ching-shih, who was very close to Chairman Mao and was a firm adherent of his theoretical and political guidelines. Moreover, Ko had been organizational secretary of the party, a member of the Political Bureau, and a deputy minister.

At the same time there were two disciples of Liu Shao-chi within the party leadership of Shanghai: Chen Pei-hsien, Municipal Committee secretary, and Tsao Ti-chiu, a member of the secretariat and deputy mayor of the city. They maintained a line which was incompatible with Chairman Mao's. Thus we can say that there had long been an acute conflict between two lines in Shanghai, a conflict which on several occasions had actually come to blows: for example, in 1951–1952, in the period of agricultural collectivization, and in 1957–1958, at the time of the Great Leap Forward. Liu's agents had been opposed to collectivization in the outlying districts of Shanghai. They were no less hostile to the subsequent trend toward changing the system of ownership in private industry and commerce, and they remained adamant until, with Mao's great call for the transformation of private into public commerce, they realized that the movement could no longer be stopped and resigned themselves to it.

How the new invasion of capitalism came about

Their strategy of opposition was to give the capitalists virtually unlimited freedom, on the principle of a collaboration between public ownership and private profit. As Lin Piao showed in his report to the Ninth Congress, in some sectors of the country the state administration was socialist only in form; in fact, power wasn't in our possession but was controlled by a handful of capitalist-roaders. A textile factory in Shanghai, for example, had been managed in pre-Liberation days by a fairly important capitalist. He had worked out a system of internal administration which was practically a carbon copy of the old capitalist system of management—with bonuses, fines, and above all, punitive measures against workers who failed to conform to the pace of production or abide by the apportionment of tasks, or who didn't have a submissive attitude toward the managers of the factory. After Liberation the system had remained in effect, its rules and regulations prominently displayed by the capitalist in his office, just as his grandfather had done before him. In 1954 Mao undertook an investigation of this factory; he read this list of regulations with its absurd standards and announced that it served the capitalists' interest to continue to control and oppress the workers. *Who is serving whom?* That was the key question. And the rules were removed from the wall. Was this case an exception? No, for in fact at this time a number of capitalists were commanding authority and laying down the law in the factories.

Why did certain leaders take the capitalist road? How can we account for their support of the capitalists? Some background is necessary here. The national bourgeoisie has a contradictory nature. During the democratic revolution it may, due to its oppression at the hands of the "compradors," be sympathetic to the revolution on a political level. On this basis a specific policy was followed with regard to the national capitalists: those who had done their part were given assistance, and we adopted a positive political attitude toward them; some of their representatives even entered the Consultative Congress or the National People's Congress. Similarly, after ownership changed hands they cooperated in the reform of working conditions. However, in the process of this transformation of the system of ownership, a sharp conflict developed around two questions: *Who is transforming whom? How is an enterprise to be run?* The bourgeoisie lost no time in showing that it would put up a fight over these issues. Mao's three points indicated the policy to be followed: defend the revolution by launching a counterattack in the countryside, aiming first at the "three evils," then at the "five evils."

[The "three evils" were the vices typical of government officials: corruption, waste, and bureaucracy. The "five evils" were offenses committed by capitalist businessmen who at that time were not completely absorbed into the socialist system: bribery of officials, tax evasion, theft of state property, cheating on government contracts, stealing economic information for private speculation.]

Mao's precept: Do not forget the class struggle

We have explained why certain leaders supported the capitalists. But how was it *possible* for them to give this support and why did they continue to do so even after Chairman Mao's investigation? Because they had the backing of Liu Shao-chi. Liu made his own visit to the factory Mao had inspected and gave instructions that countermanded the Chairman's. He didn't go into the workshops to talk things over with the workers, but instead went straight to pay his respects to the capitalist, who was still director of the factory. Just as "by dissecting one sparrow one can learn the anatomy of all sparrows," so an analysis of this factory reveals the nature of the general situation in the country. From 1957—struggle against bourgeois elements—through 1959—struggle against right-wing opportunists—up to the difficult years of 1960–1962, the proletarian camp was continually besieged, and the proletariat offered steadfast resistance. In other words, there has always been a conflict between two lines; under the dictatorship of the proletariat, the class struggle goes on. During the difficult years the state went through from 1960 to 1962—bad harvests, the USSR's unilateral treaty violations, followed by the withdrawal of all technical aid—the two agents of Liu Shao-chi who held top positions both in the municipal government and in the party, united their efforts in a drive to restore capitalism. At this point the conflict became particularly acute. On one side, the attack of the bourgeoisie; on the other, the counterattack of the proletariat. During this difficult period, in fact, Liu's two agents sought to reconsolidate their power by embracing the attitudes of the bourgeoisie in the political sphere and by attacking the proletariat. In the industrial sphere they followed the economist line, advocating bonuses and incentives, a very slow rate—a snail's pace—of development, and the necessity of foreign aid. In the sphere of agriculture, they supported the principle of small holdings, allowed the establishment of free markets for the sale of produce, and defended the free sale and purchase of land when the property was below a certain acreage. This struggle was clearly reflected in the Tenth Plenary Session of the Eighth Congress of the Chinese Communist Party in 1963. It was there that Mao gave this command: we must not forget the class struggle. Ko Ching-shih of Shanghai, a proponent of Mao's revolutionary line, took the Chairman's instructions as his guide in promoting the workers' struggle there, and thanks to this mobilization of the masses the schemes to make the city a tactical base in support of the restoration of capitalism were frustrated. So it was that following the Tenth Session, the working class and the people of Shanghai, under Mao's guidance, led the way in the antibourgeois and anticapitalist offensive: the conflict became a head-on collision.

The antibourgeois struggle begins at the Peking Opera

The first attack on bourgeois ideology took the form of a reshaping of the Peking Opera. In Shanghai, an investigation of the Peking opera *Taking Tiger Mountain by Strategy* was begun—an examination of the work from an ideological point of view, exposing all the fallacies it contained. In the field of culture and art, Chiang Ching (Mao Tse-tung's wife) played a major role. And so it was that the first antibourgeois offensive was mounted in the cultural sphere. The campaign against *Tiger Mountain* was a powerful example of the struggle between the two lines in the literary and artistic field. A group under Chiang Ching's leadership was given the task of revising the text of the play. Once the alterations had been made, *Tiger Mountain* was presented at the National Festival of Peking Opera on Contemporary Themes in 1964. [According to what Kuang Hsin reports in a section of the book *On the Revolution in Peking Opera* (Peking, 1968), while the workers, peasants, and soldiers were delighted with this transformation, the revisionists of Shanghai, wishing to discredit it, and the "great patron of the sinister line in art and literature," as well as the party leaders taking the capitalist road, heaped scorn on the play, saying, among other things, that "it has been made totally insipid." Mao subsequently attended a performance of the play, and this tremendously encouraged the revolutionary comrades of the theater group and gave them new strength.

[In early 1965 a question arose over the publication of a polemic against the play *Hai Jui Dismissed from Office.* Mao had requested a disavowal of this play by its author, Wu Han, deputy mayor of the city of Peking, a man who had been publishing articles indirectly attacking Mao for a long time. *Hai Jui Dismissed from Office* was a historical drama alluding to the dismissal of Minister of National Defense Peng Teh-huai, who had been ousted in 1959; it alleged that Chairman Mao had removed him in a fit of rage, that questions of rivalry were involved. In the play Mao was depicted as an aged anachronism, incapable of appreciating the talents of his counselors and unjust in his methods of leadership. In reality, Peng had been an advocate of the Soviet alliance and had been part of a nascent anti-Maoist faction. This faction's quarrel with Mao Tsetung revolved around the Chairman's military judgment, his appraisal of new weapons such as the atom bomb; hence it had nothing but scorn for the statement that the atom bomb "is a paper tiger."]

Comrade Chiang Ching went to Shanghai to discuss the matter. Furthermore, in 1966, with the authorization of Lin Piao, she called a meeting of cultural and artistic representatives from the People's Liberation Army, and the report issued by this important conference was the primary factor in creating a favorable climate of public opinion for the Cultural Revolution. Without the preparation of the masses, a Cultural Revolution would have been unthinkable. During this phase of preparing public opinion, the struggle between the two lines was already raging within the organization. The report on art was an important aspect of the ideological battle which began between Ko Ching-shih, on the one hand, and Chen and Tsao, on the other. But Ko Ching-shih's untimely death in February 1965 enabled Chen and Tsao to gain control of the organs of administration, seizing the position of first secretary of the party as well as that of mayor of Shanghai. They went to great lengths to prevent the publication of the article criticizing *Hai Jui Dismissed from Office.* The contents of this article had already been brought up for discussion in the Shanghai secretariat of the Chinese Communist Party. Chen and Tsao had objected to the clarity and explicitness of its perspective, maintaining that the last section, which dealt directly with political questions, was inadmissible. The others had fought for it to be published in its entirety. Finally, with the backing of Chairman Mao's headquarters, the article was published. ("Did Mao read it and did he approve?" we inquire. Our host nods his head.) After the death of Ko Ching-shih, Chen Pei-hsien became first secretary of the Communist Party of Shanghai. This article aimed a direct blow at the revisionist and reactionary Peng Chen, a supporter of the arch-revisionist Liu Shao-chi. The first secretary informed Liu and Peng Chen's henchmen that the article had been published on Mao's orders, explaining that the Chairman had personally made the decision to publish it.

A most complex struggle, fraught with ambiguities

("Did they come right out and say this?" we ask. "No," he replies, "the political struggle was extremely complex.") Chen played the role of "informer," but he did so while "waving the red flag." Besides, it has always been a feature of the inner-party struggle that despite the clash between the two lines no one ever spoke out against the proletarian line, for that would have meant exposing oneself as overtly revisionist and being branded as such. Hegel says: "Those who cry the loudest sell the worst merchandise." They cried the loudest, so to speak, and continued to identify themselves with Chairman Mao Tse-tung. An inner-party struggle does not develop as openly as you might imagine. If it had we would quickly have identified them as reactionaries, even disguised as "wavers of the red flag." In politics, in the course of a struggle like ours, the battle is fraught with ambiguities.

By the time of the Central Committee's "May 16 Circular," the preparation of public opinion had been completed and a mass movement of vast proportions was developing all over the country. The "May 16 Circular" unmasked Peng Chen and Liu Shao-chi, refuting their absurd and reactionary theories. On the national level, the group which had usurped the power of the party secretariat was stripped of its authority following the publication of this circular, and the new group favoring the Proletarian Cultural Revolution was formed. [This remark reveals that for a while Mao was in a minority within the party secretariat, and that the majority which subsequently formed around him was unmistakably and firmly evidenced in the leadership's very general acceptance of the "May 16 Circular" and later, on August 8, 1966, of the "Sixteen-Point Decision." In his book *Histoire de la révolution culturelle prolétarienne en Chine*, Jean Daubier, in contrast to Edgar Snow and Joan Robinson, questions whether Mao was ever in the minority. However, it must be pointed out that when Snow returned from a trip to China in 1971, he reported, on the basis of a somewhat abbreviated conversation with Mao (published in *Epoca* in April 1971), that Mao's objective situation had deteriorated to a point where the most important positions of power had been lost, that "in 1965, for example, he couldn't prevail on the Peking press—controlled by the party—to publish an important article whose purpose was to launch the propaganda phase of the Cultural Revolution. Mao had to have it published in Shanghai in pamphlet form. It was Liu and his allies on the Central Committee who commanded the state, the unions, the party school, the political and bureaucratic 'cadres,' always in Mao's name." During this same conversation, Mao told Snow that "at the time of their last discussion (May 1965) he had lost control in a variety of areas: propaganda, the urban and provincial party committees, and most of all, the Peking Municipal Committee." To be sure, the Chinese I have spoken with in China declare positively that Mao was never, at any moment, in the minority. But we must realize that for a Chinese comrade fighting in the Cultural Revolution, Mao's directives were infallible. This is why the Chinese simply refuse to pose the problem in terms of whether Chairman Mao was in the minority or the majority in the top organizational levels. And besides, these terms are really products of our own language, not theirs. (On this question, see the Conclusion below.)]

Following the "May 16 Circular," the great mass revolution went into action: it began in Peking, with the tatzupao at the university on June 1, followed by Mao's tatzupao on August 5. The flames of revolution began to rise among the students.

There are certain analogies between the course taken by the Cultural Revolution in Shanghai and in Peking. The mass movement of the Red Guards unfolded, first in the universities, then in the middle schools. By means of tatzupao, a campaign of criticism was mounted against revisionists in high places, but without identifying them by name; as time went on, however, the most exalted personages—Liu Shao-chi and his two agents in Shanghai—were singled out as targets of the struggle and were called by their full names.

The politicization of the masses

But it had taken a difficult process of elucidation to arrive at this point. At first things weren't so clear. Between late June and early July, Liu Shao-chi, taking advantage of his leadership position, attacked the young students. In Shanghai, Liu's agents, whose power was considerable, backed up Liu's repressive measures against the students, suppressing their movement through the use of work teams. Why were they successful in suppressing this movement? Because their *political prestige* was still intact; because they professed to share all the virtues of Mao's proletarian headquarters, parading these virtues as if they were their own. They claimed that the article that had been published against *Hai Jui Dismissed from Office* had been approved by the Shanghai party secretariat. And they said that in this way Shanghai had made an important contribution to the Cultural Revolution. [This account of the struggle contradicts the theory of certain Western experts that the Cultural Revolution was a kind of "shadowboxing." To say that Liu Shao-chi also appealed to the Red Guards in order to demonstrate his agreement with Mao amounts to saying that the mayor of Shanghai used the same method in good faith. The struggle, however, increasingly took the form of an open battle between *revisionists* and *pro-Maoists.* Why, in 1964, was there such unanimous approval of the creation of Peng Chen's famous committee for the "Cultural Revolution"? This account, which reveals the enormous difficulties involved in *unmasking* the enemy's line, gives us an answer: the Liu Shao-chi faction was able to take over not only the language of the revolution, but the revolutionary organizations as well.] And yet, there was no way to transform falsehood into truth. As the struggle developed, these agents, for all their cleverness and cunning, were unmasked. The masses began to wonder about them: if they are such resolute supporters of the Cultural Revolution, then why are they simultaneously repressing the mass movement? Meanwhile, other factors were coming into play: in 1966 the Red Guards of Peking went south to Shanghai and established revolutionary links with the Red Guards there, as well as with the working class in many factories, thus extending the scope of the movement. [When the Peking Red Guards arrived in Shanghai, the two leaders greeted them with a singular lack of enthusiasm; in fact, they called them gangs of toughs, stirred up the workers against them, and did their utmost to drive them from the city. On August 3, the Red Guards went as a delegation to the city hall but were refused admittance. So they surrounded the building from then until September 4, enraging Chen and Tsao, who called on their supporters to come to the rescue. Blows were exchanged; there were serious clashes and considerable bloodshed. But the Peking Red Guards succeeded in establishing contacts with some of the young people, especially among those workers who had hounded the "work teams" of Liu's agents and who had, as a consequence, been "blacklisted." The Red Guards publicized the "Sixteen-Point Decision," particularly the passage which said: "Cast out fear. Don't be afraid of disturbances. The masses must liberate themselves."]

Why was it possible in some measure to stifle the Red Guard movement in Shanghai? What happened? There are general contradictions and particular ones; every city, moreover, has its own characteristics. Liu's two agents displayed the astuteness and duplicity that was the special hallmark of the bourgeoisie of Shanghai; the methods they employed were not rigid, but flexible; the capitalists of Shanghai were slyer than foxes, and in the inner-party struggle the revisionist leaders of Shanghai showed themselves to be more subtle and skilled at deception than anyone else. When we say, for example, that they suppressed the student movement in Shanghai, what we mean is that they did so by a kind of sleight-of-hand, for they certainly didn't succeed in their objective of mobilizing the army against the students. Compared to Shanghai, the Peking student movement was more advanced, chiefly because Peking is the site of Chairman Mao's proletarian headquarters and also because the Peking student movement has historically been in the vanguard, as evidenced by the fact that the "May 4 Movement" began in the capital. [On May 4, 1919, thousands of students assembled in Tien An Men square to protest China's semicolonial position of dependence, and the workers went on strike in support of their movement.]

Then the great movement recovered its strength. Two phases were involved: first, the Central Committee of the Seventh Congress held its Eleventh Session and Chairman Mao gave the call to arms by writing the tatzupao "Bombard the Headquarters"; then the "Sixteen-Point Decision" was issued. Thus it was clearly stated that the mass movement was invincible, that the masses were "right to rebel," and that this rebellion was a revolution in the service of the proletarian dictatorship. During this session of the Central

Committee, the *coup de grâce* was delivered to the bourgeois headquarters and its line suffered a conspicuous defeat. However, while the reactionary bourgeois line may have been defeated within the Central Committee, and while the majority of the Central Committee members may have approved Chairman Mao's line, a far more protracted struggle was necessary if this reactionary line was to be vanquished within the organizations at the base.

The Red Guards: which the true, which the false?

> Within the party, opposition and struggle between different ideas occur constantly; they reflect the contradictions between the old and new things in society.
>
> —Mao Tse-tung

Now, let's get back to the story. I'll resume at the point where the Peking Red Guards arrived in Shanghai. No class ever leaves the stage of history voluntarily, and what Liu's agents in fact did in this period was to mingle with the masses, acting as agitators among the students and workers. Some of them were won over, and one misguided faction was goaded into creating a conservative organization. To complicate matters, this faction too called itself "Red Guards." The student movement was thus divided into two groups of Red Guards. There are well-known instances of similar experiences in the international Communist movement: revisionism is capable of adopting revolutionary slogans for counter-revolutionary purposes. When the class movement is on the rise, the revisionists wave the red flag higher, the better to strike it down. The only way to distinguish between right and wrong is to arm oneself with Marxism-Leninism, with the thought of Mao.

Despite this divisive stratagem, the students followed the revolutionary road and large numbers of the masses who had been hoodwinked became aware of the trap being laid for them. The thing that opened their eyes was precisely the example set by the "negative teachers," Chen and Tsao. The students, who had embarked on the correct course, gradually developed from a minority into a majority. Shanghai, more than any other Chinese city, demonstrates to us how hard, complex, and tortuous the class struggle can be, for the struggle that took place there set the pattern for the future of the whole country.

When the two agents of Liu began to feel their strength waning, they made the mistake of openly inciting the workers to fight against the students; and it was precisely this maneuver which provided the objective stimulus for the working class of Shanghai. These agents might be compared to those who lift a rock only to drop it on their own feet. The workers' rebellion in Shanghai began in the textile industry—at Textile Factory No. 17, to be exact—and for this, too, there is a historical reason: the textile workers are the most concentrated in China, they have the greatest wealth of experience and the longest traditions of struggle. [At the Ninth Congress, two workers from Textile Factory No. 17 in Shanghai, and two from Textile Factory No. 30, were elected to the Central Committee.] Up to this point, the workers had, for the most part, stayed out of the struggle; now they began to move. In November, the establishment of the Shanghai Revolutionary Rebels' General Headquarters was a great spur to the workers' participation in the Cultural Revolution. It mustn't be forgotten that Shanghai, with its 1.2 million industrial workers, is the country's principal industrial city. The birth of the "rebel headquarters" marks the sharpest point of the struggle between the two lines. [The "headquarters" occupied the party offices, right next door to the Municipal Committee offices, from which the "two agents" refused to be budged.]

The role of the working class of Shanghai

The experience of the Cultural Revolution in Shanghai confirms that although students can play a role in the revolution, the working class constitutes the decisive force. Naturally, the Revolutionary Rebels' Headquarters wasn't recognized as legitimate by the two agents; in fact, they even attempted to split its ranks. Thus when Mao sent Municipal Committee members Chang Chun-chiao [since the Ninth Congress a member of the standing committee of the Political Bureau] and Yao Wen-yuan—who had been summoned to Peking—back to Shanghai, they found themselves faced with two workers' organizations. One of these had been founded by the agents of Liu Shao-chi and even called itself by a name used by Mao in his investigation of the peasants' movement in Hunan—another example of the way revolutionary terms can be used to fight against the revolution. The lesson that can be drawn from this is that one must pay attention not only to the form but also to the content: although the workers' organization created by the revisionist leaders was known as *Chihweitui*—which is another way of saying "Red Guards"—its content was still reactionary.

Between late November and early December, the entire city of Shanghai was swept by an extremely fierce and strenuous debate in which the key issue was whether the "two" followed Mao's revolutionary line, as they claimed, or the bourgeois reactionary line. More than a million persons were involved, mainly workers, and work and home life were suspended while people participated, night and day, in the discussion. The rebel workers' organization had 400,000 members; the conservative organization, which described itself as "revolutionary loyal-to-Mao," had 600,000 to 800,000. Fights broke out in homes, inside families, on buses. The mobs which formed in the streets caused traffic jams. When trolleys picked up workers with opposing viewpoints, the conductors stopped the vehicles and joined in the discussion. Workers were arguing as they emerged from the factories. The whole city stayed up until two in the morning; the night was filled with debates; nobody went to bed. The struggle was extended into families, between fathers and sons, husbands and wives. Did these domestic quarrels "come to blows"? Probably not, but after a few hours of argument a husband and wife might not be on speaking terms for a while. The city was in turmoil: transportation halted, the port temporarily closed, electric power cut off. The enemies of the revolution, whose control of the municipal offices made them masters of the city, turned Shanghai upside down. [Incidents were not uncommon: when the Rebel Headquarters decided to send a delegation to Peking to report on the situation in Shanghai, Chen and Tsao stopped the train north of Anching station on November 9, 1966, with demonstrators they had mobilized for this express purpose. The delegates were arrested and detained until Peking sent orders for their immediate release and the city officials received a message ordering them to cease and desist. Other serious incidents took place at Hangchow, where an attempt was made to derail a trainful of Red Guards bound for Peking. During the night, a soldier of the People's Liberation Army, Tsai Yun-hsien, who was guarding the route, saw that the revisionists had laid a post across the rails to bar the locomotive's path. He raced onto the tracks to remove the obstacle, but the engine was unable to brake in time and he was crushed. On the hills of Hangchow I saw a large building in which they were preparing an exhibition dedicated to this soldier—who hadn't been a party member and who was given this honor posthumously—whose sacrifice was a reminder of how harsh the struggle had at times become. Tsai Yun-hsien's eighteen-year-old brother asked to be allowed to take his place in the ranks of the army.]

What made the mass revolution possible?

This revolution, marked by the advent of the broadest democracy under the dictatorship of the proletariat, is a revolution in the way men think. How was such a revolution possible? For two reasons. First, because Mao is our leader and the Cultural Revolution was under his personal direction. The revolution spread from top to bottom, from bottom to top, following a great mass line. The entire population had an opportunity to distinguish the true Marxism from the false. The second reason is that during the Cultural Revolution, the army, created by Mao and led by Lin Piao, was always on the side of the revolutionary masses. Liu Shao-chi wanted to mobilize the army against the masses but he was unable to do so. So, in answer to your question ("If this hadn't been the case, would there have been a violent revolution, in the sense of the army firing on the people?"), I can only give this reply: the army may either be the instrument of the people, or the tool of repression against the people. Our people's army is not an army of repression. No matter what form the struggles took, they were essentially without violence, without armed repression, for the handful of revisionists who would have liked to bring in the army against the masses failed to obtain its support. The People's Liberation Army is the champion of the proletariat. [I quote from the article on "The Great Lessons of the Paris Commune," published in 1966 in *Peking Review*: "The proletariat can win its liberation only through armed struggle. The first rule for a proletarian who doesn't want to be a slave is: never lay down your arms." As a matter of fact, Marx wrote of the Paris Commune that its novel feature was that after the initial upsurge, the people did not lay down their arms and hence did not relinquish power to the lackeys of the ruling class. Similarly, the article quoted from at the beginning of this chapter emphasizes this point: "Political power grows out of the barrel of a gun . . . According to the Marxist theory of the state, the army is the chief component of state power. Whoever wants to seize and *retain* state power must have a strong army."] Thus, we made the Cultural Revolution with the support of the army. Political power grows out of the barrel of a gun, but it is the party which commands the gun. Does this mean that any revolution must be absolutely *without violence?* Of course not. The problem is whether this violence achieves a revolutionary objective. There are particular contradictions which are, in turn, related to more general ones. There are also broad areas of similarity which are not immediately apparent. For example, the October Revolution in the USSR took the form of an urban insurrection, making the city the hub of the revolution; in China, the encirclement of the city by the countryside gave the revolution its distinctive character. But what both cases have in common is the objective, the seizure of political power—the revolution wins victory by means of the armed struggle, by mobilizing the masses. The form is different, but the essence is the same.

As the struggle progressed, the working class of Shanghai rapidly gained ground, while the conservative organization, despite the power and influence of its supporters, was defeated. The workers raised their class consciousness and became "revolutionary rebels"; these rebels, numbering 10,000 at the start, were over 1 million strong by January 1967. In December, the great force which had been assembled under the leadership of the working class prepared to make the final assault on the bourgeois headquarters of Shanghai.

The January Revolution

The two agents of Liu Shao-chi, realizing that their resistance could no longer be sustained, turned at this point to another tactic: promoting an economist policy in an attempt to bribe, to buy off, the workers. Paternalism and economism are the enemies of the working class. They are used to try to strip it of political power, and without political power the working class is nothing. Thus, in order to avoid a loss of initiative in the political realm, the two agents pursued a certain line of action in the economic realm. They provoked strikes in an effort to cut off the supply of electricity, to bring traffic and transportation to a standstill, and, as I mentioned, they resorted to all kinds of blackmail. As it turned out, however, this policy backfired: what transpired was the very antithesis of the desired goal. These tactics, in fact, started a number of workers wondering: "How can they get away with doing all that?" Because they still hold power: political power as well as administrative, financial, and cultural power. What makes it possible for them to launch such an economic offensive? Because all the reins of economic power are still in their hands. [The "economist" wave involved the payment of bonuses, the opportunity for certain industries to withdraw funds from the banks, large, retroactive wage increases, promotions, higher wages offered to students who went to work in the factories. Company associations were planned—for the railroad firemen, for example—and the trade-union leadership was made the "conveyor belt" for these measures, designed for the creation of a labor aristocracy. The appeal to the dockers and railway workers to go on strike, to suspend work, to shut down the port, was temporarily successful, but subsequently had the rug pulled out from under it by the development of the debate over the very nature of this "economism."] The revolutionaries saw that the time had come to seize power from the two agents. We call this period of struggle the *January Revolution*. Revolutionary ideology and theory emerge out of the practice of struggle. The development of the struggle along these lines, at this particular moment, required the seizure of political power; otherwise no progress could have been made. Mao summarized the situation as follows in the

January 1967 *People's Daily* editorial: "Proletarian revolutionaries are uniting to seize political power from the handful of party leaders taking the capitalist road." This struggle for the seizure of power began in the key sectors of the docks, railways, factories, and press. In January, we seized control of the two newspapers of Shanghai, the *Shanghai Daily* and the *Liberation Army Daily.* The "Message of Greetings to Revolutionary Rebel Organizations in Shanghai" and the "Urgent Notice" were published in these two papers. From then on, these papers abandoned the reactionary economist line and unmasked the tactics of sabotage, calling on the revolutionary workers and the masses to unite. As for the radio—to answer your question—it had always been controlled by the Maoist headquarters. Without the newspapers, the two agents of Liu Shaochi were no longer in a position to make themselves heard. And so we regained influence over public opinion.

The revolutionary workers of the docks, railways, and power stations had a twofold task: revolution and production. There are many practical illustrations of the heroic battle waged by the workers during the January Revolution: some of them, backed up by the revolutionary masses, doubled or tripled their working hours. The students helped the railway workers get the trains moving again. And so rail transportation was restored and traffic returned to normal, thanks to the students, workers, and citizens who pitched in, working day and night. The urgency of the antibourgeois attack led to the formation of the Revolutionary Great Alliance,* in which

* *The Revolutionary Great Alliance.* Almost everywhere in China, the masses were so divided that "rightist" elements were able to retain power or take advantage of the vacuum on this level. In some localities, power was passed from one group to another, each portraying itself as more revolutionary than the last. Under these circumstances the ability or inability to unite the majority became the dividing line which determined whether a seizure of power was effective or not, revolutionary or not. The model of a general revolutionary offensive to seize power provided by Shanghai led to the promulgation of the slogan of the "Revolutionary Great Alliance" by Chairman Mao. *A revolutionary power,* according to Mao's conception, must be capable of *uniting the broad majority,* of resolving all the contradictions among the people so that the attack of the masses may be concentrated against the principal class enemy.

In order to prepare the way for the eventual formation of the three-in-one combi-

eleven different mass organizations took part. On January 11, 1967, the Central Committee and the State Council of Ministers sent a "Message of Greetings to Revolutionary Rebel Organizations in Shanghai," confirming the correctness of their struggle to seize power. [The January Revolution saw the birth and development of new forms of *total* democracy and offered an opportunity for the verification of these forms in practice. In Shanghai, the rebels, having rejected extremist slogans, succeeded in fortifying the solidarity of the workers and in preventing the fragmentation of their ranks. Shanghai is the model for the correction of erroneous ideas. "You have brought about a great alliance of the proletarian revolutionary organizations," says the "Message of Greetings." "You have taken firmly in your hands the destiny of the proletarian dictatorship." And the *Peking Review* of October 1967 proclaimed that: "The storm of the January Revolution is now sweeping the whole country."] Under these circumstances, once unity had been achieved both within the working class and between it and the poor and lower middle peasants, preparations began for building new structures of power in Shanghai, with the support of the leaders Yao Wen-yuan and Chang Chun-chiao, as well as of the People's Liberation Army. In February came the creation of the Shanghai Revolutionary Committee, for which the work of preparation had begun in the heat of the January Revolution. The Revolutionary Committee which thus emerged was a new organ of red power, based on the three-in-one combination of revolutionary cadres, masses, People's Liberation Army members—and destined to express the will of the people of Shanghai.

"The Revolutionary Committee is good"

The establishment of the Shanghai Revolutionary Committee

---

nations, in accordance with the instructions of the Central Committee, the Great Alliance was not to be made between groupings that belonged to different production units, but was rather to be organized according to the individual sector, enterprise, school, etc., so that the masses of each unit would be solving their own problems, not somebody else's.

had Mao's approval—he said at the time, "The Revolutionary Committee is good." [The first organ of red power in Shanghai, founded on February 3, 1967, was called the Shanghai commune, but it was later replaced by a revolutionary structure which spread all over China, the *revolutionary committee.* Though the names differ, the essence of that direct and united relationship with the masses which was so prominent a feature of the commune was (in February) to become clarified and made concrete in the revolutionary committees through the three-in-one combination.] Other revolutionary committees had already been established in Shansi and in northeastern China, experiences flowing out of the practice of the revolutionary masses there. Mao had taken these experiences and synthesized them; only when his analysis was complete had he approved the creation of the revolutionary committee. ("But hadn't the character of the revolutionary committee been determined in advance?" we inquire. The comrade replies: "We are not idealists for whom ideas, not experiences, come first; we are materialists who verify experiences in practice. I must emphasize that it was only after the seizure of power that the revolutionary committee came into existence as practice. It is rooted in a reliance on the masses, on the movement of the masses, and on their creative capacity. Mao examines these first offshoots of mass action; he studies, anticipates, and synthesizes what they might mean; the result is the dissemination of new forms and the reinvigoration of the revolution. When you say that 'the soviets were Lenin's idea,' I reply that Lenin did exactly as Mao has done. The workers' soviets arose in Russia in 1905, and the Bolsheviks regarded them as organs of revolutionary power opposed to the Mensheviks. It was not until 1917—the workers and soldiers had then won power and Kerensky could no longer give orders—that Lenin generalized the slogan "All power to the soviets," and created the possibility, through these soviets, for the exploited workers and masses to organize and run the state themselves.") The Cultural Revolution required lengthy preparation and the study of Mao's theoretical works proved vital to its success. It was the practical struggle of the people which opened the road to victory; by following the development of practice, Mao enriched and developed his theory. Mao's thought takes the line that theory guides practice: practice without theory is blind, but theory without practice is empty.

The revolutionary alliance to identify the common enemy

Following the establishment of the revolutionary committees and the great alliance of the committees at the base, still another process was necessary, one aimed at opening the eyes of the workers who had been hoodwinked. The task of the revolutionary workers' organizations was to encourage the airing of debate, to take these workers in and help them identify the common enemy. The working class thus broadened its revolutionary links, and it was only by reaching out in this way that it was able to gain mastery of the overall situation in Shanghai. Up until September 1967, there had been a whole wave of revolutionary links and various sorts of organizations had been created; then, between February and March 1968, a new wave appeared, giving birth to revolutionary committees, based on the three-in-one combination, in all sectors of the base. Once these revolutionary committees had been established, was the Cultural Revolution finished? No, it has continued in the movement of struggle-criticism-transformation, which is essentially a party matter. This movement involves purifying the class ranks, carrying out class criticism, continually sharpening the struggle between revolutionary and counter-revolutionary tendencies. The struggle is aimed against both right-wing opportunists and ultraleftists. [The ultra-left current in the mass movement was characterized by a failure to grasp the strategic and tactical necessities: in particular, a tendency toward an enormously inflated conception of the targets of the Cultural Revolution. Only a minority of the party cadres, the capitalist-roaders, ought to have been attacked. Certain representatives of the Cultural Revolution failed to understand this, bringing them into conflict with Chou En-lai. This conflict escalated when they provoked indiscriminate assaults on cadres of the party and army and committed serious offenses against the Ministry of Foreign Affairs and various embassies. The right-wing currents, especially in southern China, took advantage of these contradictions and incidents to unleash a series of violent counter-offensives during the summer of 1967.]* Let us not forget that left-wing opportunism is nothing but a form of right-wing opportunism and that the struggle waged by Mao and discussed by Lin Piao in his report to the Ninth Congress is a struggle against right-wing and left-wing deviations. The dictatorship of the proletariat has been consolidated by this movement, but we cannot allow ourselves to slacken the attack against class enemies. The moment we lose our vigilance the enemy attacks us; this explains why the revolutionary movement in Shanghai goes on, continually developing, hand in hand with the revolutionary ardor of the masses. The people are advancing.

* Jean Daubier talks about these events at some length. He writes thus of the ultra-leftists: "For young militants who had grown up in the tempestuous era of the Cultural Revolution, it was quite a temptation to see the Chinese masses as the decisive factor in revolutionary progress. Moreover, the party was in danger of being seen by them as a fossilized mechanism, harboring a considerable number of revisionist elements who were using it as a base from which to conspire against the people. However, such an interpretation distorted the facts, for on the whole the party had remained true to the Maoist line. The relatively high percentage of anti-Maoists within the Central Committee did not in the least reflect the situation on the middle and lower levels of the hierarchy, where the Chairman and his policies enjoyed the highest prestige and confidence among a vast number of party members. Furthermore, from the administrative point of view the Communist organization could not have been dismantled without posing grave risks to the economy and security of the country. Since 1967, a considerable number of local party committees had ceased to function, but this situation could not last indefinitely. Moreover, from a purely strategic point of view the Maoists would certainly have been foolish to underestimate the party cadres and to take them all on at once. In doing so they would have thrown them into the arms of the opposition, swelling its ranks. There had to be an examination of the activities and attitudes of these cadres, both at the time of the Cultural Revolution and in the past, followed by the rejection of those few who were too heavily implicated in the Liu Shao-chi line and by the retention of the great majority—those who, despite some mistakes, remained faithful to the revolutionary policy."

Four years after the January Revolution

Four years have passed since the January Revolution. During that time far-reaching changes have taken place in Shanghai. The movement for the rectification and consolidation of the party has strengthened its membership: the stale has been eliminated in order to take in the fresh. The movement for the purification of class ranks has called forth new energies. New revolutionary cadres have arisen. Relations between the party and the masses have been improved and tremendous gains have been noted. [From what I could learn, the party, which had about 18 million members before the Cultural Revolution, currently has 17 million, 10 to 20 percent of whom are new cadres who joined during the Cultural Revolution.] Only those who proved incorrigible have been eliminated from the party; whenever party members have recognized their mistakes, we have let them back in.

We in Shanghai have achieved resounding successes in "grasping revolution and promoting production." The greatest of these achievements is the wide dissemination of Mao's thought: ever broader masses of the people have grasped it in action, are studying it, and are becoming increasingly conscious of promoting the dictatorship of the proletariat. Through articles, investigative studies, and tatzupao, they are participating in the enrichment of Mao's thought. You have been able to see for yourself that in Shanghai, every citizen has become a philosopher: 10 million philosophers. When the masses absorb Mao's thought, an enormous power radiates from them.

As to the successes achieved in building socialism, I can say briefly that in the industrial sphere, production has been greatly increased and that the problems posed by the slowdowns and stoppages suffered during the sharp conflict between the two lines have been overcome. We have not only fulfilled the quotas set by the plan, but have, in some cases, surpassed them. The industrial base has been strengthened. New techniques are springing up everywhere like flowers. The naval yards of Shanghai have produced six 10,000-ton vessels during the past two years; in all the years before that they had built only two.

In the field of agriculture, there is one absolutely phenomenal development which is particularly worthy of mention: cotton production is six times higher than it was in the post-Liberation period. In some sectors of agriculture it is ten times what it used to be.

But there is still a gap between our achievements and the demands of the revolution: the revolution develops, the masses advance, the struggle must not be abandoned. The people of Shanghai still have a way to go toward realizing their ideal, the liberation of all mankind. In short, we can say that the Cultural Revolution has been the greatest movement of mass democracy in history; the party has emerged from it sounder, stronger than ever, and more closely linked with the masses.

As for myself—in answer to your question—I am just a worker on the Shanghai Revolutionary Committee. An ordinary soldier under Mao's command in the struggle for the Cultural Revolution. I don't know to what extent this description of the Cultural Revolution in Shanghai is consistent with Mao's thought, for Mao's thought has to be applied creatively, in practice and in struggle. Today I may work here, in Shanghai; tomorrow, somewhere else. Each of us goes where the needs of the revolutionary struggle call him. Sometimes we are part of a revolutionary committee, then we may go work in a factory, in industry; from top to bottom, from bottom to top. Even when, as cadres, we are at the top, we try never to divorce ourselves from the masses. Among ourselves, we engage in constant criticism and self-criticism in order to raise our consciousness of the class struggle, to transform our world outlook.

[The meeting has taken place in the tower room of the hotel. The tower's green roof ends in a sharp point which rises over the hotel like a mast. Night has fallen on the Huang-pu and the small room is dimly lit. On several occasions a smiling, round-cheeked waiter offers us hot towels for our faces. The room is shrouded in evening mist and filled with smoke. Everyone smokes—the Chinese, it seems, have only one vice: a passion for tobacco. We are a bit numb with cold, for the central heating, shut off in the afternoon, isn't turned on again until night. The comrade, in contrast, seems perfectly at ease. Once when we were pressing for information about inner-party debates, he retorted, "Perhaps you have a lot to learn about discussion," but this was the only bit of sharpness we heard from him. All the rest was nothing but graciousness and a wealth of information. He often smiled at us over his spectacles, and his small, lean face, with its delicate features, seemed to convey a friendly informality, devoid of any *official* character. He thinks of himself as simply one of the 10 million politicized citizens of Shanghai. In short, he's no different from anyone else in this city.]

13
Death of the Housewife

Women must hold up half of heaven.

—Mao Tse-tung

Lenin wrote: "The dictatorship of the proletariat is an unrelenting struggle against all the forces and traditions of the old society. . . ." Lenin was well aware that at this juncture the revolution is only just beginning. . . . It's the same as with women. Of course it is necessary to give them legal equality to begin with! But from there on, everything still remains to be done. The thought, culture, and customs which brought China to where we find it must disappear, and the thought, culture, and customs of proletarian China, which does not yet exist, must appear. The Chinese woman doesn't yet exist, either, among the masses; but she is beginning to want to exist. And then, to liberate women is not to manufacture washing machines!

—Mao Tse-tung,
in André Malraux, *Anti-Memoirs**

The freeing of women means, as Lenin said, that even a cook will be capable of governing. In China on the eve of the Cultural Revolution women had not reached that point; nor have they today. Feudalism—one of the three mountains that crush China—continues to lie heavy on the superstructure in so far as women are concerned. One problem is clear, and that is "the need to emphasize the revolutionary role of women," to quote from an article in *Red Flag* (no. 2, 1971). This article, entitled "Revolutionary Women

* Translated by Terence Kilmartin (New York: Bantam Books, 1970), pp. 463–465.—*Trans.*

Prove Their Unshakeable Determination," is based on a study of the Tungching brigade in Kwangsi province. By means of a balance-sheet drawn up for the two lines and the two classes, the article shows how Liu Shao-chi's counter-revolutionary line vis-à-vis the women's movement was defeated. However, the article goes on, the class struggle continues and women's problems are still being fought out in terms of the class struggle. Surveys have made it clear to the party committee that certain women have been used by the enemy to hamper the activities of cadres; certain women have been won over to ideas disseminated by the class enemy. Others have not yet answered the question: for whom are we cultivating the land? and think only in petty, selfish ways of how to gain privileges for their families, and so on. Moreover, in relating to this expression of class struggle, certain cadres adopted an attitude which was expressed in the following terms: "We aren't even carrying out our principal tasks properly; the problems of mothers and mothers-in-law can wait," and "Women's work doesn't concern the party as a whole," thus attributing minor importance to such work. These attitudes indicate that the question of how much or how little importance is given to the position of women, how much or how little their work is valued, of whether they are looked upon simply as labor power or as a great revolutionary force, is not an anodyne one. On the contrary, a person's approach to these questions reveals whether or not he or she understands the class struggle and applies Chairman Mao's revolutionary line. Conscious of the problems posed by women's work, and having studied Mao's teaching—according to which "We must continue to struggle against those conceptions which disregard the women's movement"—the party committee and the cadres have led people to examine the importance of women's work in the light of three considerations:

1. The problem must be dealt with in terms of the class struggle. If the proletariat does not use Mao's thought for the re-education of women, the bourgeoisie will use the corrupt thought of the exploiting classes to the detriment of women.

2. Women constitute more than half the population; unless they are fully mobilized, there can be no true mass movement.

3. Women represent a great human potential.

A study of these points has led to a broader understanding of the need for mobilizing women to make the revolution. The belief that women are "useless," that "women's work has no influence on the collectivity," along with other erroneous conceptions, is in reality a poison disseminated by Liu Shao-chi, according to whom the masses were "backward" and the class struggle had "ended."

The article lists five concrete ways in which the revolutionary role of women can be stressed:

1. By utilizing at all times the lively ideas that are being expressed by women; by organizing, to that end, various types of study programs of Mao Tse-tung thought.

2. By linking collective study and family study; by linking reciprocal study within families with collective education.

3. By organizing study groups composed of both literate and illiterate women.

4. By organizing study during farm work-breaks.

5. By organizing mutual aid in the home, with men caring for their children and taking responsibility for housework while their wives are studying.

As the article states:

> It's a question of mobilizing the women to break the chains that fetter their minds and to work in a revolutionary spirit. Because of the age-old influence of feudal ideology and the depredations of Liu Shao-chi's counter-revolutionary, revisionist line, a minority of women are still prisoners of traditional attitudes.

The Chinese are quite reticent on this burning subject, just as they are reluctant to speak about birth control. But both subjects, closely linked to the revolutionary role of women, are beginning to figure openly in the official party organs, be it *Red Flag* or *People's Daily.* The latter published, on March 3, 1971, a long article on birth control and women's health.*

---

* This article was entitled "Let Us Struggle to Improve Women's Health." It indicates clearly that the problem of women is in large part linked to the more general problem of the countryside, and that the former must therefore be dealt with in relation to the latter. (Liu's political line was to ignore the countryside.) In fact, the backwardness of women's condition in the rural areas was a serious problem, because "arduous labor, poverty, poor hygiene, and the deleterious effect on health of too-frequent pregnancies and of deliveries by traditional methods [in other words,

The condition of women, or the revolutionary role of women, has been one of the objects of the ideological transformation that has characterized the Cultural Revolution. It is closely related to the transformation of the family. It seems that Liu Shao-chi was not so much antifeminist as he was hostile to putting women in the front in production outside the home. His attitude was one that conformed to the capitalist mode of accumulation, which traditionally relegated women to clearly defined domestic roles. When Mao says that giving washing machines to women does not liberate them, the polemic with Liu Shao-chi is clear. After the tumultuous entry of Chinese women into the political struggle at the beginning of the century, and after their exemplary participation in the Long March as well as in the anti-Japanese struggle, after the widespread enthusiasm elicited by the war of liberation which led to the founding of the socialist republic and the passage of laws declaring the legal equality of women and men—after all this came their gradual retreat into the home. But during the years of the Great Leap Forward Mao encouraged women to cut the umbilical cord that tied them to domestic work, and productive activities for women, sometimes on an industrial basis, began to be organized, especially in the cities. Liu Shao-chi, who had scoffed at the tendency of the workers to "work guerrilla-style," considered the participation of women to verge on the ludicrous, and he had some of the factories closed. According to comrades with whom I spoke in Shanghai, Liu Shao-chi's

manifestations of the "three mountains of the old society," imperialism, capitalism, feudalism], had made invalids of a number of women, to the point where it limited, indeed destroyed, their ability to work." A general program of diagnosis and health care was carried out in the countryside, with emphasis on the prevention of women's ailments, simply by creating, thanks to the Cultural Revolution, a mass movement capable of confronting these problems on a political basis, not merely by relying on the "aid of specialists . . . but by involving the masses in this work," by involving the medical sector and its "barefoot women doctors."

Thus the difficulties were surmounted, including those that arose from erroneous attitudes, according to which a "concern with people's ailments" was interpreted as being contrary to the revolutionary spirit, which teaches one not to fear "either death or hardship" in "grasping revolution and promoting production." By spreading the slogan of "Prevention" it was possible to retrieve the immense potential energy "necessary for the revolution and for military preparedness."

policy of bonuses and high wages permitted a man to subsidize his wife's needs and reinstated her in the traditional role of housewife. The Chinese with whom I discussed these problems said that in the USSR a similar policy led many women to leave production and withdraw into family life, and that an analogous phenomenon can be observed in the East European socialist countries.

Mao perceived in this withdrawal a terrible danger for China, where women were just beginning to emerge from a feudal type of family life. During the Cultural Revolution, the Federation of Chinese Women (whose guest I had been in 1954) underwent an upheaval. It was, in effect, dissolved, as the trade unions had been, probably so that it could gradually become a clearing-house for grievances. In ceasing to be "political" it risked conversion into a kind of "protection of women" organization, a kind of Salvation Army. (However, more recent news from China indicates that the Federation is being reconstituted on a basis drastically different from the earlier period, in which it was a transmission belt for disseminating the platitudes of high-level bureaucratic units.) In conversations on this subject I was told that Liu Shao-chi's position had prompted many party leaders to send their wives back into the home, to adopt once more the traditional role of homemaker.

The most illuminating explanation of the sudden appearance on the political scene of Mao's and Lin Piao's wives, elected to the Political Bureau after the Ninth Congress (without having been a part of the Central Committee elected by the Eighth Congress) is undoubtedly the one that interprets it as a spectacular affirmation of Mao's line, according to which women should be in the forefront of political and revolutionary activities. Their election to the Political Bureau has had profound reverberations; it was as if they had swum the Yangtze of age-old family traditions. Everyone was highly impressed, not always favorably. It is childish to say that Mao and Lin needed their wives in order to have a majority in the Political Bureau—a claim made by some Sinologists. Instead, one should ask why these two women were elected. An answer may be found in the fact that only the wives of the two *leaders* could count on special support in highlighting the role of women at the very core of political life. Furthermore, in the political struggle that these women would be joining they would be facing, across the barricades, the wife of Liu Shao-chi. Mao's wife, Chiang Ching, a former actress, took the offensive in Shanghai, her target the bourgeoisification of the Peking Opera. Her intervention in the area of artistic work during an army meeting called by Lin Piao made her a high-level leader of the Cultural Revolution. As a member of the Political Bureau she is currently working on problems in the field of culture and art. Lin Piao's wife, Yeh Chen, who was a journalist, has become one of those responsible for the Cultural Revolution in the army, where she works in the area of ideological problems. She is also a member of the Military Affairs Committee of the Central Committee. Chou En-lai's wife, Teng Ying-chao, was re-elected to the Central Committee at the Ninth Congress. She is a veteran of the Long March (Edgar Snow spoke of her with admiration in this connection). She is currently involved in organizing women, and was deputy secretary of the Women's Work Committee of the Central Committee. Recently, apparently for health reasons, she has not been playing a leading role.

Liu's wife, Wang Kuang-mei, led the "work team" into Tsinghua University and played an important role in the rectification campaign at Taiyuan, where she led a work team that opposed Mao's line. She went down to defeat without complaint or loss of dignity, putting up a fight to the end. She has been described as a cold, beautiful, and elegant woman. Some say she is cruel and that at Taiyuan she used methods of persuasion that were not precisely ideological. Photographs taken during Liu's official visit to Indonesia, showing her dressed in a costly ballgown and dancing with Sukarno, have flooded China, distributed by the Red Guards. Mao's and Lin's wives, in contrast, wear army uniforms, a fact I was able to confirm in Peking at an official ceremony. In their dress and in their bearing, they attempt to symbolize not merely women's legal equality but their politicization, their revolutionary participation in the loftiest heights of the superstructure.

In China women keep their maiden names, and one must be very well informed indeed to know, for example, that Chiang is Mao's wife. The Chinese with whom I spoke don't accept our way of identifying women as wives, and when I spoke of "Mao's wife" they looked at me with astonishment, as if they didn't know who I meant, until I referred to her by her maiden name.

Mao's wives

Between Peking and Canton, I think often of Mao's four wives. In Peking I saw Chiang Ching, the fourth wife. The first doesn't count; she was chosen for him by his parents and he took flight after the wedding when he saw how ugly she was. In Canton I saw a photograph of his second wife, the daughter of one of his teachers, whom he loved dearly. She was captured by the Kuomintang, kept as a hostage, and then decapitated. In one of his poems, Mao calls her "my proud poplar." I saw her portrait—a sweet face, the large eyes of a child, thick hair—in a school located in the old Confucian temple (now a museum) where Mao taught the peasants in 1926. Alongside her photograph, another of a child, Mao's son, killed during the Korean War. Mao's third wife, from whom he was divorced, was a heroine of the Long March, wounded in combat fourteen times. Was she the very beautiful woman whose photograph I saw at the Canton exhibition (opened in 1969 and devoted to the history of the Chinese Communist Party)—standing between Mao and a teenager, supple as a reed, a bandolier crossing her chest, a gun in her hand, smiling proudly? I don't know what became of her. Then comes Chiang Ching, formerly a well-known actress with an opera company, who, fascinated by the legend of Mao and the heroic struggle of the revolutionaries, reached Yenan after passing through enemy lines. Since then she has lived only for him. Her entry into political life occurred in the years just before the Cultural Revolution. "Women hold up half of heaven," according to Mao, who, unlike Stalin, could count his wives among his comrades in armed struggle and political combat. But "Women must conquer half of heaven," he added. This field of action has constituted one of the political and ideological battlefronts of the Cultural Revolution, for women have yet to "conquer half of heaven."

Kung Peng as I remember her

Everyone who visits China becomes a collector. In 1954 I was especially interested in the lives of Chinese women, and in looking through my notes, I find a collection of ten biographies of women that I never published. I met Kung Peng at a conference on Indochina in Geneva in June 1954, before going to China. I was a member of the union of Italian women and the editor of its weekly magazine, *Noi Donne.* Kung Peng, spokeswoman for the Chinese delegation and one of Chou's closest associates, made a strong impression on me. This Chinese woman responded to assaults by the big international press with a political shrewdness sheathed in irony, and for me this was a spectacle without precedent. Kung Peng revealed to me the role that women played in a China that was just barely emerging from its Middle Ages, a role that, like a wind originating almost five thousand miles away, swept out the old myths of women's inferiority, still extant in our Western societies.

Kung Peng—and through her the new China that was being born—had destroyed all the taboos. Now caustic, now gentle, she held her own at press conferences, and her poise in the presence of a hundred journalists seemed to me to be a palpable expression of all the qualities of the feminine universe. At that time she was thirty-eight and married to Chia, the present head of the Chinese delegation that is negotiating with the USSR on frontier disputes. I remember Kung Peng's face, a firm oval with harmonious features, her hair a silky black helmet. Whenever the sometimes stormy sessions with the journalists ended, she would leave in a car with light silk curtains, and one then saw only her beautiful white, motionless hands, folded across her stomach in traditional Chinese fashion. She would no longer be smiling, and her face, filled with a pensive beauty, would be free of all tension and nervousness. She seemed to me to be absolutely sure of herself, strong and stable. What dignity she had as, self-composed and alone, she took her leave of that pack of journalists!

I saw her again in Peking during my visit in 1954. We exchanged greetings from time to time after that, and I would receive news of her whenever a journalist returned from China. She headed the foreign press section of the Ministry of Foreign Affairs and over a period of years she received dozens of foreign journalists. They have all incurred a debt of gratitude toward this woman of rare intelligence. I think that during those fifteen years China had no better representative than Kung Peng. Then the Chinese ambassador in Paris told me that she was gravely ill. Before I left for Peking, a Hsinhua release announced her death. She was buried in the cemetery reserved for the heroes and heroines of the Revolution—that was all I was able to learn in Peking. According to a Soviet journalist, she had been criticized by the Red Guards, as had other functionaries of the Ministry of Foreign Affairs. Beyond that, it was as if she had vanished. The greatest suffering I underwent in China was this search for some trace of her, any trace, which would restore for a moment this lost friend. The photographs taken of us together in Geneva seemed to me very sad and terribly faded.

Where China stands with regard to women

In 1954 the place assigned to Chinese women in government seemed unique in the world. Formerly denigrated, scorned, their crippled feet a symbol of their domestic slavery (according to Confucius' immutable message of 2,300 years ago: "Remain where you are and submit to the decrees of Heaven"), women were now becoming the masters of their country. Of 1,226 delegates to the National People's Congress, 147, or 12 percent, were women. Female ministers have headed the ministries of Justice, Hygiene, and Overseas Chinese, and Sun Yat-sen's wife occupied the post of deputy president of the National People's Congress. (Through a strange twist of destiny, one of her sisters married Chiang Kai-shek and the other married one of the biggest Chinese capitalists, who died not long ago in the United States.) Women constitute 13.31 percent of the municipal assemblies and 16 percent of the regional assemblies. Three-hundred-eighty women have been presidents or deputy presidents of tribunals. In 1961 one-fifth of the scientific workers at the Chinese Academy of Science were women, and 4 of 34 scientists honored by the Academy in 1957 were women.

In 1954 I met Che Liang, Minister of Justice, who had been imprisoned and tortured by Chiang Kai-shek and on whose head the Japanese had placed a price of $50,000. The first woman in Shanghai to earn a law degree, she was at that time working on the divorce law. "In prison," she told me, "I was with two women, one with a life sentence and the other sentenced to death for opposing the feudal marriage laws. It was then that I thought of drawing up legislation that would liberate women from the old marriage contract. This law, stipulating equality of rights and the right to divorce, was passed by the government in 1950."

The spirit of the law, Che Liang explained to me, is one of permitting the creation of new families in which "husband and wife love each other, in which young people have the right to choose their mates. Among the many benefits the Revolution has brought to the Chinese is the right to love, for formerly marriage was nothing but a despotic contract which, by the will of the parents alone, united two strangers."

The fact that a woman occupied a post as important as that of Minister of Justice pointed up even more sharply, by contrast, the persistence of certain aspects of feudal life. I shall give some examples, so as to give an idea of the backward condition of women and the long, long road that China has had, and still has, to traverse.

In each Chinese village marriages were arranged by the purchasing family, the selling family, and an intermediary who negotiated the price to be paid for the bride. Often the bride did not have the right to meet her husband until the day of the wedding when, dressed all in red, she was presented to him. Sometimes he was a child, or even an infant in diapers, or as yet unborn. Thus the family acquired a domestic servant, and the young woman withered while waiting for her mate to reach adulthood. "She's married and waiting for her husband," people used to say. And if he were to die before reaching manhood she was considered to be a widow and was obliged to remain faithful to his memory, on pain of death, to the end of her days. Imagine the scene (as recounted in a popular Chinese song): a woman awakens in the nuptial chamber and by the light of a candle sees at her side a sleeping child—her husband. She asks, sobbing: "Is this my husband or my son?" But there was no solution, according to the elders, for the old god that lived in the moon made marriages in heaven and tied together with a red cord the feet of the young people destined to love each other; parents and intermediaries were merely the instruments of his will.

In Shanghai in 1954 the first divorce cases were being tried, and I find in my notes the following description of a hearing: a judge is questioning a woman, who holds a boy of twelve by the hand. To hear the vehemence with which she berates her daughter-in-law you would think that it is she who is suing for divorce: "When the little one caught a cold, did she take care of him? She sent him to school with fever. When he had lice, she didn't wash him with black soap. And during the watermelon season, he got a stomach-ache because she let him stuff himself." A litany of shouts and accusations. But it is the young woman who has filed for divorce. At seventeen she had married this child, who was then nine. Now she is twenty and is counting on the new law to free her so that she may marry a young villager she loves. The mother-in-law shouts: "She's cost me a fortune. She didn't take good care of the little one, she's brought me nothing but problems, and now look, she's leaving . . ." The intermediary who had arranged the marriage is attempting to make the young woman listen to reason. He is the next target of attack by the mother-in-law: "She cost me a fortune and she knows it! Besides paying the contract price, I fed and clothed her. Who's going to pay me back for all that?" The judge declares that the housework done by the young woman has already repaid the four years of her upkeep and the divorce is granted. The child goes out to play in the street with a brightly colored kite, while the young woman goes to find her fiancé.

Naturally, houses of prostitution were closed when Liberation came. There had been 237 in Peking alone. Prostitutes were sent to a re-education institute where they were cared for and where they learned reading, writing, and a skill; many of them married and had children. Some of the older prostitutes wrote a play, "The River, Frozen More Than Three Thousand Years, Has Thawed," which is in part the life story of one of them and which describes their former life in a whorehouse, the exploitation to which they were subjected by their Kuomintang pimps and thugs, and then their new life, which brought them freedom, education, and an occupation they need not be ashamed of. The actresses, themselves former prostitutes, wept as they acted their parts. A film based on this play has been shown all over China.

The entire population participated in this campaign to free the former prostitutes, known as "little sisters," with none of the false piety that characterizes dispensers of charity. In Shanghai, which had 800 brothels, most of the former prostitutes now have an occupation. The principal causes of their misfortunes—poverty, hunger, ignorance—have been destroyed.

During that period, the Chinese cities seemed to me to be capable of releasing incredible liberating forces among the women. Besides, there was in Shanghai and elsewhere a long tradition of struggle against the Japanese, for independence, for victory in the war of national liberation and the revolution. With what heroism Chinese women have faced death!

In Shanghai I had visited an exhibition of the labor movement (closed at present) and the face that I saw there, in an old photograph, flashes across my mind: twenty-four-year-old Shen An-fan, with short hair, hands clasped across her stomach, wearing a thin striped blouse, speaks to the workers at trade-union headquarters. The armed militia protects her: it is 1927 and the workers have occupied Shanghai. This frail young girl with delicate and poignant features was later killed in the massacre ordered by Chiang Kai-shek, as were the husky workers.

The pioneering importance of those articles of the Constitution which affirm the legal equality of the sexes and the new law on marriage was such that they were often compared to the new agrarian reform measures. At that time I wrote:

> The Chinese say that if agrarian reform has freed millions of peasants from oppression by the landowners, these new laws have liberated millions of women who, during the years of feudal marriage, were deprived of all rights. These laws, these rights, were fought for in the past by working women, arms in hand, as the exhibition of the labor movement in Shanghai attests. Their courage, their contempt for death, characterize an epoch whose liberating grandeur belongs to all the people.

The women want to live: the housewife-electronic workers of Shanghai

As I think about the present situation of women in China, I begin to realize that the effort to extend and deepen sex equality has not been a linear one. If in 1954 a substantial number of women occupied high-level posts, that could have been taken as indicating that the coming changes were to be more *vertical* than *horizontal.* That impression was confirmed by the article in *Red Flag,* quoted at the beginning of this chapter, which stated that

> since Liberation, women workers have had a great deal of political experience; specifically, they have undergone the severe tests of the Great Proletarian Cultural Revolution. Their mentality has changed profoundly, and the women who are playing a role in the building of the future are now more numerous. However, certain women, affected by the poison of Liu, according to whom "women are backward," still leave their homes only to work in the fields and then go home again to prepare meals; during meetings they remain seated in a corner, silent. The party committee has organized women's meetings to remind them of the past and their brutal exploitation in the old society, and to strengthen their understanding of the dictatorship of the proletariat. All this has aroused class feelings among the broad masses of women, who understand clearly that the cruelties of the past arose from the fact that they had no power, and all the contentment of today from the fact that they can now assume power.

Since the Cultural Revolution, the intent has been to carry out a process of *horizontal* penetration, such as has characterized the revolution in other sectors of Chinese life—education, medicine, and so on. The Central Committee has 13 women members out of 170, and 10 alternate members out of 139. These proportions, in contrast with representation in the municipal and regional assemblies, may seem unsatisfactory. (The most conspicuous instance of female participation is still the one I have already pointed out: namely, two women in the Political Bureau out of a total of twenty. As for the National People's Congress, it would be best to wait for its convocation to determine the number of seats occupied by women.) We must not forget that the Cultural Revolution has effected a rigorous selection and that the movement to achieve the total emancipation of women in the horizontal sense is just beginning. Let us examine some instances of the process that is taking place at a grass-roots level.

Chapei was a subproletarian district in Shanghai, a slum such as you find in the heart of Naples—but worse. It was an overwhelming example of human degradation. It had been, furthermore, a kind of battlefield—here the Japanese had launched their attack on the city, and during the war of liberation it was totally destroyed. Today it is still shabby, with its ramshackle wooden huts, its stunted little gardens, its pecking chickens, its children playing in the dirt. It is here I visit a transistor plant, set up by neighborhood housewives, which produces silicon planar transistors and integrated circuits. In 1958, in response to the call to make the Great Leap Forward, to "come out of your homes and take the initiative," the women had taken the first step by setting up a wooden-crate factory. There were about 350 of them, mostly in their late thirties and mostly illiterate. Until 1968 they made packing cases; in February 1969, during the Cultural Revolution, they *fanshened.** After consultation with the Shanghai Bureau of Industry, they decided that they could produce high-quality transistors.

Among the members of the revolutionary committee seated around a table, I see several quite elderly women, hair sprinkled with gray; a young girl, a cadre of the Bureau of Light Industry and a former Red Guard; and one man, a technician. On a blackboard the women have written: "Welcome to the Italian comrades in the name of the revolutionary committee." I will be talking with: Wan Ti-hu of the revolutionary committee, the only young cadre; Chen, a workers' representative; Lu, a member of the plant's revolutionary committee and a representative of the revolutionary cadres; Yang; and Hsia Kuo-hsien, the only man and the leader of the plant's revolutionary committee. He has been sent by the Bureau of Light Industry.

I ask the women: "Are you re-educating him?" They all answer at once, and with warmth: "He came here because he wanted to link himself with the masses, and we like that. We agreed that he should be the leader of the revolutionary committee, and we give him our full cooperation. The fact that they sent us such a capable technician means that the higher echelons attach great importance to this plant."

"Our plant," says the young woman with the little ribbon-tied

* *Fanshen.* Literally, "to turn over (one's body)." To radically reorient one's whole being in a revolutionary direction.

braids, "is called Burning Flame; it produces wooden packing-boxes as well as different types of electronic tubes and precision transistors. When we decided to make electronic equipment, we sent ten comrades to learn the techniques in a big factory, where they familiarized themselves with the machines and precision tools. We sent two others to the university, but they were exposed to all kinds of humiliation there: the revisionist intellectuals joked about their age, telling them that it would take at least fifteen years for them to learn, that they were too old, and that it was a waste of money to send them to the university. Their contempt really angered us and we decided to do the best we could on our own, asking as little of the government as possible. So we built 34 percent of the equipment ourselves; other plants supplied 19 percent, and we purchased 47 percent. We were asked to make integrated circuits, and on June 2, 1969, we completed the first ones. Other women in the neighborhood who used to work at home—making slippers, clothing, or toys [typical home-based industries]—came to work at our plant. Now we produce two types of transistors."

The young woman puts two little round boxes on the table; in them, cushioned on cotton, two silicon wafers and two transistors, shining like jewels.

We visit one of the workshops in this plant, installed in a large and ramshackle former tenement building. The housewife-electronic workers are just as at ease with their machines as they were with their pots and pans. We are introduced to a former housewife of thirty-nine who had once succeeded in lowering the tension, instead of cutting off the current and damaging the apparatus, when the cooling tube of her 7,000-volt machine broke. She had risked her life, protecting herself only with rubber and wooden boxes. "Before," she said, "I was afraid of a simple 200-volt wall switch."

The woman in charge of the high-precision workshop for the treatment of silicon wafers is forty-nine, and used to work in the crate factory; at the beginning she couldn't even remember the names of the machine parts.

Our visit to the crate factory, where other housewives are involved in simpler work, pounding and hammering at great speed, permits us to measure the stages through which the neighborhood women have passed. Wages are roughly the same in both workshops: "One plant, one wage scale," they say. "We all help each other." The minimum wage is 20 yuan, the maximum is 40, the average 30. Such are the women of the Chapei district.

"Is the factory making a profit?"

They laugh. "Our crate production was providing us with a surplus, which is always the basis of financing, and the overall income of the entire operation is much higher than what we have to lay out for wages and other expenses."

The women in this plant work according to a plan developed in consultation with the central state administrative body. They began in 1958, with no plan; today they produce 160,000 transistors a year.

The Chinese don't say much about the actual functioning of their economic system, about planning. It appears that their plans function unhampered by those restrictive mechanisms which govern the dynamics of productive life in other planned economies. Even though the Chinese economy is highly planned, a very large margin is left in which the creativity of the work units may express itself. The advantage of such a system lies in the fact that in going from cooking to electronics the housewives, for example, have transformed the life of the neighborhood. The plant is a center for practical experience and study, where students, technicians, and workers meet. Production increases and a labor force that in another society would remain idle is used. Furthermore, the social milieu of these women is transformed. At the heart of the transformation there is not only a new conception of women's condition, but also of the revolutionary character of woman's role vis-à-vis marriage, children, husband.

I ask, "Do the women easily accept their role as workers?"

Lu (gray-haired, lined face, manager of a toy factory until she joined the revolutionary committee) answers: "We are trying to resolve this contradiction, with the help of the Cultural Revolution. The weight of tradition is still heavy and we must raise the class consciousness not only of women but also of men. In accordance with the capitalist line, Liu Shao-chi favored a policy of high wages for men while women stayed in the home. His policy led many leaders' wives to stay home. After the withdrawal of the Soviet technicians, Liu Shao-chi closed down many factories set up by housewives, who then returned to their kitchens. But as the Cultural Revolution advances, the number of women who want to participate in political activity continues to grow. Within the family unit there's still a lot to be done: women work hard and we help them by insisting that men share household responsibilities. As for the family, there too the weight of tradition is still felt."

The young comrade interrupts: "There's still a revolution to be made in the family. We have to criticize it from a revolutionary point of view, based on the destruction of the five old concepts and their replacement by the five new concepts: (1) Destroy the notion of the uselessness of women and replace it with the idea that women must fearlessly conquer half of heaven; (2) destroy the feudal morality of the oppressed woman and the good mother and instill in its place the ideal of revolutionary proletarians; (3) destroy the mentality of dependence and subordination to men and instill the firm determination to free oneself; (4) destroy bourgeois concepts and replace them with proletarian concepts; (5) destroy the concept of narrow family self-interest and instill in the family the open proletarian concept of the nation and the world."

These five principles are constantly quoted in China in relation to the question of women, by the official party press and elsewhere.

"The women must be reminded of what life was like in the old society," commented old Lu. "In our family we often get together and talk about the cruelties and wretchedness of the life we used to live. My husband was arrested and tortured more than once by the Japanese. He used to pull a ricksha. In 1952, the last ricksha pulled by men, like beasts of burden, was sent to a museum. Now my husband works in a grain enterprise, and he too teaches our children about the class struggle.

"We have six children; the eldest, 25, is a worker; the 20-year-old, a girl, completed her junior middle school diploma in 1966 and she works on a farm; the third got his diploma in 1968 and is in the People's Liberation Army; the fourth is a junior middle school student; the fifth and sixth attend primary school. I consider myself a very happy woman."

"What do you want for your children?"

"I want them to carry on the cause of revolution in our country and I want them to help build the world revolution. I want my daughters, as women, to be able to conquer half of heaven. I want our family to reject all forms of selfishness and to put all our strength into advancing the socialist revolution. In our family gatherings we learn to consider the individual and the family in relation to society. We learn not to fear physical pain or death, not to forget the past, and not to forget for a single moment to defend the dictatorship of the proletariat.

"But within families there's a struggle between the old and the new. Not everyone in a family has the same ideas. Often contradictions arise that have to be resolved, and there too we have to struggle against selfishness and criticize revisionism. Chairman Mao teaches us that when all is said and done there are only two conceptions of the world, the proletarian and the bourgeois. It's the same in the family. The discussions we have help to change the conception of the family so that the proletarian approach will be victorious." *

The women of the Peng Pu district don't sew buttons on anymore

Corruption, law-breaking, the arrogance of intellectuals, the wish to do honor to one's family by becoming a white-collar worker and not dirtying one's hands anymore, all these stu-

* With the division of labor . . . in its turn based on the natural division of labor in the family and the separation of society into individual families opposed to one another, is given simultaneously the distribution, and indeed the *unequal* [emphasis added] distribution (both quantitative and qualitative), of labor and its products, hence property: the nucleus, the first form, of which lies in the family, where wife and children are the slaves of the husband. . . . Further, the division of labor implies the contradiction between the interest of the separate individual or the individual family and the communal interest of all individuals who have intercourse with one another. . . . And out of this very contradiction between the interest of the individual and that of the community the latter takes an independent form as the *State*, divorced from the real interests of individual and community."—Marx and Engels, *The German Ideology* (New York: International Publishers, 1947, pp. 21, 22, 23.—*Trans.*).

> pidities are only symptoms. . . . The cause of them is the historical conditions themselves.
>
> —Mao Tse-tung,
> in André Malraux, *Anti-Memoirs**

The revolution in the Chinese family begins with the transformation of the housewife's role, with involving her in the production process, and with uprooting the idea of the family as a self-centered entity. Lu, our interpreter, sees his family twice a year: his wife lives in Canton, he in Peking; they have two children, aged four and ten. Such separations are not common in the countryside—they occur among cadres only, since the state must be able to send them rapidly wherever they are needed. Lu explains that separated families have two months of vacation per year, rather than one, and it is broken up into several periods. He goes on to say that such separations are acceptable because the demands of the collectivity outweigh those of the family. However, they are the exception and not the rule: Chao, for example, lives in Peking with his wife. But the family as a sacrosanct unit, separate from the social collectivity, no longer exists in China.

With the Cultural Revolution the proletariat has intervened in ideology, bringing a revolution in the very conception of the family, and transcending once and for all that condition which led Engels to say that women are doubly proletarians, first in relation to society, and second in relation to men.

The Peng Pu community, with its 130 apartment buildings, was organized in 1958. Fifteen thousand people live here, 3,500 workers from a local steel mill and electric generator plant and their families. In 2,630 of these families both the father and the mother work. The remaining housewives are those the Cultural Revolution is attempting to organize and introduce into production.

It is Sunday and this Shanghai neighborhood, its children playing outdoors, has a festive air. Since 1959 there has been a network of services in operation here: two vegetable stores, two grain stores, a department store, a dry goods store, a pharmacy, a restaurant, and a big market. There are two primary schools with 4,000 pupils, and a middle school with a student body of 2,000. The hospital has

* *Anti-Memoirs*, p. 460.—*Trans.*

forty-three doctors in attendance, and their primary concerns are preventive medicine and birth-control services.

The district is described to us by a young woman—smiling, likeable, and vigorous—who, we are told, "had the honor of being a delegate to the Ninth Congress of the Communist Party."

"Today the housewives of this district have a higher level of consciousness than before," she says. "All they used to think about was their children, or about getting a gas stove or some beautiful bamboo baskets or new woolen trousers. Now they're interested in important affairs of state. Two hundred and eighty of them work in the neighborhood daycare center, which looks after five hundred children. The factories have daycare centers too, but the women workers, after they've weaned their babies, would rather leave them in the neighborhood centers. The charge is 2.50 yuan a month, which is paid for by the mother's work center. We've set up, using Mao's guidelines, several 'housewife production teams.' Five hundred and eighty-six women under the age of forty have jobs in the neighborhood work centers. Some make radios, others shoes; we also have some women constructing a building. They get bricks either by salvage or by making them in an inexpensive kiln."

We visit the work centers and when we are leaving we see a little old man, dressed in a handsome blue cotton suit and surrounded by children. Our young escort points to him and says, "Before the Cultural Revolution the 108 retired workers who live here led an idle life. They spent their time in the restaurant, they had tea with their grandchildren, and in the morning they did exercises. In the summer they sat under the trees, catching a breath of fresh air; in the winter they just sat around. 'With a good glass of wine and a bite of meat,' they would say, 'we'll live to be 96.' Each one thought only of himself and felt no connection with society. Now they take courses on Mao's thought, they tell about their life in the old society, they criticize their former attitudes, and in the morning they take the children to school or to the park. They've given up the old exercises. [Now I know why I haven't seen the parks crowded at all hours with elderly people doing gymnastics, as I had in 1954.] Now they get their exercise by sweeping the street or directing traffic with little red flags."

In fact, all Shanghai is full of little old men of military bearing, meticulously dressed, directing traffic; and we even see some on guard duty in front of the building where, in 1921, the Chinese Communist Party was founded.

Wandering through the district, I note that the network of social services is indeed extensive. There are public laundries, dress-making and dry-cleaning establishments (where clothes are also mended and buttons sewn on). Laundering and ironing a dress costs 5 fen. A meal in a restaurant costs 40 fen, 20 in the factory canteen, and children get four meals a day for 20 fen. "Dressing and feeding ourselves," the young comrade explains, "costs very little. In our family of five, we spend 60 yuan a month, although my husband earns 114. Rice is 16.50 yuan for 50 kilos, and we eat 22-yuan-worth of rice a month. We can have meat and fish every day—prime quality meat costs 1.80 yuan and fish 60 fen.

"The neighborhood is administered by a revolutionary committee, and there are also thirteen street revolutionary committees. Every neighborhood has had cadres since 1956, but it wasn't until 1968 that we had the first really democratic elections. For us the basic task is to spread Mao's thought, raising the level of class-consciousness within families, making them more receptive to the revolution, extending the limited domestic horizons of the women. That's why all the elderly in the neighborhood give courses on their life in the old society, under capitalism. These courses are very well attended, especially those where the women talk about the terrible conditions they were condemned to. There's a seventy-five-year-old comrade here whose life was a tragic example of that oppression: she tells young people about it three or four times a week.

"The apartment buildings and everything else are collective property; we make decisions about new housing and the state pays construction costs. And we, through our organizations, are the architects and the builders."

This neighborhood really and truly bears witness to the death of the housewife. There isn't one woman who is willing to stay home and drudge, and that's at the very heart of the question of how women can be fully emancipated through their incorporation into the production process. Because that removes them from the first form of the division of labor which, according to Marx, characterizes the family.

In the new workshops where small machine tools are made in collaboration with a big factory, housewives have constructed a building with bricks they either salvaged or made themselves. Fifty-seven women went to a factory to learn production methods; soon, two hundred more will follow them. A "production team" has organized a small shoe factory—three rooms where the women sew, assemble, and package fine shoes of leather and suede, some of them wool lined, as well as children's shoes. They earn 30 yuan per month. What they earn is not as important as the fact that they can, through this activity, emerge from behind the walls of domesticity where they were formerly kept. This little plant also works in collaboration with a large factory that passes orders on to it. It functions as a collective and wages are set by the group itself.

Other women, older ones, seated at long tables, assemble portable radios, the parts of which are supplied them by a Shanghai factory. In this instance too, it was a "production team" of women which organized the project. There are also women making toys. No one remains at home. They have worked out a form of team rotation so that some groups work Sundays, as is the case today.

"By mobilizing women, you can achieve tremendous things," the young neighborhood organizer tells us. (Clearly a person of broad experience, she continues to inspect the work being done, giving advice and making suggestions as she speaks with us.) "Mao says that there is no difference between men and women and that they can do the same work." And turning to the four men in our little group of visitors, she addresses them with some degree of irony: "Don't you agree?"

"Yes, yes! Oh, yes!" they hasten to answer, somewhat discomfited by this unexpected attack.

"Women are more capable than men," says my husband enthusiastically, intent on outdoing them.

"No, not at all," she answers. "Women too must study, like men." No "feminist" she.

We are going to visit old mother Hu, a neighborhood resident. Her apartment is spotless and I am reminded of what Curzio Malaparte wrote: "In Chinese homes there is never a single object out of place, never a rip in a curtain nor a crease in a tablecloth, never a wrinkle in a bedspread or a shirt. Even old newspapers are not crumpled but are torn up." In mother Hu's home there are many portraits of Mao on the walls. In the kitchen, an infant in his arms, a man is stirring a pot with a long spoon; he is her son-in-law. His wife, formerly a housewife, is at work, and he, following Mao's precepts, is doing the cooking and caring for his child.

In Shanghai there are 120 new housing projects for workers where the revolution of the housewife is in full swing.

On the Docks

The destruction of the archetypal housewife finds its expression in China today in a highly popular political personage: Fang Haichen, the heroine of the opera *On the Docks*, thirty-six years old, secretary of the party committee of the ninth brigade of the port of Shanghai. The role is played by the singer Li Li-fan, who is very beautiful and is endowed with a splendid voice. This opera, which I saw in a packed theater in Shanghai, was written in 1964 and has been revised several times. It focuses on the political education of a young student, Ma Hung-liang, who is employed as a dock worker and considers this work to be beneath him. He longs to ship out and sail around the world. His shortcoming is not a serious one, but if each young dock worker were to make such a choice, how would the port of Shanghai function? The female lead is the secretary of the party and undertakes the young man's political education. She is the "revolutionary pivot" of the play, the center of its action, which takes place in two acts and twenty scenes. Her role is unequivocal in this drama of absolute conviction, a conviction expressed by means of words alone, with a total absence of violence. The two conduct a lively dialogue as they experience various episodes of port life (such as an act of sabotage perpetrated by the old accountant, who, permeated by bourgeois ideology, makes an accomplice of the young man in his plan to introduce glass slivers into bags of flour that are to be shipped to an African country as a gift of international solidarity from the Chinese people).

"You can't destroy old ideologies with a club," the party secretary sings heartily, addressing this advice to Ma's uncle, who favors strong-arm methods. And the entire audience applauds wildly. Near me, a young girl, clinging to the edge of her seat, claps her hands when Ma sees the light, or when the party secretary sings about the proletarian internationalism which animates the port of Shanghai—the port into which China receives its imports and from which it sends aid to Africa, Asia, and Latin America (boats loaded with rice reach Cuba in thirty days); and she applauds with added enthusiasm at the party secretary's political flexibility.

I realized that most of the audience has already seen this opera several times; Chao knows it by heart. Millions of people sing the familiar arias, and it has been performed over and over again for families, schools, factories, the army. Its popularity stems from its rejection of violence and disciplinary constraints as a method of persuasion.

Yang, soldier of the People's Liberation Army, is the protagonist of another opera, *Taking Tiger Mountain by Strategy.* He is the most popular person in the Peking Opera, the one everyone wants to emulate. After 1964 the libretto was revised, eliminating some of the hero's weak points, certain moments of abandon, certain doubts in the confrontation of tasks; he became the personification of the invincible Chinese citizen of today. *On the Docks* symbolizes the entrance of women into the superstructure, into political action. In the 1971 plastic pocket calendars, Fang Hai-chan is depicted in a dock scene. She sings, her arms raised and a white kerchief around her neck, docker-worker-style. In her right hand she holds a scroll with the resolutions of the Tenth Session of the Eighth Congress of the Central Committee, in which Mao declared that "We must not forget the class struggle." Chao tore out the page of the calendar in which this scene was depicted and offered it to me—the Chinese, with no need for words, can indeed be perceptive—and I keep it in my briefcase.

I saw another revolutionary opera, *The White-Haired Girl,* which was also revised during the Cultural Revolution, and *The Red Detachment of Women,* a kind of Western-style ballet, but with purely Chinese music, dance, and acrobatics. Chinese concerts can also be looked upon as revolutionary performances. I heard one of China's (and the world's) greatest pianists, Ying Chen-nung, play with a symphony orchestra conducted by Li Te-lun, eminent in his own right. They played "classical" selections and themes from the Peking Opera for an audience of soldiers, workers, peasants, and students. (The piano has been introduced into Chinese orchestras, alongside traditional Chinese instruments.)

A foreigner might well be astonished by the fact that the public attends the same five or six revolutionary operas and ballets repeatedly, and always responds with the same intense emotion. Every time that a red cardboard sun rises on stage, or a red flag is raised, the entire audience applauds. It made me think of those superb Gregorian chants intoned by the multitudes—the only dramatic form in which their own inner struggles were presented. Similarly, these dramatic performances correspond to the inner tensions, the reflections, which fill the minds of the Chinese during their work. In one sense such a theatrical presentation frees them; in another, it supplies them with ideas, triumphal songs and hymns, assurances to speed them on their way.

There isn't a trace of alienation in China, nor of those neuroses or that inner disintegration of the individual found in the parts of the world dominated by consumerism. The Chinese world is compact, integrated, an absolute whole. (We must remember that in our own countries leisure-time activities constitute one form of alienation added to another, to that of the division of labor. Thus there is, on the one hand, a *commitment* to compulsory work with no intrinsic meaning, and, on the other, a liberation from work. The day is divided into two parts: that of alienated wage labor, and that of empty freedom—alienation in another form, i.e., freedom lacking rationale, aside from that of negating the first part, with its absurd accompanying exhaustion. Thus we experience, in the course of our divided day, the sum total of our alienation. In this connection, *Capital* comes to mind.* For the Chinese, however, the mode of capitalist production has been overturned, the division

* Marx points out that bourgeois economists are so hemmed in by the ideas of a given historical stage of development of society that the need for the *objectification* of the social forces of labor seem to them to be inseparable from the need for the *alienation* of those forces of living labor.

between labor and knowledge, between manual and intellectual labor, between theory and practice, between city and countryside, has been abolished, and leisure time thus has become an integral part of their revolutionary choice or inclination.)

Revolutionary operas are not performed for city dwellers only. We had to wait almost a week for the troupe that was performing *On the Docks* to return to Shanghai at the end of their long season performing in peasant communes. It is as if the La Scala or Metropolitan Opera companies were to perform in our villages.

The performers are anonymous; there is no longer a cult of the star. Yang, whose face appears on posters all over China, is called simply "Comrade Yang," and it was not until much later that I learned that his name was Tang Hsien-lin. At the end of each performance the entire company appears on stage and, waving the little red book, sings "The East Is Red," as the audience, on its feet, applauds.

A theater ticket costs from 20 to 60 fen; a movie from 10 to 20. The plays that are produced are also filmed and televised, so revolutionary dramatic productions are seen simultaneously in villages, schools, factories, army posts. Everyone, regardless of age, can be an actor. The three-year-olds in the Peng Pu daycare center, still unsteady on their little legs, sing Yang's ballad, wearing short white cloaks and carrying wooden rifles. Yesterday, quietly pulling back a curtain in the lobby of Hoping Hotel, I watched a group of young people learning *On the Docks* under the guidance of the Shanghai Opera director. They had come from a far-off commune, they told me, and they were singing, learning dance steps, rehearsing lines. Hundreds of such troupes are learning operas and ballets which they will present to audiences in the remotest regions of China.

Love in China

On my return from China I was constantly asked, "What about love? Does it exist in China?" And I would answer, "Heavens, where do you think all those children come from? Why make such a fuss over this question?" If we apply to China some of our current conceptions concerning relations between women and men, we will never succeed in understanding the situation. For example, an Italian who was very much attracted to his young Chinese interpreter decided to express his feelings to her. He came straight to the point. Her reaction was one of total stupefaction, and she asked, "What do you mean? I simply don't understand you. I'm a revolutionary cadre of the Chinese state." Women as objects do not exist in China. For the Chinese woman, held for centuries in the vise of customs, rites, usage, and cruel convention, love is now a matter of free choice.

In the *Economic and Philosophic Manuscripts of 1844*, Marx, after saying that marriage is "*certainly a form of* exclusive private property," adds:

> In the approach to *woman* as the spoil and handmaid of communal lust is expressed the infinite degradation in which man exists for himself, for the secret of this approach has its *unambiguous*, decisive, *plain* and undisguised expression in the relation of *man* to *woman* and in the manner in which the *direct* and *natural* species relationship is conceived. This direct, natural, and necessary relation of person to person is the relation of *man* to *woman*. . . . In this relationship, therefore, is *sensuously manifested*, reduced to an observable *fact*, the extent to which the human essence has become nature to man or to which nature to him has become the human essence of man. From this relationship one can therefore judge man's whole level of development. From the character of this relationship follows how much *man* as a *species being*, as *man*, has come to be himself.*

In China, love on the part of both women and men, civilian and soldier alike, seems to express itself in an almost abnormal timidity, in blushes and childlike naiveté. I have seen couples in the parks who, at most, hold hands, a plastic briefcase full of books between them. There is a kind of mysterious attractiveness in the sweetness and purity that emanate from them. In the expression of their intimate sentiments, they show a great restraint which often leaves one wondering what they are feeling. To display their sentiments, to reveal them to the world, would be to spoil them—it is as simple as that.

---

* Karl Marx, *The Economic and Philosophic Manuscripts of 1844* (New York: International Publishers, 1964, pp. 133, 134—*Trans.*).

It is often said in the West that Chinese women have lost their femininity, simply because they don't measure up to our Eurocentric concept of the feminine. I have seen many Chinese women pulling carts, moving logs in paper mills, and transporting rocks; and I have seen many political and intellectual women. The beauty of the Chinese woman—beauty or ugliness, according to our standards, as exemplified by Brigitte Bardot or Marilyn Monroe—is essentially a question of style. The Chinese woman is almost always beautiful; her style generally lies in a way of being, an air, an inner strength both human and fragile, which render her beautiful, sometimes very beautiful. This style often expresses itself in her elegantly shaped hands, and it is hard to understand how such fine, delicate hands have not become roughened. In order to judge a Chinese woman one cannot rely on the usual criteria but must rely on intuition; then one realizes that they are very beautiful, with that enduring inner vitality that leads them to seek out new ideas, strike out on new paths, and create their own patterns.

In China men and women marry at about the age of twenty-five; late marriage is another measure, in addition to birth control, which is designed to help in family planning.*

Love suffers no coercion; an effort is made to avoid the uncontrolled growth of families, especially in the countryside. But as birth-control devices reach the rural areas, late marriage will no longer be necessary. In the cities, most young people are familiar with them. Surely we cannot assume that the immense gatherings of Red Guards in Peking culminated in a simple exchange of slogans between the young women and the young men!

---

* Propaganda in favor of birth control is now very widespread. It is carried out on a mass scale in the countryside, under the direction of health teams charged with preventive care in the area of women's ailments. There have been certain organizational difficulties, as attested to by an article in *People's Daily* of March 3, 1971: "Is it possible to carry out the work of diagnosis and health care [women's ailments] and that of family planning? At first, opinions were divided. Some comrades said, 'We're already too involved with diagnosis, we'll never make it.' Nonetheless, the majority of comrades who consider that propaganda in favor of late marriage, birth control, and family planning is of great importance feel that this work can be done."

After the "Red Guards," the women

I believe that the problem of women plays a larger role in Mao's thinking now than it did in the past. It has been said that he is beginning to study the thrust of the women's liberation movements in the United States and other Western societies. In any case, he seems very concerned. What does this revolt of women that is spreading throughout the world consist of? In China, Mao realizes that women are changing, evolving, demanding and taking their rightful place, even if not yet sufficiently. Recently he has noted on several occasions that China is a completely different world, where women who formerly had only one task—caring for their children—are at present doing "strange things," engaging in "unheard-of occupations." They are parachutists, pilots of fighter planes, electronics engineers; they join the army and become officers; they are even captains of seagoing vessels. Mao wrote in 1927 that the old authoritarianism of the husband, especially in the countryside, was beginning to crumble. He told the women that times were changing, that women and men were equal, that anything a man can do, a woman can do too. He is concerned with the mass of women for the same reason he was concerned with the peasant masses: among the exploited they were the most exploited. In his famous *Report on an Investigation of the Peasant Movement in Hunan,* in 1927, Mao described the situation of the Chinese woman as objectively revolutionary, and he condemned outright the power of husbands and of men over women in general. In a tradition-bound country like China it was necessary to uproot a pernicious discrimination which began 2,500 years ago. Confucius said: "There are only two categories of inferior beings: the nobodies (*hsiao jen*) and women." Women were always under the guardianship of men. Fathers, husbands, sons, or other men exercised control over women—the perpetual minors. This control by men even gave them power over life and death. The binding of feet arose from the desire to resemble a famous imperial concubine and thus to "please" a man. This binding process spread rapidly, for it accentuated the state of women's subjection, since a woman with bound feet could not take a step alone. In order to make the suffering tolerable, bound feet came to be considered a distinguishing mark of feminine nobility. Servants, whom men needed, and peasant women in the field did not have bound feet; but they could not expect advantageous marriages. The women themselves willingly accepted this torture and mothers remained deaf to the complaints of their martyred daughters. Confucian philosophy did not recognize polygamy as the Koran did, but in reality monogamy was a sign of poverty, and the men who had the means took, in addition to a legitimate wife, one or more concubines—and they, at the whim of their masters, could be returned to their servant status. Women were such contemptible beings, according to Chinese tradition, they were condemned to such misery, that the wretched women of Shanghai, on giving birth to a girl, would drown her like a litter of kittens—a fate rarely applied to a son. We must not forget that the Chinese used to fear demons and that these demons were beings in whom the feminine element *yin* prevailed over the masculine element *yang*. When a boy was born, the peasants tricked the demons and kept them away by giving the infant a girl's name. Whereupon the demons would flee, because they scorned such miserable prey.

In China women are now winning half of heaven and their situation has been totally transformed. However, there still exist traces of superstition among women, of exaggerated deference to men, who are considered to be privileged beings, and women still display a certain timidity in regard to undertaking political leadership roles. "In the rural areas," Mao said in a recent conversation, "women still prefer to have boys. If the firstborn is a girl, the woman will have another child. And if the next one is a girl, the mother will try again. This can go on until the arrival of the ninth child, and since the mother will then be forty-five, she will at last decide to give up." (This is one of the difficulties in trying to spread the use of birth control.) "This attitude," Mao concluded, "must be modified, but it will take time."

Mao has expressed very strongly his wish that women achieve total, not merely legal, equality, an equality born of a revolution in the condition of humankind. Similarly, he shows a great interest in unleashing the torrent of feminine energy. One may well wonder if, after stimulating the youth to be the promotors of the Cultural Revolution in the schools, a *new* cultural revolution in the bosom of the family will not have as protagonists the Chinese women themselves? But isn't a women's revolution already under way? Didn't Mao write a poem in 1961, full of tenderness for the young girls in military uniform:

> How bright and brave they look, shouldering five-foot rifles
> on the parade ground lit up by the first gleams of day.
> China's daughters have high-aspiring minds,
> they love their uniforms, not silks and satins.*

---

* From *Ten More Poems of Mao Tse-tung.—Trans.*

14

The People's Army: Political Power Grows Out of the Barrel of a Gun

Without a people's army the people have nothing.
—Mao Tse-tung

In the dictionary of accepted notions about China, the most widespread is that of the hidden strength of the army. Lin Piao is depicted as a mysterious priest, a "guardian of ideology" who held power, the party, and Mao himself within his grasp. So as to obtain his support, Mao is supposed to have appointed him his "successor." As Mao's closest companion, he became the Dauphin, the heir, as if a hereditary monarchy still existed in China. Throughout this book, I have endeavored to explain that Mao's persistent concern during the Cultural Revolution has been to mold the "successors to the revolutionary cause" and that these successors number *millions.* First and foremost are the youth, destined to absorb the revolutionary qualities (an entire chapter of the little red book is entitled "Cadres" and is devoted to the qualities of these successors, with quotations drawn from "On Khrushchev's Phoney Communism," etc.): in other words, all those who shall see to it that China *does not change color.* That Lin Piao, Mao's closest collaborator, possessed the qualities of these "successors," that he exemplified dedication to the revolution and was a champion of the antirevisionist struggle, and that Mao had designated him as such, did not in the least signify (undoubtedly this is another twist of the Chinese language, mechanically translated and interpreted) that Lin Piao was "appointed" or "elected" as head of the party and state. It meant that he stood as a model of those revolutionary virtues which should characterize the people's army.*

* See "Postscript 1972."

In our society, the most familiar image of the army is a traditional one, that of people who can do nothing but take up arms, people who are the direct instrument of an oppressive power—an image of more or less simpleminded soldiers, colonels, and generals who are nothing better than despots in the barracks. The "cultural value" of combat for the Chinese army—its *wenhua*, or the fact that it has engendered a revolutionary *culture* "in the course of the armed struggle and in the creation of an entire theory of the strategy and tactics of people's war," as Lin Piao put it in 1965—is not understood by us. When it is learned that the Chinese people's army is employed in factories, agriculture, medicine, naval construction, the university, culture, and theater,* the automatic conclusion is that the party no longer exists in China, and that power is in the hands of the military. With our exclusively European culture, accustomed as we are to the putsches of colonels and the nightmares of military coup d'états, we have difficulty in accepting this simple truth: that the Chinese people's army—born of the civil war, educated during the longest armed revolution of contemporary history, organizational center of civilian life throughout all the liberated zones, and symbol of revolutionary purity and sacrifice—is amalgamated with the party. Together they form a single unit, "like a fish in water," to use Mao's expression.

When Mao drew up his "Resolution on the Army" for the Fukien Congress in 1929, he was probably aware of the spirit of Engels' statement in "Conditions and Perspectives of a War of the Holy Alliance Against Revolutionary France in 1852" that "the emancipation of the proletariat will also have a military expression. It will create a new and original method of war." "Political power

* In the fall of 1959, immediately after Peng Teh-huai's replacement by Lin Piao, the play *Hai Jui Scolds the Emperor* was performed in Peking. In 1961, the author, Wu Han, published a sort of continuation of this drama entitled *Hai Tui Dismissed from Office.* The emperor, the target of the attack, was Mao, and Peng Teh-huai was represented as "the courageous and honest man who has fallen into disgrace." In 1966 a meeting of the army's Cultural Commission on the Arts turned its attention to the play, and used it as a basis for its first attack against bourgeois ideology (see the chapter on the revolution in Shanghai). In the West, scandalized indignation and furor: "Just think," said the newspapers, "what would happen if our military turned its attention to opera, theater, and dance . . ."

grows out of the barrel of a gun," asserts Mao, summarizing the entire historical experience of the Chinese Revolution, during which the people's army never once laid down its arms, either in conquest of revolutionary power or in its defense. "The first condition of the dictatorship of the proletariat," wrote Marx in "Seventh Anniversary of the International," "is the existence of a proletarian army. It is on the battlefields that the working classes must win the right to their emancipation." And Engels in "On Authority": "Would the Paris Commune have lasted a single day if it had not made use of this authority of the armed people against the bourgeois? Should we not, on the contrary, reproach it for not having used it freely enough?"

Mao Tse-tung's celebrated thesis—political power grows out of the barrel of a gun—should therefore be restored (as Mao himself saw that it was), to its central place within the Marxist doctrine of the state: "The man who wishes to seize and retain the power of the state must possess a strong army." In *State and the Revolution*, Lenin, quoting Engels, asked: "Has the oppressed class arms?" "The revolution must be armed," continues Mao, "to defeat the ever present threat of counter-revolution, and the army which accepts this class struggle to rid itself of class oppression will lead it with a new spirit." What spirit? "The sole purpose of this army is to stand firmly with the Chinese people and to serve them wholeheartedly." Mao adds: "Military deeds are but one way to accomplish political tasks. . . . The Chinese Red Army is an armed body responsible for carrying out the political tasks of the revolution."

For a long time, then, the Chinese Revolution has in practice been asserting the very opposite of the thesis that the gun controls the party. It is, Mao has reiterated consistently since 1929, the party that commands the gun. On the fortieth anniversary of the founding of the army, the editorial in the *Liberation Army Daily* said: "Our army must be placed under the absolute leadership of the Chinese Communist Party and must be guided by the thought of Mao Tse-tung. The principle that it is the party which commands the gun must be applied, since it is inadmissible that the gun should command the party."

It is thus the duty of the observer to try to show how the people's army is the least "military" of armies among all the "model armies" known to us. Besides, it is only from this point of view that I can even attempt to delineate its distinctive features for the Western reader, inasmuch as we were cut off from the "military face" of the army during our trip and were given an opportunity to become familiar only with its "political face." We came to know this face through conversations we had, wherever we went, with scores of soldiers, members of the three-in-one combinations on the revolutionary committees.

The attitude of these soldiers during our meetings was one of modesty; their contributions to the discussions were unpretentious, and they remained in the background in relation to the worker or peasant political leaders. There was nothing of the soldier's arrogance or air of superiority in their bearing. What seemed to animate them was the determination to serve as a moral example, like Yang, the hero of *Taking Tiger Mountain by Strategy*, a warrior who fought against the Kuomintang, liberating and organizing the peasants. We saw soldiers involved in the hardest kinds of work: digging in the countryside, transporting grain and all kinds of furniture on carts, checking tickets at the entrance to a movie theater, leading children in drills at a school. No other army would have accepted these duties. We discussed this at great length, especially with the soldiers at the Nanking Bridge, at the dockyard at Tientsin where a 10,000-ton ship was being constructed, on revolutionary committees in schools, in factories, and above all, with a comrade at the tourist agency in Peking, as well as with his counterparts at the tourist office in Canton.

It is our impression that for these men in green uniforms, *the primacy of politics* is the basis of their entire training. This is not a slogan but the key enabling us to understand them, and it is summarized by the well-known phrase according to which the army must *serve the people.* The appeal which Mao addressed to the army on January 28, 1966, is a political appeal: "The People's Liberation Army must sustain the immense left-wing masses." And this is what the army has done in the course of the Cultural Revolution, establishing itself as "the central pillar of the dictatorship of the proletariat." Mao's leadership and the army's support of the revolutionary left, we were told on several occasions, made the victorious outcome of the Cultural Revolution possible. The revolutionary "three-in-one combination" which seized power during the Cultural Revolution is an alliance in which the army has always played an integral part in accordance with the directive: "From the summit to the base, in all sectors where power must be seized, representatives of the armed forces and the militia must participate in the formation of the three-in-one combination."

In this army without ranks, it is impossible to distinguish the soldier from the officer. It was only after a good deal of looking that we saw the single detail which distinguished the ordinary soldiers: they have no pockets in their jackets. So whenever we met a soldier, my husband and I would ask each other: "Did you see whether he had any pockets?" or else we would say: "I got the impression that he had pockets. . . ."

It is often forgotten outside China that the Cultural Revolution actually began to prevent the army from becoming "a privileged corps, a professional army, separated from the people." Ranks have been eliminated, and the officers, from generals on down, have reaccustomed themselves to sharing the soldiers' barracks and campbeds, as they did during the Yenan period, when they all lived in caves.

The struggle within the army before the Cultural Revolution was to "once again make the military sphere subordinate to the political sphere"—the exact opposite of what is said in the West. This struggle commenced with the "four firsts" Lin Piao proposed in 1960, "to increase the power of political and ideological work in the army." The four firsts were: (1) as between man and weapons, give first place to man; (2) as between political and other work, give first place to political work; (3) as between ideological and routine tasks, give first place to ideological work; (4) as between ideas in books and living ideas, give first place to the latter.

It was the Cultural Revolution which fomented the spirit of the "three democracies" in the political, economic, and military spheres within the army. (We noted that the "three-eight working style" as it is practiced in the army is one of the principles of behavior in the May 7 schools.) Political democracy means that from the political point of view, ordinary combatants are the equals of their leaders and are free to criticize them, express opinions about them, and pass judgment on their work in the army. Democracy in the economic sphere is put into action through a committee elected by all the soldiers of a company. This committee participates in the leadership of the company through management of commissary and production services, supervision of stocks, auditing of accounts, and waste disposal. Democracy in the military sphere, between officers and soldiers and between soldiers, means that mutual aid during instruction is as compulsory during combat as it is after the battle: generals, colonels, and ordinary soldiers, shoulder to shoulder, study together, weighing the results of the battle.

The people's army makes the primacy of the political sphere its key principle. At the time of the Cultural Revolution (and even afterward) the risk that it would become a professional army solely devoted to military tasks was eliminated. Not only were all forms of hierarchy and paternalism erased through the elimination of military "stripes," but all forms of "discipline" and traditional subordinate relationships were erased as well. At the same time, according to the statements of military experts the world over, this army without ranks and lacking traditional military discipline is the most disciplined in the world.*

"But if there aren't any ranks, how does a soldier recognize his commanding officer?"

"He recognizes him just as the worker recognizes the leader of the revolutionary committee or the person in charge of his shop. He personally knows him from his work, and not because of some external rank or 'stripe.' "

"How can discipline be maintained where hierarchical relationships between superiors and subordinates have been abolished?"

"Discipline in the Chinese army is strong because it is something

* We give here the text of the famous "military" song which relates the soldier's ideal rules of conduct. This song is called "The Three Main Rules of Discipline and the Eight Points for Attention" and is quoted in the *People's Daily* editorial of December 1, 1971: "All revolutionary soldiers must remember the three main rules of discipline. First, obey orders in all your actions; second, do not take a single needle or piece of thread from the masses; third, turn in everything captured. We must apply the three main rules of discipline. We must remember the eight points for attention: Speak politely; pay fairly for what you buy; return everything you borrow; pay for anything you damage; do not hit or swear at people; do not damage crops; do not take liberties with women; don't mistreat captives."

conscious, because it is not due to the presence of sergeants in the barracks, but because it is born of a political commitment to defend proletarian power."

The soldier at the tourist agency

This discussion of the army was all the more interesting since my companion was a military man. He represents the army in the three-in-one combination, and is the director of the national tourist agency in China.

We are in Peking. The comrade-soldier from the tourist office has invited us to lunch in a private room at the Peking Duck. He is twenty-eight years old, although he looks no more than twenty. He wears the olive-green uniform, his cap pulled low over his forehead—not once did he remove it, not even during the meal. His face is round, open, the cheeks slightly pink, with a few fine lines around the eyes. His very delicate hands contrast with his tall and robust build. But, above all, it is his eyes which strike us, at times ironic and hard and yet filled with optimism. From time to time he suddenly grows sad, making him appear even more intelligent and human. We begin by discussing our trip and he says to us: "You see, comrades, we are in a socialist country. In China the tourist agency, which maintains contact with all foreigners, is under the direction of the party." It is as if he wants to make us understand that what appears as "tourism" on the surface is, between comrades, solely and exclusively *political.*

In Europe, people would perhaps be amazed to learn that this soldier keeps perfectly up to date with what is published about China in Communist Party newspapers in the West.

"Do you receive *Unità*?" I ask him at one point.

"Of course I do."

Then he explains to me that they not only receive it, but follow it closely. "You offended us several times," says our companion, "after our Tenth Plenum. We limited our answers to two articles in *People's Daily*. *Unità*'s comments on our Ninth Congress were also ridiculous," he adds. (He may have said "derisive"—I don't understand the interpreter very well.)

"How can we renew our bonds of friendship?"

"You Westerners attack the concept of the parent party, the leading party, but when we attack it you tell us we are anti-Soviet. You even add that we want to become the leading state, and you write in *Unità* that we are for a policy of 'Sinocentrism.' Isn't this a contradiction? We are in favor of a policy of respect toward large and small parties, large and small countries, without meddling, without interference, without 'models.' "

"With regard to small countries, comrade-soldier: when Mao's statement of May 20, 1970, was made public, I quoted it at meetings I held in Naples during the campaign for regional elections. I recall how warmly people applauded the passage where Mao said that imperialism feared even the rustle of leaves in the wind, and how even a small people could conquer a great nation. And this statement of Mao's was published in its entirety in *Unità*."

"We are aware of that," says the soldier, his round face brightening like that of a child. "So let's drink together," he concludes, raising his glass of red wine: "To friendship between our two peoples."

The famous glazed duck arrives: a solid piece, shining like barley sugar. The waiter lays the platter before us as if it is some rare spectacle. Then he takes it away and brings it back carved into serving pieces. Like a courteous host, the soldier-comrade shows us how to lay a piece of duck in a small crepe, cover it with a small piece of scallion, top it with a thick spicy sauce, and roll it up. He does this first for Alberto and then for me.

"I know that in your youth," he says, turning toward me, "you fought as a guerrilla. Did you wear a uniform?"

"No, I was never in uniform. We were an underground group, and our guerrilla organization operated in the *barrios* of Rome during the German occupation. I was in the fifth underground zone."

He looks at me softly and with sympathy, then says: "I hope that you will return to that springtime of your youth . . ."

I cough slightly and bury my head in my plate. My soldier-comrade goes on to say that he believes in internationalism, in the struggle of peoples, in guerrilla warfare, and in the rescue of the Western proletariat. But, in his flexible and far-seeing way, he immediately adds: "People must study the experiences of other countries, not automatically transposing them, but molding them to their own realities. They must acquire their own experience."

He then asks us some questions about the popular demonstrations against Nixon's visit to Rome. He lets out a rollicking laugh when he learns that the American President was forced to go by helicopter to his official visits at Quirinal and the Vatican in order to escape encirclement by throngs of hostile crowds: "People consider American imperialism to be the irreducible enemy force against which they must struggle," he comments.

What strikes me about him—accustomed as we are to looking upon the soldier as a simple warrior—is the political acumen and sharpness of his mind. For me, the face of the people's army is that of this soldier without stripes (although he does have pockets), who must be a high-ranking officer and who at the tourist agency where he serves as the army representative acts as an important intermediary in contacts with foreigners. In my mind I continue to call him a soldier-general.

The history of the struggle for a correct military line

Within the army the battle between the revisionist and proletarian lines lasted approximately from 1950 to 1960. There is no doubt that it is here that the Cultural Revolution has its strongest roots. Peng Teh-huai, Minister of Defense, and Lo Jui-ching, Chief of Staff, asserted that "military instruction is in itself already political—politics of the highest order." The Maoist concept of "people's war" was called backward, and these men went so far as to suggest that Mao was a fanatic whose ideas had become outmoded in this era of nuclear weapons. The atomic bomb a paper tiger? What a ludicrous argument. Undertake a people's war today? Pure folly. But that is what the generals belonging to Peng Teh-huai's group maintained. Mao retorted by continuing to uphold his unshaken strategic vision: Revolutionary war is the war of the masses; and as such it can only be conducted by mobilizing these masses, and it is only by depending on them that it can be won. The opposition praised modern military and technical concepts and said that it would be better to send the people's militia back to work in the fields since its members "abandoned the land at harvest time." In short (as the *Liberation Army Daily* asserted on November 16, 1968), these men "set bourgeois strategy and tactics above revolutionary strategy and tactics." Khrushchev, for his part, as the leaders of the commune in Canton reminded us, was insisting that "the militia represents nothing more than mouths which must be fed"; it was not by chance that we were reminded of this statement, since, as we shall see, opposition between the two lines dated from the distant past.

For Mao, weapons are an important but not decisive factor of war; the decisive factor is men and not material. On the contrary, the military-technical line of Peng Teh-huai would have had national defense rest on a nuclear agreement with the USSR while supporting on other fronts the "triple pacifist line and cutbacks" attributed by the Chinese to Liu Shao-chi. According to an article published in July 1967 by *Liberation Army Daily*, this triple pacifist line, developed between 1961 and 1962, provided for a pacifist attitude toward American imperialism, toward modern revisionists, and toward reactionaries (at that time referring to the Indians), and cutbacks in aid to revolutionary peoples engaged in struggle. The acceptance of the hypotheses of Peng Teh-huai and his chief of staff would have implied choices along the Soviet model: priority would be given to heavy industry, power would be given to technicians, there would be specialization, a hierarchy in the army, etc. In 1959, Peng Teh-huai was relieved of his duties as Minister of Defense and replaced by Lin Piao. But it was not until after the split with the USSR and the unilateral Soviet denunciation of nuclear assistance agreements, and following American aggression in Vietnam (in which the Chinese saw the threat of *escalation* toward their own borders), that the choice between the two lines became clearcut. The line of *people's war* was the following: the entire country had to become a nation of soldiers; the militia was to cooperate with the People's Liberation Army and would be constantly strengthened against possible aggression.

On the surface, the Chinese army numbers 2.8 million men. But the "people under arms"—the people's militia—includes about 30 million combatants. We understood just what this Chinese people's militia is in our face to face encounters with it in each factory, in each school, in each urban district, in each village. It includes women, and children who can shoot as well as the hero of any Western. It is an army which knows its territory, tree by tree, hole by hole, which has dug and continues to dig, as we saw them doing, the shelters and caves for their guerrillas. While fully dependent on the army, the militia represents the *people who hold the territory*, and who prevent conquest of China by a foreign invader. For Mao, army and militia *must advance like a single man.* Mao thus defends the principle of people's war in the modern age: that not only must there be a powerful army, but that it is equally important to create divisions of the people's militia everywhere; then, should imperialism invade China, it will be denied all freedom of action.

When the Cultural Revolution entered its active phase, Mao called upon the army to support the left. The army was ready for his appeal and made it its own. Once its representatives had entered into the triple alliance, with few exceptions it remained faithful to its historical role as "a pillar of the dictatorship of the proletariat." * So well did it perform that Lin Piao can now assert that "the People's Liberation Army firmly supports the proletarian revolutionaries."

In his famous speech of September 3, 1965—"Long Live the Victory of People's War"—given on the occasion of the twentieth anniversary of victory in the War of Resistance against Japan, Lin Piao retraces the history of the Chinese people's army. This is the most complete document available on the subject. In the text he describes the ups and downs of the army, its internal contradictions, its struggles against right- and left-wing opportunism in confrontation with the Kuomintang and during the War of Resistance against Japan, as well as the struggle regarding political principles which at the time was to lead the army (among others) into a *united front:* "History shows that within the united front the Communist Party must maintain its ideological, political, and organizational independence, adhere to the principle of independence and initiative, and insist on its leading role." The experience of the Second Revolutionary Civil War demonstrated that when the strategic concepts of reliance on the peasantry and building revolutionary

* On this, see Daubier, *Histoire de la révolution culturelle en Chine.*

bases throughout the countryside were applied, "there was an immense growth in the revolutionary forces and one red base area after another was built." Furthermore:

> In these base areas we built the party, ran the organs of state power, built the people's armed forces, and set up mass organizations; we engaged in industry and agriculture and operated cultural, educational, and all other undertakings necessary for the independent existence of a separate region. Our base areas were in fact a state in miniature. . . . In the war of liberation we continued the policy of first encircling the cities from the countryside and then capturing the cities, and thus won nationwide victory.

Lin Piao goes on to discuss the role of the army:

> During the Anti-Japanese War our army staunchly performed the three tasks set by Comrade Mao Tse-tung, namely, fighting, mass work, and production, and it was at the same time a fighting force, a political work force, and a production corps. . . . By their exemplary conduct they won the wholehearted support of the masses, who affectionately called them "our own boys."

Lin Piao concludes that Comrade Mao's theory of people's war was proved by the long practice of the people's war, led by the Chinese Communist Party and comprising the War of Resistance and the two revolutionary civil wars, which together lasted twenty-two long years, and which "constitute the most drawn-out and most complex people's war led by the proletariat in modern history, and it has been the richest in experience."

The participation of the army—loyal to Chairman Mao's line—during the Cultural Revolution was carried out with the utmost political determination, but for the most part without giving way to violent demonstrations contrary to the principle "Serve the people." As Chou En-lai recently affirmed, when the Cultural Revolution in certain localities degenerated into open conflict between factions, at first with the use of sidearms, then guns, and eventually mortars, the army lost thousands of men before deciding to use its own weapons to suppress factional struggles. (The two incidents which created the greatest stir on the subject of the army as protagonist—Daubier speaks of them in his book—occurred during July and August 1967 in Wuhan. In one case, the army supported the

"Million Heroes," a group created at the time of the Cultural Revolution; but Mao repudiated this support in a message addressed to the population through the navy. During the course of the summer of 1967 another extremely confusing situation arose in Canton. The city was split for or against the "Committee for Revolutionary Alliance." The people's army, invited to intervene and forced to take up arms against organizations favoring the Committee for Revolutionary Alliance, was accused by the ultra-left of having supported counter-revolutionary forces by dissolving the Committee. Chou En-lai, however, approved this measure when he arrived in Canton. This second episode, unlike the first, shows that the army was working in close collaboration with the left-wing forces in Mao's headquarters.) Be that as it may, the line generally followed has been that favoring the re-education and reabsorption of opposition forces in accordance with the practice the Chinese army has traditionally followed. Mao afterward deplored (in a rambling interview with Edgar Snow in 1970) that in the struggle between factions, the army practice of not taking prisoners but of actually giving them money to return home (in effect since the Yenan era), has at times been forgotten. In effect, Mao said that the instances of maltreatment delayed the phase of party transformation and restructing which should have been the essential aim of the Cultural Revolution. (Both Mao and Chou En-lai, in their recent interview with Snow, specifically mentioned that they did not wish to ascribe any official significance to their remarks.)

The function of the army has been rather complicated, especially on the political level. In fact—as throughout the entire history of the Chinese Communist Party and throughout the Cultural Revolution—since the outbreak of the struggle against the right as represented by Liu Shao-chi and his disciples the army has been very much on guard and has taken a firm stand against clearly defined ultra-leftist factions born, through a highly complex process, during the most bitter phases of the Cultural Revolution. The best known and in a certain sense the most dangerous case was that of the "May 16 Group." From what is known, this group was led by Yao Teng-shan and Hsu Yen, two Chinese diplomats in Indonesia. They returned to China after displaying great courage during an attack on the Chinese embassy by anti-Communist Indonesian soldiers and were received by Mao. Playing on the prestige they thus obtained, they drew up plans, apparently in concert with leaders on a much higher level—the secret May 16 Group. After a time this group succeeded in taking over the Ministry of Foreign Affairs. Their tactic was "to use Chairman Mao so as to fight against him." As a matter of fact, they made continual reference to a literal interpretation of the famous Central Committee circular published on May 16, 1966, in which Mao denounced the existence of "Khrushchev-style persons" ("persons," not "a person") at the top of the party. They attacked a series of leaders, not only Liu, but Chou En-lai and Lin Piao, calling them ultra-leftists. The "group" found an audience within as well as outside Peking, and succeeded for a time in influencing certain actions of Chinese foreign policy. The attack against the British consulate in Peking on August 20, 1967, when the office of the English chargé d'affaires was set ablaze, is one of the actions attributed (disapprovingly) to them. In May, the ultra-leftists had twice ransacked the Ministry of Foreign Affairs looking for evidence to denounce Chinese foreign policy, not only that pursued by Chen Yi, but also that sponsored by Chou En-lai. But above all, in my opinion, it was the unity of the army that the May 16 Group sought to undermine. On August 1, 1967, the anniversary of the People's Liberation Army, an editorial appeared in *Red Flag*—whose editor and assistant director was Kuang Feng, one of the fanatics involved—devoted to the need to "oust a handful of Khrushchev people hidden within the army." The text, distributed in leaflets and broadcast over the radio, was presented as a kind of directive emanating from the Central Cultural Revolution Group. The risk was considerable (at that point Mao personally issued a directive to repudiate and eliminate the group), for by aiming at creating division within the army, pillar of the revolution, the May 16 Group was leading China into a state of veritable chaos.

One of the most important tasks of Chairman Mao's partisans, with the aid of the People's Liberation Army, was to unmask this group and its followers. This was done in a harsh political struggle, initially directed toward isolating the group, later toward salvaging through persuasive means those who had been taken in by the ultra-leftist slogans. In addition to the names of Yao Teng-shan and Hsu Yen, some China experts have added those of certain national leaders elected during the Chinese Communist Party's Ninth Congress. But as yet these disclosures have not been officially confirmed by the Chinese. Furthermore, I do not believe that the disclosure of these names—and some rather important names at that—which would at present create a scandal, is of such great importance, knowing the aversion of the Chinese leaders to thrusting names under the spotlight of criticism, and the time they waited before revealing Liu Shao-chi's name. The problem is a political one. What appears most important is the fact that the May 16 Group was in time defeated, and the task of salvaging those who had been touched by the slogans of the ultra-left, in particular the young Red Guards, has since been undertaken with great success through a campaign of "struggle-criticism-transformation." This campaign got under way in 1967 and is still fighting "left" opportunism and ultra-left deviations, against which Mao fired the first shot of the political struggle—at the same time that he saw the enemy in right-wing revisionism and opportunism (Liu Shao-chi). (In articles published in *People's Daily* on July 1, 1971, in *Red Flag*, and in the *Liberation Army Daily* on the party's fiftieth anniversary, there are numerous allusions to the ultra-left line of Wang Ming and Li Li-san, which appear to be indirect attacks against this line.)

In the course of the Cultural Revolution the army was called upon to renew those indissoluble bonds of unity with the people which marked the entire revolutionary tradition (those of a "fish in water"). It now gives its unconditional support "through concrete action" to the proletarian revolutionaries by internalizing the key directive (grasp revolution and promote production). It has committed itself to work in factories, in the fields, in schools, in hospitals, on construction sites, wherever there are economic construction efforts to be supported or sacrifices to be shared. "The army loves the people, and the people support the army"—we have seen this written on the walls of factories. "Political power grows out of the barrel of a gun" was the phrase which followed us everywhere. It is embroidered on tapestries, painted in the streets, as well as in stores and theaters, it hangs in bedrooms and even in the elevators in Canton.

The people's army, symbol of total dedication, total heroism, thus supports the revolutionary left; it sustains the *red rebels* and the entire mass of people who have flung themselves into the struggle. Standing before the people as a symbol of total self-sacrifice (as the force which liberated them from the hated enemy in the longest war in history), it supports the people and remains at their side. These bonds are strengthened through commentaries in the press, through articles, and through the writings of simple soldiers telling not only of their work experiences (acupuncture, systems of cultivation, management of army experimental enterprises, new systems of industrial work), but of political problems as well. This is affirmed by the *People's Daily* article of May 10, 1970, written by Hsing Hsi-li under the title of "Study and Defend the Philosophy in the Work of Aiding the Left." He begins as follows: "I joined the People's Liberation Army in 1965. In my shop I was a cook. In October 1968 I was sent to the Jinpong factory in Tientsin with the task of supporting the left . . ." Hsing Hsi-li is one of the thousands of soldiers we have seen humbly working among the masses from one end of China to the other.

From the political point of view the regular Chinese army is a highly selective corps. Each year only a minute portion of an enormous enlistment of eighteen-year-old youths—from 9 to 15 million—can be admitted. The others often join the militia. The selected soldiers are mainly of peasant or worker origin. To join the army is an honor. Each Chinese family with a son in the army proudly showed us his portrait. Ten- or fifteen-year-old children who drilled with the soldiers or with the people's militia proudly told us: "With our people's army we are learning resistance warfare against invaders." Then they described to us the military drills they performed during their vacations or on holidays. Needless to say, to Soviet witnesses this army was proof of a frenzied heroism on the borders of the Usuri. The films of the terrifying contests between the Chinese and the Soviets, which were shown to us in a private room at the Hsin Chiao, are frightful documents. These documentaries have been shown throughout China and are known to the majority of Chinese, including the children. A soldier wearing a fur cap with the red star, flinging himself headlong through the snow to the attack, gun in hand, was engraved on the stamps which we put on our postcards. This is an army which arms itself and yet works for and with the people. Like the legendary Anteus, the army loses its strength the moment it lifts its foot from the land, that is, from the moment it is separated from the people who gave birth to it.

Although the Chinese people are constantly preparing themselves for possible war, China is neither an aggressive nor a conquering nation. In 1963 Chen Yi declared that "Chinese troops will never cross the country's borders to export the revolution." The revolution must be propagated through ideology and not invasion. Mao's famous *atomic bomb–paper tiger* phrase (which is profoundly correct on the political level, insisting as it does that neither the people nor China disarm in view of the nuclear power of the United States and the quasimonopoly of the two "great powers") was also born of the polemic against the bourgeois military strategy which only took into account new weapons of destruction. Even though China has now "added" its own atomic force to the power of thc people, thereby breaking the nuclear monopoly of the Russians and West, it is known that since 1960 Chou En-lai has been asking that a summit conference be held banning the manufacture of nuclear weapons. For their part, the Chinese assert, atomic weapons are *only a defense*. Why did you develop them? Snow asked the Chinese prime minister in late 1970. Chou En-lai responded:

> In the first place, it must be borne in mind that our tests are limited to what is strictly necessary. Their purpose is to end nuclear monopoly and blackmail and to prevent an atomic war. This is why whenever we carry out a test, we state at the same time that in any event, whatever the circumstances, China will not be the first to use nuclear weapons. We reiterate our proposal for a summit conference in the course of which all countries of the world, *large and small*, would conclude a treaty banning such weapons and providing for their total destruction, the first step to be taken being an agreement banning their use.

While unceasingly proclaiming their nonaggressive intentions and the absence of any spirit of conquest, China makes American imperialism tremble, as we saw after Chou En-lai's visit to Hanoi. Referring to the United States on the day after the invasion of Laos, Chou proclaimed that the peoples of Indochina and of the

People's Republic of China are "united like lips and teeth." Henceforth it would be not only the Chinese atomic bombs but the entire Chinese people who were under arms, this immense people capable of holding an immense territory, who are striking terror into the heart of America after the disastrous experience that country has already met in Vietnam.*

---

* A number of articles written by American military experts and specialists in Chinese affairs in Hong Kong (the "China watchers") draw a picture of the organization and strength of the Chinese army and, consequently, of China's nuclear armaments. These articles are extensively reproduced in *La Documentation française*, no. 63, 1971, and according to the information culled from them, the figures would be as follows:

ARMED FORCES. *Regular army:* 2.8 million (United States: 3.5 million); *people's militia:* 30 million; *atom bombs:* 50 to 100; *missiles with nuclear warheads:* experimental, not yet operative.

In greater detail:

Land army: 120 divisions (3 divisions = army, 1 division = 12,000 men); 5 armored divisions, 2 divisions of paratroopers.

Air force: 100,000 men (2,600 aircraft in all); 150 light IL-28 jet bombers; 1,800 MIGS 15, 17, and 19, as well as a few MIGS 21; a few TU-4 bombers (a Russian reproduction of the 1946 B-29).

Navy: 120,000 men, 8 divisions of marines with a total strength of about 80,000 men; 1,000 ships, vedette boats, and small destroyers; 500 aircraft; 200 submarines with a radius of action of about 10,000 miles; 3 G-type submarines (able to launch 3 missiles).

According to the same sources, starting in 1966, when its own equipment had been updated, the army's basic weapons were Soviet-type AK-47 guns and SK-2 carbines. Each unit is also equipped with B-40 and B-42 rocket launchers, the efficiency of which has been demonstrated by the Vietnamese combatants in South Vietnam. Added to all this are 60-, 82-, and 120-type mortars, 105- and 122-type rockets, 57- and 75-type recoilless cannons, and lastly, heavy field artillery and anti-aircraft batteries. The armored divisions, previously equipped with T-34 tanks and SU-100 offensive cannons, are today made from Soviet model T-54 tanks. These are, however, constructed in China, and Pakistan has been supplied with a number of them by way of military assistance.

With regard to nuclear weapons and missiles, the authors of the articles assert that they are not sufficiently well informed about their development in China, and that surprises could be in store for us—as in October 1964 (the use of U-235 before any plutonium explosions) or in June 1967 (the release of an H-bomb from an aircraft).

A farewell dinner in Canton

We are invited to a kind of farewell dinner in Canton by a comrade who is a veteran of the war against Japan. It is our guess that he too represents the People's Liberation Army at the tourist agency, although he is not in uniform. It is evident that in a border area such as Canton where "spies abound," his role is extremely delicate. Chao tells me that he had a long past as an *old* cadre, but he hardly seems old at all, and finally tells us that he is fifty. Although very modest when speaking about himself, we succeed in learning of his long experience on the battlefield. From the south, where he had arrived from Hopei, he had again set out for the north. Later the army returned to the south to liberate China from the Japanese, and here he has remained. He speaks of Canton with enthusiasm: "A glorious city where five thousand martyrs died during the massacre perpetrated by Chiang Kai-shek. It was from the south, from Hunan, Yunnan, Kwangsi, and Kiangsi that the spark of the struggle which was to set the prairie ablaze was struck." I tell him that the echo of the heroic battles of the proletariat in Shanghai and Canton reached us through Malraux's novels, as children in fascist Italy. Living under the dictatorship, we learned of the pride of the Chinese revolutionaries in admitting they were Communists, and the sacrifice of five thousand martyrs remembered in a simple monument I had seen that day in Canton.

The comrade—perhaps he is a general—wears the same dress as everyone else. He smiles at us, watching us with small penetrating eyes; his expression is witty and pleasant, and he seems surprised to find us more likeable than he had expected. We talk about the Cultural Revolution, and he says: "I think there is one thing which you should remember above and beyond everything else which you

---

On the basis of present information, it appears that it will not be until 1975 and later that a Chinese deterrent force will become credible with an adequate number of MRBM's, IRBM's, and/or ICBM's, the introduction of the first atomic submarine, the possession of seven to ten type-G missile launching submarines, and about forty type-W submarines, equipped with surface-to-surface missiles.

have seen, and that is that this revolution is the most important form of mass democracy history has ever known."

The restaurant where we are eating is called the Garden of the South and is located in a remote but very beautiful spot. Little bridges with arches span miniscule lakes. Tall bamboos screen pavilions and gardens while the moon filters through the winter mist. It is hard to imagine myself here in these surroundings right out of a painting discussing such terribly concrete subjects. Chao hands me the menu, saying: "If you have a friend, its safe to send him here, he'll be all right." We are all very gay, one reason being that we are proposing toasts with *maotai* (a sorghum liquor aged for many years) which is drunk "to the last drop" (*kanpei* as the Chinese say). The Chinese do not normally drink, especially the young people, and Lu finds it very difficult to keep up with us and empty his glass after each toast. Our fighter-comrade drinks a toast to friendship between our two countries. He says that Italy's recognition of China is due to the latter's growing prestige and to the struggles of the Italian people. We drink another toast to the visits of many other Communist fighters and friends of China, for *seeing* is more important than *reading* whatever we can write: "Have confidence," we say, "you have lived through a terrible period of encirclement, but friendship for China has always been the deepest feeling of the European and world proletariat, workers, peasants, and intellectuals."

They thank us. We are perfectly aware of what a blow the isolation imposed on them by external circumstances has been (on the one hand, hostility from old enemies, on the other, the hostility of most other Communist parties). The problem is to build a bridge, and this will not be easy. I remember something an exceptional witness, Dr. Jerome Franck, said about China at one of the hearings held by Senator Fulbright: "The first and probably most difficult step is psychological. We must re-examine the image we have formed about China . . . bearing in mind from a historical viewpoint the humiliation it has suffered. Undoubtedly, we must be prepared to go further and to accept from them a kind of symbolic humiliation." At times during the course of this trip I thought that I could have felt "symbolically humiliated," but in actuality this never happened: I was overly conscious of that historical humiliation, both former and more recent, which China had endured at the hands of that part of the world to which I belong.

Chao interrupts my reflections. He says that our trip has been especially useful for the relations which have been established between *them and us*, and "we," that little pronoun, acquires a broader meaning (or so I hope) than what our modest persons may signify. With these words, the comrade-fighter raises his glass, says "*kanpei*," and together we drain our glasses.

Postscript 1972

Following the cancellation of the October 1, 1971, parade celebrating the anniversary of the founding of the republic, the most varied assumptions were made in the West as to the relationship between the army and the party. Some even went so far as to hypothesize the liquidation of Vice-Chairman Lin Piao and his closest collaborators. So far as it is known, no official statement has been published by the Chinese *outside of China*. I use the word *outside*, abroad, because there is nothing to exclude the possibility that the party, the army, and the entire Chinese population are well informed (as has occurred on other occasions) of events which may have taken place, and that they have openly and heatedly discussed them. An article which appeared in the three most important Chinese publications on December 1, 1971, under the title of "Sum Up Experience in Strengthening Party Leadership," can furnish valuable criteria for an understanding of the essence of the political questions over which confrontation most probably occurred—a confrontation, moreover, which is not new to the history of the Chinese Communist Party and which involves the respective roles of the party and the army and the relationship between them, given Mao's long-standing assertion that "the party commands the gun, and the gun must never be allowed to command the party."

Let us compare the contents of this article with the *disclosure of new events* that have occurred in China. On October 1, 1971, contrary to normal practice, no speech was made by Lin Piao. Only Chou En-lai was observed strolling with Mao's wife through the gardens of the Summer Palace in the pictures released by the Chinese news agency abroad. Chiefs of staff had not appeared in public since mid-September. The ceremonial formula linking Vice-Chairman Lin Piao to Chairman Mao in the leadership of the Chinese Communist Party's Central Committee was altered, and at the present time the party's Central Committee is under the sole leadership of Chairman Mao Tse-tung. At the same time, both in China as well as abroad, the special October 1 edition of the magazine *China Pictorial* appeared on newsstands with Mao and Lin Piao on the cover. Captioned, as in the past, Mao's "closest comrade in arms," Lin Piao was not, however, referred to as vice-chairman of the party. It is not only impossible to analyze something about which one is *ignorant*, but in addition it is not honest. A Chinese puzzle? It would be better to confine ourselves to the texts. The January 1, 1972, statement on the party-army relationship leads to the conclusion that there is no reason to assume that Lin Piao has been able to escape criticism or responsibility for his errors committed during the Cultural Revolution, and that the *shadow* surrounding Lin Piao and other major military leaders goes hand in hand with the *renewed insistance* and the exceptional energy with which the *need is reaffirmed for the People's Liberation Army to remain subject to party control and to "further increase its political capability."* In the article published on December 1, Chang Kuo-tao is mentioned four times, as if to warn him that a soldier may also be tainted with "splittism" (Chang Kuo-tao was in fact the man who seriously challenged Mao's prevailing position during the Long March by attempting to divide the army).

In the 1972 New Year's Day editorial published in *People's Daily*, *Red Flag*, and *Liberation Army Daily*, we read:

> In accordance with Chairman Mao's line on army building, the Chinese People's Liberation Army should strengthen army building and energetically grasp military and political training so as to raise its political and military qualities higher. It is necessary to strengthen militia building. It is necessary to *support the army and cherish the people, support the government and cherish the people*, and thus strengthen army-government and army-civilian unity. It is necessary to deal resolute blows at the disruptive activities of the counter-revolutionaries. The army men and the people throughout the country should conscientiously study the international situation and the par-

ty's line and policies in foreign affairs, *heighten our vigilance, defend the motherland,* be well prepared against wars of aggression and firmly smash all imperialist and social-imperialist plots of aggression and subversion.

With regard to the ideological and political struggle and in an attempt to develop a critical analysis of revisionism and to rectify the style of work, the article posits in highly explicit terms the continuance of the struggle between the socialist and capitalist paths, between that which fosters a strengthening of party leadership and that which rejects and weakens this leadership. Open reference is made to "intriguers, rumormongerers, and conspirators who cannot bear the light of day":

> It is essential, in line with Chairman Mao's teaching, to take the following as the important content: *Practice Marxism, and not revisionism; unite, and don't split; be open and aboveboard, and don't intrigue and conspire.* Whether to practice Marxism or to practice revisionism has always been the crux of the struggle between the two lines. . . . It is necessary to integrate theory with practice, and link past struggles with current ones so that we can make a still clearer distinction between Chairman Mao's Marxist-Leninist line and policies and the anti-Marxist-Leninist line and policies of Liu Shao-chi and other swindlers, between the materialist theory of reflection and idealist apriorism, between the socialist road and the capitalist road and between what helps strengthen party leadership and what weakens or rejects it. Chairman Mao has always advocated being open and aboveboard. Liu Shao-chi and other swindlers, engaged in counterrevolutionary activities for the purpose of restoring capitalism, are extremely isolated in the whole party and the whole army and among the people throughout the country, and they cannot bear the light of day; they can therefore only resort to intrigue and conspiracy, and rumormongering and mud-slinging. By insisting on being open and aboveboard we will be able to detect and resist the antiparty and antipopular evil wind and constantly strengthen the unity of the party.

Here we find the key terms which were counterposed against the first important article of December 1, terms which have evidently served since October 1971 to sustain the political debate which centers on party members but which has been extended to the masses—not only because of the well-known course of political discussions in China, but in addition, as disclosed in the January 1, 1972, editorial because this was the eve of the *first meeting of the Fourth National People's Congress, and consequently, an "electoral" campaign to elect delegates to the new assembly was in full swing.*

To conclude, it appears advisable to quote an extremely lengthy extract from the December 1 article, in addition to the passages already cited, in order to follow the initial stages of this development through a first-hand acquaintance with the documentary evidence.

> In line with the great leader Chairman Mao's instructions, "*Read and study seriously and have a good grasp of Marxism*" and "*Carry out education in ideology and political line,*" the whole party has unfolded a movement for criticizing revisionism and rectifying the style of work and deepened it step by step since the second plenary session of the Ninth Central Committee of the party. The movement has attained marked results and achieved great victory. By seriously reading works by Marx, Lenin, and Chairman Mao, the masses of party members, and particularly senior party cadres, have heightened their consciousness of class struggle and the struggle between the two lines and of continuing the revolution under the dictatorship of the proletariat, and have gone a step further in exposing and criticizing such swindlers as Liu Shao-chi. New party committees at various levels have generally been established and the struggle-criticism-transformation in the Great Proletarian Cultural Revolution is developing in depth. Rallying all the more closely around the party Central Committee headed by Chairman Mao and advancing along the line of unity for victory of the Ninth National Congress of the party, the whole party, the whole army, and the people of the whole country have continued to win new successes in the socialist revolution and socialist construction.
>
> The communique of the second plenary session of the party's Ninth Central Committee called for strengthening party building and "giving further play to the leading role of the vanguard of the proletariat." . . .
>
> In order to fulfill our party's glorious tasks still better, the party committees at all levels must sum up their experience in earnest so as to continue to strengthen party leadership over all kinds of work.
>
> What are the main questions to be stressed in strengthening party leadership?
>
> It is imperative to strengthen party concept. Chairman Mao

teaches us: "*The Chinese Communist Party is the core of leadership of the whole Chinese people. Without this core, the cause of socialism cannot be victorious.*" Our party is the vanguard of the proletariat; it is the highest form of class organization of the proletariat. Of the seven—industry, agriculture, commerce, culture and education, the army, the government, and the party—the party gives leadership to the first six. Party committees at all levels should exercise centralized leadership in all fields of work . . . Chairman Mao regards party building as one of the three principal magic weapons for the Chinese Revolution and *helping to strengthen, and not discard or weaken, the leadership of the Communist Party* as one of the most important political criteria for distinguishing fragrant flowers from poisonous weeds. In the complicated class struggle and the struggle between the two lines, every party member and every revolutionary must firmly bear in mind Chairman Mao's teaching: "*We must have faith in the masses and we must have faith in the party. These are two cardinal principles. If we doubt these principles, we shall accomplish nothing.*" It is especially necessary for members of party committees at all levels to strengthen party concept and place themselves within the party committee and not outside it, still less above it.

It is imperative to carry on education in ideology and political line in a deepgoing way. Chairman Mao has pointed out on many occasions: *The correctness or incorrectness of the ideological and political line decides everything.* Policies are the concrete embodiment of a political line. Fundamentally, strengthening party leadership means the firm implementation of Chairman Mao's proletarian revolutionary line and policies. The history of inner-party struggle between the two lines shows that the representatives of the bourgeoisie always change their tactics in an attempt to substitute their opportunist line and policies for the party's Marxist-Leninist line and policies and substitute their bourgeois program for the party's proletarian program, and thus to bring about a change in the character of the party, turning it from a proletarian into a bourgeois party, and achieve their criminal aim of liquidating party leadership and undermining the Chinese Revolution. This is an inevitable reflection of the class struggle in society. . . .

It is imperative to strengthen the unity of the party. Chairman Mao has all along stressed the importance of *being able at uniting with the great majority* and regarded the unity of the party as the most essential factor in winning victory in the Revolution and construction. Had it not been for the correct principle of unity of the

Seventh Party Congress, the new democratic revolution could not have achieved victory. And had it not been for the line of unity for victory of the Ninth Party Congress, the fruits of the Great Proletarian Cultural Revolution could not have been consolidated and developed. . . . Chen Tu-hsiu's patriarchism, Chu Chiu-pai's punitiveness, Li Li-san's "my word is law," Wang Ming's "ruthless struggle and merciless blows," Chang Kuo-tao's splittism and warlordism, and the "striking at many in order to protect a handful" practiced by Liu Shao-chi and other swindlers like him have all caused tremendous harm to the unity and unification of the party. . . .

Be open and aboveboard. Chairman Mao pointed out long ago: "*We Communists have always disdained to conceal our views.*" All party comrades, and it goes without saying for senior party cadres, must be frank and forthright politically. At all times one ought to state one's political views openly and, on every important political issue, express one's position, either for or against, adhering to what is right and correcting what is wrong. This is a question of the party's style of work and of party spirit. As chieftains of opportunist lines are engaged in splitting activities, they are bound to resort to conspiracies and intrigues. In his famous talk in 1964 on bringing up successors, Chairman Mao pointed out: "*Beware of those who engage in intrigue and conspiracy. For instance, men like Kao Kang, Jao Shu-shih, Peng Teh-huai, and Huang Ke-cheng were to be found in the Central Committee. Everything divides into two. Some persons are dead-set on conspiring. They want to do this, so that's that—even now there are such persons at it! That there are persons conspiring is an objective fact and not a question of whether we like it or not.*" In our party's history, those bourgeois careerists, conspirators, and persons having illicit relations with foreign countries, who clung to opportunist lines and engaged in conspiracies, could not but bring ruin, disgrace, and destruction upon themselves in the end.

It is imperative to strengthen the sense of discipline. Discipline is the guarantee for the implementation of the line. In summing up our party's struggle against Chang Kuo-tao's opportunist line, Chairman Mao pointed out: "*Some people violate party discipline through not knowing what it is, while others, like Chang Kuo-tao, violate it knowingly and take advantage of many party members' ignorance to achieve their treacherous purposes. Hence it is necessary to educate members in party discipline so that the rank and file will not only observe discipline themselves, but will exercise supervision over the leaders so that they, too, observe it, thus preventing the recurrence of cases like Chang Kuo-tao's.*" We must bear firmly in mind this historical experience, resolutely carry out the party's unified discipline stipulated in the party constitution, and resolutely carry out "The Three Main Rules of Discipline and the Eight Points for Attention" formulated by Chairman Mao . . .

It is imperative to *practice Marxism-Leninism, and not revisionism.* To practice Marxism or to practice revisionism? The struggles between the two lines within our party, in the final analysis, boil down to this question. Why is it that some people are fooled and taken in during the struggle between the two lines? The fundamental reason is that they do not read and study seriously and cannot distinguish materialism from idealism and the Marxist line from the opportunist line. This is an extremely profound lesson. Comrades throughout the party, senior party cadres in particular, must follow Chairman Mao's teachings, continuously persist in reading and studying seriously, have a good grasp of Marxism, consciously remold their world outlook, combine study with revolutionary mass criticism, constantly raise their ability to distinguish between genuine and sham Marxism, and carry out Chairman Mao's revolutionary line ever more consciously. . . .

Under the leadership of the Central Committee headed by Chairman Mao and along Chairman Mao's proletarian revolutionary line, let us *unite to win still greater victories!*

15

China's International Strategy in a Bipolar World

With the possible exception of some of our Chinese comrades, no one among the group gathered with us around the table at that Canton restaurant could have imagined that only a few months later unusual foreigners—the members of an American ping-pong team—would come to China, nor that their visit to Peking would inaugurate what would be called "ping-pong diplomacy." There have been numerous attempts to interpret this event, each of them expressing contradictory attitudes: some see it as a rallying by China to "Khrushchev's peaceful coexistence"; others are like orphans deprived of a revolutionary guide which could only sustain its immaculate purity as long as it remained a sort of beleaguered fortress.

No one saw the most *Chinese* significance: the paper tiger was invited to play with celluloid balls. Naturally, I am not in a position to say whether the Chinese themselves saw it this way, but the possibility cannot be excluded. It is clear, however, that we must go beyond this bit of humor.

There are undoubtedly numerous keys which can help us to understand China's international strategy. Personally, I feel that the best key, the one which is closest to reality and is consequently the most useful in understanding this new and different world which is China, is to always bear in mind the historical experience of the Chinese Revolution. I think this enables us first of all to understand the Chinese internal situation and the significance of the political aftermath of struggle which accompanied and caused it. In addition, it enables us to understand the general line of China's international strategy.

The Yenan experience is often referred to as one of the major starting points in the attempt to understand certain objectives of the Cultural Revolution. It seems to me that it would be just as much to the point to speak of this experience in connection with certain features of Chinese foreign policy. But this would carry me too far afield, and it is for this reason that I prefer to take something closer and better known to us in the attempt to outline, according to the criterion of the importance which the Chinese ascribe to practical *experience*, some of the general lines of what has been called *China's international strategy*. I wish to speak of the point of departure represented by the Bandung Conference of 1955. Ten years after the end of the Second World War, on April 18, 1955, the first conference of Afro-Asian countries got under way in Bandung, Indonesia. Seventeen years have passed since then, but the Bandung Conference still marks the entrance on the historical scene of the peoples' liberation movements of Africa and Asia and represents the first impetuous rising of countries still oppressed or scarcely liberated from the foreign yoke against the international imperialist and capitalist system.

What does this "spirit of Bandung," to which the twenty-nine countries meeting there gave lasting life, consist of? It was based on five fundamental principles which it would be useful to recall since, as we shall see, they left their mark on Chinese foreign policy, even if not in an always clear and distinctive fashion. They are: (1) respect for the fundamental rights of man as well as for the goals and principles of the United Nations Charter; (2) respect for the sovereignty and territorial integrity of all states; (3) equality of all races and nations both large and small; (4) nonintervention and noninterference in the domestic affairs of other countries; (5) no recourse to acts or threats of aggression or to the use of force.

What then was Bandung? If one tries to define its significance, I believe one could say that Bandung was essentially an attempt to establish a common political and strategic platform for the great majority of countries emerging from the disintegration of the colonialist system, countries which, during precisely this period, were beginning to be called the "Third World." China itself, while pursuing different paths from the others—in other words, the path of victorious revolution—was also emerging from the disintegration of the colonialist system and participated in this meeting—not, however, in pursuit of power, but because China was an *integral and fundamental part* of the Third World. Moreover, this was what the majority of countries at Bandung felt the Chinese presence to mean. To be sure, China's prestige was already great. But I do not believe it can be said that China attempted to impose its hegemony through its prestige. The "five points" of peaceful coexistence, which were born of this conference and which, moreover, quite faithfully recapitulate the principles subscribed to by Nehru and Chou En-lai, did and continue to exemplify the point of view of a correct formulation of relationships between different countries having different political and social systems. These same principles have consistently remained as the basis of Chinese foreign policy, as the major leaders of the People's Republic have affirmed on all occasions.

Does this mean that the Chinese today envisage a return to Bandung? I think we all realize that "a lot of water has flowed under the bridge," and that numerous events have occurred since then. We are in a totally different situation. But something valuable has remained: the "five points" and the possibility—or, better still, the necessity—of continuing to make them the connective tissue of Third World unity against all kinds of foreign dependence. But I believe that we can even go one step further. I believe it can be asserted that everything which has occurred from Bandung up to the present day confirms and justifies China's strategy as a Third World nation. During the past seventeen years, the Bandung front has been defeated mostly because the majority of countries which participated in the meeting have accepted the hypothesis that foreign aid from the developed world will solve the problems of underdevelopment. The acceptance of such a hypothesis was clearly not the result of an *error* on the part of the leadership groups. It was a class choice inherent in these groups: between the path chosen by equals, codified in the "five points" and consistently adhered to by China, and the path of *effective dependence* on the developed world, not only on an economic level but very often politically as well. The second path seemed (and to a large extent was) the most suitable choice for the majority of the countries emerging from the disintegration of the colonialist system, and they considered it the only possible way to escape or at least to program an escape from their underdevelopment. Hence the breakup of the great Bandung front, and in essence the break between India and China (October 1971), and the Indian invasion of East Pakistan, a violation of the sovereignty of a state. Even if it is true that self-determination was unequivocally expressed by vote and that East Pakistan's right to self-determination has been crushed by the government of Yahya Khan, no one can be unaware of India's expansionist designs and its desire to make East Bengal an "anti-Chinese bastion" (with the support of the USSR). Both the principle of nonintervention in the internal affairs of other countries and the right of peoples to emancipation have been violated.

If today we reread some of Nehru's writings from the Bandung period (I am thinking, for example, of *Conversations with Nehru* by Tibor Mende), it is not difficult to discover the signals warning of the break. This was the period when one spoke of "the great challenge," the outcome of which was supposed to determine the future of Asia: the challenge between the method of *Indian democracy*, as it was called, and the method of *Chinese revolutionary violence*, to adopt the slanderous tone then in vogue. But these were only words. Behind them lay a very definite reality: the attempt to make India, thanks to a massive concentration of foreign aid, the country most qualified to demonstrate to all Asia a path opposed to that of China, and to thereby discredit the "Chinese way" so as to isolate and defeat it.

What has been the result of this type of relationship between the developed and underdeveloped worlds? We can all see for ourselves: the difference between development and underdevelopment has increased and continues to grow ever more in favor of the developed world, to the detriment of the underdeveloped peoples. *Except in one instance: China.*

Chairman Mao and the other Chinese leaders rightly continue to reiterate—as I have said in these pages—that China is a poor country. As Mao said in April 1958, "Apart from their other characteristics, the outstanding thing about China's 600 million people is that they are 'poor and blank.' This may seem a bad thing, but in reality it is a good thing. Poverty gives rise to the desire for change, the desire for action and the desire for revolution." It is true that China is a poor country. More precisely, as Deputy Minister of Foreign

Affairs Chiao Kuan-hua recently stated in his first speech before the United Nations, it is an *underdeveloped country* in which a *profound developmental process* is going on. I am convinced that among all the countries present at Bandung, China is the nation which has gone the furthest along the road to development.

In the seventeen years since Bandung, then, the underdeveloped world has regressed while China has gone forward. But there is another element which seems to me to be extremely important: *the fact that the developed world, and above all the capitalist world, is losing the hegemony of power which has been based on its political policy of aid.* These three factors taken together make it easy to understand—or so it seems to me—the meaning of the *Chinese choice,* as a Third World nation. It is a choice which aims to restore to the forefront the need for the Third World to rely on its own resources to attain its independence, liberty, and development. In this sense, and only in this sense, can one speak of a *return to Bandung.* The present situation is one no longer characterized by the disintegration of the colonialist system alone; it is also marked by the objective crisis of the hegemony of the developed world based on an aid policy and systems of alliances with the leadership groups of a large part of the Third World.

This is, to my way of thinking, the meaning of the *Chinese choice.* And if we wish to speak in terms of political strategy, I believe that a *strategic choice* is also involved.

From this choice, I believe, originated China's refusal to be considered as—and to actually become—a great power and its polemics against the superpowers. It is a choice that contains both an example and an invitation: the example of a China that has relied on its own strength, and the invitation to liberate the world from the logic of power. It is for this reason, I believe, that those who view the world as moving from a bipolar toward a tripolar phase are in error. "At no time, neither today nor ever in the future, will China be a superpower subjecting others to its aggression, subversion, control, interference, or bullying," said Chiao Kuan-hua in his speech to the United Nations. As far as the problem of *nuclear monopoly* is concerned, here too the question for China is one of "smashing" it, period. According to China, the superpowers, although endlessly talking about disarmament, are in fact engaged in the daily increase in their armaments. On the subject of *disarmament,* as well as in discussions of their own nuclear weaponry—which is *not that of a superpower*—China's official position, expressed to the United Nations by the Deputy Minister of Foreign Affairs and the cause of open confrontation between the Soviets and the Chinese within the halls of the United Nations, is as follows:

> China will never participate in the so-called nuclear disarmament talks between the nuclear powers behind the backs of the nonnuclear countries. China's nuclear weapons are still in the experimental stage. China develops nuclear weapons solely for the purpose of defense and for breaking the nuclear monopoly and ultimately eliminating nuclear weapons and nuclear war. . . . I once again solemnly declare that at no time and under no circumstances will China be the first to use nuclear weapons. If the United States and the Soviet Union really and truly want disarmament, they should commit themselves not to be the first to use nuclear weapons. This is not something difficult to do.

So for the foreseeable future, the world will certainly not be a tripolar one. Not only becausc there will be more than three poles, not only because each of the three alleged candidates to "tripolarism" seeks different things, not only because China rejects this position, but above all because the world itself, the entire world, rejects this view. One need only look at the Vietnamese experience to become convinced of the truth of this last statement. Whether the world in which we live or shall live be a bipolar, tripolar, or multipolar one, or whether it becomes any of these, I do not believe that the Vietnamese will ever waive the right to have the final say on questions of their own war or peace. The Chinese are the first to realize this. It is for this reason that on occasion of Pham Van Dong's visit to Peking, during Chairman Mao's meeting with the delegation led by the prime minister of the Democratic Republic of Vietnam (November 20, 1971), full Chinese support of the *seven points* of the Provisional Revolutionary Government of South Vietnam was confirmed, and it was reiterated that the only people qualified to hold a dialogue with the United States with regard to Vietnam are the Vietnamese.

This is not to be a tripolar world, then, if by this unfortunate expression we understand a world in which three decide for all. In any event, I do not believe that China's intentions lie in that direction, and this is clearer than ever when China proclaims that it is a *part of the Third World.*

But does that perhaps mean that China seeks to isolate itself within its own untouched world—or within a vaster world, whose frontiers would be identical with the frontiers of the Third World? I do not believe this at all. China is within the world, within the vast and terrible world in which we all live. It is within this world that it formulates policy. But how? What are the guiding principles? *China needs peace and wants peace.* This is China's *other strategic choice.* China is thus a representative and an example of peace. China has neither troops nor bases beyond its borders, as Chou En-lai has stated. This is an eloquent example in a world smothered by military blocs. Obviously no one labors under the delusion that one example is sufficient to cause others to follow suit, but this is not the problem. When discussing the situation as it actually exists, the Chinese idiom is more credible than the language spoken by the others. Therein lies the strength of China's political position in the world.

But China is not merely content with talk. For example, in the face of American aggression in Vietnam, China did not hesitate in offering all necessary political and material aid. And as aggression spread to all of Indochina, Chinese aid likewise was extended to the entire peninsula. I have already pointed out that at the time of the invasion of lower Laos, when it appeared that the Americans were seeking to launch a deadly attack against North Vietnam itself, the Chinese, through Prime Minister Chou En-lai, indicated their determination to face the most severe national sacrifices. This same phrase was reiterated during Pham Van Dong's visit to Peking in November 1971:

> At any time and under any circumstances, the Chinese people will, as always, unite together, fight together, and win victory together with the fraternal Vietnamese, Laotian, and Cambodian peoples. The Vietnamese people are bound to triumph! U.S. imperialism will certainly be defeated!

Thus it is within the context of the strategic choice of peace that Nixon's trip to Peking must be judged. Much has been written and said on the subject. But it is my feeling that the best criterion to correctly assess an event of such importance is to discuss the preliminary steps which the Chinese believe must be taken to normalize relations between China and the United States. These preliminaries have frequently been stated by Chou En-lai and other Chinese leaders, most notably during their meetings with Italian political figures: *withdrawal of all American forces from Vietnam and the Indochinese peninsula, from South Korea, from the Taiwan Strait and from Taiwan itself, which has remained an inalienable part of Chinese territory; steps must also be taken against the very real prospect of a rebirth of Japanese militarism.* These preliminaries do not only involve the normalization of relations between Washington and Peking: they also have a more general significance. In other words, they indicate the method China intends to use in pursuing its strategic choice of peace—a method which, through unceasing struggle, pursues the goal of making the concrete application of the "five points" of peaceful coexistence genuinely possible within Asia and beyond. I am convinced that the Chinese are the first to realize that this goal will not be attained in a day or in a year. But the Chinese also understand from their own immediate experience that in the end it is resistance based on principle and not capitulation which will prevail. The UN "affair" illustrates this subject. If the Chinese had been willing to compromise, for example, on the principle of their sovereignty over Taiwan, they would have long since been admitted to the United Nations. But Peking chose the road it had followed before, during, and after the Cultural Revolution. And ultimately China won, despite all the efforts made by the United States to delay yet again this historical event. It is rather interesting to note here that the battle for China to enter the United Nations occurred while Nixon's envoy was in Peking, which led to the widespread belief that China would agree to make the Chinese presence at the United Nations more palatable to the Americans by consenting to the temporary presence of Chiang Kai-shek's representatives. Those who maintained this position were certainly mistaken, and must today recognize that the Chinese never lose sight of the need to struggle at the bargaining table. The official communique published at the end of Nixon's trip to China clearly falls within this framework.*

The Third World's strategic choice at the moment of the crisis in political hegemony based on the policy of foreign aid; the strategic choice of peace—these are the two criteria from which one must set out to define the Chinese presence in today's world. Furthermore, as a logical and essential corollary we must necessarily add China's refusal to join the great powers. The choice, then, is of a world which is neither bipolar, nor tripolar, nor multipolar, but is *a world without poles.*

Is such a position useful, correct, and fruitful? I personally believe that it is. For fundamentally, no matter how one views the world born at Yalta, a world defined by the birth and the development of the policy of opposing military blocs, I think it can be universally recognized that this world is in crisis, and that increasingly widespread demonstrations of intolerance bear witness to the depth of this crisis. Such a crisis has repercussions not only within the countries which have themselves engendered this policy, but is reflected in relationships between them.

Why is this world in crisis? I think it is due to two major factors. First, because the growth and spread of national consciousness no longer allows large countries to decide the fate, the politics, and the internal organization of smaller countries. But such a situation

* This historical sense of the new world situation, and of China's political engagement in a new context, is highlighted in the New Year's Day editorial quoted earlier: "Never before did U.S. imperialism find itself in such a plight. Its counter-revolutionary global strategy has suffered one defeat after another. Its powers of aggression have been enormously weakened by the magnificent victories of the people of Vietnam, Laos, and Cambodia in their war against U.S. aggression and for national salvation, by the growth of the struggle of the Palestinian and other Arab peoples against U.S.-Israeli aggression, by the rise of the revolutionary mass movement of the American people, and by the upsurge of the world people's struggle against U.S. imperialism. The profound change in the balance of forces between the United States on the one hand and Japan and the West European and other capitalist countries on the other has intensified their fight to shift their crises on to each other and their scramble for markets and sources of raw material. And the United States is faced with its toughest challenge in the twenty-six postwar years. All this has aggravated the political, economic, and social crisis in the United States.

will probably continue to occur, as is shown by the war between India—behind whom stands a great power, the USSR—and Bangladesh. But, to judge from how rapidly the crisis in this policy has developed, I do not believe that this situation will go on indefinitely. The vote for China in the United Nations was one of the most resounding and significant revelations of this crisis. Second, because the world which emerged from Yalta and which is defined by a system of opposing military blocs has failed to achieve *two* of its major objectives, namely, to insure peace and the free choice of all peoples, and to bridge, or at least to reduce, the gap between the developed and underdeveloped worlds. It is within the context of such a world in crisis that China acts to further and to make another world possible, one in which the field of action of the dependent countries would be broadened, and where the field of action of the great powers would be limited, as would their complicated system of "confrontation and collusion," with all the consequences such a system has produced in today's world and with all the changes it has wrought.

In connection with China's international strategy, one point seems especially important in order to understand the Chinese reality: *China's way of acting in the world.* At the time of the Cultural Revolution China was widely regarded by the lazy-minded as being the fomenter of revolutions, while after the Cultural Revolution, *after the first Cultural Revolution,* China appeared to equally lazy minds as a country which had renounced its interest in furthering revolution. It is my view that the first is as false a judgment as the second. The Cultural Revolution was an internal Chinese accomplishment. It was a struggle for political power between two roads, two classes, and two lines. At the same time it is clear that the Cultural Revolution spoke out to all those throughout the world who were concerned with the problem of continuing revolution under the dictatorship of the proletariat. People talked about the years of China's vacuum and absence during the Cultural Revolution. I think this is incorrect. China's presence today is assured by its position on the international stage, not only in the area of theory and ideology but in the field of strategy as well. China's interlocutors have become other states. Even during those years, in fact, China's presence was felt as a stimulus to the growth of the anti-imperialist forces, as an intense ideological impetus to furthering the struggle against capitalism. In a revolutionary sense, China was the people's representative, appealing to revolutionary forces to carry on the struggle, and presenting, through the Cultural Revolution in class relationships, an alternative to that offered by *technological-consumer* societies.

In this sense the Cultural Revolution has been an international accomplishment, and as such is related to China's overall international strategy. But all those who believed that China had become a new *guide* to revolutions throughout the world were either intentionally or otherwise in error. It could be said that a historical era has ended, the era of the *parent party* or the *guide state*, the era when each decision by the USSR automatically had direct repercussions on the movement, on the Communist parties, and on other socialist countries. The era of a common strategic structure which became organizational (the Comintern) and which hinged upon a *single country*, has ended. What remains is the unity of problems within the class struggle at the world level, the unity of the anti-imperialist struggle, as in Vietnam. In this regard, there are few speeches as enlightening as that given by Chou En-lai during Pietro Nenni's visit to China in November 1971. Through the venerable socialist leader, Chou refuted this description of the Chinese position as a *guide* and *center* to the entire European worker and socialist movement. Here is how *Avanti!* of November 20, 1971, reported it:

> Chou En-lai cited certain past experiences to support the thesis that as soon as international movements and organizations come into existence, national revolutions break down. This occurred a century ago with the Paris Commune, an attempt which coincided with the disintegration of the First International. In 1917 the October Revolution took place after the failure of the Second International, and the Chinese Revolution occurred after the breakup of the Third. This is the reason why the Chinese leadership feels that worker movements must rely on their own resources and that bilateral contacts between worker movements are preferable to a single international organization. In other words, Marxist truths must be integrated with the practical experience applicable to each country. It is for this reason, as we all know, that the Chinese reject the idea of a world Communist

> "center." We cannot support, said Chou En-lai, the theory that Moscow is the "center" any more than we want others to regard us as the "center." We hope and believe that the various revolutionary movements will rely on their own resources. There is no single revolutionary movement which can create *the* revolutionary line.

It is for this reason that those who felt betrayed by China after the Cultural Revolution have either intentionally or otherwise been in error. China has not been, nor is, nor wishes to become, a *guide country*—neither before, nor during, nor after the Cultural Revolution. As for a China which has become "less revolutionary" —those who idealize or underestimate the complexity and ambiguity of situations which have developed in Ceylon, the Sudan, and in East Pakistan (where subsequent events indicate the enormous conflict which would have seethed in this cauldron if China had made a move)—today the most traditional revisionist arguments (China seeks only to undermine the USSR) are heard together with cries from the far left and from neo-Trotskyites who speak in terms of revolutionary betrayal. A new smokescreen has been raised by the *right-left* (ultra-leftists move right to revisionist positions) to eclipse the value of China's presence in the international arena.

China freely offers the fruits of its own experience to all revolutionaries, but it has no intention of dictating to anyone. Nor does it wish to intervene in favor of one or another revolutionary or pseudo-revolutionary group. Furthermore, China is convinced that in any new world situation which may arise, one must seek to discover the interests which the great powers have at stake and how they operate. This concept was stated in the course of a speech given by Chiao Kuan-hua at the United Nations on November 16, 1971, when he asserted:

> The essence of the Middle East question is aggression against the Palestinian and other Arab peoples by Israeli Zionism with the support and connivance of the superpowers. . . . No one has the right to engage in political deals behind their backs, bartering away their right to existence and their national interests.

The practice of relying only on one's own strength, of "standing on one's two feet," is equally applicable here. The Chinese recognize, as do all Marxists, that the revolution cannot be exported and that socialism cannot be imposed through the intervention of one or another *guide country.* People should not deceive themselves by thinking that China is prepared to intervene in one part of the world or another, or to aid directly one or another conflagration which is or seems revolutionary. China's contribution to the revolutionary movement lies in its presence in the world, in its determination to make its experience and its reality known to all, in the aid it furnishes to countries which are subject to imperialist aggression—as was the case in Korea, and is the case in Vietnam—and *last but not least,* in the general lines of its foreign policy. This is why, in the last analysis, a policy which strives to dismantle the system of opposing military blocs, to diminish the preponderance of the great powers, and to affirm in practice the principle of *nonintervention* in the internal affairs of other countries, represents an enormous contribution both to the free choice of peoples and, consequently, to the revolutionary choices which are not encumbered by the burden of outside intervention and the politics of spheres of influence.

16

The Chinese Communist Party: Protagonist and Objective of the Cultural Revolution

> Man has arteries, veins, and a heart which enable his blood to circulate, but he also needs lungs to breathe, to expel carbon dioxide and absorb fresh oxygen; he rejects what is foul to absorb a new substance—this is what assures him of life. Without the elimination of wastes and the injection of new blood, the party cannot be vital.
>
> —Mao Tse-tung

Roundtable with the party committee at Factory No. 17 in Shanghai

From the political point of view, this is Shanghai's most important factory. During the Cultural Revolution it was the first in Shanghai to have a group of "rebel workers" and to seal the alliance between workers and revolutionaries. It was the first factory to successfully carry out the "rectification" of the party; its factory committee was elected in May 1968, and was one of the first in China. One of its workers was elected to the Central Committee during the Ninth Party Congress. His name was Wang Huan-wen; he was thirty-five years old and was the author of the factory's first tatzupao.

Few people are allowed to visit this factory. Participating in the discussion were Yu Tien-huan, leader of the party committee and deputy representative of the revolutionary committee; Lu Yun-ken of the party committee; Chen Tou-keng, revolutionary committee member; a young girl, Wang Wen-hsin, secretary of the Young Communist League (also restructured at this factory); Tu Tien-hsin of the factory's revolutionary committee; Su Yu-chi, of the Shanghai Rebel Workers' Brigade, which is connected with the city's Workers' Revolutionary Rebel Headquarters. They all took part in the discussion. I will not identify the speaker each time since the same arguments repeatedly crop up in the remarks of the various participants.

First of all, some background information about the factory and the party within the factory. Eight thousand people are employed here, including workers and office employees. The party membership is 1,060. Eighty new members were accepted during the Cultural Revolution—before there were 1,000 party members, but 20 percent have since been dismissed or suspended. There are thirty-one cells corresponding to the administrative divisions of the factory, and in each shop there is a committee to coordinate the various cells. Immediately above this is a section committee of thirteen members, instead of nine as before. Only one of the former members of the leadership committee remains. Of the others, some have gone to work elsewhere, others have retired, while still others have become militants at the base. Among the new members there are veteran party fighters as well as young political cadres. The new members of the leadership committee were chosen after open discussion with the workers who were not members of the party. For the first time, workers elected to the leadership committee remain workers—before, those leadership committee members who were workers were exempt from all production work.

"How did the struggle within the party develop during the Cultural Revolution?" we ask.

"The Cultural Revolution is a vast movement to consolidate and strengthen the party. It cannot be accomplished in one day. In following Mao's line, the working masses have little by little reached the stage of *rebellion.* Engels has said that a revolution is the most authoritarian thing in existence. Factory leaders no longer enjoyed any prestige, but a long and bitter struggle was necessary to strip them of their power. The conquest of power began in 1966, but in January 1967, this power, although paralyzed, still remained in the hands of revisionists. The January Revolution finally tore it away from them. These leaders have been sent back to the masses, criticized, and their pernicious influence entirely neutralized. We have created the revolutionary committee on the basis of the three-in-one combination. This was the initial transfer of power in Shanghai: the assumption of power by the rebel working class."

"What have been the phases of this struggle, and who has taken the initiative?"

"Lu Yun-ken and I put up the first tatzupao, which had more than 1,000 characters. We were the first to rebel against the party committee after the Central Committee circular of May 16, 1966. Then there was June 12; the old party committee was committed to its revisionist path, leading the masses astray. It was aided by a 'work team' which was the source of the repression against us; there were penalties, 'black lists,' and so on. There were more than one hundred disciplinary regulations in force at the factory, inherited from the period of capitalist domination. But where there is repression, there is also rebellion. We were only two at first, then thirty, and then hundreds; in November 1966 there were more than a thousand rebel workers. But a single factory is not enough; we contacted other factories, the entire district, until at last we were large enough to create a mass revolutionary organization: the Workers' Revolutionary Rebel Headquarters. The revolutionary spark was stalking the revisionist cadres. They understood the danger and tried first to sabotage production, then to buy off the workers: they offered them shoes, bicycles, watches, various consumer items. Then they adopted the 'economist' line: increases in salary, the promise of individual well-being. Finally, they completely lost their heads and both the party committee and the trade unions, heeding the directives of the leaders of the revisionist group in Shanghai, called upon the workers to stop working, to block water supplies coming in to the factory, to block transport, etc. For some days everything was paralyzed. The struggle was terrible, tearing the working class to pieces."

"But how did those workers, those comrades who had initially opposed your action, become reunited with you?"

"That, too, was a gradual thing. First of all, you must understand this concept: the class struggle under the dictatorship of the proletariat takes on new characteristics, and the division within the party and working class was based on this. Some people understood this, some accepted it passively, and others deliberately maintained that once the dictatorship of the proletariat had been established, the only enemies to be reckoned with were those outside rather than those within. Party members, persuaded of the correctness of Mao's line, were unaware of the danger stalking the party; the party now ran the risk of becoming perverted to the extent that it was no longer a revolutionary party but was a party of production. We claimed to be members of a revolutionary party, of a party that would pursue revolution under the dictatorship of the proletariat. But the comrades could not be convinced that they had chosen the wrong path, the path of Liu Shao-chi. A good number of them were hesitant, uncertain, and disoriented."

"Weren't you afraid of breaking party unity?"

"No. Mao teaches us not to fear dissension within the party. On the contrary, Liu Shao-chi was preaching 'peace within the party'; this was nothing but opportunism. Mao had begun the struggle against this concept of 'internal peace' long before. In his article 'Combat Liberalism,' he denounced eleven forms of liberalism, including saying as little as possible while knowing perfectly well what is wrong, and seeking only to avoid blame. And Mao warned against those who are aware of their mistakes and yet make no attempt to correct them. These are the philistines, who are on the road to degeneration, for if they do not mend their ways, they will cease to be revolutionaries."

"Has the struggle only taken place within the party?"

"No. Those contradictions within the party arising from the struggle between two lines have been exposed and directly related to the masses' concrete struggle, thereby enabling them to decide on the basis of concrete political experiences rather than abstractions. Our rectification movement was carried out completely in the open and everyone participated. Chairman Mao has said that each cell should initiate a rectification movement, but the masses must participate, not only a few members of the party. The masses must participate in meetings and give their opinions, even those who do not belong to the party. Thus, the movement began in public view, and was a movement which led to the expulsion from the party of all those degenerate elements, and to the assimilation of new elements, so that new blood would circulate within the veins of the party."

"How can there be rebellion against leadership in a party which abides by the concept of democratic centralism? Isn't there a contradiction between rebellion and party discipline?"

"No. It was Liu Shao-chi who preached unconditional allegiance to the party, servility toward its leaders, and discipline without discussion. No attention was paid to the opinions of the masses, and the leadership was bureaucratic. In our factory, for instance, although one of Liu's agents had been criticized by the masses, he had been promoted by the leadership to the rank of section manager. Another revisionist was appointed director of evening courses. Criticism by the masses made no difference. What mattered was the protection enjoyed by this higher-up and his friends. This is a typically bureaucratic practice: the masses do not count, and leaders support each other against the masses. Liu said: 'The masses are backward.' Mao says: 'The masses are the true heroes.' The bureaucratic concept must be changed if the masses are to be mobilized. Why is it that in Shanghai today a few telephone calls at eight in the morning can assemble tens of thousands of people within a few hours? Why do thousands of Red Guards rush off to Peking? Neither Liu nor Teng Hsiao-ping could have made it happen, even in the days when, thanks to their 'work teams,' they controlled the factories and the students. Do you know why? Because this blind discipline within the party is a bourgeois discipline, a slave discipline, and can only be exercised over a relatively limited number of people who depend on the bureaucratic apparatus. Those who impose a discipline of this sort can hardly inspire that *active and conscious obedience* which can mobilize in the blink of an eye hundreds of thousands of people to combat a common enemy. Only proletarian discipline can achieve this, a conscious and open-eyed discipline. Liu spoke of 'serving the party.' Mao speaks of 'from the masses to the masses.' The party has gradually acquired a new discipline, a proletarian discipline."

"How was this new discipline born?"

"It was born in revolt, in the ability to rebel against revisionism and against errors."

"How can discipline be born in revolt?"

"You may not be able to understand it. Let's see if we can explain it better. While 'revolutionary rebels' were steadily reacting against sabotage, political debate began among the masses. We had Mao's support—he sent us a message of greeting to the rebels of Shanghai—as well as the backing of the People's Liberation Army. The rebels began to understand the concept of revolt. Adherence to the party was no longer an act of faith and discipline. Why does a Communist fight? What was the correct line, what was the false line? What was needed, a party that applied the mass line or a bureaucratic party? A party which raises class consciousness or a party which advocates material well-being? The struggle crystallized around the criteria for factory leadership. Management by the masses, or management by technicians? Collective leadership or the leadership of specialists? Priority to politics or priority to economics? The revolt was triggered by these concepts; tatzupao appeared and soon became a powerful form of expression for the working masses. The party philosophy is a philosophy of struggle. The party has become an instrument of political and ideological struggle, no longer one of organization. If we think only of our cotton, of our turnips, of production, of the routine application of directives, the Communist Party will be destroyed and our comrades lost. Before, our comrades would say: 'The people's army is strong enough to attack the enemy if necessary. Our situation here is good. Our duty is to increase production. Our mentality is a class mentality, and we are loyal to Mao. What more should we do?' "

"Can you give us a concrete example of this rejection of rebellion?"

"At the beginning of the Cultural Revolution many party members had already started down the wrong path, but even more serious was that they failed to understand their errors. Take the case of this one comrade, a party member, a worker from his earliest youth—he had entered our factory when he was nine years old, he had known a life of suffering and deprivation. When faced with the action of the 'revolutionary rebels,' he was disoriented. He said: 'Under Mao's leadership, our life has improved from day to day. Why should we call ourselves rebels? Against whom? Against socialism? Against the proletarian class?' He would not come to terms, and we had some tough political clashes at the factory. The rebel workers criticized him, but he continued to fail to understand. He would stand under the portrait of Mao and, pointing with his finger, he would say: 'Me, follow any other line than Mao's? I'd rather die. I want to defend Chairman Mao with all my heart. I just can't understand your rebellion against the Communist Party.' Later, during the rectification and party consolidation movement, this comrade finally came to understand from the many discussions that class consciousness was not enough, that the individual must participate in the struggle if the proletarian revolution under the dictatorship of the proletariat is to make any progress. Otherwise, it's like having eyes but not seeing, ears but not hearing. It is in this way that the level of consciousness among party members has been raised. We have eliminated egoism and the influence of economism and bureaucratism. We have learned that to be a fighter is to think of both our country and the world revolution, to fight until the exploitation of man by man is eliminated throughout the entire world, until all of mankind is liberated."

"What is the climate now in the party section at the factory?"

"Before, the party ran the risk of losing sight of the class struggle under the leadership of the proletariat and the world revolution. Today, our party knows that every inch of thread spun, every inch of material woven represents a contribution to the world revolution. Here is another example. A comrade had been working at our plant for sixteen years. He had joined the party, but the world revolution hardly existed for him. He had several children; he worried a great deal about his family and precious little about revolution. Now he has rid himself of his egocentric interests and Communism has become his primary concern. Youths and those no longer young have entered the party. Some of them are serving on the factory's leadership committee. Before, under Liu's bureaucratic organization, this was impossible. The good Communist, the 'good fighter' who wanted to make his way, had to show absolute loyalty to his immediate superior for many long years."

"I would like to return to the question of democratic centralism. Its operation poses acute problems for other Communist parties. In many parties, anyone who wrote a tatzupao against a party leader would risk expulsion."

"The principle of democratic centralism is the key principle of our party. But it must represent a true synthesis of democracy and centralism. Liberty must be exercised under one leadership. Democracy must be guided by centralism; but without profound democracy centralism does not exist, there is only bureaucracy. The Cultural Revolution is a true democratic action; it is the mobilization of hundreds of thousands of people under the dictatorship of the proletariat. Does democracy mean the abolition of all political leadership? No, on the contrary, it is the strengthening of Chairman Mao's leadership. Democratic centralism has not been destroyed, but consolidated. How? By the tatzupao, by broad discussions, by the masses' expression of their opinions. You must dare to hold opinions different from those of leading official organizations, and dare to speak out; you must dare to think, dare to act. The tatzupao, a new weapon in the class struggle, is a bond between centralism and democracy. In our statutes, we define democratic centralism as 'liberty and discipline.' It is democratic centralism that assures both the people and the party of a strong democracy, a *proletarian democracy* under the dictatorship of the proletariat. It is a democracy directly affecting not only party members but the masses as well; a democracy of the revolutionary masses, expressing themselves through their tatzupao, discussions, criticisms, and proposals. Centralism is represented by the revolutionary headquarters, headed by Chairman Mao. The revolutionary masses participate in our struggle. They want the revolution to go forward; they want no part of revisionism. The principle of democratic centralism clearly assumes a class character."

"On what basic principles did you reconstruct the party, especially at the beginning, when existing organizations had been overthrown?"

"In 1967 major discussions were held: who should belong to the core of leadership? Some people said that since their organization was the first to rebel, they should be the core of leadership. Others claimed that they had greater ability or were more numerous. Our experience shows that Communists have never abandoned their leadership; when necessary, they have on occasion replaced those mass organizations which had ceased to function. Likewise, Mao has never failed in his leadership role. Liu Shao-chi's line has merely succeeded in sowing disturbances in our proletarian revolution. The Cultural Revolution was directed by the Communist Party, even though the party itself has been seriously affected by it. 'The party is the core of leadership,' Mao has said. 'The party's power is the core of power; it is the power within the power.' This is the line that we have followed. To answer your question about recruitment of party members and the criteria involved, may I quote the following: 'Party organization must be composed of advanced elements of the proletariat; it must be dynamic, capable of leading the proletariat and the revolutionary masses, and of combating class enemies.' "

"Have you had to combat any erroneous concepts?"

"We have had to combat certain erroneous concepts. For instance, some people said: 'We have played an important role in the rebellion; we should now be able to join the party.' Others insisted: 'Those who have become revolutionary committee leaders should join the party.' Such concepts are contrary to Mao's thinking with regard to party make-up, and would alter the party's basic nature as the vanguard of the proletariat. To rectify and build this organization, it is extremely important to have a good leadership group. Another erroneous concept: to be considered a 'Communist by right.' This concept is totally contrary to the idea of the uninterrupted revolution under the dictatorship of the proletariat."

"What measures has the party taken with regard to organization?"

"We see that meetings are neither too long nor too frequent. Questions of detail should not become overwhelming. At the Ninth Congress [I realized once again that Mao's 'mysterious speech' to the Ninth Congress is a mystery only to Westerners], Mao reminded those comrades from the masses elected for the first time to the Central Committee that they must take care not to alienate themselves either from the masses or from production, and that they must carry out all their duties. We are against the overuse of meetings, and against the plurality of leadership posts."

"At the moment, how does proletarian democracy function at the factory?"

"The struggle to bring proletarian democracy to the forefront is continuing, and the bond between centralism and democracy must be strengthened in the party's practical activity. Some people have said: 'If proletarian democracy is given a free rein, there will be too many obstacles in the way of unity because of differences of opinion.' This is a throwback to one of Liu Shao-chi's theories that 'the masses are backward.' It is a return to a patriarchal style of work: work and keep silent, because we are not a party of debaters. And in Mao's words, there are those who 'fear the masses, the criticism of the masses, and the discussions of the masses.' But if the others are not allowed to speak, correct opinions can never be expressed or false ideas corrected. How then can unity through centralism be reached? For without this unity, true revolutionary unity will never exist. The question of whether to apply democratic centralism has always been the underlying question in the struggle between the two lines."

"How is democratic centralism related to the mass line?"

"By the creation of democracy on as wide a basis as possible so as to centralize the ideas of the masses."

"What is the most burning political problem?"

"Not only our fighters, but most of all our leaders, must heighten their consciousness on the question of the struggle between the two lines. The struggle has not ended, and to speak lightly of final victory in our country is a mistake. It is contrary to Leninism, and does not correspond in the least to reality. As Mao says, we are experiencing only the first of the cultural revolutions which China must experience to continue its proletarian revolution."

"What about the Young Communist League?"

"In our plant, we have created the League on the principle that it must be consolidated in the presence and with the aid of everyone. The party committee has mobilized the masses outside the League, so that the masses can express their opinion with regard to members of the League. Youths who have proven themselves in the course of the Cultural Revolution have been admitted; bad elements which had infiltrated the League have been expelled. Under the leadership of the party committee, the League has put the organization under the leadership of youths whose sound class position and dynamic revolutionary convictions set them off from the rest. The class struggle is one of the fundamental subjects which the young should be taught—this is the guideline for the League in Factory No. 17."

"As the party consolidates its leadership role within the factory, what will the role of the revolutionary committee become?"

"The party provides political leadership while the revolutionary committee is the administrative organization: the actions of the committee are under the political guidance of the party. The organ of power—the revolutionary committee—will not find its role in any way diminished in the future; rather, it will be strengthened in the way outlined in our new constitution. Between the party committee and the revolutionary committee there is a liaison group which watches over the practical leadership of the factory. The two committees share the same offices. At the moment, preparations are being made at our plant—and by all Chinese worker, military, and peasant organizations—to send delegates to the National People's Congress which will adopt the new constitution."

Our conversation has lasted more than four hours and has now ended. The atmosphere has become relaxed. In the beginning this important group of worker-leaders had seemed suspicious. We called their attention to this and the discussion had gradually become more and more spontaneous. As we are leaving, and because we have found them exceptionally open, my husband, who regrets the coldness of their welcome, says: "When we arrived, you did not shake our hands. I hope that the next time you tell us things as interesting as those you have told us today, you will shake our hands."

An embarrassed silence. I immediately add: "I would like to correct what my husband has just said. Whether or not you shake hands with us is not very important to me. Communists the world over greet each other with the raised fist [I raise mine] and that is how I salute you."

There is a brief moment of emotion. They come toward us, affectionately offer us their hands, and accompany us outside the factory.

The "public" struggle within the Chinese Communist Party

This conversation at the factory contains the essential first-hand information which I shall use to discuss the Chinese Communist Party. The question that came up time and again throughout our entire trip was: "What is the function of the party?" The Chinese always answered us firmly (sometimes irritated to hear this echo of the doubts running through the West) that "the party has always retained its leadership function," a function at times fulfilled on an individual basis by militants when the base-level organizations—even those on the highest levels—had ceased to play their role or had disintegrated under mass criticism. The struggle which was launched within the Chinese Communist Party was a public struggle, open and without deception, which took place in full view of the masses, who in the last resort are the judges. It is precisely the unusual nature of the struggle that leads Westerners to say that good leaders have been exposed to the criticism of "youngsters" (the Red Guards), of "hordes of rebels," or even of "bands of ragged peasants."

In reality, it was the Communist Party which directed the Cultural Revolution, the first revolution under the dictatorship of the proletariat. The Chinese state that for the working class the Paris Commune was the first experience with power; it was defeated, but the teaching of the Commune is eternal. They quote Marx: "If the Commune should be destroyed, the struggle would only be postponed. The principles of the Commune are eternal and indestructible."

And Mao: "The salvos of the October Revolution brought us Marxism-Leninism. The Cultural Revolution is a revolution carried on under the dictatorship of the proletariat to consolidate its power."

In his speech at the time of the fiftieth anniversary of the October Revolution, Lin Piao said that Mao Tse-tung's most original contribution to Marxism was precisely this concept of revolution under the dictatorship of the proletariat:

> Comrade Mao Tse-tung has not only enriched Marxism in the area of the conquest of political power by the proletariat. He has also made a creative contribution to its development, marking a new historical era when he tackled the most important problem of our time: the consolidation of the dictatorship of the proletariat, the struggle against all danger of restoring capitalism.

Shanghai: visit to the first party headquarters

Our first visit in Shanghai is to a modest gray stone house in the former French concession—where in 1921 the Chinese Communist Party had been founded by twelve of the forty-seven Communists then in China. The entrance to No. 108 Wang-Tse Street is open. Outside, a dense crowd with what appears to be an intention similar to ours. Everyone applauds when we enter, greeting us as comrades. We are very moved.

We cross a small courtyard and enter the room where the first party congress was held. A small bare room, it is like a village sacristy, with a round table covered with a white cotton tablecloth. On the table, a teapot and twelve cups. Around it are twelve wooden stools. Everything is exactly as it was on that July 1, 1921, our guide tells us. He adds that the meeting had been abruptly interrupted when the participants became aware that a French spy had penetrated the house. They dispersed, and the Constitutional Congress of the party was concluded out on Lake Shaohsing, under the pretext of a boating party.

The comrade gives us the names of the twelve delegates to the First Congress of the Chinese Communist Party* and tells us that

* Following is the list which was given me in Shanghai. The notations in parenthesis have been added by me.

Mao Tse-tung, from the province of Hunan (Mao was elected Chairman of the Central Committee of the Chinese Communist Party in January 1935 at the time of the Tsunyi Conference, during the Long March).

Tung Pi-wu, from Wuhan (currently vice-president of the Republic).

Ho Shu-heng, from the province of Hunan (shot by the Kuomintang in 1934).

Chen Tan-chin, from Wuhan (executed in 1943 by the Kuomintang in Sinkiang with a brother of Mao Tse-tung).

Wang Shu-mei, from Chinan.

Teng En-min, from Chinan (killed during the civil war against the Kuomintang).

Li Han-chun, from Shanghai (executed by the Kuomintang in 1927).

Chang Kuo-tao, from Peking (left the Chinese Communist Party in 1938 for the Kuomintang; living in Hongkong).

Liu Jen-ching, from Peking (expelled from the Chinese Communist Party in 1937 for "right-wing tendencies").

five of them died during the revolutionary struggles, another died a natural death, and four became traitors.

On the wall of the little room, two of Mao's renowned phrases: "A single spark can start a prairie fire," and "In China the Communist Party was born, an epoch-making event." Our guide tells us: "Mao has related Marxism-Leninism to the practice of the Chinese Revolution." In 1921 Mao was one of the delegates from the province of Hunan where in April 1918 he had founded in Changsha the revolutionary cultural organization, Hsingmin. From the start, Mao's struggle was directed against right opportunists who insisted that the Communist Party should be restricted to the spread of Marxism-Leninism, that it should operate within legal channels, that worker centers should be organized but not the vast masses. This tendency was represented by Chang Kuo-tao and Lin Jen-ching, who were students at Peking University. At the same time, Mao fought against the opportunist adventurism of the left. What type of party should be built? A proletarian party with Marxism-Leninism as its great weapon, said Mao, and he had the following included in its statutes: "The duty of the party is to create the proletarian revolution and to establish the dictatorship of the proletariat in China." He drew attention to the fact that Liu Shao-chi joined the party late in 1921 while a student in Moscow, and in *Thirty Years of the Chinese Communist Party*, the author Hu Shao-mu presents Chen Tu-hsiu as the party founder, neglecting to add that although he was elected secretary by those present at the First Congress, he did not participate in person (he had not wanted to leave Canton where he was teaching), and that not until he was elected secretary-general did he actually go to Shanghai. At the Third Congress in 1923, Chen Tu-hsiu said that the founding of the Chinese Communist Party had been "improvised," thereby es-

---

Chen Kung-po, from Canton (shortly after rejoined the Kuomintang; head of the pro-Japanese Nanking government in 1944; shot in 1946 by the Kuomintang).

Chou Fo-hai, from Canton (died in prison in 1948 after collaborating with the Japanese).

Li Ta, from Shanghai (left the party from 1923 to 1949; was accused of being an anti-party element during the Cultural Revolution; died in 1966).

In 1921 Chou En-lai was in France where he helped to found the Chinese Socialist Youth Group among Chinese worker-students.

tablishing an error as fact.* Mao was elected party chairman on January 6, 1935, and Lin Piao says that he was the true founder of the party.

In an article published in *People's Daily* on July 1, 1971, the fiftieth anniversary of the Chinese Communist Party ("Commemorate the Fiftieth Anniversary of the Communist Party of China"), Mao's victory in 1935 is presented as a victory over the "left" opportunist line of Wang Ming, who was nothing but a pseudo-Marxist.

> When the Red Army arrived in Tsunyi in Kweichow in January 1935, during the Long March, an enlarged meeting of the Central Committee of the party was held. This was the great historical meeting at Tsunyi which put an end to the domination of Wang Ming's "left" opportunist line in the central leading body and established Chairman Mao's leadership over the entire party. In this way, the party line was brought back to the correct Marxist-Leninist path, but to reach this point, so much blood was shed, and at what a terrible price!
>
> The Tsunyi meeting marked the growth from childhood to maturity for our party. After this meeting under the direction of our great leader, Chairman Mao, it was possible to bring the 25,000-li Long March, famous throughout the entire world, to a victorious end. During this Long March, the First Front Army of the Red Army formed a detachment to resist the Japanese invasion and marched to northern Shensi. It increased the determination of the entire people to resist the aggression of Japanese imperialism. Later, our party defeated the line of Chang Kuo-tao who was proposing that another Central Committee be created and that the Red Army be divided. In October 1936 the Second and Fourth Front armies arrived in northern Shensi and joined up with the First Front Army and with the Red Army of that area. At this time, the Red Army had fewer than 30,000 men, having dropped from 300,000. Our party's forces had temporarily dropped in number, but qualitatively speaking, they were stronger than before, thanks to the correct line.

The era of the Long March, and later that of the entire revolutionary future of China, was born with Mao and the approval of the correct political line. This justifies Lin Piao's statement men-

* In 1929, Chen Tu-hsiu was expelled from the Chinese Communist Party for "rightist tendencies." He then founded a Trotskyist group. He died in 1942.

tioned above. According to his summary of the political vicissitudes of the Chinese Communist Party at the Third Congress, the history of the party is that of the struggle which pits the Chairman's Marxist-Leninist line against the right-wing and left-wing opportunist lines existing within the party.

Volumes have been written on the history of the Chinese Communist Party and most of the authors have tried to retrace its stages. Within the framework of the present book, we shall limit ourselves to describing the contemporary history of the party. We shall attempt to focus on one essential question: the role of the party in the Cultural Revolution, and the revolutionary criticism to which the party has been subjected. To the leader who wants a political key which will enable him to penetrate the past and present of the Chinese Communist Party's half century of existence, we offer this inspiring quotation (taken from the *People's Daily* article on the fiftieth anniversary of the Chinese Communist Party):

> The fifty-year history of the Chinese Communist Party proves that the success or defeat of a party depends on the line it follows. Even if it has conquered power, it will lose it if its line is incorrect, and when it does not have the power, it will ultimately conquer it if its line is correct. But a correct line is not a gift from heaven; it is not born nor does it develop quietly and spontaneously; it exists in contrast to erroneous lines and it develops by struggling against them.

I would also like to warn the reader against comparing the rectification and consolidation campaign of the Chinese Communist Party with the experiences of the Stalinist and post-Stalinist Communist Party. In this regard, the Chinese Communist Party keeps its distance, and counterposes another model of revolutionary leadership, a revolutionary core, or, better still, a vanguard with its roots in the masses, a vanguard which does not substitute itself for the masses. The so-called Sino-Soviet conflict can be more easily understood in this light.

The Communist Party in the Cultural Revolution and proletarian democracy

The party is the protagonist and objective of the Cultural Revolution. "It is right to rebel," says Mao. This is the first time in the history of Marxist-Leninist parties that a Communist Party head has made such a statement. To this first directive—rebel against leaders who are following the capitalist road—another has been added, one which is fraught with political and theoretical consequences: the party must not be transformed into a new race of "overlords" (see the chapter on the May 7 schools). Brought forth during the phase of the dictatorship of the proletariat, the Cultural Revolution is the first revolution to have arisen in this fashion. It strengthens the dictatorship of the proletariat while simultaneously diminishing the purely coercive power of the state apparatus—the representative but also ideological apparatus which is the party—and fosters the intervention of the proletariat in ideology. The Cultural Revolution deepened the ties between party and masses. It marks the triumph of the mass line. And it is the period which will initiate broad democracy for the masses of the Chinese people, for an entire people who want socialism, and the end result will be what the Chinese call a "people's," rather than a socialist, democracy. Mao states:

> After the socialist transformation of the means of production, the class struggle between the proletariat and bourgeoisie will last a long time; it will encounter vicissitudes, and it will at times become a very bitter struggle. This must be our starting point. . . . In this way the contradiction between the forces of production and relationships of production, and their clash with the superstructure, will continue to exist within all of human society for as long as a mode of production shall exist. Within a given mode of production, we find the reproduction of relationships based on authority and subservience, on leadership and obedience within which capitalist relationships of production are produced.

Without this movement "from the masses to the masses," authoritarianism and arbitrary leadership will again be built up within the party, and it will become a paternalistic and authoritarian party, bureaucratic and privileged—in other words, a party detached from the masses.

It was Mao who first set forth the principle that without party leadership, no revolution can succeed. So there is no ambiguity with regard to the role of the party. The party, however, is not a metaphysical entity, an immutable historical category. On the contrary, it must reflect history. "Divergences, the struggle of various ideas within the party, continue to exist," says Mao, "as a reflection within the party of class contradictions, of the contradictions of the old and the new, exactly as they exist within society. Without these contradictions within the party and the ideological struggles to resolve them, the life of the party would come to an end." Mao speaks of two kinds of unity which must be achieved: the first within the party, the second within the people. Both may be obtained on the basis of the mass line. "Let the people talk," says Mao. "The sky's not going to fall, and you won't be thrown over. And what will happen if you don't let them talk? One of these days you'll be overthrown." "The party cadres," he continues, "should not act like the lord of Shih who loved dragons but died of fear whenever he saw one. For years they talked of socialism, but now that it's here, they're afraid." Who fears socialism? "China's Khrushchev. Continually talking about mass movements, but as soon as the masses were actually mobilized, he lost his head, pouring out his abuse against them, treating them as bands of idlers." For Mao Tse-tung, the *assumption of power cannot be called a definitive success if it is limited to structures*: "The assumption of power by ideological means is absolutely necessary if consolidation of the working classes' power and hegemony is the goal." To accomplish this decisive political leap, the leading role must revert to the masses; this has nothing, as it is generally believed in the West, to do with any form of spontaneity. Lin Piao says that the mass revolutionary movement is naturally correct; for among the masses, right- and left-wing deviationist groups may exist, but the main current of the mass movement always corresponds to the development of the society involved, and is always correct. The role of the party in destroying "spontaneous" illusions lies in the quality of its leadership assumed during the socialist revolutionary process. This role consists in transforming dispersed rebel movements into a revolutionary current capable of overcoming contradictions. "Revolution is the resolution of contradictions," affirms the Chinese Communist Party. And it is through the party that the proletariat becomes transformed into the dominant class.

This *internal* relationship between party and masses is precisely what defines a revolutionary party, the party of the dictatorship of the proletariat. And it is from this relationship that the proletariat is exalted to its position of hegemony in the class structure. In Lenin's words: "The dictatorship of the proletariat is nothing other than the transformation of the proletariat into a ruling class." All historical experience demonstrates—and the Cultural Revolution attests—that the party is the dominant element in the dictatorship of the proletariat; it is its core of leadership, its vanguard, but only to the extent that its relationship with the masses is established on the basis of proletarian democracy and only insofar as proletarian democracy is nurtured by the *mass line* now awaiting its concrete application. This concept of the party-masses relationship does not limit the fundamental role of the Marxist-Leninist party, but rather broadens its political scope and practical application; it opens the party "to new blood from the proletariat," suppresses all feelings of superiority, all presumptions of "educating the people"; it consolidates the hegemonic role of the party on the broadened basis of proletarian democracy.

Among other things, the struggle against Liu Shao-chi was motivated by his erroneous conception of the party, a conception quite close to that of the Stalinist and post-Stalinist party. Recourse to the masses is the vital contribution made by the Cultural Revolution in its theory and practice. It is not a concept that appeared overnight, but one which was fully incorporated into each stage of the Chinese revolution. *For what characterizes the Chinese Communist Party and Mao Tse-tung's thought on the whole,* is the position accorded to the masses, the role given them within the party, which is equal to the role of the party in guiding the masses. Throughout its history, the party has been the primary battleground, and Mao's line has never wavered in this regard: the party should be built upon the mass line; it should be subject to the criticism of the masses; it should never substitute itself for the masses who must liberate themselves. The struggle waged by Mao on the party front can hardly be considered a new chapter, the "chance discovery" of a "group" struggling against another "group" in the equivocal game of a "palace revolution" all the more mysterious for being Chinese. This interpretation is not only due to ignorance. It reflects a "Thomist" vision of the party as a revealed truth, as a scholastic entity: the party which "cannot be touched," the party which is always right, an unalterable and incorruptible entity, an infallible ruling group—those who criticize the party become its enemies. This type of party, the "pure revolutionary archetype," has certain inalienable or what might be called "biological" characteristics. By the sole fact of its existence, it objectively produces more and more revolution, more and more socialism, in keeping with its so-called natural function. To Mao, on the contrary, the party is a force acting within a historical context, and as such it is the theater where the struggle to define a just revolutionary line takes place; it is a living body which can change for the worse and deteriorate, which can fall prey to the revisionist sickness if it does not struggle against it, and which, like all living bodies, needs oxygen and must eliminate carbon dioxide.

It is difficult to understand why this idea of *destruction-construction*, among the greatest of Mao's contributions to dialectical thought ("one divides into two" within the party) has aroused so much furor. Mao has been called a blasphemer, a heretic, and a schismatic: he has been accused of trying to destroy the party (which he says is as precious as the pupils of our eyes). We, on the contrary, saw a party which had emerged from the rectification campaign more dynamic and robust than ever. Mao's concept of the party is completely antidogmatic, the most Leninist concept one could hope to find fifty years after the October Revolution. And so it must appear to those who, together with the Chinese, mourn Lenin's premature death: "But Lenin died in 1924, far too early to have brought practical solutions to any one of a number of great problems," said *Red Flag* (no. 7, 1967). The "mass line" concept has become purposefully confused. In actual fact, as Bettelheim explained in *Les Temps modernes* (April 1971), it is a "return to the fundamental positions of Marx . . . abandoned both in practice and in theory by social democracy and by a pseudo-Leninism that had long forgotten the essence of Lenin's teachings, which dogmatically quoted a few of his texts—especially those which made the party master of the masses, in pedagogical terms at first, and in more absolute terms later on."

To dispel some of the more outrageous errors, and to understand the remote origins of the Cultural Revolution, Mao's texts on the rectification movement within the party, written during the 1940s, should be read or reread. There are two series of these documents. The first series, written in Yenan, date from 1941–1942: "Reform Our Study," May 1941; "Rectify the Party's Style of Work," February 1942; "Oppose Stereotyped Party Writing," February 8, 1942. In these texts, Mao deals with divergences within the party, left- and right-wing deviations, petty-bourgeois ideology and work styles under the mask of Marxism-Leninism, subjectivist and sectarian or liberal tendencies, stereotyped forms, and the slavish application of foreign models.

The Party and revolutionary language

In "Oppose Stereotyped Party Writing," Mao explains the style of language he has chosen. It is the linguistic origin of the little red book and the tatzupao:

> [In our country] foreign stereotypes and foreign dogma came into being. Running counter to Marxism, certain people in our party developed the foreign stereotype and dogma into . . . stereotyped party writing. . . . Some of our comrades love to write long articles with no substance, very much like the "footbindings of a slattern, long as well as smelly." Why must they write such long and empty articles? There can be only one explanation: they are determined the masses shall not read them. . . . Stereotyped party writing is . . . dead language. . . . Many of our comrades doing propaganda work make no study of language. Their propaganda is very dull. . . . Why do we need to study language and . . . spend much effort on it? Because the mastery of language is not easy and requires painstaking effort. First, let us learn language from the masses. The people's vocabulary is rich, vigorous, vivid, and expressive of real life. . . . What did Dimitrov say? He said: "We must learn to talk to the masses, not in the language of book formulas, but in the language of fighters for the cause of the masses, whose every word, whose every idea reflects the innermost thoughts and sentiments of millions."

In the same speech Mao praised the use of pamphlets; he explained how they must be written, how they were written by Russian workers, and how they incorporated their political demands. This is the idea behind the tatzupao, which Mao contrasts with the stereotyped style. He recounts how at the end of 1894, together with the worker Babushkin, Lenin wrote the first pamphlet on agitation, calling upon the workers of a St. Petersburg factory to strike.

The other series of texts dates from 1942 to 1944. It was directed at the Political Bureau and deals with party history. It stirred up considerable debate and discussion, which continued through preparations for the Seventh Congress in 1945. This Congress witnessed unprecedented party unity.

Already in 1943 we find Mao stating one of the essential principles of the Cultural Revolution, that of "from the masses to the masses." In "Some Questions Concerning Methods of Leadership," we read:

> In all the practical work of our party, all correct leadership is necessarily "from the masses, to the masses." This means: take the ideas of the masses (scattered and unsystematic ideas) and concentrate them (through study turn them into concentrated and systematic ideas), then go to the masses and propagate and explain these ideas until the masses embrace them as their own, hold fast to them and translate them into action, and test the correctness of these ideas in such action. Then once again concentrate ideas from the masses and once again go to the masses so that the ideas are persevered in and carried through. And so on, over and over again in an endless spiral, with the ideas becoming more correct, more vital, and richer each time. . . . In the present rectification movement we must correct these defects and learn to use the methods of combining the leadership with the masses and the general with the particular in our study . . .

During the Cultural Revolution these texts came to be the basis of the revolutionary criticism directed against Liu Shao-chi's line. Before the war Mao wrote "On Correcting Mistaken Ideas in the Party" (republished in 1967), which became an incisive weapon in the struggle against subjectivism, dogmatism, and empiricism, against individualism and factionalism, against "the bookish spirit of self-important, but in actual fact, ignorant intellectuals, for the knowledge of workers and peasants is often quite superior to theirs." It was in this same spirit that in 1942 Mao analyzed the policy to be used in dealing with intellectuals: "The only way," he wrote, "is to orient them toward practical work, to make practitioners out of them, and to convince those involved in theoretical work to enter upon the study of important practical problems."

The struggle against the erroneous conception of the party

We know that the German social democrats (Kautsky) placed theory above practice and the party above the masses. We know that Stalinism makes the party the trustee of the truth, the repository of absolute power which it exercised through an authoritarian apparatus and which repressed any initiative by the masses. All Chinese criticism of Liu Shao-chi is aimed at this concept of the party. Liu wished to transform the party—the instrument of the class struggle—into a self-improvement school for bureaucrats, a career springboard in order to rise after an apprenticeship as severe as that of the Jesuits, to the highest echelons of power. This was an attack on the Stalinist concept of the party, as indicated by an important speech (almost unknown in the West) given in April 1967 before the "Bethune-Yenan Rebel Brigade Inspired by the Thought of Mao Tse-tung," and published in *East Wind* in July 1967. This speech presents a platform for debate on the Cultural Revolution:

> For a long time now Mao has carried on the struggle against a mentality reigning within the party, one which is personified by Liu Shao-chi. What exists is a system of supposed ideological relationships; they were established within the Chinese Communist Party during the 1940s, following a visit to Moscow by a certain An Chi-wen, then assistant director of the organizational section of the Central Committee; he had been sent there by his chief, Liu Shao-chi. He returned from his trip with an excellent and modern system of party organization. The system was put into effect by a small minority of cadres. It was at this time that the struggle began between the two points of view. Many resisted and boycotted this system which gave the role of surveillance and control of the masses to the party. Mao has always supported a different concept: the party and its members should be subject to the control and criticism of the masses. But for a long time the struggle was carried on in such a way that few clearly understood that what was involved was a struggle between two opposing lines.

Precisely so that this mass criticism itself should reveal the completely political scope of this struggle and should in effect disavow

Liu Shao-chi's concept of the party, and consequently of the masses, Mao issued the following directive during the years 1966–1967, the key years of the Cultural Revolution: Liu Shao-chi's book, published in 1939 and entitled *How to Be a Good Communist*—which, according to the revolutionary rebels, should have been entitled *How to Make Your Career by Using the Title Communist*—should be criticized by everyone, but in a positive manner, and by relating its problems to the central question of the political struggle. For this reason the book was then reprinted (several new editions had already been issued with modifications and additions), and was sold not only in bookstores but in the streets so that *every Chinese* would be able to read and criticize it. This extremely rigorous and direct manner of involving an entire people in the criticism of Liu Shao-chi's theoretical guidelines is also expressed in the speech to the Rebel Brigade. We refer to it because of its organic character and the official importance given it in *East Wind*, even though Western journalists (for instance, Wilfred Burchett in *Africasia*) wrote in 1971 that there were ultra-left elements, such as Rittenberg, in the Brigade and that they were expelled in 1968.

In the speech to the Rebel Brigade, the question of how to become an expert in making revolution was posed.

> According to Liu Shao-chi, the young revolutionary must pass through a long period of promotions and training before emerging as a mature and complete revolutionary. Whoever follows this path will receive both compensation and favors. But he must show his obedience and be unconditionally loyal and faithful to his superiors, whoever they may be. He must never bring up any personal demands in an attempt to gain the respect and spontaneous help of other members of the party or of his superiors, and the protection of the leadership. In other words, Liu Shao-chi says: be reasonable and believe in me; do not think in terms of personal demands, we shall take care of you; we shall see to it that your loyalty is recompensed. . . . In his book, the author fails to admit the possibility of error on the part of the leadership; the impression is created that it is only the masses, the simple members of the party, who are to be criticized and corrected. It was in this way that Teng Hsiao-ping [former party secretary] protected those who for the sake of their careers demonstrated real devotion to him. . . . The rebels revolted against this blind and

unconditional obedience which failed to examine the line followed by the ruling group. They asserted that it was this tendency that had led the revolutionary movement down the path of Khrushchev revisionism. . . . A person who obeys blindly cannot be called a Marxist. Wherever there are slaves, there are masters. If you notice a blind obedience among party members, you need only look a little higher, and you will surely see who is exacting this blind obedience and who is the master of these slaves. In Liu Shao-chi's kind of cadres, slave and master play complementary roles at all levels. The secretary of the party cell must blindly obey the higher-level party secretary; if you look toward the top, the secretary is a slave, but if you look down, toward the masses, he is a master exacting blind obedience from his slaves. This is inevitable.

Let us transpose this onto an international plane, to the rest of the working-class movement. This type of discipline (even if there is an error, even if the party secretary makes a mistake, even if the majority errs in its decision, you are not entitled to refuse to obey) created unhealthy relationships at all levels. It happened, for instance, that a Communist Party leader, well known for his dictatorial character and harshness toward comrades, was called to Moscow by Khrushchev and sent back with his instructions—the instructions of a slavemaster; he demanded for himself the same blind obedience which he showed toward his master. These are manifestations of bourgeois discipline; it is the type of organization required by the bourgeois system. What is needed, on the contrary, is the establishment of an authentically proletarian revolutionary discipline.

It is right to rebel

It was not easy to lead the party to rebel. In a party where disciplinary regulations were strict, where self-discipline and self-conditioning had been carried to great lengths, where repression was ruthless, as demonstrated by the criticism directed toward Liu Shao-chi, many were afraid and hesitant. What will happen tomorrow? What's going to become of me? Why aren't things going the way they should? they ask. At stake in the struggle was the development of consciousness. For Mao, triumph at the top in the struggle against Liu Shao-chi was of no interest. If the revolution, like all true revolutions, was to attain its goal it had to be carried out by the masses: a revolutionary choice "between two classes, two roads, two lines" born in the heat of struggle, in an immense outburst, the politicization of millions of people. To transform man's conception of the world and of himself, as well as the concept of party, and to strengthen the dictatorship of the proletariat in China, there must be total revolution and promotion of production. Old habits must be changed: obedience must be unlearned, or disobedience learned, the democratic centralism which had become bureaucratic centralism overthrown; for the minority there must be the end of passive subjection to the majority while the latter was following an erroneous line. "Be subject to the will of the majority even if the truth is on the side of the minority? Absolutely not," wrote *People's Daily* on June 16, 1967, in an article entitled "Down with Slavishness; Strictly Observe Proletarian Revolutionary Discipline":

> Sacrifice truth, renounce principles, capitulate before the "majority" even when it is wrong? That is 100 percent opportunism. Chairman Mao says: "Throughout history new and correct things have often failed at the outset to win recognition from the majority of people and have had to develop by twists and turns in struggle." When truth is with the minority, the minority should uphold it, fear no attack, and unswervingly struggle for it. Our great leader Chairman Mao is a brilliant example. When he was attacked by the opportunists such as Chen Tu-hsin, Li Li-san, Wang Ming, and others, by using the so-called majority Chairman Mao constantly upheld the truth, persisted in a principled stand, and waged uncompromising struggles against them.

At times, one must *oppose the party* in order *to defend it*. All solutions which involve leaving the party and abandoning the struggle can only be considered an opportunist choice, a manifestation of petty-bourgeois anarchism. Throughout his life as a loyal Communist, Mao has demonstrated that the decisive battle has been fought within the party.

Can it be said, as Liu Shao-chi does, that whoever opposes the leadership sabotages democratic centralism? No, for democratic centralism is the broadest of democracies. Without democracy, there can be no correct centralization. *Obedience or debate?* To this Mao replies that directives which are in opposition to the revolution must not be unconditionally accepted; on the contrary, they must be resolutely challenged. The key word is *challenge*. But in rejecting what must be changed, in welcoming the new, in the challenge and disobedience, right and left deviations must be opposed. One seeks to reject nothing, the other to reject everything. In rejecting servility, we must not fall into anarchism. These positions are apparently contradictory, but in reality they are one and the same, and extremes of either kind must be avoided. Anarchy and ultra-leftism are the two faces of revisionism. While Liu Shao-chi was in power, his accomplices preached servility; once they lost power, they tried to spread anarchy, sow confusion, and oppose the dictatorship of the proletariat. How then shall we carry on rectification of the party against right and left deviations? It must be done *publicly*, says Mao. The doors of the party must be opened to enable the masses to express themselves; leadership must be strengthened, the level of understanding of the cadres raised, support found among the masses, and right and left deviations opposed. The transformation of democratic centralism into proletarian democracy demands protracted work; one must be experienced in the struggle, familiar with the many vicissitudes, defeats, and victories sustained or won by millions of Communists; it is a task of destroying and rebuilding the party, a task of rectification and consolidation, as the Chinese say; it is the greatest mobilization of masses that history has ever known. The decisions made by the Ninth Congress are found in synthesized form in Article 5 of the statutes, a sort of codification of the right to dissent, something absolutely new within the statutes of a Communist Party:

> Party members have the right to criticize and to make proposals to party organizations and leaders at all levels. Should a party member hold divergent opinions regarding decisions or directives of party organizations, he is entitled to maintain his reservations; he is further entitled to bypass the authority he has criticized and render an account to higher-level organizations, up to the Central Committee and its Chairman. A political atmosphere must be created in which centralism and democracy, discipline and liberty, unanimous will, individual satisfaction, and life itself concurrently reign.

Against a parent party and for a true internationalism

In terms of the international movement, this party which arose from the Cultural Revolution and the Ninth Congress brought to an end the subordination of one party to another under the pretext of numerical importance. It brought to an end all unwarranted interference by one country in the domestic affairs of another: the armed intervention in Czechoslovakia was called "sinister big-power chauvinism" in Lin Piao's report. It brought an end to the notion of a socialist "model" which could be valid for everyone. The Chinese rejected the idea of a "guide party" or patriarchal party, as Lin Piao calls the Soviet Communist Party—a notion which has long dominated relations within the socialist camp.

With regard to "their model"—with regard to the Chinese myth, as we call it in the West—the Chinese were the first to reject such idealizing and idealism. Mao underscores the differences and historical and political disparities existing between the structures of different countries and different parties.

During the course of our conversations about the party, we gathered that one of the accusations hurled by other Communist parties which most irritated the Chinese was the following: China aspires to become a sort of "guide state." They pointed out to us how this was the opposite of what they had proclaimed—the end of the parent- or guide-party concept—and to their own internationalist view that each country, large or small, has the right to autonomy and independence. In fact, Mao's statement of May 20, 1970, on the role of small countries goes much farther than a simple judgment of the world political situation. What is true for countries is also true for parties. "The relations between all countries and between all parties, big or small, must be built on the principles of equality and noninterference in each other's internal affairs," said Lin Piao in his report to the Ninth Congress.

The Chinese are certainly aware of the fascination their experience holds for the proletariat and youth throughout the entire world. Both because they believe that "modesty strengthens and presumption weakens," and particularly because of the historical and dialectical method which they follow, they do not ask to be copied. They are content to put within the reach of others whatever part of the Chinese revolutionary heritage they may find useful. Spending a few weeks in their company, you come to learn that they dislike imitations. Their only desire is that the proletariat advance along the socialist road. In the March 18, 1971, editorial commemorating the Paris Commune these basic principles which form the heart of the internationalist movement and of interparty relationships are recalled:

> A proletarian party should, in accordance with the basic principles of Marxism-Leninism, use the Marxist-Leninist stand, viewpoints, and methods to carry out deepgoing investigations and study of the class relations in society, make concrete analyses of the present conditions and the history of its own country and the characteristics of the revolution in that country, and solve the theoretical and practical problems of the revolution independently. It is necessary to learn from international experience, which, however, should not be copied mechanically; a proletarian party should creatively develop its own experience in the light of the realities of its own country. Only thus can it guide the revolution to victory and contribute to the cause of the proletarian world revolution.

The new Constitution

In April 1969 the Ninth Congress of the Chinese Communist Party met. Very young revolutionaries sat beside the old guard and the army delegates. Elections to the Political Bureau and amendments to the party statutes ratified the victory of the line of Mao Tse-tung and Lin Piao.* The reconstruction of the party was now

---

* Mao Tse-tung became chairman of the Central Committee of the Chinese Communist Party. Lin Piao became vice-chairman. The Political Bureau (with Mao Tse-tung, Lin Piao, Chen Po-ta, Chou En-lai, Kang Sheng as members of the Standing Committee) was composed of the following: Mao Tse-tung, Lin Piao, Yeh Chun (wife of Lin Piao), Yeh Chien-ying, Liu Po-cheng, Chiang Ching (wife of Mao), Chu Teh, Hsu Shih-yu, Chen Po-ta, Chen Hsi-lien, Li Hsien-nien, Li Tso-peng, Wu Fa-hsien, Chang Chun-chiao, Chiu Hui-tso, Chou En-lai, Yao Wen-yuan, Kang Sheng, Huang Yung-sheng, Tung Pi-wu, and Hsieh Fu-chih.

almost complete. The nuclei of the Chinese Communist Party on the revolutionary committees created a comprehensive network of cells. Today, following the local congresses, party committees have been reconstituted in twenty-two out of twenty-nine provinces and in the three autonomous cities of Peking, Shanghai, and Tientsin.*

The provincial political bureaus came into existence at the end of 1970; they now cover almost the entire country. Various movements and campaigns continue to exist and even develop (study of the "Thought of Mao Tse-tung," of the "four and five perfections," congress of activists, etc.) parallel to this, sustaining and increasing the enthusiasm and vitality of Chinese political life in the Cultural Revolution.

The new Constitution which the National People's Congress will be called upon to ratify within the next few months proclaims that the proletarian state is irrevocably placed under the leadership of the Communist Party. Marxism-Leninism and the thought of Mao Tse-tung contain the theoretical principles guiding all political philosophy. The Constitution establishes the forms of central and local power of the new state as they have emerged during the Cultural Revolution. The Constitution thus sanctions new organizations, such as the revolutionary committees. Among the recognized rights of citizens is the right of the individual to express his point of view freely, to write tatzupao, to appeal to the masses, to organize large-scale debates, and to express himself fully within the framework of proletarian democracy. In accordance with a statement by

* The list of provincial congresses held through June 1971 includes: Yunnan, from May 31–June 3; Hopei, from May 17–20; Sinkiang, from May 7–11; Shansi, from April 7–11; Peking, from March 10–15; Chekiang, from January 20–28; Kirin, from March 18–24; Shantung, from April 1–5; Hupei, from March 23–28; Fukien, from March 30–April 3; Tsinghai, from March 6–11; Shensi, from February 28–March 5; Honan, from March 2–8; Kansu, from February 11–17; Kwangsi, from February 9–16; Liaoning, from January 9–13; Anhui, from January 15–21; Shanghai, from January 4–10; Kiangsi, from December 18–26, 1970; Kwangtung, from December 18–26, 1970; Kiangsu, from December 19–26, 1970; Hunan, from November 24–December 4, 1970.

Chou En-lai quoted in *Epoca* (February 1971), the Constitution also guarantees the right to strike.*

---

* According to information given to us, about 1 percent of former party members are considered "irredeemable"; those definitively expelled (the gravest political punishment) are estimated at between 2 and 5 percent. Before the Cultural Revolution, the Chinese Communist Party had 17.5 million members. After its Ninth Congress it had approximately the same number because new members ("the new blood in the body of the people") had been accepted.

17

Mao's Children

In the courtyard of the Red Torch Primary and Middle School in Canton—located in the Tung Shan section in the middle of the old city, a dazzlingly white district recalling some little villages in Apulia—the schoolchildren were playing "dynamite-carrying guerrilla." This is a Chinese version of our relay races. A cord, stretched at a certain height, is supposed to represent a river; on one of its banks floats a red flag. Holding under his arms a little bag stuffed with rags and with the word "explosives" written all over it, the child must jump over the cord; if he falls, the dynamite explodes and his mission has failed. If he doesn't fall, he passes the "explosives" to one of his little comrades on the run and begins again. Their cheeks on fire, the schoolchildren run around breathlessly and vie with each other to see who can jump the highest. Almost no one falls.

These are Mao's children. His successors. The six- to ten-year-olds in the primary schools, and the ten- to fourteen-year-old students in the junior middle schools. Girls and boys together, they are the Chairman's Little Red Guards, the generation which the world will face in another five or ten years. Their game over, they run toward us crying, "Ni hao" (How are you?); they take our hands, talking all at once, as if we can understand what they are saying. Through the windows along a balcony, we see several classes at work—the school has 1,500 pupils—and as soon as our heads come into view, the children, quivering with repressed curiosity, spring up and applaud. We sit in on several lessons.

In one of the junior middle school classes, a twelve-year-old child-teacher speaks to his comrades—who listen with the greatest respect—of the "fighting hero, Tung Sun-jen, martyr of the war of liberation," a soldier who was unable to place an explosive charge under an enemy-held bridge and blew himself up with the bridge. "The external situation," says the boy, "did not allow the comrade to accomplish his mission. He wanted to put the charge under one of the bridge's piers, but he couldn't find a hole to slide the explosives into, and they kept falling into the water. How do you think the soldier took the role of the internal cause upon himself?" Several students raise their hands, and one plump little girl, dressed in a short quilted jacket, answers: "Comrade Tung thought that the entire Chinese people were leading a life of repression, and that if this life was prolonged one minute more, the suffering of the people would increase by as much. He therefore used his own hands to blow up the bridge. He based himself on the internal cause as long as the external cause was unfavorable."

I ask the child-teacher, a very intelligent and quite handsome boy, perfectly at ease amid instructors and visitors, how he became a teacher.

"By following Mao's method: officers teach soldiers, soldiers teach officers, and soldiers teach soldiers. We participated in the three-in-one combination, setting up the curriculum, which also includes lessons given by students. Now we take turns giving these lessons. When we teach, the teachers listen to us [I saw that their teachers did indeed listen to them attentively]. We follow the example of the People's Liberation Army. Every class has its soldier-teachers. Students teach voluntarily, but they are elected each week by their comrades. So they give a one-hour lesson two or three times a week."

"Would you tell me," I ask the class, "what you feel is new at the school since the Cultural Revolution?"

Several hands go up. I point to an enthusiastic youngster—"That one, please," I say to the interpreter—and the little boy speaks up right away:

"Before, there weren't any child-teachers. The shops where we do our manual work are all new. Workers come to the school to give classes. And teachers go to the factories to receive worker education."

In another class, I ask: "Were you afraid of your instructors before the Cultural Revolution?"

Sun Yi-min, thirteen years old, a member of the revolutionary committee which runs the school, answers:

"In the past we were a little afraid of the teachers, and we didn't dare criticize them. But since the Cultural Revolution, student-teacher relations have been transformed. Instructors are teaching for the revolutionary cause, and students are studying for the revolutionary cause. This common goal unites students and teachers. After each lesson there are critical comments about the class and about the program. The teacher can criticize his students, but students can criticize the teacher as well."

"Before," says Chu Ma-yen, a Red Guard and another member of the school's revolutionary committee, "teachers prepared their lessons shut up inside their offices, drinking tea and smoking cigarettes. Result: they talked a lot, but the students did not understand much. Now we often prepare the lessons together."

In the principal's ground-floor office we meet with the revolutionary committee of the Red Torch School. There are four student representatives (three boys and one girl) on the committee. They are the ones I have just seen in class, and I continue to question them, because they, above all, are the children of Mao, the Chinese of tomorrow, and can "show me the future." I never manage to catch them out: they are quick, combative, and extremely intelligent. And there is nothing "learned" about what they say; they really know everything from the inside, since they themselves have participated in the organization of the school, in modifying programs and courses of study, in restructuring the school together with worker-teachers and soldiers, and even in re-educating teachers. Conflict has existed between students and teachers, and the children calmly corroborate this in the teachers' presence. The struggle did on occasion become quite bitter. I was told in Peking that after being convicted of revisionism by their students, some teachers had had ink smeared over their faces and dunce caps placed on their heads as a mark of dishonor. I don't know what happened in this particular school, but I have no doubt that students made life very difficult for the "revisionist" teachers.

"In actual practice," I ask, "how would a revisionist teacher act?"

"He would say that there is no education without punishment."

The students add that they had written several tatzupao on the subject. One senior middle school student, a member of the revolutionary committee at the May 7 Middle School in Shanghai, had already told me that teachers would use "the rod and slap method instead of the ideological method." The students' grievance book at that school is pretty much summarized by a tatzupao I copied. It explains the Cultural Revolution among the young thus:

> During class, when discipline leaves something to be desired, some of our teachers suddenly assume a threatening air; they take out the rod, striking it against the desk like deaf men, or use their hands instead. This we will no longer permit. This does not mean that teachers should refrain from severely criticizing infractions of discipline: on the contrary, such disturbances should be criticized. But how can they threaten us by waving rods and banging on desks? How can they treat us like this? Such things should not happen in our socialist schools. We think that teachers should patiently and scrupulously perform their ideological duties with their students. Teachers should reflect and say to themselves: Can the rod and hand replace ideological work? No, they can never replace it.

"We, too," says Sun Yi-min, "attacked this problem. We think that when you brandish a rod or bang on desks, we are even less convinced. We realize that if banging is the only thing a teacher knows, he lacks authority. Anyone can scream and bang on a desk. Chairman Mao teaches the opposite: to convince others, you must persuade them, not force them. The only result of force is that you've coerced rather than convinced. Even the Little Red Guards at our school wrote some tatzupao against punishment."

The teachers at the Red Torch School, slightly embarrassed perhaps by what the children have said about them, are not in any way less convinced that the revolution in teaching has shown positive results and that the students have been justified in fighting authoritarianism in the schools. One rather pretty young woman, a mathematics teacher, explains to us:

"What the children say is true: a new relationship has been forged between the students and us. Before, we scarcely paid attention to what happened to them at school. For example, I once gave a mathematics assignment and the children, who had not understood the lesson, made some mistakes. To punish them, I prohibited them from going swimming in the afternoon; I thought that it would be more valuable to force them to remain in class so that they could go over their mathematics lesson. But the students were of a different mind and rebelled. They were right: a single lesson is not enough to understand; knowledge is acquired gradually. I did not agree, and wanted to impose my authority. The children then organized for my benefit a course on the thought of Mao, and since then I have never again used similar methods . . ."

"Before," a little girl interrupts, "the teachers did not give students an education based on reason, and they did not explain to us what they were doing. Now things have changed: teachers consult students, and we help each other. If the characters a teacher writes on the blackboard are barely legible, the students raise their hands, and the teacher criticizes himself for his own neglect."

"How have you simplified the curriculum?"

The student An Yen-chen explains:

"We have reduced the years of study. Primary education has been reduced from six to five years, and the junior and senior middle school courses each last two years instead of three. The curriculum has been simplified and practical training helps us to gain a better understanding of our courses. Before, there were some very difficult lessons in electricity; now with the practical training we receive at the school shop, this subject, like mechanics, has become a lot simpler."

Comrade Ho, a worker and member of the school's revolutionary committee, on loan from a weaving equipment plant in Canton, has reorganized these programs with the help of the teachers. We gather that Mao's Little Red Guards are his fervent supporters, and the students on the Red Torch revolutionary committee listen enthralled as he gives us the following explanation:

"We realized that history, geography, literature, mathematics, and physics were taught at the elementary level and then repeated in middle school. Now the primary school has a single course in 'basic knowledge,' while the study of various other subjects is reserved for the junior and senior middle schools. Furthermore, the children enter middle school with many advantages gained from their practical experience acquired in the shops as youngsters. In the five primary grades the children actually learn manual labor. Workers and peasants come to tell them about life under the old society, and the children prepare their lessons with them. The class struggle constitutes the major subject of our courses. When they leave school the students are going to mingle with workers and peasants in their practical work. We follow the teachings of the People's Liberation Army, and we cultivate the style of heroic behavior which is the rule in our army."

I ask him if he has encountered any difficulties in his new task as school organizer.

"Under the old society," says Ho, "the working class was exploited and dominated by the capitalists. Now the party and Chairman Mao have given us the glorious task of educating the young. When I arrived I was petrified, but then I thought of the confidence Mao had placed in the working class and how he had entrusted it with the education of the successors to the revolutionary cause, our children. I then resolved to perform this task, which for me was a revolutionary task. Naturally I encountered enormous difficulties. But you learn to swim by swimming. That's what I did. And my efforts have been supported by revolutionary teachers, soldiers, and students . . ." And the worker turns to smile at the student members of the revolutionary committee.

Accompanied by the students and teachers from the committee, we go to visit the school shops, where the very little ones, screwdrivers in hand, are struggling to assemble and disassemble some switches. In another shop, students aided by worker-teachers are busying themselves around a small electric lathe, making heavy screws. The students take turns doing a week of manual labor. We enter the school's little foundry, where primary and junior middle school students are being initiated into the blacksmith's art: they heat the iron, hammer it against an anvil, and fashion simple pieces. A sixteen-year-old boy and a twelve-year-old girl take turns hammering the metal that a third child holds firmly on the anvil with tongs. In a shop class, a worker gives a lesson on the structure of certain machine tools.

In Shanghai, a worker at the May 7 Middle School was teaching English he had learned abroad (in all the Chinese schools I visited, the foreign language that is commonly taught is English). That school also included a carpentry shop and a center where elementary medical instruction was given. The students divided their time equally between factory and field, helping workers and peasants. Teachers accompanied them, for they too were simultaneously performing educational and manual work: there are no longer any old-fashioned teachers, for all instructors are being re-educated and are learning to relate theory to practice. I remember a rather stout man with spectacles, a physics teacher, telling me how during an electrical blackout at the school he had found himself unable to restore the power despite the fact that on paper he was perfectly familiar with this kind of problem. The worker-teacher responsible for re-educating him had then taught him to make repairs of this type. This experience provoked a crisis in this teacher, who realized to what extent his knowledge had been pure book-learning.

We again meet with the revolutionary committee, and I broach a touchy subject: grades and examinations.

"Liu's revisionist line," says little Chu Ma-yen, "attached the greatest importance to grades. Later on we came to understand the true goal of study. Since then grades have scarcely counted at all because more often than not they indicate a level of knowledge acquired from books; it is more important to raise the ideological level of the students. We have exams, of course, but the questions are *open* ones, and we know them in advance. Just answering them is not enough; we have to prove our degree of political initiative."

"Could you give me an example?"

"Well," says Hu Yun-chen, "a teacher asks which is the lighter in an alloy, copper or aluminum. Suppose a student doesn't know that aluminum is the lighter metal and is used to make airplanes. What if he answers: 'I know that my country needs copper to defend itself from the danger of possible aggression.' Even if he has not given the exact answer to the question, he can pass."

"The system of examinations continues to exist," says another teacher, Comrade Wan, a former principal, "but grades are given according to the child's political development. Let us assume that there are ten questions: if the child answers five of them with a show of initiative and creativity, he can obtain the highest grade; on the other hand, should he answer ten questions in a bookish and unoriginal way, he will receive a lower grade."

In fact, all the classes we visit—history, literature, writing (which consists of extremely complex ideograms)—are taught in conjunction with examples and questions involving political behavior: "Why has the Tachai brigade performed well?" After answering questions concerning agriculture, soil, irrigation, and seeding, the children propose their own solutions, giving primary importance to political aspects as they have learned from the thought of Mao. Thus they must be able to answer the question: "Who can summarize why the Tachai brigade has transformed heaven and earth?"

A little red book sits on each desk, even on those of the youngest ones who don't as yet know how to read. They lay their little hands on the books as if "knowledge" were there. What then does the application of Mao's philosophy consist of? I read on the blackboard: "The rearguard can be transformed into the vanguard. Failure is the source of success. Happiness is born of unhappiness. Misery is also a vital impulse which can change the world. From laziness action can be born. From fear courage and contempt for death can be born."

These dialectical principles of politics or of a new morality are assimilated by each child as he learns how ideology can be transformed through improvement in personal behavior. Encouraged by teachings centered on morality and the primacy of politics, the students at the Red Torch School have learned totally new attitudes toward themselves and society.

"When we break a chair," says Hu Yun-chen, "we repair it ourselves in the carpentry shop. If we tear our clothing, we figure out among ourselves how to mend it. We cut each other's hair when it becomes too long. We take care of each other's minor illnesses using acupuncture. The older students in the basic medicine program are Red Guard doctors and can give injections, massages, perform simple acupuncture, and can also look after the people of the district. Applying the thinking of Mao, we write tatzupao criticizing bourgeois ideology or analyzing a problem so we can solve it. The student Li Chi-chen, who has studied and applied Mao's works daily, has written tens of thousands of characters setting forth his ideas."

This Li Chi-chen, a Red Torch student, is a model of sorts for his comrades, who recount how after reading Mao's "three constantly read articles," once school had ended, went to the station with other little comrades and swept the waiting room, sidewalks, and offices. "Every day, even Sundays, or when a typhoon was blowing, he cleaned the station premises. The railway workers would ask us our names and we would answer that we were the servants of the people. Where do you come from? We are from Chairman Mao's university. One day, one of the students left his satchel at the station and our railway comrades discovered his name. They wrote to the school to single out this fine example."

These teachers tell us that they were totally unaware of what was going on and only learned of the work performed by the students from the letter of thanks written by the railway comrades at the Canton station.

"There are many, many similar examples," says Ho, the worker-comrade. "Their moral growth is healthy, and their families think that children nowadays are far more advanced with regard to cultural, agricultural, and industrial matters. But the children also fight against the egotistical concept of family, against the backward mentality of certain parents; they hold political meetings with their fathers and mothers in an attempt to share with their families the problems of a socialist society. We have created a liaison committee between parents and the school which holds meetings regularly. The parents are extremely satisfied and say that the children now 'carry spades and know how to work the land, pick up hammers and know how to work iron, hold pens and know how to criticize the bourgeoisie, carry rifles and know how to make war.' We are educating the successors of the proletarian revolution to bury imperialists and revisionists the world over. We have organized a group of red doctors here, and we make the children participate in military exercises to give them a fighting spirit. The school year lasts about ten months—from February to July and from September through December; during both winter and summer vacations the children are often sent to billets and camps run by the People's Liberation Army to drill with the soldiers and share their lives."

At the May 7 Middle School in Shanghai (44 classes, 2,390 students, 180 teachers), a scrawny, unforgettable boy, Li She-je, a Red Guard doctor, accompanied me through the school's medical service, where, with a number of other thirteen- to fifteen-year-old comrades, he was studying and practicing acupuncture. They punctured each other on the calves or arms with remarkable earnestness. A few patients, adult workers, came to be "acupunctured" or massaged by the students, who skillfully examined vertebrae, backs, and napes. They certainly must have been effective, since the sick of the area all presented themselves at the dispensary. Li She-je proudly carried his medical kit across his back.

"When we have learned medicine well, we shall go with our remedies into the rural areas, to the east and west of the country, to help the peasants. And should we get sick, we will be able to heal ourselves all alone, with acupuncture and our medicines. The soldiers of the People's Liberation Army have taught us to serve the people, and the 'barefoot doctors' have taught us to practice medicine. Each brigade at the school has a student-Red Guard doctor. There are sixty thirteen- and fourteen-year-old Red Guard doctors at the school, and from the beginning of the Cultural Revolution until the end of 1971, more than 350 students have been trained. More than 200 students have already learned acupuncture. At present, each of us has an acupuncture needle, medicinal herbs, and our two hands to give massages. We can *serve the people.*"

I asked him what he had in his kit. He drew out a red case filled with needles, a small tin box with cotton wads soaked in alcohol, a plastic ear with twenty acupuncture marks, and a book on herb-based remedies. (The children showed me their wonderful laboratory and the plants from which they extracted medicines: they are already capable of producing twenty such remedies. In the bottles filled with alcohol, I saw a white snake, leeches, and a frog.) Finally, he took the inevitable little red book from his kit. After systematically laying everything out on the table, he rested his hand on the little book—the habitual gesture of Chinese children—and said:

"Since the Cultural Revolution we have introduced our children to the military life. We have taught them simple drills: target practice, marching, self-defense in case of ambush. Of course, a child's major interest continues to be his studies, but he must also learn the military exercises that will increase the readiness and preparedness, indispensable in case of war."

I turned toward the child doctor: "Is it true? Do you know how to shoot at targets?"

"Of course!" replied Li She-je, piqued by the tone of my question. "We must know how to shoot in order to open fire on revisionism and imperialism; we must be ready for everything. If enemies dare to attack us, we schoolchildren shall go to the front to hunt and fight the aggressor."

These are *Mao's children.* What will happen in five or ten years if Mao or another revolutionary Chinese leader calls them to Tien An Men square? Millions of fervent warriors will rise all over China: an invincible tide. Raised during the Cultural Revolution, they have been passionately educated in courage, heroism, devotion, loyalty, sacrifice, purity, modesty, and contempt for death. This is the milk that has nourished them—a dizzying array of virtues signifying political commitment rather than a "good conscience." No other people in the world possesses them to such a degree, and in comparison with our old world which, like Ugolino, seems at times to devour its children, new generations of young Chinese shall be the "North Stars" of what will undoubtedly be a very different future.

Lessons have now ended at the Red Torch School (they last from 8:15 to 11:30 in the morning and from 2:30 to 4:00 in the afternoon). The children have lunch at home and leave school in lines, striding rhythmically, singing, following a red flag. In their sneakers or open sandals, with their short, worn little jackets patched with different colored materials, their Red Guard armbands, and the triangular insignia of Mao's Little Red Guards—at times held on with a safety pin—they file past, heads high, prouder than West Point cadets.

18

Farewells at the Frontier

Everything happens very quickly. We get up at six o'clock. When the Canton train pulls into the Hong Kong frontier station, at the little Lo Wu bridge, it is only half-past ten. Chao, Lu, and Comrade Chin from Canton accompany us past the customs house to the entrance to the bridge, the forward line of the "front" which separates China from the rest of the world. It is a gesture of friendship, they told us the evening before, with a very simple solemnity. In the train we sang "Bandiera Rossa," but my voice broke with emotion.

In the ultra-modern station on the Chinese side we eat a last meal together. In view of the time—10:40 A.M.—it is not so much a meal as a last gesture of understanding after two months of living together. The room is spacious, with a light green carpet, showcases filled with the works of Mao and Chinese magazines, and the usual photographs on the walls. In contrast with the beginning of my trip, everything now seems like a familiar scene, or, better yet, like a mirror in which the extraordinary face of this extremely complex China which I have come to know from within is reflected.

I turn to my Chinese comrades. "Before leaving we'd like to say one last thing," I tell them. "Bring other people to China, open your doors. The truth about China ought to be known, and you'll make new friends. The world must know what we have seen."

I would have liked to make them understand that China needs the world less than the world needs China, but all I say is, "You're much more important than you think."

We eat in ten minutes. Then we are asked to go through customs. In our case the formalities are reduced to the minimum. No customs officer asks us if we have film or photographs; no one looks through our bags. At the office we change all the yuan we have left, as Chinese money may not leave China, and in exchange we receive Hong Kong money which we are to use for the rest of our trip. Now we have to head for the train waiting on the other side of the bridge, which must be crossed on foot. At the entrance to the bridge Chin makes the others stop, saying, "Here's the line of demarcation." Everything happens in a few seconds, as if the film projector jams just as we are preparing to go ahead together once more.

"Well, good-bye," we say. For the first time we embrace and kiss. And it is not only our friends we are embracing—it is China.

"China's immense, and we shan't easily forget it," says Alberto. "For you, it's exactly the opposite—it will be easy for you to forget us. Don't!"

"We won't forget you," Chao answers.

They also seem to be touched. But did they understand that we too, as a kind of "barefoot doctor" of politics, have tried to shatter the "curtain of ignorance" and the isolation of China in order to return it, in all its reality, to the center of our discussions, to link this tremendous experiment with the great convulsion of the worker movement in the West? The best is behind us; a painful unknown awaits us.

I turn around furtively, for in spite of my efforts my eyes are filling with tears which I feel rolling down my cheeks. Ashamed of this weakness, I decide not to turn around again and continue walking. When I am finally sure they can no longer see my emotion, I turn around. They are standing there, all three of them, waving, their silhouettes outlined against the light at the entrance to the bridge. I continue to walk and turn around, turn around, while they become smaller and smaller. Then we are swallowed up in the tunnel. When we come out, there they are for the last time, at the other end, framed by the arch of the gallery as in the oval gates of Hangchow, all three of them already so far away, their arms raised.

I arrive at the English frontier station with its emblem of Her Britannic Majesty. I am so distraught that the policemen and policewomen look at me quizzically. In the train going to Hong Kong, a young Chinese in uniform does his best to sell us American cigarettes, whisky, chocolate, "everything you don't find in China," like water to the thirsty. We stubbornly refuse. I press my face against the window so that the two foreign diplomats, a man and a woman, chatting at the end of the car will not see me. During the trip, I try in vain to make myself invisible, but everyone sees that I am crying. A fat Arab stares at me. The only words I can say in answer to Alberto's questions are: "These tears come from far away. You know, so much mud has bespattered the ideal of Communism. . . . The tanks against Prague, the humiliation of the last few years, the sarcastic remarks of the class enemies. The distant source of these tears—I'll understand it better later—is the age-old rage, terror, and helplessness. But these tears aren't bitter—on the contrary, they're *positive*. They're a kind of bath, a liberation. I lived *with them*, I looked around, studied, debated. I traveled from one end of China to the other, and now that I'm leaving them, I start to cry like this—I can't help it!"

Through the window I see the first Chinese women dressed in Western style: high heels and miniskirts on legs more suited to pants. Western fashion is merciless. The women of China are more elegant in their cotton outfits! These young "Westernized" Chinese women seemed to be weighed down by the spray on their bouffant hairdos and the heavy makeup on their small faces; they looked like aged pagan idols.

Hong Kong is a leap backward in time, a leap of a quarter-century: the face of Shanghai or Canton before the Liberation. It has everything: townhouses like cathedrals, eye-catching skyscrapers *à la* Miami Beach, superdeluxe shops with jewels for millionaires, newsstands with pornographic magazines, fabulous sports cars, prostitutes, beggars, and the Chinese porter, like a coolie, who totters under the weight of our baggage hanging from a shoulder pole. As in the old days in Shanghai, he too lives off the foreigner. Our baggage is heavy and the porter seems about to faint. We help him by carrying some of the bags, and so, following one after the other, we reach the superb Mandarin Hotel. When the hotel's Indian doorman—dressed in red-leather boots, white turban, and Bengal Lancer jacket—sees the porter he begins to scream, chases him away with a look of hatred, and calls the elevator boys—Chinese children, dressed in flashy gold-braided uniforms. A woman begs from us, and an old man with a humble smile holds out a servile palm to accept a small coin. An American passes by, wearing a big white ten-gallon hat *à la* Lyndon Johnson, a Havana cigar in his mouth and a diamond ring on his finger. And he is supposed to be worth more than any one of the 800 million Chinese? He is, to be sure, unshakeably convinced that he is.

"So it begins all over again," I say to myself. The class system, the rulers and the ruled, human solitude heaped up like the stones of a pyramid in order to support a few elite at the top. I want only one thing: to flee from Hong Kong, this boxed-in city of bureaucratic civilization. Haven't I already seen all this? Haven't I already seen this populace squeezed onto junks, living like schools of fish between Kowloon and the island of Hong Kong, and these little Chinese boys who dive down to the bottom to pick up with their teeth the local half-dollar which a rich tourist in a boat has thrown to them? I picture the schoolchildren at Red Torch.

The West has made Hong Kong its outpost, its China-watchers reminiscent of people who follow the migrations of birds with field glasses. They buy the smallest scrap of information about China. They work at Harvard University and at the China desk of the State Department. Everything they glean is fed into gigantic computers. Then they calculate the incidence of the various hypotheses in order to discover the "constants" of the future China. As everyone knows, they are completely mistaken, and their task is a labor of Sisyphus. After China, Hong Kong has the violence of debauchery. Future centuries should preserve it just as it is, mummified like Pompeii, a "window of the West."

We are unable to avoid an invitation from diplomats and journalists who want to see the two people who have just returned from Mao's China—as if we were two exotic birds! We accept because we want to talk about China right away. But the women are chattering like magpies in the salon.

"A quarter-inch pearl! Another one that's even larger! Then there's a flat one that's one-third of an inch—extraordinary! I'm going to buy it tomorrow. I just adore Chinese jewelry, and the jade statues that have just come in . . ."

They talk about counting calories, how to cut out fats—"Die of hunger, maybe, but lose weight, because the new styles . . ." They are wearing maxi-dresses, lace stockings, and boots that came up to their thighs. Boots in the tropics! How unnecessary, how superfluous! But it's the style here, as it is in Paris and London.

"Don't you think the Chinese women have lost all their charm?" the men ask us. "With their military helmets, their braids, and their trousers with baggy seats . . ."

"No, they have such an intensity, such deep strength . . ."

"What does their strength have to do with me? Can their muscles help them to lift me? It must be an amazing experience to be lifted by a Chinese woman!"

The women make little noises of tenderness, then very quickly resume their chatter—boots, jewelry, hairdos, maxi-dresses, their diets. These are our women, the women of the technocratic society! I think of the Chinese women at work, shovel or pick in hand, or operating heavy machines—Red Guards, doctors, worker-students. Are they not the *real* women? I wonder what these creatures are under their little curls and impeccable makeup, a vacuum in their heads, an absence of any ideas with the exception of "ideas" directed toward their husbands, their current love affairs, the magic of sex, and the raising of their children in the class religion.

The only young Chinese girls in the room are the two maids who serve the meal! Our hostess speaks of them gently as she would of trained chimpanzees. "This evening I made them take off their jackets. They're cold because their arms are bare, and they don't know what they're doing—they're serving from the right instead of from the left." White blood, yellow blood. I help myself from the plate offered me by one of the young girls. Looking up into the likeable, familiar face, I say "Hsieh hsieh"—thank you. She looks at me in amazement and without saying a word reminds me that we're *on the other side.* I am overcome by a familiar dull feeling of revolt, and with my first bite of lobster I feel nauseous, as if I am eating raw meat like a Western cannibal.

"Excuse me," I say. "I can't eat it."

"I understand." An Italian diplomat comes to my assistance. "People do have odd dislikes. When I was in Paris, it was several years before I could bring myself to eat oysters."

Then the completely hypocritical conversation resumes. A journalist gaily relates the story of the Pope's trip to Hong Kong in search of the "new Christianity." I burst out laughing, and everyone looks at me in astonishment.

We leave at two o'clock in the morning. It is the first time in fifty days that I have gone to bed at such an hour, dazed, after having wasted five hours on nonsense—five hours that could have been used for study or work. The return to the West through the funnel of Hong Kong is coldly instructive and savage.

During the night I watch the mountains of Kwangtung lightly silhouetted on the horizon. On the other side a people is marching with a light step and with fervor toward the future. This people may be the incarnation of the new civilization of the world. I can only say that China has made an unprecedented leap into history. I tell myself that I am fortunate, very fortunate. Not only have I crossed those mountains, I have lived inside the skin of this country, I have felt the beating "red hearts" of a million simple people, ordinary people, "fanatics," "ascetics," and "heroes," symbols of a new revolutionary intensity, who are rewriting the history of their country and, in many ways, the very history of the world. What is the best way to understand and love them? Is it not to return to our own countries, to the world of which we are the children and the protagonists, and to change it?

19

Conclusion: Some Theoretical and Political Questions

It now becomes necessary for me to move away from the political testimony contained in this book and to extract from it several fundamental questions in order to illuminate them; to step away from the narrative, and hence from the immediate reality of China, in order to compare it with our own. I must *step back in order to draw closer.* I should like in this way to put some of the questions I have raised into the context of Marxist theory and the history of the worker movement.

The revolution in the superstructure under the dictatorship of the proletariat

In order to understand completely the significance of the Cultural Revolution from the point of view of Marxist theory, we must go back to the theses of Marx and Engels concerning the state (the destruction of the bourgeois state, the revolutionary overthrow of its ideological as well as repressive apparatuses). In the words of the *Communist Manifesto*: "The Communist revolution is the most radical rupture with traditional property relations; no wonder its development involves the most radical rupture with traditional ideas."

On the eighteenth anniversary of the People's Republic of China, an editorial in *People's Daily* said: "On the ideological level the defeated classes still have major powers and are controlling new positions." How are we to strip them of their power—that is, in the words of Gramsci, how are we to establish *the ideological hegemony of the proletariat?*

This is the fundamental problem the Cultural Revolution is attempting to solve, on both the theoretical and practical levels. For the first time in history the proposed solution is that of a new revolution, this one to be achieved under the dictatorship of the proletariat. The dictatorship of the proletariat is not an idyllic period. Lenin calls it the most heroic war of the new class against a past whose power lies in the force of habit. It was these words which gave Mao the concept he used to "dramatize" the Cultural Revolution: who will overcome, the proletariat or the bourgeoisie? As Mao says:

> The class struggle between the proletariat and the bourgeoisie, the class struggle between the different political forces, and the class struggle in the ideological field between the proletariat and the bourgeoisie will continue to be long and tortuous, and at times will even become very acute. The proletariat seeks to transform the world according to its own world outlook, and so does the bourgeoisie. In this respect, the question of which will win out, socialism or capitalism, is still not really settled.

And the *People's Daily* article mentioned above says: "The *heroic struggle* of the proletariat should be used to destroy the ideological system of all exploiting classes. For this purpose we must inevitably advance toward an antagonistic confrontation."

The official Chinese text published at the time of the centenary of the Commune recalled that "socialist society covers a considerably long historical period. Throughout this period, there are still classes, class contradictions, and class struggle. The struggle still focuses on the question of political power. The defeated class will still struggle; these people are still around and their class still exists." The Chinese have been deeply convinced by their experience in building socialism of the truth of that other famous saying of Lenin: "The corpse of the bourgeois society cannot be placed in a coffin and buried. This corpse is decomposing among us; it is rotting and contaminating us." (*Red Flag*, February 1967, quotes this text as a reference point for the Cultural Revolution.)

Mao allows no doubt to exist concerning this theoretical position. In each of his statements he puts forth the Marxist-Leninist doctrine according to which it is clear that a class does not become truly dominant unless it has made its own ideology the dominant one (compare not only the Chinese experience but also that of the

USSR), although Marx and Lenin himself (in *State and Revolution*) did not succeed in projecting the vital questions they raised into the actual development of a socialist state. It is in accordance with this teaching that the Chinese place the ideological battle in the forefront and give priority to politics. This is translated on the theoretical level by one of Mao's sixteen points, "Grasp the revolution and promote production," which, on the practical level, sets the decisive note of the Cultural Revolution.

As an extension of the thinking of Marx and Lenin on the destruction of the state, the Cultural Revolution is defined from the theoretical point of view as an antagonistic confrontation with a handful of "bourgeois" over the takeover of power—for the purpose of destroying the bourgeois or petty-bourgeois ideological system which, like the phoenix, is being constantly reborn from its ashes. For in order to create the ideology of the proletarian class it is not enough to have destroyed private ownership of the means of production. Lenin pointed out that it is not until power has been won that the struggle begins. Sixteen years after the conquest of socialist power, the Chinese launch the struggle to reinforce the dictatorship of the proletariat. They define this struggle dramatically, like every revolution; it is "a question of life or death" that China does not change color.

The phenomenon unfolds dialectically on two levels, that of structure and of superstructure. The link between the structure (the economic base) and the superstructure (state-ideology) must remain indissoluble: "Grasp the revolution and promote production." This is a classic Marxist concept. According to the Chinese there will always, in every society, be a contradiction between what is progressive and what is regressive, even at the highest stage of communist society, where class contradictions will no longer exist because classes will no longer exist. There will be a contradiction between what is just and what is unjust, between what is scientific and what is unscientific. Similarly, the contradictions between the forces of production and the relations of production, and their contradictions with the superstructure, will continue to exist in every human society as long as production relations continue to exist. But does the reproduction of the social relations of production take place solely on the level of the socioeconomic structures, or is it not also engendered in large part by the political superstructure and the ideological apparatus which is established in close relationship with it? "The 'seizure of power' during the phase of the dictatorship of the proletariat cannot be considered successful if it does not go beyond the level of organization. Only by seizing power ideologically can we consolidate power in the domain of organization," according to an editorial in *Wenhui Pao*, August 30, 1967. This is the struggle for power on the ideological level.

In his essay "On Contradiction," Mao deals with this theme of the continuation of revolution under the dictatorship of the proletariat, a theme which is one of the key problems of socialism: how to consolidate the dictatorship of the proletariat, prevent the restoration of capitalism, and work creatively toward the fixed, ultimate goal of reducing the power of the coercive and ideological apparatuses of the state—*until the latter withers away*—by lessening their repressive nature and carrying the revolution to their very heart by an "intervention of the masses in the superstructure." Furthermore, in carrying out this revolution the masses effect a revolution in their own mentality, in their conception of the world and of the individual. It is not enough to seize power (seize the state apparatus, i.e., the repressive state apparatus). By seizing power a class becomes dominant, but this class will prove to be incapable of transforming the relations of production in a revolutionary sense if it does not succeed in making its own ideology the *dominant* one. A dominant class does not impose its ideology as long as it does not transform the state ideological apparatus in addition to the production relations. This, for example, is the meaning of the criticism directed by the Chinese toward education and culture: if the state ideological apparatus is not transformed into an apparatus serving proletarian ideology, it continues to be the vehicle of bourgeois ideology, producing bourgeois and petty-bourgeois individuals. To be sure, this is not a matter of sliding into a theory of the determinism of the superstructure and ideology. But what must be clearly understood is the place of ideology in class relationships, in the transformation and continuity of production relations, and an examination must be made of how ideology finds its political existence in the apparatus, what are the functions of the state, that is, of the ruling class.

The Chinese have clearly understood that revolution consists not only of "Soviet power plus electrification," but also of a revolution in ideology, in the "state ideological apparatus." This expression "state ideological apparatus," which I have already used in this book to define the superstructures within the Cultural Revolution, is borrowed from Althusser (see the article in *La Pensée* of October 1970). Althusser's study, which is explicitly inspired by Gramsci, will aid us in our effort, as we have defined it, to *step back in order to draw closer* to the Cultural Revolution by rising to a theoretical level.

Gramsci should be reread in the light of the Cultural Revolution. The manner in which he poses the theoretical problem of class hegemony provides a key to the interpretation of the thought of Mao Tse-tung during the Cultural Revolution, especially with regard to the transformation of class hegemony into proletarian democracy and the limitation of the repressive aspect of the state.

Althusser's conclusions concur in part with those of Gramsci, and together they undoubtedly constitute the most serious theoretical elaboration available in the West to help us understand unprecedented events in the history of the proletariat and to place them in the context of Marxist-Leninist theory. For Althusser, the state ideological apparatus is aimed at creating consensus among the "dominated," but, precisely because it presupposes a relationship between dominating and dominated groups, it retains a subtle element of coercion. In Gramsci's thinking, the opposition is more clearcut (as between two successive stages of a single unitary historical development) between the coercive function, linked to the "economic-corporate" stage, and the hegemonic function. For Gramsci the latter is not exhausted in the state, and even when its center of impulse is found within the state, it enlarges the latter's sphere of intervention, infiltrating other so-called private organizations in such a way as to restrict the coercive elements (See *Lettere dal carcere*). This is why, in Gramsci's thinking, the highest model of hegemony (and, consequently, of the state ideological apparatus, in accordance with Althusser's formula) is not strictly speaking that of the capitalist state, but that of the socialist state. This is, therefore, a model which is much closer to certain formulas used *by* the Chinese Cultural Revolution than to others utilized *for* bourgeois society (for instance, the "repressive tolerance" Marcuse speaks about). In *Note sul Machiavelli,* Gramsci says: "Among the numerous accepted meanings of the term 'democracy,' the most realistic and most concrete one seems to me to be the one which can be defined in relation to the concept of hegemony." Within this context Gramsci includes the Marxist theme of the gradual withering away of the state as a repressive and coercive power (the Communist stage). Gramsci continues: "It is possible to imagine the withering away of the coercive state as the increasingly important elements of a controlled society assert themselves." This does not prevent hegemony itself from appearing in the beginning as a "corporate economic primitivism" and, on the cultural level, as causing an activity which is "above all negative, a criticism of the past . . . tending to cause us to forget and destroy." (Moreover, this is exactly what happens with the Cultural Revolution when it declares that it is impossible to build without destroying the past, be this in the classroom, or in art, theater, literature, etc.)

But there is another and perhaps more profound difference in emphasis between Gramsci and Althusser. It lies in the indication of the historical moment when the function of hegemony (or the organization of consensus around a social group) becomes possible. In *Note sul Machiavelli,* Gramsci tends to attribute it also to the political party as such, and thus believes it to be equally possible *before the actual conquest of state power* by a given social class. Althusser, on the other hand, implicitly postulates the "statist" character of every effective ideological activity. The conquest of power then becomes a necessary condition for the organization of consensus by way of the state ideological apparatus (and the very function of the political party, now renewed). Seen from this angle, Althusser's concept seems closer than that of Gramsci to certain strategic Chinese concepts.

We must remember that in China the party is the dominant apparatus, under the dictatorship of the proletariat, and that the ideological apparatus is controlled by the party. But at the same time, the party, as the vanguard and core of leadership ("the relationship between party and masses must be an internal rather than external one; this is why the party is more of a core of leadership than a vanguard," Bettelheim writes) is neither a metaphysical category nor a Thomist *credo*. In China the struggle is raging within the party itself, a party which cannot be regarded as it is in the USSR (hence its functional defect), as the all-encompassing driving force of politics and administration. The proletariat "intervenes" in the party, the ideological apparatus of the power system, and elsewhere. The dominant party of the proletarian revolution fulfills its task, which is to reinforce the dictatorship of the proletariat, by accomplishing its own revolution as a ruling apparatus, and by opening its structures to the masses. (Criticism of the party and electoral replacements of committees and other party organizations is done *in the open*, with the participation of workers who are not members). This is the confirmation of an ever vital *mass line* which opens the party to "the new blood of the proletariat." Or, if we prefer, the hegemonic role of the party is strengthened in the vast confrontation which is proletarian democracy. Here again we perceive that this is different from the form of proletarian dictatorship adopted in the Soviet Union: the soviets plus the party as vanguard. There the party assumes the role of absolute leader, to the point where it stands above the masses (this is Stalin's pseudo-Leninism) and places them under the control of its apparatus. In China the party is the instrument of the revolution, not of the administration, and in this way its Leninist character is fully restored. But in this party, which by the mere fact of its existence cannot be the perfect prototype of a revolutionary guide, the line of a Liu Shao-chi may attempt to introduce the deviationist concept of a "party of administration, not of revolution." This revisionist deviation finds *the direct material basis* for its attack in the choice of a model for industrialization similar to the capitalist model (as the only one adopted by all societies born of the Industrial Revolution): that of accumulation. The capitalist accumulation model inevitably reproduces production relations in which hierarchical forms and the subdivision of positions of authority are crystallized, re-establishing a system of upper and lower strata, particularly through a new breed of specialists and "technocrats." Henceforth, it is not even enough to reject "the model of revisionist industrialization," or even to create another, revolutionary, model if we do not at the same time carry the revolution over into the social relations governed by production and thus into the entire ideological apparatus, including the party.

Even if those who see the party as an infallible and incorruptible guide find this fact difficult to accept, the revolution in ideology must still simultaneously intervene even in the party's vanguard and *ideological apparatus.*

Like the revolution in the classroom, the revolution in culture (theater, literature, art, information, the press, and science) underlies the revolution within the more strictly ideological and political superstructures (as a matter of fact, the Cultural Revolution began in 1964 as a cultural battle against the Peking Opera, then exploding in the schools, mobilizing the Red Guards, etc.). Althusser suggests the following list of ideological state apparatuses (a fairly complete list of the structures which should be dealt with in the revolution within the superstructure): "Education, family, the army as a people's army rather than professional one." Let us add: the union as an ideological apparatus, women's groups, youth groups, athletic associations. One could, writes Althusser, "ask by what right can we regard as *state* ideological structures institutions which for the most part have no public status but are simply *private* institutions." As a conscious Marxist, Gramsci had already foreseen this objection:

> The distinction between public and private is a distinction within the bourgeois legal system and is valid in the [subordinate] sectors in which the bourgeois system of law exercises its "powers." . . . The state, which is the state *of* the dominant class, is neither public nor private; on the contrary, it is the condition of any distinction between public and private. . . . Private institutions are perfectly able to "function" as state ideological apparatuses.

I shall return to the three state ideological apparatuses, the first of which, education, provides an invaluable example to anyone wanting to understand the Chinese Cultural Revolution. But first I shall go back to what Gramsci has said (in "Gli Intellettuali e l'organizzazione della cultura") concerning the role of education and the intellectuals, as an ideological apparatus, both in bourgeois society and in a socialist society still infested with the miasmas of the past:

> A fundamental characteristic of any group which aims to become dominant is its struggle to assimilate and to "ideologically" win over traditional intellectuals. Such assimilation and conquest are all the more rapid to the extent that the group in question elaborates and at the same time secretes organic intellectuals within its ranks . . . The distribution of various types of schools (academic and vocational) throughout the "economic" territory and the diverse aspirations of the various groups across the social scale determine and shape the production of the various branches of intellectual specialization. Thus in Italy the rural bourgeoisie gives rise in large measure to civil servants and members of the liberal professions, while the urban bourgeoisie produces technicians for industry. Consequently, northern Italy produces mainly technicians, and southern Italy produces chiefly civil servants and members of the liberal professions.

In his *La Pensée* article, Althusser also examines "the ideological state apparatus which plays the dominant role, although one hardly perceives it, so silent is its music—namely, the school." Starting in kindergarten, it takes children of every social class and from that tender age onward, using new methods and old, it inculcates "skills" (French, arithmetic, natural history, the sciences, and literature) sugar-coated with the dominant "ideology," and it does this for a number of years—the years in which the child is most "vulnerable," trapped between the family state apparatus and the school state apparatus. The young person is inculcated with the knowledge which determines his or her social status—worker, peasant, office worker, civil servant, manager, specialist, technician, administrator, professional ideologist, etc.—and each group is "equipped with the ideology suitable for the role it is to fill in the class society."

The revolution of teaching in China has shown that this type of parthenogenesis and reproduction of the traditional class ideological apparatus ran the risk of being perpetuated within the socialist school system exactly as in the bourgeois schools. If the proletariat does not impose its revolutionary ideology, the selection of pupils will be done in accordance with the criteria mentioned above: the son of the worker will be a worker, the son of the peasant will be a peasant, the son of the intellectual an intellectual, and so forth for the various occupations. (As I said, at Tsinghua University before the Cultural Revolution, 60 percent of the total number of students receiving university training did not belong to the working class.) The revolution in education has broken down all petty-bourgeois distinctions, on the one hand by reforming and reversing the mechanisms of selection (the vast majority of the students now come from the working classes), and, on the other, by closely linking theory and practice, manual work and intellectual labor, and thus destroying the distinction between *homo sapiens* and *homo faber* spoken of by Gramsci.

Petty-bourgeois "degradation" within the family takes place in the domain of the superstructure. Whereas the political sphere of the proletarian state is destined to move toward ever more advanced stages under the dictatorship of the proletariat, the "private" character of the family clashes with the "public" nature of power and acts as a retardation factor. For this reason the family must also be revolutionized and actively made to participate in Gramsci's "civil society."

To bring the revolution to the army may seem incomprehensible unless we take into account the chief characteristic of the Chinese army: it is a people's army which places politics before military practice. With the choice of a classic military strategy comes the danger of making the army a traditional fighting unit (a risk introduced by Peng Teh-huai), with the concomitant choice of giving priority to heavy industry and returning to an internal hierarchy involving the separation of the troops from their officers. We are then even liable to see the re-establishment of the bourgeois concept of a professional army. (In *State and Revolution* Lenin wrote that the bureaucracy and the standing army are "parasites" in the body of bourgeois society.)

From the Marxist-Leninist point of view, the entire theoretical significance of the Cultural Revolution can be summarized as follows: using Marx and Lenin as a starting point, China has learned by experience that the destruction of the bourgeois state and of its repressive and ideological structures must continue without interruption, because of the terrible force of tradition which is reborn and proliferates like a poisonous mushroom even under a system of collective ownership of the means of production. Thus collective ownership is completely inadequate as the sole guarantor of the development of proletarian dictatorship, and we can witness in it the reproduction of a system of social relations between individuals which once again divides them into haves and have-nots.

Proletarian democracy

If one accepts these observations up to this point as a working hypothesis and as notes for research, their synthesis on the level of political theory will be that the Cultural Revolution, the goal of which is the consolidation of the proletarian dictatorship, accompanied by a decline in the state's function of political coercion, thanks to the intervention of the proletariat in existing ideological structures. It sets in motion the inexhaustible participation of the masses, which accelerates and puts into concrete form the appearance of that proletarian democracy of which the Chinese speak. How else, moreover, are we to define the politicization of the masses which I saw during my trip? The moment the masses no longer fear coercion from the state apparatus, proletarian democracy begins to establish itself.

It is here, on the level of consensus, that the mass line conceived by Mao more than forty years ago undergoes its broadest development. This unprecedented reliance on the masses might merely conceal a pedagogical and academic character were it not based on a concrete social practice, did it not explode within the heart of the ideological apparatuses. "The essence of the revolution in the state bodies," says Mao, "consists in securing their link with the masses."

On the question of proletarian democracy, it seems to me that one of the most interesting contributions is made by Bettelheim in a study which appeared in *Les Temps modernes* (April 1971):

> Historical experience seems to show that the dominant element in the dictatorship of the proletariat is of necessity the ruling party. The latter alone can be organized around a proletarian line and function in accordance with the principles of democratic centralism. This is why the proletarian character of power, although it is dependent on the forms of state organization, rests above all on the existence of

> proletarian democratic relationships between the party and the masses (which brings us back to the concept of the mass line) as well as within the party. Such relationships cannot be written into the statutes of an organization; they can be developed only through long class struggles, and must be constantly strengthened by concrete struggles directed against the *separation* of power structures from the masses. . . . The constant reliance on the masses, therefore, seems to me to be the most decisive contribution made by the theory and practice of the Chinese Revolution. . . . In conclusion, it seems to me equally important to emphasize two questions which are closely linked. First, Mao Tse-tung's conception of the relationship of the party to the masses in no way lessens the *fundamental role* of a Marxist-Leninist party in the struggle for socialism; exactly the opposite is true. Secondly, Mao Tse-tung restores to the decisive concept of the "*dictatorship of the proletariat*" its *true significance*, a significance which had been completely obliterated by Stalinist practice, namely, that this dictatorship is also, and of necessity, *the broadest democracy for the masses of the people*, that is, for the people as a whole, for the proletariat and for all the classes which are fighting at its side and which have a stake in socialism, hence for the great majority of the people of a country. Dictatorship as repression should be exercised only over a tiny group of people, while the broadest masses of the people should have the most complete freedom of speech and demonstration, *including the freedom to be mistaken*. . . . Politically, these two points seem to me to be decisive, because for well-known historical reasons the concept of the dictatorship of the proletariat has been grossly distorted, the term being used to designate a dictatorship exercised over the masses, whereas its content is completely different. What the Chinese Revolution reminds us is that the dictatorship of the proletariat is nothing other than *proletarian democracy*, democracy for the broadest masses of the people.

The fact that the proletarian masses do not possess revolutionary consciousness as a metaphysical endowment, but that the function of leadership is, if necessary, exercised from above and by the party, does not in any way contradict the principle of "from the masses to the masses": it makes short work of the spontaneity and anarchy that people thought could be identified with the Cultural Revolution. The role of the leadership nucleus within the party is to "concentrate the correct ideas of the masses" by distilling them from the latter's experience and then returning them to the masses in a developed form, carrying these ideas once again from the masses to the party, in an endless unbroken dialectical relationship. According to Lin Piao, "We must consider ourselves an integral part of the revolutionary force; at the same time, we must continually regard ourselves as a target of the revolution."

At this point a question arises: What about Mao? Is he not regarded as a demigod? Doesn't a cult of Mao exist in China?

The "cult of Mao"

In such a rigorously Marxist context, doesn't the "cult of Mao" reintroduce that "false consciousness" which for Marx and Engels was inherent in the concept of ideology (whereas for Lenin the term also designates the authentically revolutionary consciousness of the proletariat)? In the West it is said that if in Chinese ideology we find constant exaltation of, and obsessional recourse to, Mao's thought, is there not a danger of a "personality cult" and hence of "false consciousness," even if the results are positive? Then another question is asked: if the participation and politicization of the Chinese masses in the realm of ideology are positive factors (particularly when compared to the depoliticization, political opacity, and absenteeism of the masses in Soviet and other socialist societies), isn't the creative drive of the Chinese masses continually and exclusively inspired from above, is it not linked exclusively to Mao and his cult?

To answer this question, I think we must first posit a concept, one which underlies all of the preceding observations: that of the qualitative leap represented by the Cultural Revolution—the transition from ideology as it is understood and practiced in a class society, to ideology as it should be practiced in a socialist society. A decisive point for the demonstration of a truly revolutionary function of the political organization and all the ideological structures born of the Cultural Revolution is precisely the fact that all forms of "false consciousness" in what we designate here as a "cult" have been surmounted. For when we Westerners speak of a cult we mean something which would be the exact opposite of the creative initiative of the masses, and would be contrary as well to Mao's philosophy (as it is summarized by the "mass line").

Let us first clarify one point: is it correct here to use the expression (or the phraseology) "personality cult" as used by Khrushchev? First, the term prevents us from understanding the Chinese, who vigorously reject it because, they say, Khrushchev invented it and then used it in his own way for as long as he held power. Second, the expression is not Marxist. It masks the true problems that arose in the USSR, namely, the re-establishment of Leninist party life and leadership, and the relations between structure and superstructure in Soviet society. In the third place, if by the term "cult" we understand a certain prestige relationship existing between a revolutionary leader and the masses, a kind of "cult" (esteem, respect) toward the leader is necessary to the extent that his words must carry weight.

One day when we were discussing these problems, the Chinese said to my husband, "Your articles in *Unità* will be influential only to the extent that an esteem or a certain sort of cult exists toward you among your readers." We laughed, but the meaning was clear. Our influential interlocuter then added, in a polemical tone: "Let's end the hypocrisy—doesn't this type of 'cult' also exist in your own societies toward leaders? When one of them gives a speech, isn't his picture published in the newspapers? When he holds a press conference, aren't pictures of him all over television? And what about the 'cult' surrounding Churchill, Roosevelt, and de Gaulle when they were still alive? The man in charge has always felt a psychological-political need to be admired, especially in times of historical crisis. It's not a 'Chinese' phenomenon, a 3,000-year-old admiration for the emperor which has been transferred to Mao, 'the son of heaven,' but a universally widespread and sometimes profoundly human factor. The need to unite everyone around Mao, especially during the period of the Cultural Revolution, was a political necessity. Now it no longer seems as urgent."

To explain the "cult" as the prestige of an important individual, the Chinese quote Lenin: the political consciousness of the proletariat comes to it from without. They also quote the famous thought that no class in history has come to power without having found within itself the political leadership and vanguard capable of organizing and leading the movement. The Chinese are opposed to any exaggerated role of the individual, but they reaffirm the principles of Leninism in relationships among leaders, the party, class, and masses.

To explain everything we find negative in the "personality cult" more precisely, we would have to change the terminology used by Khrushchev and speak instead of a "dogma" imposed by the leading individual. Such dogmatism was characteristic of Stalin, but it is the antithesis of the spirit of Mao. Here we return to the heart of the problem.

From the viewpoint of the workers' movement, clarification of this point is absolutely essential. The question of the omnipresence of Mao, which in the eyes of many people appears as a "cult-dogma" with overtones of Stalinism, must be cleared up. A preliminary distinction must be made between Mao and *Mao's thought*. The thought is distinct from the man; it will survive him, as Marxism survived Marx and Leninism survived Lenin. All the prophets who proclaim the crumbling of China when Mao disappears will see that his thought will continue to mold the thinking of millions of people, as was the case for the thinking of Confucius—with the difference that Mao is a Marxist-Leninist theoretician.

But this distinction between person and thought, though important, is not enough. I must reaffirm a concept which was verified throughout my entire trip: Mao's thought is the opposite of Stalinist dogmatism. Mao is the Marxist theoretician who possesses to the highest degree a feeling for differences in situations, for combinations of circumstances, for reality, for inequalities. *Difference* and *inequality* (according to an expression of Althusser's in a still unpublished text) are the two concepts which dominate Mao's thought, within a system of thought which follows the major themes of Marxist philosophy. "People are right to rebel: this is the first lesson of Marxism." This is one of Mao's ultra-concentrated formulations; it is also the one which best expresses the break with the dogmatism of Stalin.

In the chapters on the party, education, philosophy in the factory, and the army, I tried to show, in the living reality of the masses, this revolutionary and exceedingly antidogmatic lesson taught us by the Cultural Revolution.

Dogma and revolutionary line

The objective role of Mao Tse-tung's thought is the ideological arming of the masses. In the USSR, on the other hand, the official apparatus had recourse to Stalin so as to increase the ideological repression of the masses. The bourgeoisie, and especially its radical-leaning social-democratic wing, has acquired the habit of comparing Mao with Stalin in order to make them both symbols of dictatorship and oppression. But does not the "prudery" shown by these ultra-democrats with regard to China serve to mask their own role as prostitutes in the active service of the liberal bourgeoisie?

There is a *radical difference* between Stalin and Mao. Stalin was the personification of dogmatism, authoritarianism ("the cadres decide everything"), the state apparatus, the cult of technology ("technology decides everything"). He was the "apparatchik" raised above the masses. The apparatus he directed did not hesitate to use repression against the workers and peasants, and it enjoyed tremendous advantages. Mao is basically antidogmatic and antiauthoritarian. He gives the initiatives of the masses priority over the state apparatus; he insists on the principles of equality; and he reiterates that the party cannot take the place of the masses, and that *the masses must liberate themselves.*

When Communists make mistakes, the Chinese Communist Party attempts to save them, based on the directive that "95 percent of the cadres are healthy." This is exactly the opposite of the Stalinist work of destruction. In "Our Study and the Current Situation," written in 1944, Mao explains:

> We should lay the stress not on the responsibility of certain individual comrades, but on the analysis of the circumstances in which the errors were committed, on the content of the errors. . . . this should be done in the spirit of "learning from past mistakes to avoid future ones" and "curing the sickness to save the patient," in order to achieve the twofold objective of clarity in ideology and unity among comrades.

Many Chinese cadres whose positions were very different from those of Mao remained in the party, and even on the Central Committee. Thus, after the line they were supporting was rejected, Li

Li-san and later Wang Ming remained members of the Central Committee. They were removed at the Ninth Congress, but they are apparently still members of the party, at least if we are to believe the English magazine *Broadsheet* (March 1970), the organ of the China Policy Study Group. The names of revisionist leaders, publicly announced at meetings in China, number not more than four or five (Liu Shao-chi, Teng Hsiao-ping, Peng Chen, and two or three others); actually, only one name appears everywhere: that of Liu Shao-chi.

In Peking we were told that Chen Yi, who still held the title of Minister of Foreign Affairs but was no longer exercising the functions of that office, is supposed to have told Mao that he did not have the courage to attend the Ninth Congress because of the hostility he sensed and because of what he feared was going to happen. "No, on the contrary," Mao replied, "you must go, you'll represent the opposition." When the former head of Tsinghua University replied to the revolutionary committee for the tenth time, "No, I don't want to participate in the work of running the university; I'm convinced you're wrong and are leading the university to its ruin," the revolutionary committee and the head exchanged greetings, and the head then returned to his work in the university truck shop, while the revolutionary committee went about managing university affairs.

For the person who has emerged from an experience similar to mine in China, the objective role of Mao's thought seems the opposite of a dogmatic catechism. As can be seen in all the evidence I have collected, this thought arms the masses ideologically and provides a continuous link between theory and practical experience. Mao's aversion to book learning has long been common knowledge (see in particular an article written in 1941), and the reading of the little red book, when it is merely insipid repetition, is criticized and ridiculed at public meetings. Arming of the masses with an ideology and placing them in a position to adapt themselves to Marxism-Leninism and the thought of Mao Tse-tung is much more than simply asking them to recite quotations; it means exerting a steady pressure in the direction of a new revolutionary consciousness which prevents them from submitting to orders opposed to the building of socialism. Theses such as those on "blind obedience," "against servility in the party," "against docile obedience to leaders" (see the chapter devoted to the party), completely contradict the idea that party members must be "docile tools," "respect the majority no matter what line it chooses," accept any solution at all for the sake of peace (for "internal peace"), in short, be disciplined, sheep-like functionaries completely lacking in independent judgment of party policies. Mao tirelessly preaches the value of rebellion; he approved the first "red rebels"; he sent a message of greeting to the rebel workers of Shanghai. It is in rebellion that the Cultural Revolution effects a new takeover of power.

Where is Stalin in all this? With Stalin's methods, a few days would have sufficed to eliminate Liu Shao-chi. But Mao rejects these methods, just as he rejects every "palace revolution." Khrushchev himself was overthrown in a single night, to our great astonishment and that of the Soviet Union. I still remember the headline in the London *Sunday Times* (I was waiting for the results of the English elections): "Wilson in, Khrushchev out." The Cultural Revolution is a discussion launched from above, but its evolution is *not planned in advance*. It is taking place among millions of men, among the masses, in complete freedom.

The method of discussion: here the Cultural Revolution has made a completely new contribution to the workers' movement. It has done this by placing texts which supply all the terms of the debate in the hands of the masses. Liu Shao-chi's work, *How to Be a Good Communist*, became, as we have seen, one of the bases of every debate about the party. The basic texts of Khrushchev have been disseminated throughout China. The Chinese even say that Peking is the only city where you can find the complete works of Khrushchev—they are not available in Moscow. The Chinese called to our attention the fact that all the Soviet attacks against the Chinese, as well as the full exchange of letters between the Chinese and Soviet Communist parties at the beginning of the break, were published in full in Peking. I was constantly told in China that if the Soviet Union really wanted to begin discussion of the Sino-Russian disagreement, they should make the texts of Mao Tse-tung available to the masses of their own country for discussion. In short, the story that the Chinese read only the works of Mao seems false and unfounded. In China, freedom as *viewed from* *the left* means public debate *at all levels.* As I have already said, it is the broadest political debate in history. And by necessity it signifies the maturing of the masses in the fire of struggle, a maturing process which is to make class consciousness increasingly lucid. For Mao, a victory won from above would have been of no interest. "This revolution aims not only to dismiss a handful of people; it is a major revolution in the superstructure." * The revolution—every true revolution—is born within the masses. Here alone it can *achieve its ultimate goal*: to revolutionize the mentality of human beings thoroughly and to give them a revolutionary drive based on a sound choice, achieved in the fire of the struggle "between two classes, two roads, and two lines."

In this context the Cultural Revolution, which like any political struggle is a struggle for power, is in no way a surprise attack inside a "forbidden city." On the contrary, Mao's struggle against a ruling faction of the party, the leader of which was Liu Shao-chi, began at least as early as 1958, the period of the Great Leap Forward. At that time Mao did not in any way appear as a demigod; he was a member of the minority. He succeeded in winning victory for his line by patiently modeling a new superstructure which would lead the masses to express their own opinion on a valid option of socialist construction for China. The defeat of Liu's economist-revisionist line was accomplished during a political struggle within the masses. We said earlier that when Mao, in a spectacular gesture, wrote his Marxist-Leninist tatzupao, the keynote of which was "bombard the headquarters," the workers and students did not know where the enemy was, that they asked the location of the headquarters to be bombarded, that they wondered who could pos-

* *People's Daily,* July 1, 1971. This same article continues: "The Cultural Revolution could also be called the 'Second Chinese Revolution.' At first many comrades did not fully understand this Great Proletarian Cultural Revolution. When the masses rose in revolt and split into two groups which clashed violently, people thought for a time that the country was in a state of complete chaos. Some even asked why, since just a small group consisting of Liu Shao-chi and his accomplices had usurped some of the powers of the dictatorship of the proletariat, Chairman Mao did not simply order them dismissed. But then why make use of such a method [the Cultural Revolution]? Experience has shown that dismissal, a system which is very often used, cannot solve the problem."

sibly oppose the "revolutionary headquarters of Mao" and support the other one, which was only later defined as bourgeois. Only after August 16, 1966, did the Red Guards begin to write the name of Liu Shao-chi on the walls of Peking University. The struggle was long and difficult, and it was a life-and-death struggle, as the Chinese say, a struggle destined to bring about the emergence from this political turmoil of a critical analysis in both factory and classroom. Everything—the party, the unions, the Communist Youth League, economic and political choices—had to be passed through the sieve of criticism. The masses had to become conscious of deviations, latent degeneration, and—the gravest possible danger for a Chinese—the *return to the past.* The contradictions exploded in the course of the political debate carried on by the masses.

The Cultural Revolution was nothing other than this attempt to disseminate and raise class consciousness; the thought of Mao Tse-tung is in fact nothing other than the effort to disseminate a living Marxism-Leninism, without which the march toward socialism is impossible. It is the absolute condition for socialism that it be taken over by the masses; it has an absolute need to express itself politically among the masses. I spoke at length of the tatzupao spread over the walls of factories and cities. Like science and technology, Marxism-Leninism (including its philosophy) should not be a field reserved to specialists. This body of phenomena—dissemination of ideology, participation of the masses in the field of ideology, freedom from all fear toward the ruling apparatus, the awakening of a genuine proletarian democracy—has absolutely nothing to do with Stalinism.

A critique of Stalinism from the left

Two other points seem to me essential for the history of the Marxist-Leninist workers' movement. The first is that the Chinese have offered concrete and sustained criticism of Stalinist policy and have constantly followed a policy which is different from, and often in opposition to, the one which Stalin attempted to impose upon Mao Tse-tung and the Chinese Revolution. History has taken it upon itself to show the serious errors of this Stalinist line. The second point is that Chinese critique of Stalinism is *from the left* (a concept which Althusser elaborates in an as yet unpublished text), whereas all Western criticism, including that of certain leftist or Trotskyite groups, is from the right.

It is true that the critique of Stalin in China remains incomplete. The presence of likenesses of Stalin may mislead us. For many of us, this unfinished critique is irritating. But when one expresses critical opinions of Stalin's policy in China—and this happened to us—one is listened to attentively. In the recent article commemorating the Paris Commune, there are dozens of quotations from Marx, Engels, and Lenin, but Stalin's name is mentioned only once, and that out of historical necessity, to say that Lenin founded the first socialist state and Stalin reinforced it. Not once during our short trip did we hear Stalin quoted, whereas Marx and Lenin, not to mention Mao Tse-tung, were quoted abundantly. The criticism leveled at Stalin in a 1967 *Red Flag* article entitled "Notes for a Major Historical Document" speaks of "Stalin's theoretical defects." This is a discreet criticism, but one which throws a light "from the left" on the accusations made by the Chinese against Stalin. In stating that complete victory in all areas of the economy is an accomplished fact, in talking about the end of the class struggle, in saying that contradictions between social groups are decreasing and that economic tensions are disappearing, and in claiming that the social nature of the means of production fully corresponds to the social nature of the process of production, Stalin forgot, on the theoretical level, that the problem of knowing *who* is going to win the revolutionary victory still remains to be solved, that this is the task to be accomplished under the dictatorship of the proletariat, and that if the problem is not solved correctly, there is a danger that the bourgeoisie will return to power. When, in contrast, Stalin began to speak of a worsening of the class struggle within the socialist society, it was only to make this the "ideological" motivation for a repression generated from above.

Where, if not precisely here, are the roots of Khrushchev's "usurpation of the party and the state," for which the Chinese hold the Soviet Communist Party responsible? If we consider, as the Chinese do, that Liu Shao-chi (defined as China's Khrushchev) is, when all is said and done, a more "right-wing" Stalin, we can deduce that revisionism follows directly from Stalinism. And are not Stalin's errors (even if he is called a "fervent proletarian revolutionary") those very faults of which Liu Shao-chi is accused?

In 1936, at the time Stalin was proclaiming the internal cohesiveness of the USSR, stating that there were no longer any contradictions within the people, police repression was beginning. *If there are no enemies within, there are foreign agents*; if there are no contradictions within the people, it is because the class struggle is being stirred up from without by agents who are sabotaging socialism—whence the obsession with espionage, plots, and betrayals, whence the purges and the repression. But when Khrushchev characterized Stalin as a bloodthirsty imbecile, the Chinese were irritated because the definition seemed to them hasty and non-Marxist. The Chinese reproach Stalin for having abandoned Leninism in party life, suppressed collective leadership, used methods of government which separated the party from the masses, practiced authoritarianism with regard to other Communist parties, and granted privileges to technicians and high-ranking politicians. The Chinese said that in the Soviet Union people were content to denounce the violence and liberate the prisoners of the Stalinist era, and after that "de-Stalinization" was considered finished. Actually it had not even begun. Here "Khrushchev revisionism" found fertile soil. In reality there is a continuity rather than a break between Stalin and Khrushchev.

If we examine matters closely, we find that the Chinese harshly condemn Stalin's errors. In the light of the Cultural Revolution, we understand that for Mao, Stalin's mistake was the break with the masses, the repression of their initiatives, a policy of coercion practiced during the transitional phase—precisely at the time when in order to consolidate the dictatorship of the proletariat it was necessary to broaden consensus, strengthen class hegemony, and politicize the masses in order to create a genuine proletarian democracy. If, as Bettelheim says, constant reliance on the masses is the fundamental characteristic of the Cultural Revolution, Stalinism is exactly the opposite. While until now the Chinese have not wanted to openly make a critique of Stalin from the left, they have firmly fought against criticism of Khrushchev leveled from the right. But Mao's speech "On the Correct Handling of Contradictions Among the People," one year after the Twentieth Congress, already revealed a conception which is fundamentally different from the Stalinist conception of development during the socialist phase. This divergence from the Soviet type of development has become increasingly radical.

Thus the Cultural Revolution is explained not only by the problems which arose during the fifty years of history of the workers' movement, but also by the crisis of Stalinism in the USSR and in the socialist countries, especially Czechoslovakia and Poland. The Chinese are constantly re-examining these experiences in the light of day-to-day practice. When they take the road opposed to the Stalinist road, domestically as well as on the international level of relationships among the parties, they are making a *critique from the left*. They have followed such a road throughout their entire revolutionary history, and especially during their Cultural Revolution. The Chinese refuse to see in the Stalinist road a socialist "model" valid for all other Communist parties. At the same time they reject the subordination of the Communist parties to Moscow, the concept of the patriarchal or guide state. They advocate autonomy for every country and every party within the framework of a strong internationalism which permits each country and each revolutionary party to profit by what is best in the revolutionary heritage of the other parties.

In connection with this last point, is it necessary to recall a fact which is common knowledge? The relations between Mao and Stalin were always bad. Stalin never believed in the socialist revolution in China—until its victory; but he took a great interest in China in terms of the defense of the Soviet frontiers. In the twenties, thirties, and forties, and as late as 1945, the Chinese Communists suffered personally from Stalin's mistakes, the Chinese said in "On the Question of Stalin," which dates from 1963 and which is the article most favorable to Stalin that can be found. Stalin refused to understand Mao's strategy with regard to the peasants, and the "Report on the Peasant Movement in Hunan" was rejected by the Communist International and by Stalin personally as a non-Marxist analysis. Mao seemed to Stalin to be a kind of rebel chieftain at the head of peasant hordes, rather than a Marxist-Leninist. Borodin, who settled in Canton in 1923 as an agent of the International, was, according to Mao, a man who understood nothing of the peasants. When Mao is accused of having adapted Marxism to China, he is actually being paid a tribute which distinguishes him from foreign models. Mao has never made a dogma out of Marxism; he understood that the scientific principles of Marxism and Leninism formed the theoretical basis which made it possible to solve the particular problems of the revolutionary transformation of Chinese society. After this, is it necessary to recall that according to the most authoritative Marxist theoreticians, with the essay "On Contradiction" Mao gave Marxism its most advanced contemporary elaboration?

To return to the relations between Mao and Stalin, it must be remembered that in 1945 Stalin believed that Chiang Kai-shek's 2.5-million-strong army was going to scatter the numerically very inferior and poorly armed Communist troops; hence the advice to Mao to give up the struggle and enter the Chiang Kai-shek government as a minority group. On the eve of Japan's surrender (August 15, 1945), Stalin had signed a thirty-year treaty of alliance with Chiang Kai-shek, by which the Soviet Union recognized Chiang's government as the sole legitimate Chinese government. The story is told that during the war of liberation Stalin had sent Mao a treatise on the method of conducting a partisan war, and that Mao handed the work to Liu Shao-chi with the remark, "Read this if you want to know what you have to do to get us all killed."

In his *History of the Cold War*, André Fontaine writes that the Soviet press, which had shown great discretion toward China, did not begin to echo Mao Tse-tung's words until 1947, and then very suddenly. Until the entrance of the people's forces into Peking, Stalin continued to believe in Chiang Kai-shek's victory, a repeat of the elimination of the Communists in 1927. But in victory after victory the people's army upset Chiang's forces everywhere, and on October 1, 1949, the People's Republic of China was born. In the following year, on the occasion of Stalin's sixtieth birthday, Mao went to Moscow, and on February 14, 1950, he signed a treaty of mutual assistance for thirty years, against every threat coming from Japan or from any state allied with Japan.

In conclusion, the Chinese Communist Party was never, at any moment in its history, a Stalinist party—even if Mao and the Chinese gave Stalin his due, especially for the way he waged the struggle during the Second World War.

What Mao represents to the Chinese

I have written at length about the presence, throughout China, of portraits of Mao. The Chinese use them to decorate their homes, the machines in their shops, their bicycles, buses, trains, hotels, the carts in which they haul wood, and here and there place Mao's portrait in the fields, cities, and even the pagodas. Even if this enthusiasm, as we noted earlier, will in the future inevitably lose some of its "feverishness"—which the Chinese link to the intensity of the political struggle—it is still necessary to go beyond surface appearances. It seems to me that this phenomenon is explained first of all by the importance of Mao's thought, and then by what Mao the human being represents to the Chinese. This Marxist theoretician both led socialism to victory in China, and for twenty-two years fought the longest guerrilla war in history, tearing China away from feudalism, capitalism, and colonialism. When the Chinese say that their "spiritual atomic bomb is Mao's thought" (I heard it in a film), the expression may seem ridiculous to us, but it simply confirms the importance of Mao's presence in the long and difficult struggle of the Chinese working class and the Chinese people. For hundreds of millions of Chinese, once slaves of a feudal, colonial regime, Mao, the leader of the People's Liberation Army, quite simply represents freedom, and the feeling of the Chinese people toward him is one of boundless gratitude. Certain youthful portraits depict a dreamy, visionary, handsome Mao, in military uniform or in a blue tunic; he reminds us of Che Guevara, who aroused so much enthusiasm among the younger generation. But Guevara, unfortunately, did not win his war. Mao won socialist power by theory and weapons. Moreover, Mao, after founding the socialist state in 1949, has been its theoretical and political leader for twenty years. Imagine a Lenin who after the October Revolution directed the construction of the Soviet state for more than twenty years! What is difficult (especially for certain political leaders) to understand is that for the Chinese Mao represents a *synthe-*

sis of the entire theoretical and practical experience of socialism from its origins until the present day. To be sure, it is a "Chinese" synthesis, but perhaps it is not exclusively Chinese. As soon as we consider Mao's work from this point of view, we begin to glimpse the real relationship between Mao and his people. In the eyes of the Chinese, Mao has the same stature and the same prestige as Lenin. Who would talk today about a cult of Lenin?

When Snow asked Mao, at the beginning of 1965, if the Soviet accusation of a "cult of personality" had any basis in fact, Mao answered that perhaps there was some. But Snow added that the phenomenon is more complex than foreigners are willing to admit. And Mao in his rambling conversation with the American writer at the end of December 1970, is supposed to have said that the reason he had felt a reinforcement of the "cult" was necessary was political: it had been necessary to stimulate the masses in order to dismantle the anti-Mao party bureaucracy at that time when he had lost control of many controlling levers in certain regions and provinces, and even in Peking. But he now felt that things were different, and that this "cult," which seemed necessary at the time, must diminish. He wants no more flattering titles. He wants only to be called "teacher," that is, "educator," "schoolmaster," as he was in the beginning. Snow further says that Mao is supposed to be "embarrassed" by this cult around his portraits, and he is supposed to have very frankly demonstrated this during the parade of October 1, 1970.* This would seem to confirm the idea that in 1967 it

---

* During the past months those interviews with Snow in which Mao takes up this question of "cult" have been translated into Chinese and submitted to cadres for study and discussion. The cancellation of the October 1 parade, the privilege and glory of the capital, occurred suddenly in 1971. Nevertheless, this ceremony had been frequently changed, starting in 1959 with the cancellation of the military parade, and later during the Cultural Revolution with the deepening politicization and greater moderation. That the October 1 parade—an impressive and "exclusive" event in the capital which has celebrated the national liberation holiday since 1950—has been replaced by popular demonstrations throughout the entire country (festivities which share something of the style of the July 14 festivities in France or the July 4 celebrations in the United States) could perhaps indicate a decision to coordinate the movement toward a decentralization of power, a movement begun in 1958 and extensively developed during the Cultural Revolution.

was Mao himself who suppressed the expression "great teacher, guide, commander-in-chief and helmsman," which appeared in the communique announcing the explosion of the first H-bomb. It seems certain that Mao does not abuse his immense popularity. The party, the state, and the nation make use of Mao rather as they would a mediator, because of his power of communication (for us completely unimaginable) with the masses—masses, as I have said, among whom he enjoys the prestige of a Lenin, to the point where at times people have been able to use his name purely as a tool. It even happened that Liu Shao-chi and his partisans, while in practice opposed to Maoism, made great use of the cult of Mao! From this comes the well-known phrase, "waving the red flag to oppose the red flag."

One element of Mao's strength is that he takes a long-range view of history, in terms of hundreds and thousands of years, and places himself, not without irony, in the context of this infinity. In 1965, in that conversation with Snow, he noted that the people of the democratic-bourgeois period were superior to those of the feudal era, and said that people of future generations will have knowledge far superior to that of our contemporaries. Then he added that, "A thousand years from now all of them, even Marx, Engels, and Lenin, would possibly appear rather ridiculous." This is how Mao sees himself in relation to history and to the future of China and the entire world.

What about the Great Proletarian Cultural Revolution? It merely paves the way for the stages of a revolutionary future which belongs to the dialectics of history. "The Great Proletarian Cultural Revolution," Mao said in 1967, "is only the first of a series. There will of necessity be several of these revolutions in the future . . . The cadres of the party and the people must be careful not to believe that everything will go well after one, two, three, or four cultural revolutions. We must maintain a particularly keen intensity, and never relax our vigilance."

Will this first cultural revolution, of which we are the contemporaries and the witnesses, be victorious? I think I can answer that the victory was won from the moment the revolution came into existence. Paraphrasing Marx on the subject of the Commune, we may say that the principles of the Cultural Revolution could not be destroyed, and that they will be current as long as the working class has not achieved its liberation.

Liberation from all schemas and models

To understand the Cultural Revolution better, and to attempt to analyze its method (instead of being satisfied merely to declare that one wishes to do it), we must first of all know the facts, for without them no theoretical and political analysis is valid. The purpose is not only to avoid the temptations of exaltation and despair, but above all to liberate oneself from all schematic thinking. This is the first revolutionary experience which has taken place under the dictatorship of the proletariat, and as such it is destined to acquire a universal scope and validity. Let us forget the unfortunate phrase "Chinese model," which merely places obstacles in the way of the person who wishes to understand it. This is not a prototype but a vital and continuing process which marks a turning point in the socialist revolution. For many militants, and for leftists uninformed of what is going on in China, or worse yet, nurtured on distorted information, an understanding of the Cultural Revolution cannot be acquired easily and quickly. I, for my part, have attempted to relate facts, to help the reader to catch a glimpse, in particular, of the long-term consequences of the events as they are already seen everywhere in China.

To speak of an "apologia for a myth" or a "noncritical approach" in connection with such a plan seems to me to be an error of method. Such reflexes have their origin both in old mystifications and in the habit, intellectual as well as political (Stalinist), of considering that "the line" has been laid down once and for all in black and white, with the necessary red and blue pencil marks, even for a great process which is still continuing.

Others place the cart before the horse and, before going more deeply into the study of the Cultural Revolution, declare that it cannot be a solution, even while recognizing that it provides an alternative for anyone who wishes to escape from the crisis connected with the Stalinist system. Thus they cunningly substitute a new preconception for the possibility of objective analysis.

Finally, there are those who do not wish "to be burned twice." Bitter personal memories combine with their emotion in the face of the Chinese experience and the traumas left over from by-gone attitudes of triumph when the Communist parties claimed to be linked to the USSR by an "iron bond," as Togliatti said.

It seems to me that among the leftists of the West there are two hypocritical attitudes with regard to China. There is the attitude of those who are frightened and grimace when they see intellectuals doing manual labor. Then there is the attitude of the politicians, for whom China must remain a taboo subject out of fear of contaminating the proletariat of our own countries with the "Yellow Peril." Both are obeying an old reflex: deep down they believe that the Chinese could liberate us from our political helplessness and pull our chestnuts out of the fire. By a curious transference, those who are most obstinately denying the universal scope of the Chinese revolution identify with those who supported and still support the thesis of the exportation of the revolution; supposedly it is now the turn of the Chinese revolution, since the Soviet revolution let the moment slip by.

Then there are those who love an imaginary China, an absolute socialist "model," sometimes anarchistic, sometimes libertarian and without a Communist Party, a kind of perpetual motion of the masses in which the withering away of the state is supposed to have already occurred. These are the supporters of the flight forward and of perpetual defeats. However, they have already had mishaps; they went from Khrushchevism to anti-Khrushchevism, from Castroism to anti-Castroism, and their current unconditional and mindless Maoism is undoubtedly just another passing phase. Having seen the corruption of the world and having had their fill of everything they demand of the society of consumption, the people who frequent the left-wing salons of Paris, Rome, London, and New York dream of China as a last refuge. In a bad Italian film one of the characters who has just tried an experiment—sleeping with his wife and her lover—asks, "How will it all end?" "That's obvious," the friend answers. "It will end with the arrival of the Chinese, and with them purity will return . . ." The Chinese do not seem to have the slightest idea of the use to which they are put in the West:

to each his own. The Chinese would certainly be very surprised by this. When one alludes to it, they change the subject.

We could continue this list of ways of looking at China. To those mentioned we should add the bourgeois Sinologists who are following the Chinese experience as if it was in a test tube, and who are personally as interested in Marxism-Leninism-Maoism as I am in the habits of beetles. Then there is the literary set, full of stylistic subtleties, frivolous laughter, and embellishments which have scarcely changed since the eighteenth century: this group now wishes to make us feel how immeasurably Asian and distant China is. (Moravia's book, written, according to the Chinese, after a sojourn of seven days in Peking, ends with the statement that after having fled from China like Don Juan [Moravia] before the stone guest [Mao], he at last reached Hong Kong, the city which is "a challenge to Mao Tse-tung's China or, better yet, between Mao's China and the whole world," and that he felt at home in this "beautiful, very beautiful" city whose beauty "is reminiscent of that of New York, just as the beauty of a younger sister is sometimes reminiscent of that of her senior." After having insisted on the "Confucianization of Marxist thought wrought by Mao," and after much ironic nonsense about his Chinese interlocutors, Moravia shouts with genuine enthusiasm from the terrace of his ridiculous skyscraper, "Hong Kong is a rejuvenated city.") *

There are also the generations of students who joined the struggle against capitalism at the time of the imperialist war in Vietnam. For them China speaks a language which is immediately intelligible, poses no major problem of translation, and is transmitted si-

---

* Moravia's *Cultural Revolution in China* is among the most ludicrous interpretations of the Cultural Revolution. In his view, the Red Guards, "the most inexperienced" group of the people, "catapulted, like a Second Children's Crusade, for one year, from one end of China to the other," were the chief tool used by Mao to retain his power against the faithless bureaucracy! It is well known that the Children's Crusade in the Middle Ages consisted of a throng of children who had been turned into fanatics by the religious customs. They were formed into a group and sent to the Turkish shores to liberate the Holy Sepulchre. But the waters of the Mediterranean, unlike those of the Red Sea, did not part before them, and the children were captured and sold into slavery.

multaneously throughout the world with lightning speed. Let us note in this connection that it is very true that revolutionary ideas travel by themselves. In China I often heard workers and students using slogans similar to those used by the "contesters" of May 1968—words that no one had brought from Paris to Peking. For example the machine tool workers in Shanghai punctuated certain moments of their battles during the Cultural Revolution with the phrase, "Become so angry that you grind your teeth." But these young people in the West, who are drawing closer to China with such vitality, suffer at the same time from lack of power. Their first problem is the absence of any link with the working class, with the Western proletariat and its vanguard, without which the success of a revolutionary movement is unthinkable.

Finally, there is the Communists' way, be they friends or foes of China. Perhaps they are the ones who feel the closest brotherhood with the Chinese, and who best understand China and what is happening there—whether they love or hate it and even when they approach only to reject the Chinese experience. Whether we like it or not, it is the thought of Mao Tse-tung which, objectively, in spite of all official condemnations, influences the masses of Communist cadres and, especially, the rank and file of the Communist parties, both in the East and the West.

If I understood them correctly, the Chinese refuse to "solve our problems" or give us the pattern to be followed in order to build socialism in countries such as ours. I should add that I also have the impression that the Chinese are doing nothing to support this or that organization, this or that "pro-Chinese" group, directly. Their attitude seems to be dictated by the principle that the Chinese experience is at the service of all revolutionaries, but each revolutionary must think out for himself the correct solution to the problems of the revolution in his country. This requires the fullest use of our intelligence. In "Our Study and the Current Situation," Mao wrote:

> This mechanism, the brain, has the special function of thinking. Mencius said, "The office of the mind is to think." He defined the function of the brain correctly. We should always use our brains and think everything over carefully. A common saying goes, "Knit the brows and you will hit upon a strategem." In other words, much

> thinking yields wisdom. . . . If we get rid of our baggage and start up the machinery, if we march with light packs and know how to think hard, then we are sure to triumph.

In short, we need an inventive brain which is capable of imagination. "The imagination has seized power" is the slogan from May 1968 which has the richest implications. "Lack of imagination means that one cannot even imagine its absence."

In *l'Ordino Nuovo* Gramsci wrote that we need every bit of our intelligence. This imperious and continuous appeal addressed to the movement to produce ideas, liberate the creative spirit, and awaken the imagination, is the first commandment of all the theoreticians who have developed Marxism-Leninism. This is exactly what Mao did in his constant study of Soviet and Western experiences, from the Paris Commune down to our own times—not out of a desire to imitate them but so as to draw from them the lessons suited to the *concrete situation* of China, the *particular nature* of its revolution. His message on the occasion of the one-hundredth anniversary of the Commune, sent from Peking to the world movement one month before the opening of the chapter of "ping-pong diplomacy," contains perhaps the most important appeal ever made by China to the proletariat and the peoples of the world. It reiterates the suggestion that they make the revolutionary outlook their primary concern for the present, basing their work on the fundamental principles of Marxism. At the same time, the appeal calls upon the movement to analyze the specific features of its own revolution, to study its own history, to make a concrete analysis of its specific situation, totally independent of any "model," to adopt the revolutionary experience of other countries as its own in order to fuse it with one's own reality, *not by transposing it mechanically.**

* The editorial in *People's Daily, Red Flag,* and *Liberation Army Daily* on the fiftieth anniversary of the founding of the Chinese Communist Party, first confirms "the universal truth of Marxism-Leninism," that "the basic question of the revolution is that of power, and that the principal duty and highest form of the revolution is the seizure of power by force." Then it raises the problem of learning "how this duty, which varies in accordance with the concrete situation of each country, must finally be carried out in China." There follows a specific reference to Lenin: "In November 1919, basing his remarks on the great experience of the October Revolution, Lenin told the Communists of the Eastern peoples, in his *Report Made to the Sec-*

Mao fears mechanical transposition like the plague. Throughout his work he repeats the theme so dear to him: *inequalities, differences.* Thus, the results obtained *by* and *under* different conditions, *by* and *in* "concrete conditions" must be rejected, for these solutions are valid in the precise content of their results only for the conditions which engendered them. The "single model" can become yet another, paralyzing trap, even if this model happens to be China. (This is contrary to the belief expressed in all the mythologies that Mao may have the solutions to our problems.) But at the same time, we must preserve "like the pupils of our eyes" everything that is *universal* in Marxist theory—a universality resulting from the cumulative (unequal and different) particular experiences of the entire movement. For this reason we must cling to the conviction that the peoples of the world need solid revolutionary ideals (ranging from the French Revolution down to the Commune, from the October Revolution to the Chinese Revolution and the epic of the Vietnamese people), so that they will know about these events and their theoretical and practical application from within, and will draw from their enthusiasm the strength needed to nourish their own heritage of struggles and ideas.

It is precisely this search for the universal in the particular that, in my opinion, constitutes Mao's sensitivity to the currents that are shaking the world—this despite the fact that he has almost never left China, with the exception of two trips to the USSR and the countries of Eastern Europe. It also underlies the close attention he pays to the emotions and reasons that lead peoples to rebel, to the oppression-rebellion-humiliation-revolt mechanism, especially in the small nations, but even in the big nations, such as the United States, where a capacity for struggle is appearing, especially among the young people, in which Mao has persistent confidence. This

ond Russian Congress of the Communist Organizations of the Eastern Peoples that, 'You must take the individual differences existing in your homelands into account. Adapting your work to the specific conditions which do not exist in the European countries, you must learn to apply the general theory and practices of Communism.' " Lenin stressed that this was "a task which had never before been assigned to the communists of the world." It is obvious, the article concludes, "that if we did not link the universal truth of Marxism-Leninism with the actual experiences of the revolution in the country, we would be unable to concern ourselves with the problems of the seizure of power and the victory of the revolution."

manner of *listening to the peoples of the world*, a practice which is sometimes cruelly lacking in other great powers, characterizes the international vision of China.

The fact is that Mao was and has remained 100 percent Leninist. It is precisely for this reason that he was able to be a non-Stalinist (like Gramsci, who from the depths of his prison and in the most tragic isolation refused to be a Stalinist, paving the way in his *Notebooks* for an original development of Marxism-Leninism) and to ensure the progress of Leninism by arriving at unprecedented conclusions and developments through Leninist analysis based on a concrete situation different from that of the USSR. From this point of view the Chinese revolution has passed through stages which the Soviet solution had barely suggested. (Mao elucidates aspects of Lenin's thinking that until now had been inadequately explained by contributing new ideas to the latter's work, or by stressing poorly elaborated aspects of the work, using Marxism-Leninism as a basis.) The decisive contribution of the Chinese revolution to the development of Marxism—a contribution which became particularly important after the Cultural Revolution—is that it has offered a solution which is extraordinarily rich in lessons concerning the fundamental problem of the socialist transition: that of the place and role of the masses, the party and the state in the exercise of the dictatorship of the proletariat. Mao's thought is to *be Leninist elsewhere* (than in the USSR). Mao himself, his life and his history—in short, everything he represents—is summarized in this burning question: *How is one to be a Leninist today elsewhere* (than in the USSR)? Needless to say, when one is able to *be a Leninist elsewhere*—not only under other conditions but precisely during the developmental phase of the dictatorship of the proletariat —rather than merely *copying Lenin* one is working toward the *advancement* of his ideas.

Appendix

Excerpted from a letter of the Central Committee of the Communist Party of China of February 29, 1964, to the Central Committee of the Soviet Union

The question of aid

We have always had a proper appreciation of the friendly Soviet aid which began under Stalin's leadership. We have always considered that the Soviet people's friendly aid has played a beneficial role in helping China to lay the preliminary foundations for its socialist industrialization. For this the Chinese Communist Party and the Chinese people have expressed their gratitude on numerous occasions.

In recent years the leaders of the Communist Party of the Soviet Union (CPSU) have habitually played the benefactor and frequently boasted of their "disinterested assistance." When commemorating the fourteenth anniversary of the signing of the Sino-Soviet Treaty of Friendship, Alliance, and Mutual Assistance in February this year, *Pravda*, *Izvestia*, and other Soviet propaganda media again beat the drum to the same tune. We have not yet made a systematic reply in the press, but we must point out that, so far from being gratis, Soviet aid to China was rendered mainly in the form of trade and that it was certainly not a one-way affair. China has paid and is paying the Soviet Union in goods, gold, or convertible foreign exchange for all Soviet-supplied complete sets of equipment and other goods, including those made available on credit plus interest. It is necessary to add that the prices of many of the goods we imported from the Soviet Union were much higher than those on the world market.

While China has received aid from the Soviet Union, the Soviet Union on its part has also received corresponding aid from China. No one can say that China's aid to the Soviet Union has been insignificant and not worthy of mention. Here are some examples:

Up to the end of 1962 China had furnished the Soviet Union with 2,100 million new rubles'-worth of grain, edible oils, and other foodstuffs. Among the most important items were 5,760,000 tons of soya beans, 2,940,000 tons of rice, 1,090,000 tons of edible oils, and 900,000 tons of meat.

Over the same period, China furnished the Soviet Union with more than 1,400 million new rubles'-worth of mineral products and metals. Among the most important items were: 100,000 tons of lithium concentrates, 34,000 tons of beryllium concentrates, 51,000 tons of borax, 270,000 tons of wolfram concentrates, 32.9 tons of piezoelectric quartz, 7,730 tons of mercury, 39 tons of tantalum-niobium concentrates, 37,000 tons of molybdenum concentrates, and 180,000 tons of tin. Many of these mineral products are raw materials which are indispensable for the development of the most advanced branches of science and for the manufacture of rockets and nuclear weapons.

As for the Soviet loans to China, it must be pointed out that China used them mostly for the purchase of war matériel from the Soviet Union, the greater part of which was used up in the war to resist U.S. aggression and aid Korea. In the war against U.S. aggression the Korean people carried by far the heaviest burden and sustained by far the greatest losses. The Chinese people, too, made great sacrifices and incurred vast military expenses. The Chinese Communist Party has always considered that this was the Chinese people's bounden internationalist duty and that it is nothing to boast of. For many years we have been paying the principal and interest on these Soviet loans, which account for a considerable part of our yearly exports to the Soviet Union. Thus even the war matériel supplied to China in the war to resist U.S. aggression and aid Korea has not been given gratis.

The question of the Soviet experts

The Soviet experts working in China were invariably made welcome, respected, and trusted by the Chinese government and people. The overwhelming majority of them were hard working and helpful to China's socialist construction. We have always highly appreciated their conscientious work, and still miss them to this day.

You will remember that when the leaders of the CPSU unilaterally decided to recall all the Soviet experts in China, we solemnly affirmed our desire to have them continue their work in China and expressed the hope that the leaders of the CPSU would reconsider and change their decision.

But in spite of our objections you turned your backs on the principles guiding international relations and unscrupulously withdrew the 1,390 Soviet experts working in China, tore up 343 contracts and supplementary contracts concerning experts, and scrapped 257 projects of scientific and technical cooperation, all within the short span of a month.

You were well aware that the Soviet experts were posted in over 250 enterprises and establishments in the economic field and the fields of national defense, culture, education, and scientific research, and that they were undertaking important tasks involving technical design, the construction of projects, the installation of equipment, trial production, and scientific research. As a result of your peremptory orders to the Soviet experts to discontinue their work and return to the Soviet Union, many of our country's important designing and scientific research projects had to stop halfway, some of the construction projects in progress had to be suspended, and some of the factories and mines which were conducting trial production could not go into production according to schedule. Your perfidious action disrupted China's original national economic plan and inflicted enormous losses upon China's socialist construction.

You were going completely against Communist ethics when you took advantage of China's serious natural disasters to adopt these grave measures.

Your action fully demonstrates that you violate the principle of mutual assistance between socialist countries and use the sending of experts as an instrument for exerting political pressure on fraternal countries, butting into their internal affairs and impeding and sabotaging their socialist construction.

Now you have again suggested sending experts to China. To be frank, the Chinese people cannot trust you. They have just healed the wounds caused by your withdrawal of experts. These events are still fresh in their memory. With the leaders of the CPSU pursuing an anti-Chinese policy, the Chinese people are unwilling to be duped.

In our opinion, all the countries in the socialist camp should handle the question of sending experts in accordance with the principles of genuine equality, noninterference in each other's internal affairs, mutual assistance, and internationalism. It is absolutely impermissible for any country unilaterally to annul or scrap any agreement or contract concerning the sending of experts. Any country which violates such an agreement or contract should, in accordance with international practice, compensate the other side for the losses thus inflicted. Only thus can there be an interchange of experts on a basis of equality and mutual benefit between China and the Soviet Union and among countries in the socialist camp.

We would like to say in passing that, basing ourselves on the internationalist principle of mutual assistance among countries in the socialist camp, we are very much concerned about the present economic situation in the Soviet Union. If you should feel the need for the help of Chinese experts in certain fields, we would be glad to send them.

The question of Sino-Soviet trade

Nobody is in a better position than you to know the real cause for the curtailment of Sino-Soviet trade over the last few years. This curtailment was precisely the result of your extending the differences from the field of ideology to that of state relations.

Your sudden withdrawal of all the Soviet experts working in China upset the schedules of construction and the production arrangements of many of our factories, mines, and other enterprises and establishments, and had a direct impact on our need for the import of complete sets of equipment. Such being the case, did you expect us to keep on buying them just for display?

Moreover, in pursuance of your policy of further imposing restrictions on and discriminating against China in the economic and commercial fields, since 1960 you have deliberately placed obstacles in the way of economic and trade negotiations between our two countries and held up or refused supplies of important goods which China needs. You have insisted on providing large amounts of goods which we do not really need or which we do not need at all, while holding back or supplying very few of the goods which we need badly. For several years you have used the trade between our two countries as an instrument for bringing political pressure to bear on China. How could this avoid cutting down the volume of Sino-Soviet trade?

From 1959 to 1961, our country suffered extraordinary natural disasters for three years in succession and could not supply you with as large quantities of agricultural produce and processed products as before. This was the result of factors beyond human control. It is utterly unreasonable for you to attack China on this account and blame it for this reduction in trade.

Indeed, but for China's efforts the volume of Sino-Soviet trade would have decreased even more. Take this year for example. China has already put forward a list of 220 million new rubles'-worth of imports from the Soviet Union and 420 million new rubles'-worth of exports to the Soviet Union. But you have been procrastinating unreasonably, continuing to hold back goods we need while trying to force on us goods we do not need. You say in your letter, "In the course of the next few years the USSR could increase its export to China of goods in which you are interested. . . ." But your deeds do not agree with your words.

You constantly accuse us of "going it alone" and claim that you stand for extensive economic ties and division of labor among the socialist countries. But what is your actual record in this respect?

You infringe the independence and sovereignty of fraternal countries and oppose their efforts to develop their economy on an independent basis in accordance with their own needs and potentialities.

You bully those fraternal countries whose economies are less advanced and oppose their policy of industrialization and try to force them to remain agricultural countries forever and serve as your sources of raw materials and as outlets for your goods.

You bully fraternal countries which are industrially more developed and insist that they stop manufacturing their traditional products and become accessory factories serving your industries.

Moreover, you have introduced the jungle law of the capitalist world into relations between socialist countries. You openly follow the example of the Common Market which was organized by monopoly capitalist groups.

All these actions of yours are wrong.

In the economic, scientific, technical, and cultural spheres, we stand for relations of cooperation of a new type, based on genuine equality and mutual benefit, between China and the Soviet Union and among all the socialist countries.

We hold that it is necessary to transform the present Council of Mutual Economic Assistance of socialist countries to accord with the principle of proletarian internationalism and turn this organization, which is now solely controlled by the leaders of the CPSU, into one based on genuine equality and mutual benefit, which the fraternal countries of the socialist camp may join of their own free will. It is hoped that you will favorably respond to our suggestion.